50

Essays

A Portable Anthology

Fifth Edition

Edited by

SAMUEL COHEN

University of Missouri

bedford/st.martin's
Macmillan Learning

Boston | New York

For Bedford/St. Martin's
Vice President, Editorial, Macmillan Learning Humanities: Edwin Hill
Editorial Director, English and Music: Karen S. Henry
Senior Publisher for Composition, Business and Technical Writing,
  Developmental Writing: Leasa Burton
Executive Editor: John E. Sullivan III
Developmental Editor: Sherry Mooney
Assistant Editor: Jennifer Prince
Production Editor: Pamela Lawson
Media Producer: Rand Thomas
Production Supervisor: Joe Ford
Marketing Manager: Joy Fisher Williams
Project Management: Jouve
Text Permissions Researcher: Eve Lehmann
Senior Art Director: Anna Palchik
Text Design: Sandra Rigney
Cover Design: John Callahan
Cover Photo: Ayhan Altun/Getty Images
Composition: Jouve
Printing and Binding: LSC Communications

Manufactured in the United States of America.

1 0 9 8
f e d c

For information, write: Bedford/St. Martin's, 75 Arlington Street,
Boston, MA 02116   (617-399-4000)

ISBN 978-1-319-04372-8 (Student Edition)
ISBN 978-1-319-04430-5 (Evaluation Copy)

Acknowledgments
Text acknowledgments and copyrights appear at the back of the book on pages 448–50, which constitute as an extension of the copyright page.

Preface for Instructors

50 Essays: A Portable Anthology is a compact, inexpensive collection of classic and contemporary essays, most of which have already proven popular in hundreds of classrooms and with thousands of students. Learning how to read good writing effectively is crucial to learning how to write and think critically—and *50 Essays* is full of exceptional prose and many opportunities to practice reading, thinking, and writing about it.

50 Essays includes a core of classic essays such as Gloria Anzaldúa's "How to Tame a Wild Tongue," E. B. White's "Once More to the Lake," and Malcolm X's "Learning to Read," accompanied by fresh, recent selections such as Colson Whitehead's "The Loser Edit" and Lydia Millet's "Victor's Hall." For such a compact volume, *50 Essays* represents an extraordinary diversity of voices and genres—from polemical exhortations to personal narratives, from speeches to meditations, from nuanced arguments to humorous articles of varied length and complexity. The essays should stimulate ideas for students' own writing as they provide sound models for rhetorical analysis.

But *50 Essays* is more than just a selection of good readings: it is a versatile and practical collection designed to prompt critical thinking and writing in the composition classroom. For maximum flexibility and ease of navigation, the essays are arranged alphabetically by author, while alternative tables of contents are provided to help instructors shape courses that meet their teaching preferences. For example, one table of contents is organized by rhetorical mode (narration, description, comparison, and so forth); another by rhetorical purpose (personal, expository, argumentative writing); another by theme (ethics, gender, identity, pop culture, nature and the environment, among others); another by pairs and clusters of readings (Zora Neale Hurston and Audre

Lorde on "Women Speaking to Racism," Chimamanda Ngozi Adichie and Oliver Sacks on "Facing Death," Nicholas Carr and Malcolm Gladwell on "Mediated Lives," and more); and a final table lists the selections chronologically by the date of the essay's composition.

For students, an introduction provides advice on the key skills of active reading, critical thinking, and writing. Terms in bold throughout the introduction refer to a glossary at the back of the book—which defines important writing terms, such as audience, evidence, and plagiarism. An annotated model paper shows students how to analyze and work with multiple sources. Headnotes contextualize each reading in its writer's own place and time. As an aid to comprehension, the essays themselves are lightly glossed. Several types of assignments follow each reading and provide multiple avenues into it: questions on meaning, on rhetorical strategy, on connections between and among selections, and on ideas for further analysis and research. An up-to-date appendix on MLA-style documentation (covering the 2016 version) also helps students write their own source-based papers.

NEW TO THIS EDITION

Sixteen readings are new to this edition, including:

- **Essays on critical thinking, language, and writing** that help students reflect on their reading and become more thoughtful writers, such as Joan Didion's "On Keeping a Notebook" and Colson Whitehead's "The Loser Edit."
- **Essays on contemporary topics** that invite students to confront timely issues, including concern over police brutality in Ta-Nehisi Coates's "The Paranoid Style of American Policing" and the damage to society caused by the "Love What You Do" mantra in Miya Tokumitsu's "In the Name of Love."
- **Essays that critically examine popular culture** to make students aware of the arguments going on around them, including Dave Zirin's "Pre-Game," which explores the role of professional athletes in politics, and Cristina Henríquez's "Lunch," which invites students to her family's table to remember bygone traditions.

GET THE MOST OUT OF YOUR COURSE WITH *50 ESSAYS*

Bedford/St. Martin's offers resources and format choices that help you and your students get even more out of your book and course. To learn more about or to order any of the following products, contact your Macmillan sales representative, e-mail sales support (**sales_support@bfwpub.com**), or visit our online catalog at **macmillanlearning.com**.

Choose from Alternative Formats of *50 Essays*

Bedford/St. Martin's offers a range of affordable formats, allowing students to choose the one that works best for them. For details, visit **macmillanlearning.com**.

- To learn more about our e-book partners, visit **macmillanlearning.com/ebooks**.

Select Value Packages

Add value to your text by packaging one of the following resources with *50 Essays*. To learn more about package options for any of the following products, contact your Bedford/St. Martin's sales representative or visit **macmillanlearning.com**.

LaunchPad Solo for Readers and Writers offers instruction tailored to individual students' unique needs and features several innovative digital tools.

- **Reading comprehension quizzes** for every selection in *50 Essays*.
- **Pre-built units that support a learning arc.** Each unit includes a pre-test, multimedia instruction and assessment, help for multilingual writers, and a post-test that assesses what students have learned about critical reading, the writing process, using sources, grammar, style, and mechanics.
- **Video introductions** offer overviews of many unit topics and illustrate the concepts at hand.
- **Adaptive quizzing for targeted learning.** Most units include *LearningCurve*, game-like quizzing that focuses on the areas in which each student needs the most help.
- **The ability to monitor student progress.** Instructors can use the gradebook to see which students are on track and which need additional help.

Order ISBN 978-1-319-10219-7 to package *LaunchPad Solo for Readers and Writers* with *50 Essays* or visit **macmillanlearning .com/catalog/readwrite** for more information.

Writer's Help 2.0 is a powerful online writing resource that helps students find answers whether they are searching for writing advice on their own or as part of an assignment.

- **Reading Comprehension Quizzes for *50 Essays*.** Get reading comprehension quizzes for each selection in *50 Essays*, already included in the Writer's Help 2.0 platform.

- **Smart search.** Built on research with more than 1,600 student writers, the smart search in Writer's Help 2.0 provides reliable results even when students use novice terms such as *flow* and *unstuck*.

- **Trusted content from our best-selling handbooks.** Choose *Writer's Help 2.0, Hacker Version* or *Writer's Help 2.0, Lunsford Version* and ensure that students have clear advice and examples for all of their writing questions.

- **Adaptive exercises that engage students.** Writer's Help 2.0 includes *LearningCurve*, game-like online quizzing that adapts to what students already know and helps them focus on what they need to learn.

Student access is packaged with *50 Essays*, Fifth Edition, at a significant discount. Order ISBN 978-1-319-10218-0 for *Writer's Help 2.0, Hacker Version* or ISBN 978-1-319-10208-1 for *Writer's Help 2.0, Lunsford Version* to ensure your students have easy access to online writing support. Students who rent a book or buy a used book can purchase access to Writer's Help 2.0 at **macmillanlearning.com/writershelp2**.

Instructors may request free access by registering as an instructor at **macmillanhighered.com/writershelp2**.

For technical support, visit **macmillanlearning.com /getsupport**.

***Portfolio Keeping*, Third Edition, by Nedra Reynolds and Elizabeth Davis**, provides all the information students need to use the portfolio method successfully in a writing course. *Portfolio Teaching*, a companion guide for instructors, provides the practical information instructors and writing program administrators need to use the portfolio method successfully in a writing course. To order *Portfolio Keeping* packaged with this text, contact your sales representative for a package ISBN.

Instructor Resources
macmillanlearning.com

You have a lot to do in your course. Bedford/St. Martin's wants to make it easy for you to find the support you need—and to get it quickly.

Resources for 50 Essays is available as a PDF that can be downloaded from the Bedford/St. Martin's online catalog at the URL above. In addition to chapter overviews and teaching tips, the instructor's manual includes sample syllabi, answers to questions that appear within the book, and suggested classroom activities.

Join Our Community! The Macmillan English Community is now Bedford/St. Martin's home for professional resources, featuring Bedford *Bits* and *LitBits*, our popular blog sites that offer new ideas for the composition classroom and composition teachers. Connect and converse with a growing team of Bedford authors and top scholars who blog on *Bits*. *50 Essays* author Samuel Cohen, Andrea Lunsford, Nancy Sommers, Steve Bernhardt, Traci Gardner, Barclay Barrios, Jack Solomon, Susan Bernstein, Elizabeth Wardle, Doug Downs, Liz Losh, Jonathan Alexander, and Donna Winchell.

In addition, you'll find an expanding collection of additional resources that support your teaching.

* Sign up for webinars
* Download resources from our professional resources series that support your teaching
* Start a discussion
* Ask a question
* Follow your favorite members
* Review projects in the pipeline

Visit **community.macmillan.com** to join the conversation with your fellow teachers.

ACKNOWLEDGMENTS

Many thanks go to the instructors who helped shape this edition of *50 Essays*: Mark Arnowitz, New Jersey Institute of Technology; Alva Balthazar, Rio Hondo College; William Carney, Cameron University; Clayton Couch,

Haywood Community College; Darin Cozzens, Surry Community College; Tamera Davis, Northern Oklahoma College–Stillwater; Robert DeFrance, Long Beach City College; Denise Dumars, Long Beach City College; Erin Ergenbright, Portland Community College; Edward Fletcher, Savannah State University; Wanda Haynes, Manchester Community College; Danen Jobe, Pikes Peak Community College; Elizabeth Keefe, Gateway Community College; Sarah Kirk, University of Alaska Anchorage; Janet Krauss, Fairfield University; Carolyn Kremers, University of Alaska Fairbanks; William Lemon, Irvine Valley College; Maureen Lennon, Seneca College; Jeannine McDevit, Pennsylvania Highlands Community College; Lyle Morgan, Pittsburg State University; Suzanna Riordan, Baruch College; Amanda Ross, Central Washington University; Joanna Sit, City University of New York; Sarah Stanley, University of Alaska Fairbanks; Mike Walonen, Bethune-Cookman University; Anika Waltz-Cummings, New Jersey Institute of Technology; Sherrie Weller, Loyola University Chicago.

I would also like to thank the people at Bedford/St. Martin's who made this book possible, particularly Joan Feinberg, Denise Wydra, Karen Henry, Steve Scipione, and Elizabeth Schaaf. I would especially like to recognize the work of John Sullivan and Karin Halbert, whose vision, experience, and support made the first and second editions possible; Amy Gershman, whose hard work, good ideas, and patience are responsible for the improvements in the third; the brilliant and indefatigable Alicia Young, who also edits *Literature: The Human Experience* and deserves combat pay for having to work with me so much; and Sherry Mooney for her strong ideas and stronger patience in her work with me on this edition. Thanks also to Jennifer Prince who ably assisted Sherry. I would also like to acknowledge the help of Pamela Lawson, who guided the book through production; Anne Sussman, for her careful copyediting; Eve Lehmann for clearing permissions; and Joy Fisher Williams for her marketing insights. I would like to thank the teachers from whom I was lucky to learn how to read and write, and teach. I would like to thank my Spring 2003 Writing I students at Baruch College, CUNY, who were taught with this book in its early stages and who had a great deal of unflinchingly honest advice for how to put it together, and the students I have had the pleasure to teach since then. I would like to thank the English Department at the University of Missouri for the job, the office, and the opportunity to work with great students, and my colleagues in Columbia, especially the graduate student employees in the department who have taught the book and taught me about how it works and about how hard they work. Most of all, I would like to thank Kristin Bowen for everything she's taught me about textbooks and much more; our boys, Ben and Henry, who have grown up with this book and are now both much taller than it; and our newly adopted dog, Azalea, who has not replaced her predecessor but, like her, seems not to be bothered by the revising of textbooks as long as she can curl up at your feet while you're doing it.

Contents

CHIMAMANDA NGOZI ADICHIE, *To My One Love*   17

"My glow was gone, my poetry forgotten. I was trying to
remember what I had felt when I saw the photo of the dead
person on the wall and realized it was Nnamdi."

SHERMAN ALEXIE, *The Joy of Reading and Writing:
Superman and Me*   22

"I read anything that had words and paragraphs. I read with
equal parts joy and desperation. I loved those books, but I
also knew that love had only one purpose. I was trying to save
my life."

GLORIA ANZALDÚA, *How to Tame a Wild Tongue*   27

"Ethnic identity is twin skin to linguistic identity—I am my
language. Until I can take pride in my language, I cannot take
pride in myself."

Table of Contents
by Rhetorical Mode

Table of Contents by Purpose

Table of Contents
by Theme

xxi

Table of Contents
by Clusters and
Paired Readings

Table of Contents
by Chronological Order

Introduction for Students: Active Reading, Critical Thinking, and the Writing Process

READING, WRITING, 'RITHMETIC

Hard work, preparation, and lots of reading can add up to good writing. That is the arithmetic of writing. We become active, critical, intelligent readers and writers by carefully reading the writing that others have done and then applying what we have learned to our own writing. Reading and writing are most of what you will do in your college courses. The strongest readers and writers have learned to see these activities as inextricably intertwined. You read, you write, then you read some more, then you write again. And this pattern applies in nearly all of your classes, not just those in English and history and other disciplines that come to mind as reading and writing heavy. Math, biology, and engineering classes require the same skills. Acquiring and strengthening them at the start of your college career will help you all the way to graduation and beyond, as reading and writing are central to so many of the careers you might find yourself in a few years down the road.

This introduction will briefly consider the best ways to approach the kinds of assignments you will encounter in your college writing courses. As you read it, think about the ways you read and write now. Do you do some of these things already? Have you tried them before? Be open to the advice, but remember, it is only the advice of one teacher. Your teacher may have different ideas, just as you may, and these ideas may change. Here's an example: in the first edition of this book, I argued against reading while lying down, saying it was better to sit up so you could pay better attention and stay awake. Students, teachers, and my editor disagreed. I decided they were right. The point? As the introduction will explain, the best thing you can do with the texts you encounter in school and in the world is try both to understand them and to evaluate them, and be open to having your mind changed by them. And if you want, do so while stretched out on a nice comfortable couch.

ACTIVE READING

We read for a number of reasons. We want the news, we want information, we want to be entertained. We want to hear other people thinking. We want to be taken out of ourselves and live other lives. We also read because it is crucial to learning how to write. The poet Jane Kenyon gave this advice on becoming a better writer: "Have good sentences in your ears." To write well—to express your ideas efficiently and clearly—you need to observe how others do it. You need to see examples of the ways writers write, the techniques and forms they use. Because good writing is about more than correctness, though, you also have to observe the ways writers think. Working with ideas—handling the ideas of others and presenting your own—is the most important thing writers do, and so the most important thing for writers to learn. Since it is so important, of course, it is difficult. Life is like that. But reading examples of good writing gives you access to models: it shows writers engaging with ideas, holding them up to the light, turning them this way and that, and maybe modifying them in some way, adding something, taking something away, taking them apart entirely, offering their own instead.

To learn to do the same, however, you need to do more than simply mimic what good writers do. You need to treat their writing the same way they treat ideas. Hold their writing up to the light, turn it this way and that, figure out how it works and also how it doesn't, think about how it might be wrong—how you might think differently about their subjects. This activity is sometimes called active or critical reading.

The essays in this collection are here to be studied as models; they are also here to be read critically. While you might learn something from every essay, they are not chapters in a chemistry textbook. Your job is not to take what they say as the gospel truth. Instead, you should evaluate what you read. This doesn't mean you should treat these essays as movie critics treat movies or restaurant critics treat food: these essays aren't here for you to simply judge, to give a thumbs up or down to, to savor or spit out. Instead, you should evaluate their ideas and the way they present them as if in conversation with them. Ask questions of them, argue with their assumptions, examine how they connect their ideas, and test these connections. In learning to think this way about what writers create, you will learn to think like a writer.

There are many techniques that can help you read this way. What they boil down to is reading actively rather than passively. Think of passive reading as like watching television. While there are some good, thoughtful programs on TV, most of us watch TV passively—sitting on a couch, maybe eating, maybe doing something else simultaneously (but not our schoolwork, of course), and letting television wash over us. Active reading, in contrast, requires full attention. Posture aside, your mind needs to be sitting up straight, concentrating on the page, ready to reach down into the page and grab the words. Here are some tips to ensure that you get the most out of what you read.

WAYS TO READ ACTIVELY

Read consciously.   In addition to being awake, it is important to be conscious of the situation you are in. Why are you reading? Merely for comprehension, or for observation of the writing itself, or for argument about the ideas? What are you reading? For what purpose or occasion or publication was the piece written, and by whom? Is it a selection from someone's autobiography? Is it an article from a newspaper or an editorial? How has it been contextualized—is it in a chapter on a certain kind of writing or on a certain idea or theme? Keeping these questions in mind as you read makes you notice more, think harder, and make connections among ideas.

Read critically.   Always ask yourself what you think about the writer's arguments. Although doing this does not require you to take issue with every or any single thing an author writes, it does ask you to think of reading as conversation: the writer is talking to you, telling you what she thinks about something, and you are free to answer back.

Read with a pencil in hand. This is the best, easiest way to answer back. Many students leave their books untouched, thinking that they will remember what they read or that it is wrong to write in books or that they won't be able to sell them back at the end of the semester if they write in them. These are common objections, but consider this: you won't recall everything (nobody remembers everything he or she reads, and memorizing isn't the only or even the most important thing we do when we read); it's not wrong to write in a book (books don't have feelings, but if they did, they'd like the attention); and bookstores will buy back marked-up books (go check out the used books in the bookstore). Making marks on the page—annotating—is the surest way to read actively. Underline important passages, circle words you haven't heard of, scribble furious rants in the margin, jot down questions about content or writing strategy, use exclamation points and question marks and arrows and Xs. Grab the text with your bare hands. Reading with a highlighter is the passive version of marking your book because it is less suited to annotating and more suited to identifying chunks of text. The result of marking with a highlighter is that you haven't engaged with your reading so much as prioritized parts of it a little bit—used fluorescent yellow or pink or green to say, "Hey, there's something important here." While a highlighter might be more appropriate in your chemistry textbook, even there it can be dangerous: while checking out the used books in the bookstore, notice how often entire paragraphs and even pages are afloat in seas of highlighter ink, and ask yourself how that helped the students whose books these used to be. Pencils are also good for chewing, sticking in your hair to hold your bun together, and sliding behind your ear to make you look smart and industrious.

Use a notebook or computer. Many readers like to take notes in a notebook or computer. Although there are disadvantages to this kind of note taking relative to annotation—your marks are not right in the text and so are less immediately accessible and less immediately tied to the lines on the page—there are also advantages. You can make lengthy notes. You can copy important and well-phrased sentences (making sure to enclose them in quotation marks and to note where they came from). You can **paraphrase**[1] ideas, you can **summarize**, you can note your reactions as you read. Doing these things can make you think more about what you're reading. Some readers use a double-entry system in which they draw a line down the middle of the page, note or reproduce particular passages from the reading in the left column, and respond to those passages in the right column. Many variations on this kind of note taking are possible (and all of them, of course, can be reproduced on a computer).

An Example of Annotation and Note Taking from Brent Staples, "Just Walk on By: Black Men and Public Space" (p. 339)

Living with rage would make him crazy

Echoes the essay's title

His tension or other people's?

"Everybody"? Seems like a stereotype about white people

Over the years, I learned to smother the rage I felt at so often being taken for a criminal. Not to do so would surely have led to madness. I now take precautions to make myself less threatening. I move about with care, particularly late in the evening. I give a wide berth to nervous people on subway platforms during the wee hours, particularly when I have exchanged business clothes for jeans. If I happen to be entering a building behind some people who appear skittish, I may walk by, letting them clear the lobby before I return, so as not to seem to be following them. I have been calm and extremely congenial on those rare occasions when I've been pulled over by police.

And on late-evening constitutionals I employ what has proved to be an excellent tension-reducing measure: I whistle melodies from Beethoven and Vivaldi and the more popular classical composers. Even steely New Yorkers hunching toward nighttime destinations seem to relax, and occasionally they even join in the tune. Virtually everybody seems to sense that a mugger wouldn't be warbling bright, sunny selections from Vivaldi's *Four Seasons*. It is my equivalent of the cowbell that hikers wear when they know they are in bear country.

Strong emotion

"rare" implies that he even takes care to behave well when driving

People are comfortable with what they know

Powerful image

1. Words in **boldface** are treated in the glossary of writing terms, which starts on page 439.

Notes

Staples's essay started off making it sound like he was a criminal, but by the end I realized that was his whole point: he's NOT a criminal, yet he's often treated like one because of his race

Staples's descriptions of how he copes with people perceiving him as a threat are really illuminating but also really disheartening

I found it weird that Staples counteracts the stereotypes people have of him by using other stereotypes—e.g., the idea that cultured people who know classical music can't be criminals (I guess traditionally rap is associated with African Americans? Another stereotype . . .)

The last line of this passage is really powerful—Staples feels like he is being viewed as a hunter, when actually he's the one being hunted (he's in "bear country"). That image really emphasizes how the people reacting to him as a threat are, in reality, a threat to him . . .

Note the different kinds of entries here. The first is about the reader's changing thoughts as he reads. The second is a moment of appreciation. The third and fourth are trains of thought that start from small parts of the essay. None of these sum up the reading, though that is a good thing to do also. Instead, these entries record reactions and thoughts inspired by the essay, and—like the notes made alongside the excerpt—could serve as ways back into the essay when it is time to write about it. See page 7 for a checklist of things you can annotate and make notes about as you read. Also see the sample student paper beginning on page 11. This paper builds on the initial ideas and notes presented here; as you read it, look for ways in which the student develops his preliminary thoughts into an argument.

CRITICAL THINKING/CRITICAL READING

The previous annotation sample shows how active reading is much more than reading to understand. Summarizing what has been read is important; moving beyond summary to active engagement is something else, and it is crucial to really making use of what you've read. One name for this something else is critical thinking.

A CHECKLIST FOR ANNOTATING A READING

As you read, consider marking or taking notes on the following:

☐ Main topics
☐ Secondary topics
☐ Main points
☐ Supporting points
☐ Examples, **evidence**, or other support
☐ Ideas or ways of saying things that you like
☐ Ideas or ways of saying things that you don't like
☐ Ideas you want to think more about later
☐ References or words with which you are not familiar

Critical thinking doesn't mean being critical in the everyday sense, that is, being negative. It means being inquisitive, evaluative, even skeptical. When reading, it means thinking not just about what someone says but about the unspoken assumptions that lie behind what she says, the unnamed implications of what she says, and the way she says it. It also means evaluating—asking if you agree with a writer's implicit and explicit **conclusions**, even asking if you agree with the framing of the question asked or the topic addressed, and judging the eloquence and/or effectiveness of the writing. Critical thinking is a catchall term for a number of activities that add up to active, thoughtful engagement with a subject. For many, it is the single most important skill higher education makes possible: it allows people to actively judge and process the things they read and hear rather than passively accept them. For others, it has an arguably more powerful aspect: that of allowing individuals to accept or reject the common wisdom that is all around them, in everyday life, at work, in politics.

When applied to reading, critical thinking might be called critical reading. See page 8 for a checklist of critical reading questions, with follow-up questions, that you can ask yourself when reading critically (that is, always). While they will not all be applicable for every occasion, most will be helpful as you try to understand and evaluate others' writing.

A CHECKLIST FOR CRITICAL READING

☐ What is the writing situation? Where did the text originally appear?

☐ What is the writer's subject?

   ☐ Is she choosing to focus or not to focus on something important? Is she leaving something out?

☐ What is the writer's main point about her subject?

   ☐ Do you agree? Do you disagree? Why?

☐ What is the writer's purpose in making that point?

   ☐ What do you think of that purpose? Do you think that she achieves it?

☐ To what sort of audience does the writer seem to be addressing herself?

   ☐ Are you part of that audience? Who is, and who is left out?

☐ What are the assumptions behind the writer's treatment of her subject?

   ☐ Do you agree with them? Do you disagree? Why?

☐ What further conclusions could be drawn from the writer's point?

   ☐ Do you agree with them? Do you disagree? Why?

☐ What do you think of the way the writer makes her argument?

   ☐ Is it convincing? Logical? Does she fight fair?

☐ What can you borrow (without plagiarizing)?

   ☐ Are there particular techniques the writer uses to argue, describe, narrate, or just shape a sentence that you want to remember and use in your own writing?

THE WRITING PROCESS

As the last critical reading question indicates, writers get better by paying attention to how the writing they like works and trying to duplicate those effects in their own work. This is not the same thing as **plagiarism**: you know not to take another's work and pretend it's your own. The very best writers got so good not by copying words and ideas without giving proper credit, but by imitating other writers—their **styles**, their **tones**, their patterns of organization—and using these as starting points for developing their own voices.

Reading actively, critically, and with an eye toward borrowing helps you to become a better writer. However, nothing helps you learn to write like writing itself. While there will be a number of occasions in your academic career when you will be required to hand in formal, typed, proofread essays, take advantage of the times when you have to write informally—in class, in journals, online. Think of times when you don't have to write but could— sitting on the bus, waiting for your computer to boot up—and get out a notebook and write. Like strengthening a muscle through repeated exercise, the more you use your writing skills the stronger they will become.

This strength will help you when it is time to write formal, academic essays, and it can help to lessen anxiety about writing. Every writer, when faced with more demanding assignments, feels some form of dread, trepidation, or nervous excitement. In other words, it is far from rare for writers of all levels of experience to freeze up, space out, or throw in the towel. Many of the best ways writers have found to get past the difficulty of getting started involve recognizing that writing is a process. People often imagine a typical scene when they think of writing: they see the writer, hunched over the blank pad or in front of the blank screen, waiting for inspiration to strike, then, having been struck, finding the exact words to express this inspiration, and then, finishing, leaning back with a sigh of contentment at a job well done. Very few people actually write this way.

Rather than thinking that you must sit down and create a polished piece of work out of thin air, remember that writers can go through many stages when they write and that each stage can help produce a final product. Before you begin to write a first **draft**, try a number of **prewriting** activities, which can help you brainstorm or come up with ideas. You can work up notes or a formal or informal outline before you draft. At this point you can also make use of comments you wrote in the margins of your text. After taking a first stab at a draft, you can **revise**. As important as recognizing that you can break down the writing process into these stages is knowing that they don't have to be followed. After producing a draft, you may return to outlining and brainstorming. You can even do this as you draft: as you see your main point (your **thesis**) changing or your **argument** taking a different course, go back to your notes or outline and modify accordingly. When you get to the revision stage, when you think you might be focusing on correctness and style, you may find not only that you need to rewrite what you wrote in the drafting stage but also that you need to rethink the ideas you came up with during the prewriting stage. While smoothing out the **transitions** between your **paragraphs**, you may find they are rough because the connections among your ideas are also rough, and so you will need to smooth out your ideas before you can smooth out your expression of them.

This may all sound daunting. It shouldn't. Thinking about writing as a recursive process—one in which you loop back to the starting point as you revise and build on your work—means you don't have to try to get everything perfect the first time. It allows you to get your ideas down on paper as they come to you because you know you can always go back and change them. It allows you to think critically about your work because it never feels like it's too late to improve any aspect of it. Read as a writer reads—critically, actively—and write as a writer writes—in stages, recursively—and pretty soon (that is, before you even know it) you will be a thoughtful, fluid writer who enjoys practicing his or her craft. There is no complicated mathematical formula to explain the interrelation of critical reading, creative brainstorming, careful revision, and all of the other elements that are part of what makes good writing, but the basic arithmetic—reading + hard work = good writing—holds up.

I hope that you enjoy reading the essays in this book, and that you find that they help you with your writing. At the end of this introduction you'll find an example of an essay written in response to readings in *50 Essays*. Annotations have been added to highlight important parts of the essay—elements like the thesis statement, transitions, and a **conclusion**. Read it over for ideas about how to put together sentences and paragraphs, how to construct an argument, and how to document sources. This essay is also a good example of **synthesis**—the process of considering a number of different readings, putting them in conversation with each other, and forming your own **claim** or thesis, making your own statement. Remember, though, that there's no one model you should follow, no one way to write about anything. Examples are good, but you need to find your own voice, your own way to say what you want to say.

Schaff 1

Jonathon Schaff
Professor Cohen
English 101
17 February 2016

Dangerous Duality: How Racism Splits Us in Two
By Jonathon Schaff

I have never been told that I am a problem. I have been told
that my behavior is problematic, but no one has ever told me that
there was something wrong with me just for being me. As a white
American, I've never been avoided on the street or denied a meal
because of my skin color. Yet many African Americans have faced
and continue to face this kind of discrimination in America. Since
I am not an African American, I can only try to understand the
African American experience of living in this country, both past
and present, by submerging myself in the words and ideas of
black writers.

*Author
discusses his
own **point
of view***

Something can happen to the human mind when it is
informed that it is a problem. When people are treated differently
than the way they see themselves, the human mind creates a kind
of divided sense of self. As a result, African Americans who have
been victimized by racism oftentimes see themselves in two
different, irreconcilable ways, and that divide can have dangerous
consequences.

*Thesis
statement
makes the
author's
claim*

The idea that split identities form as a product of racism may
have been first introduced by W. E. B. Du Bois in his important 1903
essay, "Of Our Spiritual Strivings," in which he refers to a state of
"double-consciousness." Du Bois argues that blacks, forty years after
being legally freed, felt they were black and American at the same
time, and yet not both at once. Du Bois wrote:

It is a peculiar sensation, this double-consciousness, this
sense of always looking at one's self through the eyes of
others, of measuring one's worth by the tape of a world that
looks on in amused contempt and pity. One ever feels his
twoness, — an American, a Negro; two souls, two thoughts,
two unreconciled strivings; two warring ideals in one dark
body, whose dogged strength alone keeps it from being torn
asunder. (45)

*Use of
quotation
illustrates
argument of
the original
author*

Du Bois saw himself through the eyes of the white majority, and
therefore could not fully separate his own identity from the way he
was perceived by other people. Given this, it is easy to understand
how his double-consciousness formed. Du Bois suggests that being
both black and American, at least in 1903, was not only impossible
but was an intersection where violence occurred.

Schaff 2

Du Bois's essay has continued to echo in the work of black authors into the twentieth century. His ideas have persisted largely because African Americans continued to suffer indignities long after slavery was abolished. Until the 1960s, Jim Crow laws prevented blacks from having access to the same quality of life that whites enjoyed by means of segregation. Barring blacks from white swimming pools and restaurants, Jim Crow laws had a corrosive effect on the African American psyche. In his essay "Notes of a Native Son," published in 1955, James Baldwin writes about his father, a severe man and the son of a slave. Baldwin's father taught him to hate and mistrust whites because they would inevitably do blacks harm. As he grew up, Baldwin began to understand his father's bitterness and the dangers it posed. Baldwin describes an encounter at a restaurant in New Jersey that had refused to serve him and which ended in his violent attack on the waitress:

> I could not get over two facts, both equally difficult for the imagination to grasp, and one was that I could have been murdered. But the other was that I had been ready to commit murder. I saw nothing very clearly but I did see this: that my life, my real life, was in danger, and not from anything other people might do but from the hatred I carried in my own heart. (53)

Baldwin echoes Du Bois's point that the hatred involved in double-consciousness is destructive for African Americans both externally and internally. In order to curb this hatred, Baldwin says that "[i]t began to seem that one would have to hold in the mind forever two ideas which seemed to be in opposition" (64). These two opposing ideas define the African American struggle between accepting life's injustices and fighting against the corrosive powers of hate that permeated the country in the first half of the twentieth century. Would Baldwin feel the same way if he were alive today?

The work of contemporary African American authors reveals that today's society continues to inform blacks that they are dangerous and frightening. Brent Staples's 1987 essay, "Just Walk on By: Black Men and Public Space," offers a series of poignant anecdotes about his life as a graduate student and an adult. Staples recalls the fear he inspired in others as a habitual nighttime walker. He recollects crossing the street and hearing people in their cars lock their doors. He also remembers the way other people would cross the street if they were on course to pass him on the sidewalk (340). Similarly, John Edgar Wideman, a professor of Africana

Topic sentence states the paragraph's main idea

Schaff 3

studies and literary arts at Brown University, identifies with being
avoided based on his skin color in his 2010 essay "The Seat Not
Taken." The seat next to Wideman often remains empty for his entire
commute on the Amtrak train from New York City to Providence,
Rhode Island. Despite the fact that Wideman is well-dressed and can
obviously afford the expensive train ticket, he has observed that
"9 times out of 10 people will shun a free seat if it means sitting
beside me."

Author uses evidence from an outside source to support his claim

Staples and Wideman, both intelligent men and authors for the
New York Times, seem to be able to keep healthy perspectives on
who they are, but this is not easy. Staples remarks that he feels like
he travels through "bear country," late at night on the streets (342).
People take on the ferociousness of animals when they see him
coming around a corner. Wideman, on the other hand, initially claims
that the empty seat next to him is a "privilege, conferred upon me
by color, to enjoy the luxury of an extra seat to myself." Yet he
ultimately "can't accept the bounty of an empty seat without remembering why it's empty, without wondering if its emptiness isn't
something quite sad. And quite dangerous, also, if left unexamined."
The "danger" represented by the empty seat is the danger of seeing
threats where there are none, of judging and avoiding others based
solely on skin color.

Author uses summary to make a point in his own words

Because of these dangers, pressure is put on African Americans
to go out of their way to appear nonthreatening. To alert and pacify
the scared strangers he met on the street, Staples would whistle traditionally white classical music by Beethoven and Vivaldi. Viewing
himself through white eyes, Staples found a way to avoid causing
trouble. But walking down the street without whistling the *Moonlight
Sonata* should not instigate an attack. Yet this is the reality for many
black Americans. Based on how people react to their skin color,
pressure is put upon them from the white majority to behave a
certain way, even if that way is senseless, and the consequences for
failing to conform to it can result in violence.

Use of transition "because" connects two ideas

As a white person, I find it hard to imagine the world reflexively
avoiding me. It must be difficult for Staples and Wideman to not feel
as though they contribute to how people treat them or not feel as
though there is something threatening locked up inside themselves.
Neither have I ever felt the hate that Baldwin described with the
power to destroy his father nor been compelled to violence because
I've experienced injustice. Reading these authors tracing back from
over a century ago to present day has made me more conscious of the
division race still inserts into our modern lives and the emotional and

Schaff 4

personal consequences of this opposition in the human consciousness. Perhaps this lack of understanding is what enables the divide
to continue today.

If blacks throughout our nation's history have suffered
from racism, is it realistic to think that there is an end in sight?
Circumstances have changed — first slavery gave way to Jim Crow,
which has given way to more subtle forms of discrimination, which
coexist with the same old-fashioned, street-level racism Du Bois,
Baldwin, Staples, and Wideman have all felt — but the underlying
duality remains, and remains dangerous. As Baldwin put it, "I imagine that one of the reasons people cling to their hates so stubbornly
is because they sense, once hate is gone, that they will be forced to
deal with pain" (56). Even though the United States elected an
African American president, is the country truly post-racial? There is
a lot of pain that this country will have to deal with if and when it
lets go of its hate. But if the era of healing lasts half as long as the
epoch of prejudice, then we could be in for a better way of living, a
way that prefers empathy to ignorance and unity to division.

*Conclusion
sums up
main point
and extends
the author's
ideas*

*Author uses
expressive
diction
and tone in
concluding
paragraph*

Works Cited

Baldwin, James. "Notes of a Native Son." *50 Essays,* 5th ed., edited
    by Samuel Cohen, Bedford/St. Martin's, 2017,
    pp. 44–65.
Du Bois, W. E. B. *The Souls of Black Folk.* 1903. Introduction by
    Randall Kenan, Signet Books, 1995.
Staples, Brent. "Just Walk on By: Black Men and Public Space." Cohen
    pp. 339–42.
Wideman, John Edgar. "The Seat Not Taken." *The New York Times,*
    7 Oct. 2010, www.nytimes.com/2010/10/07/opinion
    /07Wideman.html?_r=0.

Readings

CHIMAMANDA NGOZI ADICHIE

To My One Love

Born in 1977 in Enugu, Nigeria, Chimamanda Ngozi Adichie is a novelist, short story writer, and nonfiction writer whose work has appeared in various publications, including the New Yorker *and the* Iowa Review. *She has authored five books, including her most recent novel,* Americanah, *for which she won a National Book Critics Circle Award. She is also the recipient of a MacArthur Genius Grant. Adichie often speaks on her experiences as an African feminist, and her TEDx talk, "We should all be feminists," was sampled in Beyoncé's 2013 song "Flawless."*

"To My One Love," originally titled "Operation," comes from the literary magazine Granta. *It was featured in their issue about storytelling, "What Happened Next." In it, Adichie expresses the perpetual shocks of young love and young loss.*

Lagos in June is steamy. But that Thursday afternoon at the *Champion* newspaper office, I did not notice how the air was like a hot, moist blanket. I swaggered and smiled, too full of accomplishment. I had just had a collection of watery poetry published by a vanity press in London. I was doing my first newspaper interview. I was 19 years old.

Kate, the woman who interviewed me, was squat, friendly, and full of praise for the poems (although she had not read them). After the questions, she told me I was a role model for young Nigerians. I glowed. She took me downstairs to have my picture taken in a wide room that smelled of chemicals. Matte photographs were plastered on the wall. Most of them were of prominent people, but there were also beggars under bridges and children playing football and soldiers by the roadsides.

"They put up the best on the wall," Kate said.

17

Later, as we left, I turned to glance again at the wall of photo-graphs, and that was when I saw it, the photo of Nnamdi. I might have let out a sound, I might have only shivered, but Kate noticed and asked if something was wrong.

I pointed. "I knew him," I said.   5

Kate shook her head. "Oh, sorry, sorry. It was an operation at the bank just across the road," she said.

I remember the splashes of blood on Nnamdi's face, his head slumped against the seat of the car; the blood was a deep gray in the black-and-white photo.

At my university secondary school in Nsukka, there were two groups of students. The staff group, which I belonged to, was made up of students whose parents were university lecturers, who lived on campus and had little money and spoke good English. The other group was the Omata. They came mostly from Onitsha and the name Omata somehow conjured the chaos of that large commercial town. Their parents were rich, illiterate traders; they lived in dormitories and often missed the first week of term. We mimicked their mixed-up English tenses, laughed at their poor grades, and mocked their bluster. And, secretly, we coveted what they had: the gold watches that we saw only on the wrists of adults, the gullibility of uneducated parents, the imported sandals that cost more than our families made in a month.

Nnamdi owned such sandals; his were a sparkly brown, almost orange, and had wedge heels. He was an archetype of the unre-fined Omata student, down to his swaying-to-the-side strut. Nnamdi was in Form 4, a popular senior student, while I was in Form 2. Of course I found him terribly attractive.

It was his friends who called me at first to say, "*Ima*, Nnamdi 10 really likes you." I was noncommittal, tough because I was expected to be. Finally, he came himself. I wish I remembered the first day I talked to him, or what we said. I remember that he walked me home after school, though, and that he said very little. I knew him because he was the kind of student everybody knew, and I had always thought him to be larger than life, taller than life. But there he was, shy beside me, looking down as we walked.

He took to escorting me home. He took to calling me GB, like most of my family and friends. "*Bikonu*, please, GB, I want you to be my wife," he said nearly every day, in Igbo. And I would say, in English, with false coolness, "I have to think about it," even though I wanted nothing more than to be his girlfriend. Later, Nnamdi would tease me about how I gave him a high jump to scale. I like to think now that he knew how much I liked him, from the beginning, and that we were equal participants in the ritual.

The afternoon I said yes, we were standing in front of my garage and he went over and plucked a flower—one of my mother's carefully preserved yellow roses—and held it out to me.

"What is this for?" I asked sharply. (I had said yes, but it didn't mean I was no longer tough.)

"A sign. I won't leave until you take it."

"I won't take it until you tell me what it means."   15

We went back and forth until Nnamdi said, in English, "It means love," and I took the flower and he added, "If your mother asks who plucked it, say you don't know." *good excuse*

I left the *Champion* office and sat in a hot taxi and looked at Lagos inching past, the hawkers pressing sunglasses against the window, the buses spitting out thick gray smoke, the cars stuck bumper to bumper in traffic. *every taxi driver does this*

"See this stupid man! He wan scratch me!" my taxi driver said, gesturing to the car beside us. Then he stuck his head out and cursed in rapid Yoruba.

I sat back, silent and sweating, and thought of Kate's words, of how we Nigerians use the word *operation* to refer to armed robberies and how it had taken on an ominous pallor. Buses were stopped and people killed in *operations* on the Benin–Lagos expressway. Houses were broken into in nighttime *operations*. Banks were raided in *operations*. One Christmas when we were traveling to our hometown, Abba, our driver made a dangerous U-turn in the middle of the expressway. "There is an operation in front!" he said, and my mother praised him for being so quick. *all Heist*

My taxi driver had stopped cursing and asked what I had been   20 doing in the *Champion* newspaper office. "Wonderful!" he said when I told him. "Small aunty like you can write book. Well done!"

I thanked him. But my glow was gone, my poetry forgotten. I was trying to remember what I had felt when I saw the photo of the dead person on the wall and realized that it was Nnamdi.

Thats awful

* * *

My friends, my smug staff friends, were appalled by how much time (Nnamdi) and I spent together. Could he even make one decent sentence? What did we talk about? they wanted to know. Even I hardly know now. He made me laugh. We fought about things I no longer remember and sometimes, when I pretended to be angrier than I was, he would threaten to throw himself in the path of a car or to kneel, in apology, at the entrance of my class. He would say this so earnestly that I would laugh. Just as I laughed when he suggested we go to a *dibia* to do the *igba ndu*, a blood betrothal that would keep us from ever breaking up. I was not familiar with it. The people in my world did not do things like the *igba ndu* rite; they sniffed at the supernatural. But the simplicity of (Nnamdi's) faith intrigued me. Nnamdi intrigued me.

Before I went to the *Champion* office that June day, I knew Nnamdi was dead. His friend Ojay had told me some months before. "Something happened to (Nnamdi," he had said. (Nnamdi) had been at the wrong place at the wrong time, the (operation) was over, the armed robbers had finished stealing from the bank, but Nnamdi had parked his car in such a way that he blocked their getaway. I didn't cry. It seemed so distant, so unlikely, and I had not seen him in years.

It was in the taxi from the *Champion* office that I began to cry. I thought about the last time I had seen him. It was at a beach in Lagos. We had not seen each other since his father had transferred him to another secondary school. We were both self-consciously, unconvincingly mature. He said he was trying to get into the University of Lagos. I said I was preparing to take my final secondary school exams. He had not changed; the tall, thin body, the narrow face, and the hooked nose were all the same.

"Do you have a boyfriend?" he asked finally.   25

"Yes," I replied, although I did not.

He had a girlfriend, too, he said, many girlfriends in fact. Before we parted, he added, "You can have as many boyfriends as you want to. But when it comes to marriage, it's me and nobody else. God made you for me. If we marry other people, thunder will strike us down."

We were no longer young teenagers, but he spoke with that old earnestness on his face and I laughed.

* * *

On my birthday, the last birthday before Nnamdi left my school, he gave me a scented satin rose in a gilded case. I hid it from my mother: It looked expensive and I feared she would ask me to return it. Later, when he gave me a ring with gold strips that curved across my finger, I hid that too. But I did not hide the card he brought when I was sick with malaria. It looked like an ordinary get-well card, one of the many my friends had sent. When you opened Nnamdi's card, though, it played an upbeat take on "Für Elise." Inside the card, Nnamdi had written in his unformed, childish hand, "To my one love GB. From your own Nnamdi."

In memoriam: Nnamdi Ezenwa

For Discussion and Writing

1. Why are Adichie's friends mystified by her relationship with Nnamdi?
2. Where in the essay does Adichie let us know when she knew of Nnamdi's death? What is the effect of the placement of this information?
3. **connections** Adichie, in "To My One Love," and James Baldwin, in "Notes of a Native Son" (p. 44), both eschew linear chronology in the structuring of their essays. Describe how time is organized in each essay, and to what effect. How would the effect be different if the essays were structured chronologically? What would be lost?
4. Sometimes we think back on the things of our past—events, relationships, ideas—and they seem, as Adichie writes of her time with Nnamdi, "so distant." Write about something from your past that feels this way to you. How clearly can you see the event or person, or how clearly can you articulate the idea or opinion? How does thinking about it make you feel? Is the feeling of distance a stable thing, or can the past sometimes feel more immediate?
5. **looking further** Memory is a much-studied and yet still mysterious phenomenon. Read up on theories of memory from neuroscience, psychology, trauma studies, and anywhere else you turn up interesting work. First, summarize these ideas and then discuss which you find more convincing. Which seem truer or more useful to you? Which seem less congenial? Why?

SHERMAN ALEXIE

The Joy of Reading and Writing: Superman and Me

Born in 1966 and raised on the Spokane Indian Reservation in Wellpinit, Washington, Sherman Alexie is one of the foremost Native American writers and the recipient of the Native Writers' Circle of the Americas 2010 Lifetime Achievement Award. He is best known for his fiction, from his first collection of stories, The Lone Ranger and Tonto Fistfight in Heaven *(1993), which won the PEN/Hemingway Award for Best First Book of Fiction, to three novels,* Reservation Blues *(1995),* Indian Killer *(1996), and* Flight *(2007), and the young adult novel* The Absolutely True Diary of a Part-Time Indian *(2007). He has also written twelve books of poems, including* The Business of Fancydancing *(1991) and his latest,* Face *(2009); screenplays, including that for the movie* Smoke Signals *(1999), with Chris Eyre; and an album, with Jim Boyd, made of songs from the book* Reservation Blues.

"The Joy of Reading and Writing: Superman and Me" displays Alexie's characteristic mix of popular culture reference and reflection on what it means to be an Indian in today's America. As you read, note how carefully Alexie crafts what at first glance might seem to be a slight essay. Note especially the way images and phrases are repeated and the effect he constructs from these repetitions.

I learned to read with a Superman comic book. Simple enough, I suppose. I cannot recall which particular Superman comic book I read, nor can I remember which villain he fought in that issue. I cannot remember the plot, nor the means by which I obtained the comic book. What I can remember is this: I was 3 years old, a Spokane Indian boy living with his family on the Spokane Indian Reservation in eastern Washington state. We were poor by most standards, but one of my parents usually managed to find some minimum-wage job or another, which made us middle-class by reservation standards. I had a brother and three sisters. We lived on a combination of irregular paychecks, hope, fear, and government surplus food.

My father, who is one of the few Indians who went to Catholic school on purpose, was an avid reader of westerns, spy thrillers, murder mysteries, gangster epics, basketball player biographies, and anything else he could find. He bought his books by the pound at Dutch's Pawn Shop, Goodwill, Salvation Army, and Value Village. When he had extra money, he bought new novels at supermarkets, convenience stores, and hospital gift shops. Our house was filled with books. They were stacked in crazy piles in the bathroom, bedrooms, and living room. In a fit of unemployment-inspired creative energy, my father built a set of bookshelves and soon filled them with a random assortment of books about the Kennedy assassination, Watergate, the Vietnam War, and the entire 23-book series of the Apache westerns. My father loved books, and since I loved my father with an aching devotion, I decided to love books as well.

I can remember picking up my father's books before I could read. The words themselves were mostly foreign, but I still remember the exact moment when I first understood, with a sudden clarity, the purpose of a paragraph. I didn't have the vocabulary to say "paragraph," but I realized that a paragraph was a fence that held words. The words inside a paragraph worked together for a common purpose. They had some specific reason for being inside the same fence. This knowledge delighted me. I began to think of everything in terms of paragraphs. Our reservation was a small paragraph within the United States. My family's house was a paragraph, distinct from the other paragraphs of the LeBrets to the north, the Fords to our south, and the Tribal School to the west. Inside our house, each family member existed as a separate paragraph but still had genetics and common experiences to link us. Now, using this logic, I can see my changed family as an essay of seven paragraphs: mother, father, older brother, the deceased sister, my younger twin sisters, and our adopted little brother.

At the same time I was seeing the world in paragraphs, I also picked up that Superman comic book. Each panel, complete with picture, dialogue, and narrative was a three-dimensional paragraph. In one panel, Superman breaks through a door. His suit is red, blue, and yellow. The brown door shatters into many pieces.

I look at the narrative above the picture. I cannot read the words, but I assume it tells me that "Superman is breaking down the door." Aloud, I pretend to read the words and say, "Superman is breaking down the door." Words, dialogue, also float out of Superman's mouth. Because he is breaking down the door, I assume he says, "I am breaking down the door." Once again, I pretend to read the words and say aloud, "I am breaking down the door." In this way, I learned to read.

This might be an interesting story all by itself. A little Indian 5 boy teaches himself to read at an early age and advances quickly. He reads "Grapes of Wrath" in kindergarten when other children are struggling through "Dick and Jane." If he'd been anything but an Indian boy living on the reservation, he might have been called a prodigy. But he is an Indian boy living on the reservation and is simply an oddity. He grows into a man who often speaks of his childhood in the third person, as if it will somehow dull the pain and make him sound more modest about his talents.

A smart Indian is a dangerous person, widely feared and ridiculed by Indians and non-Indians alike. I fought with my classmates on a daily basis. They wanted me to stay quiet when the non-Indian teacher asked for answers, for volunteers, for help. We were Indian children who were expected to be stupid. Most lived up to those expectations inside the classroom but subverted them on the outside. They struggled with basic reading in school but could remember how to sing a few dozen powwow songs. They were monosyllabic in front of their non-Indian teachers but could tell complicated stories and jokes at the dinner table. They submissively ducked their heads when confronted by a non-Indian adult but would slug it out with the Indian bully who was 10 years older. As Indian children, we were expected to fail in the non-Indian world. Those who failed were ceremonially accepted by other Indians and appropriately pitied by non-Indians.

I refused to fail. I was smart. I was arrogant. I was lucky. I read books late into the night, until I could barely keep my eyes open. I read books at recess, then during lunch, and in the few minutes left after I had finished my classroom assignments. I read books in the car when my family traveled to powwows or basketball games. In shopping malls, I ran to the bookstores and read bits and pieces of as many books as I could. I read the books my father brought home from the pawnshops and secondhand. I read the books I borrowed from the library. I read the backs of cereal boxes. I read the newspaper. I read the bulletins posted on the walls of the school, the clinic, the tribal offices, the post office. I read junk mail. I read auto-repair manuals. I read magazines. I read anything that had words and paragraphs. I read with equal parts joy and desperation. I loved those books, but I also knew that love had only one purpose. I was trying to save my life.

Despite all the books I read, I am still surprised I became a writer. I was going to be a pediatrician. These days, I write novels, short stories, and poems. I visit schools and teach creative writing to Indian kids. In all my years in the reservation school system, I was never taught how to write poetry, short stories, or novels. I was certainly never taught that Indians wrote poetry, short stories, and novels. Writing was something beyond Indians. I cannot recall a single time that a guest teacher visited the reservation. There must have been visiting teachers. Who were they? Where are they now? Do they exist? I visit the schools as often as possible. The Indian kids crowd the classroom. Many are writing their own poems, short stories, and novels. They have read my books. They have read many other books. They look at me with bright eyes and arrogant wonder. They are trying to save their lives. Then there are the sullen and already defeated Indian kids who sit in the back rows and ignore me with theatrical precision. The pages of their notebooks are empty. They carry neither pencil nor pen. They stare out the window. They refuse and resist. "Books," I say to them. "Books," I say. I throw my weight against their locked doors. The door holds. I am smart. I am arrogant. I am lucky. I am trying to save our lives.

For Discussion and Writing

1. What is Superman doing in the comic book panel Alexie remembers? Why is it important to remember this detail at the very end of the essay?

2. In paragraph 7, Alexie repeats a certain verb fourteen times. What is this verb, and what effect does this repetition have? What might Alexie be trying to say about the process of his coming to literacy, in terms of both the effort required and the height of the obstacles encountered (or, given the metaphor introduced in par. 4, the thickness of the doors that must be broken through)?

3. **connections**   In "Learning to Read and Write" (p. 125), Frederick Douglass writes, "In moments of agony, I envied my fellow-slaves for their stupidity" (par. 6). Compare this sentiment to Alexie's feelings about his fellow classmates on the reservation (par. 6). Do you think that Alexie envied his classmates? Why, or why not? How were his difficulties different from those faced by other Indians?

4. In paragraph 5, Alexie writes about himself in the third person, in effect dramatizing what happens when one writes the story of one's life. Using the third person, write about a particularly important moment or aspect of your life. Afterward, write a short reflection on the distancing effect of referring to yourself as "he" or "she." How does this type of writing help you learn about yourself?

5. **looking further**   In the final paragraph, Alexie describes Indian students sitting in the back of classes he's visited as "sullen and already defeated," saying that they "refuse and resist." Refusal and resistance are complicated concepts in this essay: Alexie refuses to adhere to the role laid out for him as an Indian and instead reads and writes, thereby resisting not simply a stereotype but a circumscribed future— and some students resist his urgings to do the same. The connections between writing and resistance are many: while we often think of writing as a way to resist forms of power, it can also be used to resist change. Pick an issue currently in the news and find pieces of writing on opposing sides. What strategies do they use? Look at style, the kind of argument, or any aspect of writing used to make the cases.

GLORIA ANZALDÚA

How to Tame a Wild Tongue

Gloria Anzaldúa was born in 1942 in the Rio Grande Valley of South Texas. At age eleven she began working in the fields as a migrant worker and then on her family's land after the death of her father. Working her way through school, she eventually became a schoolteacher and then an academic, speaking and writing about feminist, lesbian, and Chicana issues and about autobiography. She is best known for This Bridge Called My Back: Writings by Radical Women of Color *(1981), which she edited with Cherríe Moraga, and* Borderlands/La Frontera: The New Mestiza *(1987). Anzaldúa died in 2004.*

"How to Tame a Wild Tongue" is from Borderlands/La Frontera. In it, Anzaldúa is concerned with many kinds of borders—between nations, cultures, classes, genders, languages. When she writes, "So, if you want to really hurt me, talk badly about my language" (par. 27), Anzaldúa is arguing for the ways in which identity is intertwined with the way we speak and for the ways in which people can be made to feel ashamed of their own tongues. Keeping hers wild—ignoring the closing of linguistic borders—is Anzaldúa's way of asserting her identity. Pay close attention to the way she writes here, too; her style could be seen as another way in which she keeps her tongue wild.

"We're going to have to control your tongue," the dentist says, pulling out all the metal from my mouth. Silver bits plop and tinkle into the basin. My mouth is a motherlode.

The dentist is cleaning out my roots. I get a whiff of the stench when I gasp. "I can't cap that tooth yet, you're still draining," he says.

"We're going to have to do something about your tongue," I hear the anger rising in his voice. My tongue keeps pushing out the wads of cotton, pushing back the drills, the long thin needles. "I've never seen anything as strong or as stubborn," he says. And I think, how do you tame a wild tongue,

27

train it to be quiet, how do you bridle and saddle it? How do you make it lie down?

> "Who is to say that robbing a people of
> its language is less violent than war?"
> —RAY GWYN SMITH[1]

Terrible

I remember being caught speaking Spanish at recess—that was good for three licks on the knuckles with a sharp ruler. I remember being sent to the corner of the classroom for "talking back" to the Anglo teacher when all I was trying to do was tell her how to pronounce my name. "If you want to be American, speak 'American.' If you don't like it, go back to Mexico where you belong."

no comprehend

"I want you to speak English. *Pa' hallar buen trabajo tienes que*   5 *saber hablar el inglés bien. Qué vale toda tu educación si todavía hablas inglés con un* 'accent,'" my mother would say, mortified that I spoke English like a Mexican. At Pan American University, I and all Chicano students were required to take two speech classes. Their purpose: to get rid of our accents.

Attacks on one's form of expression with the intent to censor are a violation of the First Amendment. *El Anglo con cara de inocente nos arrancó la lengua.* Wild tongues can't be tamed, they can only be cut out.

OVERCOMING THE TRADITION OF SILENCE

> *Ahogadas, escupimos el oscuro.*
> *Peleando con nuestra propia sombra*
> *el silencio nos sepulta.*

En boca cerrada no entran moscas. "Flies don't enter a closed mouth" is a saying I kept hearing when I was a child. *Ser habladora* was to be a gossip and a liar, to talk too much. *Muchachitas bien criadas*, well-bred girls don't answer back. *Es una falta de respeto* to talk back to one's mother or father. I remember one of the sins I'd recite to the priest in the confession box the few times I went to confession: talking back to my mother, *hablar pa' 'tras, repelar. Hocicona, repelona, chismosa*, having a big mouth, questioning, carrying tales are all signs of being *mal criada.* In my culture they are all words that are derogatory if applied to women—I've never heard them applied to men.

* * *

The first time I heard two women, a Puerto Rican and a Cuban, say the word *"nosotras,"* I was shocked. I had not known the word existed. Chicanas use *nosotros* whether we're male or female. We are robbed of our female being by the masculine plural. Language is a male discourse.

> And our tongues have become
> dry   the wilderness has
> dried out our tongues   and
> we have forgotten speech.
> — IRENA KLEPFISZ[2]

Even our own people, other Spanish speakers *nos quieren poner candados en la boca.* They would hold us back with their bag of *reglas de academia.*

Oyé como ladra: el lenguaje de la frontera

Quien tiene boca se equivoca.
— MEXICAN SAYING

"Pocho, cultural traitor, you're speaking the oppressor's lan-   10
guage by speaking English, you're ruining the Spanish language," I have been accused by various Latinos and Latinas. Chicano Spanish is considered by the purist and by most Latinos deficient, a mutilation of Spanish.

But Chicano Spanish is a border tongue which developed natu-rally. Change, *evolución, enriquecimiento de palabras nuevas por invención o adopción* have created variants of Chicano Spanish, *un nuevo lenguaje. Un lenguaje que corresponde a un modo de vivir.* Chicano Spanish is not incorrect, it is a living language.

For a people who are neither Spanish nor live in a country in which Spanish is the first language; for a people who live in a country in which English is the reigning tongue but who are not Anglo; for a people who cannot entirely identify with either stan-dard (formal, Castillian) Spanish nor standard English, what recourse is left to them but to create their own language? A lan-guage which they can connect their identity to, one capable of communicating the realities and values true to themselves—a language with terms that are neither *español ni inglés,* but both. We speak a patois, a forked tongue, a variation of two languages.

Chicano Spanish sprang out of the Chicanos' need to identify ourselves as a distinct people. We needed a language with which we could communicate with ourselves, a secret language. For some of us, language is a homeland closer than the Southwest— for many Chicanos today live in the Midwest and the East. And because we are a complex, heterogeneous people, we speak many languages. Some of the languages we speak are:

1. Standard English
2. Working class and slang English
3. Standard Spanish
4. Standard Mexican Spanish
5. North Mexican Spanish dialect
6. Chicano Spanish (Texas, New Mexico, Arizona, and California have regional variations)
7. Tex-Mex
8. *Pachuco* (called *caló*)

My "home" tongues are the languages I speak with my sister and brothers, with my friends. They are the last five listed, with 6 and 7 being closest to my heart. From school, the media, and job situations, I've picked up standard and working class English. From Mamagrande Locha and from reading Spanish and Mexican literature, I've picked up Standard Spanish and Standard Mexican Spanish. From *los recién llegados*, Mexican immigrants, and *braceros*, I learned the North Mexican dialect. With Mexicans I'll try to speak either Standard Mexican Spanish or the North Mexican dialect. From my parents and Chicanos living in the Valley, I picked up Chicano Texas Spanish, and I speak it with my mom, younger brother (who married a Mexican and who rarely mixes Spanish with English), aunts, and older relatives.

With Chicanas from *Nuevo México* or *Arizona* I will speak 15 Chicano Spanish a little, but often they don't understand what I'm saying. With most California Chicanas I speak entirely in English (unless I forget). When I first moved to San Francisco, I'd rattle off something in Spanish, unintentionally embarrassing them. Often it is only with another Chicana *tejana* that I can talk freely.

Words distorted by English are known as anglicisms or *pochismos*. The *pocho* is an anglicized Mexican or American of Mexican origin who speaks Spanish with an accent characteristic of North Americans and who distorts and reconstructs the language according to the influence of English.[3] Tex-Mex, or Spanglish, comes most naturally to me. I may switch back and forth from English to Spanish in the same sentence or in the same word. With my sister and my brother Nune and with Chicano *tejano* contemporaries I speak in Tex-Mex.

From kids and people my own age I picked up *Pachuco*. *Pachuco* (the language of the zoot suiters) is a language of rebellion, both against Standard Spanish and Standard English. It is a secret language. Adults of the culture and outsiders cannot understand it. It is made up of slang words from both English and Spanish. *Ruca* means girl or woman, *vato* means guy or dude, *chale* means no, *simón* means yes, *churro* is sure, talk is *periquiar,* *pigionear* means petting, *que gacho* means how nerdy, *ponte águila* means watch out, death is called *la pelona*. Through lack of practice and not having others who can speak it, I've lost most of the *Pachuco* tongue.

CHICANO SPANISH

Chicanos, after 250 years of Spanish/Anglo colonization, have developed significant differences in the Spanish we speak. We collapse two adjacent vowels into a single syllable and sometimes shift the stress in certain words such as *maíz/maiz, cohete/cuete*. We leave out certain consonants when they appear between vowels: *lado/lao, mojado/mojao.* Chicanos from South Texas pronounce *f* as *j* as in *jue (fue)*. Chicanos use "archaisms," words that are no longer in the Spanish language, words that have been evolved out. We say *semos, truje, haiga, ansina,* and *naiden*. We retain the "archaic" *j*, as in *jalar*, that derives from an earlier *h* (the French *halar* or the Germanic *halon* which was lost to standard Spanish in the 16th century), but which is still found in several regional dialects such as the one spoken in South Texas. (Due to geography, Chicanos from the Valley of South Texas were cut off linguistically from other Spanish speakers. We tend to use words that the Spaniards brought over from Medieval Spain. The majority of the Spanish colonizers in Mexico and the Southwest came from Extremadura—Hernán Cortés was one of them—and Andalucía. Andalucians pronounce *ll* like a *y*, and their *d*'s tend to be absorbed by adjacent vowels: *tirado* becomes *tirao*. They brought *el lenguaje popular, dialectos y regionalismos*.[4])

Chicanos and other Spanish speakers also shift *ll* to *y* and *z* to *s*.[5] We leave out initial syllables, saying *tar* for *estar*, *toy* for *estoy*, *hora* for *ahora* (*cubanos* and *puertorriqueños* also leave out initial letters of some words). We also leave out the final syllable such as *pa* for *para*. The intervocalic *y*, the *ll* as in *tortilla*, *ella*, *botella*, gets replaced by *tortia* or *tortiya*, *ea*, *botea*. We add an additional syllable at the beginning of certain words: *atocar* for *tocar*, *agastar* for *gastar*. Sometimes we'll say *lavaste las vacijas*, other times *lavates* (substituting the *ates* verb endings for the *aste*).

We use anglicisms, words borrowed from English: *bola* from ball, *carpeta* from carpet, *máchina de lavar* (instead of *lavadora*) from washing machine. Tex-Mex argot, created by adding a Spanish sound at the beginning or end of an English word such as *cookiar* for cook, *watchar* for watch, *parkiar* for park, and *rapiar* for rape, is the result of the pressures on Spanish speakers to adapt to English. 20

We don't use the word *vosotros/as* or its accompanying verb form. We don't say *claro* (to mean yes), *imagínate*, or *me emociona*, unless we picked up Spanish from Latinas, out of a book, or in a classroom. Other Spanish-speaking groups are going through the same, or similar, development in their Spanish.

LINGUISTIC TERRORISM

> *Deslenguadas. Somos los del español deficiente.* We are your linguistic nightmare, your linguistic aberration, your linguistic *mestisaje*, the subject of your *burla*. Because we speak with tongues of fire we are culturally crucified. Racially, culturally, and linguistically *somos huérfanos*—*we speak an orphan tongue*.

Chicanas who grew up speaking Chicano Spanish have internalized the belief that we speak poor Spanish. It is illegitimate, a bastard language. And because we internalize how our language has been used against us by the dominant culture, we use our language differences against each other.

Chicana feminists often skirt around each other with suspicion and hesitation. For the longest time I couldn't figure it out. Then it dawned on me. To be close to another Chicana is like looking into the mirror. We are afraid of what we'll see there. *Pena.* Shame. Low estimation of self. In childhood we are told that our language is wrong. Repeated attacks on our native tongue diminish our sense of self. The attacks continue throughout our lives.

Chicanas feel uncomfortable talking in Spanish to Latinas, afraid of their censure. Their language was not outlawed in their countries. They had a whole lifetime of being immersed in their native tongue; generations, centuries in which Spanish was a first language, taught in school, heard on radio and TV, and read in the newspaper.

If a person, Chicana or Latina, has a low estimation of my native tongue, she also has a low estimation of me. Often with *mexicanas y latinas* we'll speak English as a neutral language. Even among Chicanas we tend to speak English at parties or conferences. Yet, at the same time, we're afraid the other will think we're *agringadas* because we don't speak Chicano Spanish. We oppress each other trying to out-Chicano each other, vying to be the "real" Chicanas, to speak like Chicanos. There is no one Chicano language just as there is no one Chicano experience. A monolingual Chicana whose first language is English or Spanish is just as much a Chicana as one who speaks several variants of Spanish. A Chicana from Michigan or Chicago or Detroit is just as much a Chicana as one from the Southwest. Chicano Spanish is as diverse linguistically as it is regionally.

By the end of this century, Spanish speakers will comprise the biggest minority group in the U.S., a country where students in high schools and colleges are encouraged to take French classes because French is considered more "cultured." But for a language to remain alive it must be used.[6] By the end of this century English, and not Spanish, will be the mother tongue of most Chicanos and Latinos.

So, if you want to really hurt me, talk badly about my language. Ethnic identity is twin skin to linguistic identity—I am my language. Until I can take pride in my language, I cannot take pride in myself. Until I can accept as legitimate Chicano Texas Spanish, Tex-Mex, and all the other languages I speak, I cannot accept the legitimacy of myself. Until I am free to write bilingually and to switch codes without having always to translate, while I still have to speak English or Spanish when I would rather speak Spanglish, and as long as I have to accommodate the English speakers rather than having them accommodate me, my tongue will be illegitimate.

I will no longer be made to feel ashamed of existing. I will have my voice: Indian, Spanish, white. I will have my serpent's tongue—my woman's voice, my sexual voice, my poet's voice. I will overcome the tradition of silence. *strong women*

independent woman

> My fingers
> move sly against your palm
> Like women everywhere, we speak in code. . . .
> —MELANIE KAYE/KANTROWITZ[7]

— Queen Ba

"Vistas," corridos, y comida: My Native Tongue

In the 1960s, I read my first Chicano novel. It was *City of Night* by John Rechy, a gay Texan, son of a Scottish father and a Mexican mother. For days I walked around in stunned amazement that a Chicano could write and could get published. When I read *I Am Joaquín*[8] I was surprised to see a bilingual book by a Chicano in print. When I saw poetry written in Tex-Mex for the first time, a feeling of pure joy flashed through me. I felt like we really existed as a people. In 1971, when I started teaching High School English to Chicano students, I tried to supplement the required texts with works by Chicanos, only to be reprimanded and forbidden to do so by the principal. He claimed that I was supposed to teach "American" and English literature. At the risk of being fired, I swore my students to secrecy and slipped in Chicano short stories, poems, a play. In graduate school, while working toward a Ph.D., I had to "argue" with one advisor after the other, semester after semester, before I was allowed to make Chicano literature an area of focus.

Even before I read books by Chicanos or Mexicans, it was the Mexican movies I saw at the drive-in—the Thursday night special of $1.00 a carload—that gave me a sense of belonging. "*Vámonos a las vistas,*" my mother would call out and we'd all—grandmother, brothers, sister, and cousins—squeeze into the car. We'd wolf down cheese and bologna white bread sandwiches while watching Pedro Infante in melodramatic tearjerkers like *Nosotros los pobres,* the first "real" Mexican movie (that was not an imitation of European movies). I remember seeing *Cuando los hijos se van* and surmising that all Mexican movies played up the love a mother has for her children and what ungrateful sons

Spanish literature

30

and daughters suffer when they are not devoted to their mothers. I remember the singing-type "westerns" of Jorge Negrete and Miquel Aceves Mejía. When watching Mexican movies, I felt a sense of homecoming as well as alienation. People who were to amount to something didn't go to Mexican movies, or *bailes*, or tune their radios to *bolero*, *rancherita*, and *corrido* music.

The whole time I was growing up, there was *norteño* music sometimes called North Mexican border music, or Tex-Mex music, or Chicano music, or *cantina* (bar) music. I grew up listening to *conjuntos*, three- or four-piece bands made up of folk musicians playing guitar, *bajo sexto*, drums, and button accordion, which Chicanos had borrowed from the German immigrants who had come to Central Texas and Mexico to farm and build breweries. In the Rio Grande Valley, Steve Jordan and Little Joe Hernández were popular, and Flaco Jiménez was the accordion king. The rhythms of Tex-Mex music are those of the polka, also adapted from the Germans, who in turn had borrowed the polka from the Czechs and Bohemians.

I remember the hot, sultry evenings when *corridos*—songs of love and death on the Texas-Mexican borderlands—reverberated out of cheap amplifiers from the local *cantinas* and wafted in through my bedroom window.

Corridos first became widely used along the South Texas/ Mexican border during the early conflict between Chicanos and Anglos. The *corridos* are usually about Mexican heroes who do valiant deeds against the Anglo oppressors. Pancho Villa's song, *"La cucaracha,"* is the most famous one. *Corridos* of John F. Kennedy and his death are still very popular in the Valley. Older Chicanos remember Lydia Mendoza, one of the great border *corrido* singers who was called *la Gloria de Tejas*. Her *"El tango negro,"* sung during the Great Depression, made her a singer of the people. The everpresent *corridos* narrated one hundred years of border history, bringing news of events as well as entertaining. These folk musicians and folk songs are our chief cultural myth-makers, and they made our hard lives seem bearable.

I grew up feeling ambivalent about our music. Country-western and rock-and-roll had more status. In the 50s and 60s, for the slightly educated and *agringado* Chicanos, there existed a sense of shame at being caught listening to our music. Yet I couldn't stop my feet from thumping to the music, could not stop humming the words, nor hide from myself the exhilaration I felt when I heard it.

There are more subtle ways that we internalize identification, 35 especially in the forms of images and emotions. For me food and certain smells are tied to my identity, to my homeland. Woodsmoke curling up to an immense blue sky; woodsmoke perfuming my grandmother's clothes, her skin. The stench of cow manure and the yellow patches on the ground; the crack of a .22 rifle and the reek of cordite. Homemade white cheese sizzling in a pan, melting inside a folded *tortilla*. My sister Hilda's hot, spicy *menudo*, *chile colorado* making it deep red, pieces of *panza* and hominy floating on top. My brother Carito barbequing *fajitas* in the backyard. Even now and 3,000 miles away, I can see my mother spicing the ground beef, pork, and venison with *chile*. My mouth salivates at the thought of the hot steaming *tamales* I would be eating if I were home.

Si le preguntas a mi mamá, "¿Qué eres?"

"Identity is the essential core of who we are as individuals, the conscious experience of the self inside."
        —GERSHEN KAUFMAN[9]

Nosotros los Chicanos straddle the borderlands. On one side of us, we are constantly exposed to the Spanish of the Mexicans, on the other side we hear the Anglos' incessant clamoring so that we forget our language. Among ourselves we don't say *nosotros los americanos, o nosotros los españoles, o nosotros los hispanos.* We say *nosotros los mexicanos* (by *mexicanos* we do not mean citizens of Mexico; we do not mean a national identity, but a racial one). We distinguish between *mexicanos del otro lado* and *mexicanos de este lado.* Deep in our hearts we believe that being Mexican has nothing to do with which country one lives in. Being Mexican is a state of soul—not one of mind, not one of citizenship. Neither eagle nor serpent, but both. And like the ocean, neither animal respects borders.

Dime con quien andas y te diré quien eres.
(Tell me who your friends are and I'll tell you who you are.)
—MEXICAN SAYING

Si le preguntas a mi mamá, "¿Qué eres?" te dirá, "Soy mexicana."
My brothers and sister say the same. I sometimes will answer *"soy mexicana"* and at others will say *"soy Chicana" o "soy tejana."* But I identified as *"Raza"* before I ever identified as *"mexicana"* or "Chicana."

As a culture, we call ourselves Spanish when referring to ourselves as a linguistic group and when copping out. It is then that we forget our predominant Indian genes. We are 70–80 percent Indian.[10] We call ourselves Hispanic[11] or Spanish-American or Latin American or Latin when linking ourselves to other Spanish-speaking peoples of the Western hemisphere and when copping out. We call ourselves Mexican-American[12] to signify we are neither Mexican nor American, but more the noun "American" than the adjective "Mexican" (and when copping out).

Chicanos and other people of color suffer economically for not acculturating. This voluntary (yet forced) alienation makes for psychological conflict, a kind of dual identity—we don't identify with the Anglo-American cultural values and we don't totally identify with the Mexican cultural values. We are a synergy of two cultures with various degrees of Mexicanness or Angloness. I have so internalized the borderland conflict that sometimes I feel like one cancels out the other and we are zero, nothing, no one. *A veces no soy nada ni nadie. Pero hasta cuando no lo soy, lo soy.*

When not copping out, when we know we are more than nothing, we call ourselves Mexican, referring to race and ancestry; *mestizo* when affirming both our Indian and Spanish (but we hardly ever own our Black ancestry); Chicano when referring to a politically aware people born and/or raised in the U.S.; *Raza* when referring to Chicanos; *tejanos* when we are Chicanos from Texas.

Chicanos did not know we were a people until 1965 when Ceasar Chavez and the farmworkers united and *I Am Joaquín* was published and *la Raza Unida* party was formed in Texas. With that recognition, we became a distinct people. Something momentous happened to the Chicano soul—we became aware of our reality and acquired a name and a language (Chicano Spanish) that reflected that reality. Now that we had a name, some of the fragmented pieces began to fall together—who we were, what we were, how we had evolved. We began to get glimpses of what we might eventually become.

Yet the struggle of identities continues, the struggle of borders is our reality still. One day the inner struggle will cease and a true integration take place. In the meantime, *tenemos que hacer la lucha. ¿Quién está protegiendo los ranchos de mi gente? ¿Quién está tratando de cerrar la fisura entre la india y el blanco en nuestra sangre? El Chicano, si, el Chicano que anda como un ladrón en su propia casa.*

Los Chicanos, how patient we seem, how very patient. There is the quiet of the Indian about us.[13] We know how to survive. When other races have given up their tongue, we've kept ours. We know what it is to live under the hammer blow of the dominant *norteamericano* culture. But more than we count the blows, we count the days the weeks the years the centuries the eons until the white laws and commerce and customs will rot in the deserts they've created, lie bleached. *Humildes* yet proud, *quietos* yet wild, *nosotros los mexicanos-Chicanos* will walk by the crumbling ashes as we go about our business. Stubborn, persevering, impenetrable as stone, yet possessing a malleability that renders us unbreakable, we, the *mestizas* and *mestizos,* will remain.

Notes

1. Ray Gwyn Smith, *Moorland Is Cold Country,* unpublished book.

2. Irena Klepfisz, "*Di rayze aheym*/The Journey Home," in *The Tribe of Dina: A Jewish Women's Anthology,* Melanie Kaye/Kantrowitz and Irena Klepfisz, eds. (Montpelier, VT: Sinister Wisdom Books, 1986), 49.

3. R. C. Ortega, *Dialectología Del Barrio,* trans. Hortencia S. Alwan (Los Angeles, CA: R. C. Ortega Publisher & Bookseller, 1977), 132.

4. Eduardo Hernandéz-Chávez, Andrew D. Cohen, and Anthony F. Beltramo, *El Lenguaje de los Chicanos: Regional and Social Characteristics of Language Used by Mexican Americans* (Arlington, VA: Center for Applied Linguistics, 1975), 39.

5. Hernandéz-Chávez, xvii.

6. Irena Klepfisz, "Secular Jewish Identity: Yidishkayt in America," in *The Tribe of Dina,* Kaye/Kantrowitz and Klepfisz, eds., 43.

7. Melanie Kaye/Kantrowitz, "Sign," in *We Speak in Code: Poems and Other Writings* (Pittsburgh, PA: Motheroot Publications, Inc., 1980), 85.

8. Rodolfo Gonzales, *I Am Joaquín/Yo Soy Joaquín* (New York, NY: Bantam Books, 1972). It was first published in 1967.

9. Gershen Kaufman, *Shame: The Power of Caring* (Cambridge, MA: Schenkman Books, Inc., 1980), 68.

10. John R. Chávez, *The Lost Land: The Chicago Images of the Southwest* (Albuquerque, NM: University of New Mexico Press, 1984), 88–90.

11. "Hispanic" is derived from *Hispanis* (*España*, a name given to the Iberian Peninsula in ancient times when it was a part of the Roman Empire) and is a term designated by the U.S. government to make it easier to handle us on paper.

12. The Treaty of Guadalupe Hidalgo created the Mexican-American in 1848.

13. Anglos, in order to alleviate their guilt for dispossessing the Chicano, stressed the Spanish part of us and perpetrated the myth of the Spanish Southwest. We have accepted the fiction that we are Hispanic, that is Spanish, in order to accommodate ourselves to the dominant culture and its abhorrence of Indians. Chávez, 88–91.

For Discussion and Writing

1. List the different kinds of languages Anzaldúa says she speaks and organize them according to a principle of your own selection. Explain that principle and what the list it produces tells us about the Chicano/a experience with language.

2. How does Anzaldúa use definition to discuss her experience with language, and to what effect?

3. **connections** Compare Anzaldúa's sense of herself as an American to Audre Lorde's in "The Fourth of July" (p. 221). In what way does each woman feel American? In what way does each not?

4. In her discussion of moving back and forth between the varieties of languages she speaks, Anzaldúa uses the term "switch codes" (par. 27). Define that term and write about situations in your life in which you switch codes.

5. **looking further** When the book from which this excerpt comes was published in 1987, much attention was being paid to multiculturalism and reactions against it—a conflict often called the "culture wars." Read up on this controversy and discuss the different political and philosophical visions informing the conflicting positions. Where do you stand on the issues raised by multiculturalism? Do you think our model today should be the melting pot, or what then–New York City mayor David Dinkins called the "gorgeous mosaic"?

BARBARA LAZEAR ASCHER

On Compassion

Barbara Lazear Ascher, born in 1946, worked as a lawyer for two years before she became a full-time writer. Her essays, which have appeared in newspapers and magazines, have been collected in Playing after Dark *(1986) and* The Habit of Loving *(1989). She has also written books about her brother's death from AIDS (*Landscape without Gravity: A Memoir of Grief, *1993) and romance (*Dancing in the Dark: Romance, Yearning, and the Search for the Sublime, *1999).*

A New Yorker, Ascher draws her examples for "On Compassion" from life in that city. The brief scenes she describes — the encounter on the street corner, the moment in the café — allow the reader to imagine the thoughts and feelings of the participants. As you read, take note of how the specific details of the city enliven her examples and the way that specificity helps the examples to illustrate her argument.

The man's grin is less the result of circumstance than dreams or madness. His buttonless shirt, with one sleeve missing, hangs outside the waist of his baggy trousers. Carefully plaited dreadlocks bespeak a better time, long ago. As he crosses Manhattan's Seventy-ninth Street, his gait is the shuffle of the forgotten ones held in place by gravity rather than plans. On the corner of Madison Avenue, he stops before a blond baby in an Aprica stroller. The baby's mother waits for the light to change and her hands close tighter on the stroller's handle as she sees the man approach.

The others on the corner, five men and women waiting for the crosstown bus, look away. They daydream a bit and gaze into the weak rays of November light. A man with a briefcase lifts and lowers the shiny toe of his right shoe, watching the light reflect, trying to catch and balance it, as if he could hold and make it his, to ease the heavy gray of coming January, February, and March. The winter months that will send snow around the feet, calves, and knees of the grinning man as he heads for the shelter of Grand Central or Pennsylvania Station.

But for now, in this last gasp of autumn warmth, he is still. His eyes fix on the baby. The mother removes her purse from her shoulder and rummages through its contents: lipstick, a lace handkerchief, an address book. She finds what she's looking for and passes a folded dollar over her child's head to the man who stands and stares even though the light has changed and traffic navigates about his hips.

His hands continue to dangle at his sides. He does not know his part. He does not know that acceptance of the gift and gratitude are what make this transaction complete. The baby, weary of the unwavering stare, pulls its blanket over its head. The man does not look away. Like a bridegroom waiting at the altar, his eyes pierce the white veil.

The mother grows impatient and pushes the stroller before her,   5 bearing the dollar like a cross. Finally, a black hand rises and closes around green.

Was it fear or compassion that motivated the gift?

Up the avenue, at Ninety-first Street, there is a small French bread shop where you can sit and eat a buttery, overpriced croissant and wash it down with rich cappuccino. Twice when I have stopped here to stave hunger or stay the cold, twice as I have sat and read and felt the warm rush of hot coffee and milk, an old man has wandered in and stood inside the entrance. He wears a stained blanket pulled up to his chin, and a woolen hood pulled down to his gray, bushy eyebrows. As he stands, the scent of stale cigarettes and urine fills the small, overheated room.

The owner of the shop, a moody French woman, emerges from the kitchen with steaming coffee in a Styrofoam cup, and a small paper bag of . . . of what? Yesterday's bread? Today's croissant? He accepts the offering as silently as he came, and is gone.

Twice I have witnessed this, and twice I have wondered, what compels this woman to feed this man? Pity? Care? Compassion? Or does she simply want to rid her shop of his troublesome presence? If expulsion were her motivation she would not reward his arrival with gifts of food. Most proprietors do not. They chase the homeless from their midst with expletives and threats.

As winter approaches, the mayor of New York City is moving   10 the homeless off the streets and into Bellevue Hospital. The New

York Civil Liberties Union is watchful. They question whether the rights of these people who live in our parks and doorways are being violated by involuntary hospitalization.

I think the mayor's notion is humane, but I fear it is something else as well. Raw humanity offends our sensibilities. We want to protect ourselves from an awareness of rags with voices that make no sense and scream forth in inarticulate rage. We do not wish to be reminded of the tentative state of our own well-being and sanity. And so, the troublesome presence is removed from the awareness of the electorate.

Like other cities, there is much about Manhattan now that resembles Dickensian London. Ladies in high-heeled shoes pick their way through poverty and madness. You hear more cocktail party complaints than usual, "I just can't take New York anymore." Our citizens dream of the open spaces of Wyoming, the manicured exclusivity of Hobe Sound.

And yet, it may be that these are the conditions that finally give birth to empathy, the mother of compassion. We cannot deny the existence of the helpless as their presence grows. It is impossible to insulate ourselves against what is at our very doorstep. I don't believe that one is born compassionate. Compassion is not a character trait like a sunny disposition. It must be learned, and it is learned by having adversity at our windows, coming through the gates of our yards, the walls of our towns, adversity that becomes so familiar that we begin to identify and empathize with it.

For the ancient Greeks, drama taught and reinforced compassion within a society. The object of Greek tragedy was to inspire empathy in the audience so that the common response to the hero's fall was: "There, but for the grace of God, go I." Could it be that this was the response of the mother who offered the dollar, the French woman who gave the food? Could it be that the homeless, like those ancients, are reminding us of our common humanity? Of course, there is a difference. This play doesn't end — and the players can't go home.

For Discussion and Writing

1. What examples of encounters with the homeless does Ascher offer?
2. Imagine and list alternative examples of encounters with the homeless that Ascher might have used. How might they have changed her essay?

3. **connections**   Both Ascher and Lars Eighner in "On Dumpster Diving" (p. 146) write about people who are down on their luck: Eighner as one who has been down on his luck himself, Ascher from the perspective of the more fortunate. How do their differing perspectives inform their essays?

4. Where does Ascher believe compassion comes from? Do you agree or disagree? Why? Can you illustrate your argument with an example from your own experience?

5. **looking further**   Our federal and state governments, due to the economic downturn of the past few years, have had to grapple with the question of how much government can and should do to assist citizens who have fallen on hard times. How have these questions been asked and answered across history and across the globe? What informs the answers? What's your answer?

JAMES BALDWIN

Notes of a Native Son

Born in Harlem in 1924, a preacher and a published writer of reviews and essays at a young age, James Baldwin became a noted writer of American prose. Though he lived abroad for much of his adult life, in Paris, Switzerland, and Istanbul, Baldwin wrote incisively and passionately about the experience of being black in America. His first novel, Go Tell It on the Mountain *(1953), drew on his youth in the church and on his relationship with his preacher father as well as on the rolling, repetitive, swelling language of the sermon. His essay collection* Notes of a Native Son *(1955) reflected further on his own life and on African American experience as well as on the literary and cultural products that have come out of that experience. Baldwin's next novels,* Giovanni's Room *(1956) and* Another Country *(1962), delved into the issue of homosexuality. In his open explorations in fiction and nonfiction of taboo subjects and often hidden but sometimes quite open prejudices, Baldwin became a model of a writer practicing thoughtful yet always heartfelt engagement with the world.*

"Notes of a Native Son" considers the hatred at the heart of race relations in midcentury America and at the heart of Baldwin's relationship with his father. That Baldwin accepts that hate as neither the totality nor the final destination of these relationships is testament to his sensibility and strength as a writer and as a man. As you read, savor the writing from line to line and paragraph to paragraph, and think about the ways in which these lines and paragraphs add up to such quietly forceful writing.

I

On the 29th of July, in 1943, my father died. On the same day, a few hours later, his last child was born. Over a month before this, while all our energies were concentrated in waiting for these events, there had been, in Detroit, one of the bloodiest race riots of the century. A few hours after my father's funeral, while he lay

44

in state in the undertaker's chapel, a race riot broke out in Harlem. On the morning of the 3rd of August, we drove my father to the graveyard through a wilderness of smashed plate glass. The day of my father's funeral had also been my nineteenth birthday. As we drove him to the graveyard, the spoils of injustice, anarchy, discontent, and hatred were all around us. It seemed to me that God himself had devised, to mark my father's end, the most sustained and brutally dissonant of codas. And it seemed to me, too, that the violence which rose all about us as my father left the world had been devised as a corrective for the pride of his eldest son. I had declined to believe in that apocalypse which had been central to my father's vision; very well, life seemed to be saying, here is something that will certainly pass for an apocalypse until the real thing comes along. I had inclined to be contemptuous of my father for the conditions of his life, for the conditions of our lives. When his life had ended I began to wonder about that life and also, in a new way, to be apprehensive about my own.

I had not known my father very well. We had got on badly, partly because we shared, in our different fashions, the vice of stubborn pride. When he was dead I realized that I had hardly ever spoken to him. When he had been dead a long time I began to wish I had. It seems to be typical of life in America, where opportunities, real and fancied, are thicker than anywhere else on the globe, that the second generation has no time to talk to the first. No one, including my father, seems to have known exactly how old he was, but his mother had been born during slavery. He was of the first generation of free men. He, along with thousands of other Negroes, came North after 1919 and I was part of that generation which had never seen the landscape of what Negroes sometimes call the Old Country.

He had been born in New Orleans and had been a quite young man there during the time that Louis Armstrong, a boy, was running errands for the dives and honky-tonks of what was always presented to me as one of the most wicked of cities—to this day, whenever I think of New Orleans, I also helplessly think of Sodom and Gomorrah. My father never mentioned Louis Armstrong, except to forbid us to play his records; but there was a picture of him on our wall for a long time. One of my father's strong-willed female relatives had placed it there and forbade my father to take it down. He never did, but he eventually maneuvered her out of the house and when, some years later, she was in trouble and near death, he refused to do anything to help her.

He was, I think, very handsome. I gather this from photo- 5 graphs and from my own memories of him, dressed in his Sunday best and on his way to preach a sermon somewhere, when I was little. Handsome, proud, and ingrown, "like a toe-nail," somebody said. But he looked to me, as I grew older, like pictures I had seen of African tribal chieftains: he really should have been naked, with war-paint on and barbaric mementos, standing among spears. He could be chilling in the pulpit and indescribably cruel in his personal life and he was certainly the most bitter man I have ever met; yet it must be said that there was something else in him, buried in him, which lent him his tremendous power and, even, a rather crushing charm. It had something to do with his blackness, I think—he was very black—with his blackness and his beauty, and with the fact that he knew that he was black but did not know that he was beautiful. He claimed to be proud of his blackness but it had also been the cause of much humiliation and it had fixed bleak boundaries to his life. He was not a young man when we were growing up and he had already suffered many kinds of ruin; in his outrageously demanding and protective way he loved his children, who were black like him and menaced, like him; and all these things sometimes showed in his face when he tried, never to my knowledge with any success, to establish contact with any of us. When he took one of his children on his knee to play, the child always became fretful and began to cry; when he tried to help one of us with our homework the absolutely unabating tension which emanated from him caused our minds and our tongues to become paralyzed, so that he, scarcely knowing why, flew into a rage and the child, not knowing why, was punished. If it ever entered his head to bring a surprise home for his children, it was, almost unfailingly, the wrong surprise and even the big watermelons he often brought home on his back in the summertime led to the most appalling scenes. I do not remember, in all those years, that one of his children was ever glad to see him come home. From what I was able to gather of his early life, it seemed that this inability to establish contact with other people had always marked him and had been one of the things which had driven him out of New Orleans. There was something in him, therefore, groping and tentative, which was never expressed and which was buried with him. One saw it most clearly when he was facing new people and hoping to impress them. But he never did, not for long. We went from church to smaller and more improbable church, he found himself in less and less demand as a minister, and by the time he died none of his friends had come to see him for a long time. He had lived and died in an intolerable bitterness of spirit and it frightened me, as we drove him to the graveyard through those unquiet, ruined streets, to see how powerful and overflowing this bitterness could be and to realize that this bitterness now was mine.

When he died I had been away from home for a little over a year. In that year I had had time to become aware of the meaning of all my father's bitter warnings, had discovered the secret of his proudly pursed lips and rigid carriage: I had discovered the weight of white people in the world. I saw that this had been for my ancestors and now would be for me an awful thing to live with and that the bitterness which had helped to kill my father could also kill me.

He had been ill a long time—in the mind, as we now realized, reliving instances of his fantastic intransigence in the new light of his affliction and endeavoring to feel a sorrow for him which never, quite, came true. We had not known that he was being eaten up by paranoia, and the discovery that his cruelty, to our bodies and our minds, had been one of the symptoms of his illness was not, then, enough to enable us to forgive him. The younger children felt, quite simply, relief that he would not be coming home anymore. My mother's observation that it was he, after all, who had kept them alive all these years meant nothing because the problems of keeping children alive are not real for children. The older children felt, with my father gone, that they could invite their friends to the house without fear that their friends would be insulted or, as had sometimes happened with me, being told that their friends were in league with the devil and intended to rob our family of everything we owned. (I didn't fail to wonder, and it made me hate him, what on earth we owned that anybody else would want.)

His illness was beyond all hope of healing before anyone realized that he was ill. He had always been so strange and had lived, like a prophet, in such unimaginably close communion with the

Lord that his long silences which were punctuated by moans and hallelujahs and snatches of old songs while he sat at the living-room window never seemed odd to us. It was not until he refused to eat because, he said, his family was trying to poison him that my mother was forced to accept as a fact what had, until then, been only an unwilling suspicion. When he was committed, it was discovered that he had tuberculosis and, as it turned out, the disease of his mind allowed the disease of his body to destroy him. For the doctors could not force him to eat, either, and, though he was fed intravenously, it was clear from the beginning that there was no hope for him.

In my mind's eye I could see him, sitting at the window, locked up in his terrors; hating and fearing every living soul including his children who had betrayed him, too, by reaching towards the world which had despised him. There were nine of us. I began to wonder what it could have felt like for such a man to have had nine children whom he could barely feed. He used to make little jokes about our poverty, which never, of course, seemed very funny to us; they could not have seemed very funny to him, either, or else our all too feeble response to them would never have caused such rages. He spent great energy and achieved, to our chagrin, no small amount of success in keeping us away from the people who surrounded us, people who had all-night rent parties to which we listened when we should have been sleeping, people who cursed and drank and flashed razor blades on Lenox Avenue. He could not understand why, if they had so much energy to spare, they could not use it to make their lives better. He treated almost everybody on our block with a most uncharitable asperity and neither they, nor, of course, their children were slow to reciprocate.

The only white people who came to our house were welfare 10 workers and bill collectors. It was almost always my mother who dealt with them, for my father's temper, which was at the mercy of his pride, was never to be trusted. It was clear that he felt their very presence in his home to be a violation: this was conveyed by his carriage, almost ludicrously stiff, and by his voice, harsh and vindictively polite. When I was around nine or ten I wrote a play which was directed by a young, white schoolteacher, a woman, who then took an interest in me, and gave me books to read and, in order to corroborate my theatrical bent, decided to take me to see what she somewhat tactlessly referred to as "real" plays. Theatergoing was forbidden in our house, but, with the really cruel intuitiveness of a child, I suspected that the color of this woman's skin would carry the day for me. When, at school, she suggested taking me to the theater, I did not, as I might have done if she had been a Negro, find a way of discouraging her, but agreed that she should pick me up at my house one evening. I then, very cleverly, left all the rest to my mother, who suggested to my father, as I knew she would, that it would not be very nice to let such a kind woman make the trip for nothing. Also, since it was a school-teacher, I imagine that my mother countered the idea of sin with the idea of "education," which word, even with my father, carried a kind of bitter weight.

Before the teacher came my father took me aside to ask *why* she was coming, what *interest* she could possibly have in our house, in a boy like me. I said I didn't know but I, too, suggested that it had something to do with education. And I understood that my father was waiting for me to say something—I didn't quite know what; perhaps that I wanted his protection against this teacher and her "education." I said none of these things and the teacher came and we went out. It was clear, during the brief inter-view in our living room, that my father was agreeing very much against his will and that he would have refused permission if he had dared. The fact that he did not dare caused me to despise him: I had no way of knowing that he was facing in that living room a wholly unprecedented and frightening situation.

Later, when my father had been laid off from his job, this woman became very important to us. She was really a very sweet and generous woman and went to a great deal of trouble to be of help to us, particularly during one awful winter. My mother called her by the highest name she knew. She said she was a "christian." My father could scarcely disagree but during the four or five years of our relatively close association he never trusted her and was always trying to surprise in her open, Midwestern face the genu-ine, cunningly hidden, and hideous motivation. In later years, particularly when it began to be clear that this "education" of mine was going to lead me to perdition, he became more explicit and warned me that my white friends in high school were not really my friends and that I would see, when I was older, how white people would do anything to keep a Negro down. Some of them could be nice, he admitted, but none of them were to be trusted and most of them were not even nice. The best thing was to have as little to do with them as possible. I did not feel this way and I was certain, in my innocence, that I never would.

But the year which preceded my father's death had made a great change in my life. I had been living in New Jersey, working in defense plants, working and living among southerners, white and black. I knew about the south, of course, and about how southerners treated Negroes and how they expected them to behave, but it had never entered my mind that anyone would look at me and expect *me* to behave that way. I learned in New Jersey that to be a Negro meant, precisely, that one was never looked at but was simply at the mercy of the reflexes the color of one's skin caused in other people. I acted in New Jersey as I had always acted, that is as though I thought a great deal of myself—I had to *act* that way—with results that were, simply, unbelievable. I had scarcely arrived before I had earned the enmity, which was extraordinarily ingenious, of all my superiors and nearly all my coworkers. In the beginning, to make matters worse, I simply did not know what was happening. I did not know what I had done, and I shortly began to wonder what *anyone* could possibly do, to bring about such unanimous, active, and unbearably vocal hostility. I knew about jim-crow but I had never experienced it. I went to the same self-service restaurant three times and stood with all the Princeton boys before the counter, waiting for a hamburger and coffee; it was always an extraordinarily long time before anything was set before me; but it was not until the fourth visit that I learned that, in fact, nothing had ever been set before me: I had simply picked something up. Negroes were not served there, I was told, and they had been waiting for me to realize that I was always the only Negro present. Once I was told this, I determined to go there all the time. But now they were ready for me and, though some dreadful scenes were subsequently enacted in that restaurant, I never ate there again.

It was the same story all over New Jersey, in bars, bowling alleys, diners, places to live. I was always being forced to leave, silently, or with mutual imprecations. I very shortly became notorious and children giggled behind me when I passed and their elders whispered or shouted—they really believed that I was mad. And it did begin to work on my mind, of course; I began to be afraid to go anywhere and to compensate for this I went places to which I really should not have gone and where, God knows, I had no desire to be. My reputation in town naturally enhanced my reputation at work and my working day became one long series of acrobatics designed to keep me out of trouble. I cannot say that these acrobatics succeeded. It began to seem that the machinery of the organization I worked for was turning over, day and night, with but one aim: to eject me. I was fired once, and contrived, with the aid of a friend from New York, to get back on the payroll; was fired again, and bounced back again. It took a while to fire me for the third time, but the third time took. There were no loopholes anywhere. There was not even any way of getting back inside the gates.

That year in New Jersey lives in my mind as though it were the year during which, having an unsuspected predilection for it, I first contracted some dread, chronic disease, the unfailing symptom of which is a kind of blind fever, a pounding in the skull and fire in the bowels. Once this disease is contracted, one can never be really carefree again, for the fever, without an instant's warning, can recur at any moment. It can wreck more important things than race relations. There is not a Negro alive who does not have this rage in his blood—one has the choice, merely, of living with it consciously or surrendering to it. As for me, this fever has recurred in me, and does, and will until the day I die. 15

My last night in New Jersey, a white friend from New York took me to the nearest big town, Trenton, to go to the movies and have a few drinks. As it turned out, he also saved me from, at the very least, a violent whipping. Almost every detail of that night stands out very clearly in my memory. I even remember the name of the movie we saw because its title impressed me as being so patly ironical. It was a movie about the German occupation of France, starring Maureen O'Hara and Charles Laughton and called *This Land Is Mine*. I remember the name of the diner we walked into when the movie ended: it was the "American Diner." When we walked in the counterman asked what we wanted and I remember answering with the casual sharpness which had become my habit: "We want a hamburger and a cup of coffee, what do you think we want?" I do not know why, after a year of such rebuffs, I so completely failed to anticipate his answer, which was, of course, "We don't serve Negroes here." This reply failed to discompose me, at least for the moment. I made some sardonic comment about the name of the diner and we walked out into the streets.

This was the time of what was called the "brown-out," when the lights in all American cities were very dim. When we reentered the streets something happened to me which had the force of an optical illusion, or a nightmare. The streets were very crowded and I was facing north. People were moving in every direction but it seemed to me, in that instant, that all of the people I could see, and many more than that, were moving toward me, against me, and that everyone was white. I remember how their faces gleamed. And I felt, like a physical sensation, a *click* at the nape of my neck as though some interior string connecting my head to my body had been cut. I began to walk. I heard my friend call after me, but I ignored him. Heaven only knows what was going on in his mind, but he had the good sense not to touch me—I don't know what would have happened if he had—and to keep me in sight. I don't know what was going on in my mind, either; I certainly had no conscious plan. I wanted to do something to crush these white faces, which were crushing me. I walked for perhaps a block or two until I came to an enormous, glittering, and fashionable restaurant in which I knew not even the intercession of the Virgin would cause me to be served. I pushed through the doors and took the first vacant seat I saw, at a table for two, and waited.

I do not know how long I waited and I rather wonder, until today, what I could possibly have looked like. Whatever I looked like, I frightened the waitress who shortly appeared, and the moment she appeared all of my fury flowed towards her. I hated her for her white face, and for her great, astounded, frightened eyes. I felt that if she found a black man so frightening I would make her fright worthwhile.

She did not ask me what I wanted, but repeated, as though she had learned it somewhere, "We don't serve Negroes here." She did not say it with the blunt, derisive hostility to which I had grown so accustomed, but, rather, with a note of apology in her voice, and fear. This made me colder and more murderous than ever. I felt I had to do something with my hands. I wanted her to come close enough for me to get her neck between my hands.

So I pretended not to have understood her, hoping to draw her 20 closer. And she did step a very short step closer, with her pencil

poised incongruously over her pad, and repeated the formula:
". . . don't serve Negroes here."

Somehow, with the repetition of that phrase, which was already ringing in my head like a thousand bells of a nightmare, I realized that she would never come any closer and that I would have to strike from a distance. There was nothing on the table but an ordinary water-mug half full of water, and I picked this up and hurled it with all my strength at her. She ducked and it missed her and shattered against the mirror behind the bar. And, with that sound, my frozen blood abruptly thawed, I returned from wherever I had been, I *saw*, for the first time, the restaurant, the people with their mouths open, already, as it seemed to me, rising as one man, and I realized what I had done, and where I was, and I was frightened. I rose and began running for the door. A round, pot-bellied man grabbed me by the nape of the neck just as I reached the doors and began to beat me about the face. I kicked him and got loose and ran into the streets. My friend whispered, *"Run!"* and I ran.

My friend stayed outside the restaurant long enough to misdirect my pursuers and the police, who arrived, he told me, at once. I do not know what I said to him when he came to my room that night. I could not have said much. I felt, in the oddest, most awful way, that I had somehow betrayed him. I lived it over and over and over again, the way one relives an automobile accident after it has happened and one finds oneself alone and safe. I could not get over two facts, both equally difficult for the imagination to grasp, and one was that I could have been murdered. But the other was that I had been ready to commit murder. I saw nothing very clearly but I did see this: that my life, my *real* life, was in danger, and not from anything other people might do but from the hatred I carried in my own heart.

II

I had returned home around the second week in June—in great haste because it seemed that my father's death and my mother's confinement were both but a matter of hours. In the case of my mother, it soon became clear that she had simply made a miscalculation. This had always been her tendency and I don't believe that a single one of us arrived in the world, or has since arrived anywhere else, on time. But none of us dawdled so intolerably about the business of being born as did my baby sister. We sometimes amused ourselves, during those endless, stifling weeks, by picturing the baby sitting within in the safe, warm dark, bitterly regretting the necessity of becoming a part of our chaos and stubbornly putting it off as long as possible. I understood her perfectly and congratulated her on showing such good sense so soon. Death, however, sat as purposefully at my father's bedside as life stirred within my mother's womb and it was harder to understand why he so lingered in that long shadow. It seemed that he had bent, and for a long time, too, all of his energies towards dying. Now death was ready for him but my father held back.

All of Harlem, indeed, seemed to be infected by waiting. I had never before known it to be so violently still. Racial tensions throughout this country were exacerbated during the early years of the war, partly because the labor market brought together hundreds of thousands of ill-prepared people and partly because Negro soldiers, regardless of where they were born, received their military training in the south. What happened in defense plants and army camps had repercussions, naturally, in every Negro ghetto. The situation in Harlem had grown bad enough for clergymen, policemen, educators, politicians, and social workers to assert in one breath that there was no "crime wave" and to offer, in the very next breath, suggestions as to how to combat it. These suggestions always seemed to involve playgrounds, despite the fact that racial skirmishes were occurring in the playgrounds, too. Playground or not, crime wave or not, the Harlem police force had been augmented in March, and the unrest grew— perhaps, in fact, partly as a result of the ghetto's instinctive hatred of policemen. Perhaps the most revealing news item, out of the steady parade of reports of muggings, stabbings, shootings, assaults, gang wars, and accusations of police brutality is the item concerning six Negro girls who set upon a white girl in the subway because, as they all too accurately put it, she was stepping on their toes. Indeed she was, all over the nation.

I had never before been so aware of policemen, on foot, on 25 horseback, on corners, everywhere, always two by two. Nor had I ever been so aware of small knots of people. They were on stoops and on corners and in doorways, and what was striking about them, I think, was that they did not seem to be talking. Never, when I passed these groups, did the usual sound of a curse or a laugh ring out and neither did there seem to be any hum of gossip. There was certainly, on the other hand, occurring between them communication extraordinarily intense. Another thing that was striking was the unexpected diversity of the people who made up these groups. Usually, for example, one would see a group of sharpies standing on the street corner, jiving the passing chicks; or a group of older men, usually, for some reason, in the vicinity of a barber shop, discussing baseball scores, or the numbers or making rather chilling observations about women they had known. Women, in a general way, tended to be seen less often together—unless they were church women, or very young girls, or prostitutes met together for an unprofessional instant. But that summer I saw the strangest combinations: large, respectable, churchly matrons standing on the stoops or the corners with their hair tied up, together with a girl in sleazy satin whose face bore the marks of gin and the razor, or heavy-set, abrupt, no-nonsense older men, in company with the most disreputable and fanatical "race" men, or these same "race" men with the sharpies, or these sharpies with the churchly women. Seventh Day Adventists and Methodists and Spiritualists seemed to be hobnobbing with Holy-rollers and they were all, alike, entangled with the most flagrant disbelievers; something heavy in their stance seemed to indicate that they had all, incredibly, seen a common vision, and on each face there seemed to be the same strange, bitter shadow.

The churchly women and the matter-of-fact, no-nonsense men had children in the Army. The sleazy girls they talked to had lovers there, the sharpies and the "race" men had friends and brothers there. It would have demanded an unquestioning patriotism, happily as uncommon in this country as it is undesirable, for these people not to have been disturbed by the bitter letters they received, by the newspaper stories they read, not to have been enraged by the posters, then to be found all over New York, which described the Japanese as "yellow-bellied Japs." It was only the "race" men, to be sure, who spoke ceaselessly of being revenged— how this vengeance was to be exacted was not clear—for the indignities and dangers suffered by Negro boys in uniform; but everybody felt a directionless, hopeless bitterness, as well as that panic which can scarcely be suppressed when one knows that a human being one loves is beyond one's reach, and in danger.

This helplessness and this gnawing uneasiness does something, at length, to even the toughest mind. Perhaps the best way to sum all this up is to say that the people I knew felt, mainly, a peculiar kind of relief when they knew that their boys were being shipped out of the south, to do battle overseas. It was, perhaps, like feeling that the most dangerous part of a dangerous journey had been passed and that now, even if death should come, it would come with honor and without the complicity of their countrymen. Such a death would be, in short, a fact with which one could hope to live.

It was on the 28th of July, which I believe was a Wednesday, that I visited my father for the first time during his illness and for the last time in his life. The moment I saw him I knew why I had put off this visit so long. I had told my mother that I did not want to see him because I hated him. But this was not true. It was only that I *had* hated him and I wanted to hold on to this hatred. I did not want to look on him as a ruin: it was not a ruin I had hated. I imagine that one of the reasons people cling to their hates so stubbornly is because they sense, once hate is gone, that they will be forced to deal with pain.

We traveled out to him, his older sister and myself, to what seemed to be the very end of a very Long Island. It was hot and dusty and we wrangled, my aunt and I, all the way out, over the fact that I had recently begun to smoke and, as she said, to give myself airs. But I knew that she wrangled with me because she could not bear to face the fact of her brother's dying. Neither could I endure the reality of her despair, her unstated bafflement as to what had happened to her brother's life, and her own. So we wrangled and I smoked and from time to time she fell into a heavy reverie. Covertly, I watched her face, which was the face of an old woman; it had fallen in, the eyes were sunken and lightless; soon she would be dying, too.

In my childhood—it had not been so long ago—I had thought her beautiful. She had been quick-witted and quick-moving and very generous with all the children, and each of her visits had been an event. At one time one of my brothers and myself had thought of running away to live with her. Now she could no longer produce out of her handbag some unexpected and yet familiar delight. She made me feel pity and revulsion and fear. It was awful to realize that she no longer caused me to feel affection.

The closer we came to the hospital the more querulous she became and at the same time, naturally, grew more dependent on me. Between pity and guilt and fear I began to feel that there was another me trapped in my skull like a jack-in-the-box who might escape my control at any moment and fill the air with screaming.

She began to cry the moment we entered the room and she saw   30 him lying there, all shriveled and still, like a little black monkey. The great, gleaming apparatus which fed him and would have compelled him to be still even if he had been able to move brought to mind, not beneficence, but torture; the tubes entering his arm made me think of pictures I had seen when a child, of Gulliver, tied down by the pygmies on that island. My aunt wept and wept; there was a whistling sound in my father's throat; nothing was said; he could not speak. I wanted to take his hand, to say something. But I do not know what I could have said, even if he could have heard me. He was not really in that room with us, he had at last really embarked on his journey; and though my aunt told me that he said he was going to meet Jesus, I did not hear anything except that whistling in his throat. The doctor came back and we left, into that unbearable train again, and home. In the morning came the telegram saying that he was dead. Then the house was suddenly full of relatives, friends, hysteria, and confusion and I quickly left my mother and the children to the care of those impressive women, who, in Negro communities at least, automatically appear at times of bereavement armed with lotions, proverbs, and patience, and an ability to cook. I went downtown. By the time I returned, later the same day, my mother had been carried to the hospital and the baby had been born.

III

For my father's funeral I had nothing black to wear and this posed a nagging problem all day long. It was one of those problems, simple, or impossible of solution, to which the mind insanely clings in order to avoid the mind's real trouble. I spent most of that day at the downtown apartment of a girl I knew, celebrating my birthday with whiskey and wondering what to wear that night. When planning a birthday celebration one naturally does not expect that it will be up against competition from a funeral and this girl had anticipated taking me out that night, for a big dinner and a night club afterwards. Sometime during the course of that long day we decided that we would go out anyway, when my father's funeral service was over. I imagine *I* decided it, since, as the funeral hour approached, it became clearer and clearer to me that I would not know what to do with myself when it was over. The girl, stifling her very lively concern as to the possible effects of the whiskey on one of my father's chief mourners, concentrated on being conciliatory and practically helpful. She found a black shirt for me somewhere and ironed it and, dressed in the darkest pants and jacket I owned, and slightly drunk, I made my way to my father's funeral.

The chapel was full, but not packed, and very quiet. There were, mainly, my father's relatives, and his children, and here and there I saw faces I had not seen since childhood, the faces of my father's one-time friends. They were very dark and solemn now, seeming somehow to suggest that they had known all along that something like this would happen. Chief among the mourners was my aunt, who had quarreled with my father all his life; by which I do not mean to suggest that her mourning was insincere or that she had not loved him. I suppose that she was one of the few people in the world who had, and their incessant quarreling proved precisely the strength of the tie that bound them. The only other person in the world, as far as I knew, whose relationship to my father rivaled my aunt's in depth was my mother, who was not there.

It seemed to me, of course, that it was a very long funeral. But it was, if anything, a rather shorter funeral than most, nor, since there were no overwhelming, uncontrollable expressions of grief, could it be called—if I dare to use the word—successful. The minister who preached my father's funeral sermon was one of the few my father had still been seeing as he neared his end. He presented to us in his sermon a man whom none of us had ever seen—a man thoughtful, patient, and forbearing, a Christian inspiration to all who knew him, and a model for his children. And no doubt the children, in their disturbed and guilty state, were almost ready to believe this; he had been remote enough to be anything and, anyway, the shock of the incontrovertible, that it was really our father lying up there in that casket, prepared the mind for anything. His sister moaned and this grief-stricken moaning was taken as corroboration. The other faces held a dark, non-committal thoughtfulness. This was not the man they had known, but they had scarcely expected to be confronted with *him*; this was, in a sense deeper than questions of fact, the man they had not known, and the man they had not known may have been the real one. The real man, whoever he had been, had suffered and now he was dead: this was all that was sure and all that mattered now. Every man in the chapel hoped that when his hour came he, too, would be eulogized, which is to say forgiven, and that all of his lapses, greeds, errors, and strayings from the truth would be invested with coherence and looked upon with charity. This was perhaps the last thing human beings could give each other and it was what they demanded, after all, of the Lord. Only the Lord saw the midnight tears, only He was present when one of His children, moaning and wringing hands, paced up and down the room. When one slapped one's child in anger the recoil in the heart reverberated through heaven and became part of the pain of the universe. And when the children were hungry and sullen and distrustful and one watched them, daily, growing wilder, and further away, and running headlong into danger, it was the Lord who knew what the charged heart endured as the strap was laid to the backside; the Lord alone who knew what one *would* have said if one had had, like the Lord, the gift of the living word. It was the Lord who knew of the impossibility every parent in that room faced: how to prepare the child for the day when the child would be despised and how to *create* in the child—by what means?—a stronger antidote to this poison than one had found for oneself. The avenues, side streets, bars, billiard halls, hospitals, police stations, and even the playgrounds of Harlem—not to mention the houses of correction, the jails, and the morgue— testified to the potency of the poison while remaining silent as to the efficacy of whatever antidote, irresistibly raising the question of whether or not such an antidote existed; raising, which was worse, the question of whether or not an antidote was desirable; perhaps poison should be fought with poison. With these several schisms in the mind and with more terrors in the heart than could be named, it was better not to judge the man who had gone down under an impossible burden. It was better to remember. *Thou knowest this man's fall; but thou knowest not his wrassling.*

While the preacher talked and I watched the children—years of changing their diapers, scrubbing them, slapping them, taking them to school, and scolding them had had the perhaps inevitable result of making me love them, though I am not sure I knew this then—my mind was busily breaking out with a rash of disconnected impressions. Snatches of popular songs, indecent jokes, bits of books I had read, movie sequences, faces, voices, political issues—I thought I was going mad; all these impressions suspended, as it were, in the solution of the faint nausea produced in me by the heat and liquor. For a moment I had the impression that my alcoholic breath, inefficiently disguised with chewing gum, filled the entire chapel. Then someone began singing one of my father's favorite songs and, abruptly, I was with him, sitting on his knee, in the hot, enormous, crowded church which was the first church we attended. It was the Abyssinia Baptist Church on 138th Street. We had not gone there long. With this image, a host of others came. I had forgotten, in the rage of my growing up, how proud my father had been of me when I was little. Apparently, I had had a voice and my father had liked to show me off before the members of the church. I had forgotten what he had looked like when he was pleased but now I remembered that he had always been grinning with pleasure when my solos ended. I even remembered certain expressions on his face when he teased my mother—had he loved her? I would never know. And when had it all begun to change? For now it seemed that he had not always been cruel. I remembered being taken for a haircut and scraping my knee on the footrest of the barber's chair and I remembered my father's face as he soothed my crying and applied the stinging iodine. Then I remembered our fights, fights which had been of the worst possible kind because my technique had been silence.

I remembered the one time in all our life together when we had 35
really spoken to each other.

It was on a Sunday and it must have been shortly before I left home. We were walking, just the two of us, in our usual silence, to or from church. I was in high school and had been doing a lot of writing and I was, at about this time, the editor of the high school magazine. But I had also been a Young Minister and had been preaching from the pulpit. Lately, I had been taking fewer engagements and preached as rarely as possible. It was said in the church, quite truthfully, that I was "cooling off."

My father asked me abruptly, "You'd rather write than preach, wouldn't you?"

I was astonished at his question—because it was a real question. I answered, "Yes."

That was all we said. It was awful to remember that that was all we had *ever* said.

The casket now was opened and mourners were being led up the 40 aisle to look for the last time on the deceased. The assumption was that the family was too overcome with grief to be allowed to make this journey alone and I watched while my aunt was led to the casket and, muffled in black, and shaking, led back to her seat. I disapproved of forcing the children to look on their dead father, considering that the shock of his death, or, more truthfully, the shock of death as a reality, was already a little more than a child could bear, but my judgment in this matter had been overruled and there they were, bewildered and frightened and very small, being led, one by one, to the casket. But there is also something very gallant about children at such moments. It has something to do with their silence and gravity and with the fact that one cannot help them. Their legs, somehow, seem *exposed*, so that it is at once incredible and terribly clear that their legs are all they have to hold them up.

I had not wanted to go to the casket myself and I certainly had not wished to be led there, but there was no way of avoiding either of these forms. One of the deacons led me up and I looked on my father's face. I cannot say that it looked like him at all. His blackness had been equivocated by powder and there was no suggestion in that casket of what his power had or could have been. He was simply an old man dead, and it was hard to believe that he had ever given anyone either joy or pain. Yet, his life filled that room. Further up the avenue his wife was holding his newborn child. Life and death so close together, and love and hatred, and right and wrong, said something to me which I did not want to hear concerning man, concerning the life of man.

After the funeral, while I was downtown desperately celebrating my birthday, a Negro soldier, in the lobby of the Hotel Braddock, got into a fight with a white policeman over a Negro girl. Negro girls, white policemen, in or out of uniform, and Negro males—in or out of uniform—were part of the furniture of the lobby of the Hotel Braddock and this was certainly not the first time such an incident had occurred. It was destined, however, to receive an unprecedented publicity, for the fight between the policeman and the soldier ended with the shooting of the soldier.

Rumor, flowing immediately to the streets outside, stated that the soldier had been shot in the back, an instantaneous and revealing invention, and that the soldier had died protecting a Negro woman. The facts were somewhat different—for example, the soldier had not been shot in the back, and was not dead, and the girl seems to have been as dubious a symbol of womanhood as her white counterpart in Georgia usually is, but no one was interested in the facts. They preferred the invention because this invention expressed and corroborated their hates and fears so perfectly. It is just as well to remember that people are always doing this. Perhaps many of those legends, including Christianity, to which the world clings began their conquest of the world with just some such concerted surrender to distortion. The effect, in Harlem, of this particular legend was like the effect of a lit match in a tin of gasoline. The mob gathered before the doors of the Hotel Braddock simply began to swell and to spread in every direction, and Harlem exploded.

The mob did not cross the ghetto lines. It would have been easy, for example, to have gone over Morningside Park on the west side or to have crossed the Grand Central railroad tracks at 125th Street on the east side, to wreak havoc in white neighborhoods. The mob seems to have been mainly interested in something more potent and real than the white face, that is, in white power, and the principal damage done during the riot of the summer of 1943 was to white business establishments in Harlem. It might have been a far bloodier story, of course, if, at the hour the riot began, these establishments had still been open. From the Hotel Braddock the mob fanned out, east and west along 125th Street, and for the entire length of Lenox, Seventh, and Eighth avenues. Along each of these avenues, and along each major side street—116th, 125th, 135th, and so on—bars, stores, pawnshops, restaurants, even little luncheonettes had been smashed open and entered and looted—looted, it might be added, with more haste than efficiency. The shelves really looked as though a bomb had struck them. Cans of beans and soup and dog food, along with toilet paper, corn flakes, sardines and milk tumbled every which way, and abandoned cash registers and cases of beer leaned crazily out of the splintered windows and were strewn along the avenues. Sheets, blankets, and clothing of every description formed a kind of path, as though people had dropped them while running.

I truly had not realized that Harlem *had* so many stores until I saw them all smashed open; the first time the word *wealth* ever entered my mind in relation to Harlem was when I saw it scattered in the streets. But one's first, incongruous impression of plenty was countered immediately by an impression of waste. None of this was doing anybody any good. It would have been better to have left the plate glass as it had been and the goods lying in the stores.

It would have been better, but it would also have been intolerable, for Harlem had needed something to smash. To smash something is the ghetto's chronic need. Most of the time it is the members of the ghetto who smash each other, and themselves. But as long as the ghetto walls are standing there will always come a moment when these outlets do not work. That summer, for example, it was not enough to get into a fight on Lenox Avenue, or curse out one's cronies in the barber shops. If ever, indeed, the violence which fills Harlem's churches, pool halls, and bars erupts outward in a more direct fashion, Harlem and its citizens are likely to vanish in an apocalyptic flood. That this is not likely to happen is due to a great many reasons, most hidden and powerful among them the Negro's real relation to the white American. This relation prohibits, simply, anything as uncomplicated and satisfactory as pure hatred. In order really to hate white people, one has to blot so much out of the mind—and the heart—that this hatred itself becomes an exhausting and self-destructive pose. But this does not mean, on the other hand, that love comes easily: the white world is too powerful, too complacent, too ready with gratuitous humiliation, and, above all, too ignorant and too innocent for that. One is absolutely forced to make perpetual qualifications and one's own reactions are always canceling each other out. It is this, really, which has driven so many people mad, both white and black. One is always in the position of having to decide between amputation and gangrene. Amputation is swift but time may prove that the amputation was not necessary—or one may delay the amputation too long. Gangrene is slow, but it is impossible to be sure that one is reading one's symptoms right. The idea of going through life as a cripple is more than one can bear, and equally unbearable is the risk of swelling up slowly, in agony, with poison. And the trouble, finally, is that the risks are real even if the choices do not exist.

"But as for me and my house," my father had said, "we will 45
serve the Lord." I wondered, as we drove him to his resting place,
what this line had meant for him. I had heard him preach it many
times. I had preached it once myself, proudly giving it an interpretation different from my father's. Now the whole thing came
back to me, as though my father and I were on our way to Sunday
school and I were memorizing the golden text: *And if it seem evil
unto you to serve the Lord, choose you this day whom you will
serve; whether the gods which your fathers served that were on the
other side of the flood, or the gods of the Amorites, in whose land ye
dwell: but as for me and my house, we will serve the Lord.* I suspected in these familiar lines a meaning which had never been
there for me before. All of my father's texts and songs, which I
had decided were meaningless, were arranged before me at his
death like empty bottles, waiting to hold the meaning which life
would give them for me. This was his legacy: nothing is ever
escaped. That bleakly memorable morning I hated the unbelievable streets and the Negroes and whites who had, equally, made
them that way. But I knew that it was folly, as my father would
have said, this bitterness was folly. It was necessary to hold on to
the things that mattered. The dead man mattered, the new life
mattered; blackness and whiteness did not matter; to believe that
they did was to acquiesce in one's own destruction. Hatred, which
could destroy so much, never failed to destroy the man who hated
and this was an immutable law.

It began to seem that one would have to hold in the mind forever two ideas which seemed to be in opposition. The first idea
was acceptance, the acceptance, totally without rancor, of life as
it is, and men as they are: in the light of this idea, it goes without
saying that injustice is a commonplace. But this did not mean
that one could be complacent, for the second idea was of equal
power: that one must never, in one's own life, accept these injustices as commonplace but must fight them with all one's strength.
This fight begins, however, in the heart and it now had been laid
to my charge to keep my own heart free of hatred and despair.
This intimation made my heart heavy and, now that my father
was irrecoverable, I wished that he had been beside me so that I
could have searched his face for the answers which only the
future would give me now.

For Discussion and Writing

1. Identify all of the different stories Baldwin tells in "Notes of a Native Son."

2. How does Baldwin relate the story of his relationship with his father to the story of the relationship between black and white America?

3. **connections**   When Ta-Nehisi Coates's book *Letter to My Son* was published, reviewers often compared his writing to Baldwin's. Read Coates's "The Paranoid Style of American Policing" (p. 99) alongside "Notes of a Native Son." Compare the word choice, the structure and rhythm of the sentences, and the use of rhetorical devices. Do you see similarities in the way the two authors write? Do you see differences?

4. Write about a moment in your life when you were extremely angry. How did you handle it, and what does the experience tell you about yourself now?

5. **looking further**   It is one thing to handle yourself well when you are angry; it is another thing for a large group of people to handle itself well in the face of extreme provocation and injustice. Research the history of nonviolent protest. What has enabled such movements to avoid letting their anger lead them to meet violence with violence?

JAMES BOSWELL

On War

Born on October 18, 1740, in Edinburgh, Scotland, James Boswell was a biographer and diarist, a lawyer and a lord. He preferred the urban lifestyle and studied law at the University of Edinburgh and the University of Glasgow before going on to practice in Edinburgh for seventeen years. Among his literary achievements are The Life of Samuel Johnson, *published in 1791, and his more than seventy essays in the* London Magazine.*

In "On War," which he composed in 1777 after viewing the Arsenal in Venice, Boswell reflects on the "irrationality of war" and how, despite that lack of reason, humanity continues to "prepare instruments for the destruction of our species at large." As you read "On War," consider the relevance of this reading today, and what it has to say about the wars we continue to fight.

While viewing, as travelers usually do, the remarkable objects of curiosity at Venice, I was conducted through the different departments of the Arsenal; and as I contemplated the great storehouse of mortal engines, in which there is not only a large deposit of arms, but men are continually employed in making more, my thoughts rebounded, if I may use the expression, from what I beheld; and the effect was, that I was first as it were stunned into a state of amazement, and when I recovered from that, my mind expanded itself in reflections upon the horrid irrationality of war.

What those reflections were I do not precisely recollect. But the general impression dwells upon my memory; and however strange it may seem, my opinion of the irrationality of war is still associated with the Arsenal of Venice.

One particular however I well remember. When I saw working-men engaged with grave assiduity in fashioning weapons of death, I was struck with wonder at the shortsightedness, the *caecae mentes*[1] of human beings, who were thus soberly preparing the instruments

1. Latin for aimless or unseeing mind. [Ed.]

of destruction of their own species. I have since found upon a closer study of man, that my wonder might have been spared; because there are very few men whose minds are sufficiently enlarged to comprehend universal or even extensive good. The views of most individuals are limited to their own happiness; and the workmen whom I beheld so busy in the Arsenal of Venice saw nothing but what was good in the labour for which they received such wages as procured them the comforts of life. That their immediate satisfaction was not hindered by a view of the remote consequential and contingent evils for which alone their labours could be at all useful, would not surprise one who has had a tolerable share of experience in life. We must have the telescope of philosophy to make us perceive distant ills; nay, we know that there are individuals of our species to whom the immediate misery of others is nothing in comparison with their own advantage—for we know that in every age there have been found men very willing to perform the office of executioner even for a moderate hire.

To prepare instruments for the destruction of our species at large, is what I now see may very well be done by ordinary men, without starting, when they themselves are to run no risk. But I shall never forget, nor cease to wonder at a most extraordinary instance of thoughtless intrepidity which I had related to me by a cousin of mine, now a lieutenant-colonel in the British army, who was upon guard when it happened. A soldier of one of the regiments in garrison at Minorca, having been found guilty of a capital crime, was brought out to be hanged. They had neglected to have a rope in readiness, and the shocking business was at a stand. The fellow, with a spirit and alertness which in general would, upon a difficult and trying emergency, have been very great presence of mind and conduct, stript the lace off his hat, said this will do, and actually made it serve as the fatal chord.

The irrationality of war is, I suppose, admitted by almost all 5 men: I almost say all; because I have met myself with men who attempted seriously to maintain that it is an agreeable occupation and one of the chief means of human happiness. I must own that although I use the plural number here, I should have used the dual, had I been writing in Greek; for I never met with but two men who supported such a paradox; and one of them was a tragick poet, and one a Scotch Highlander. The first had his imagination so in a blaze with heroic sentiments, with the "pride, pomp, and circumstance of glorious war," that he did not avert to its miseries, as one dazzled with the pageantry of a magnificent funeral thinks not of the pangs of dissolution and the dismal corpse. The second had his attention so eagerly fixed on the advantage which accrued to his clan from the "trade of war," that he could think of it only as a good.

We are told by some writers, who assume the character of philosophers, that war is necessary to take off the superfluity of the human species, or at least to rid the world of numbers of idle and profligate men who are a burden upon every community, and would grow an insupportable burden, were they to live as long as men do in the usual course of nature. But there is unquestioningly no reason to fear a superfluity of mankind, when we know that although perhaps the time "when every rood of land maintain'd its man" is a poetical exaggeration, yet vigorous and well directed industry can raise sustenance for such a proportion of people in a certain space of territory, as is astonishing to us who are accustomed to see only moderate effects of labour; and when we also know what immense regions of the terrestrial globe in very good climates are uninhabited. In these there is room for millions to enjoy existence. In cultivating these, the idle and profligate, expelled from their original societies, might be employed and gradually reformed, which would be better surely, than continuing the practice of periodical destruction, which is also indiscriminate, and involves the best equally with the worst of men.

I have often thought that if war should cease over all the face of the earth, for a thousand years, its reality would not be believed at such a distance of time, notwithstanding the faith of authentick records in every nation. Were mankind totally free from every tincture of prejudice in favour of those gallant exertions which could not exist were there not the evil of violence to combat; had they never seen in their own days, or been told by father or grandfathers, of battles, and were there no traces of the *art of war*, I have no doubt that they would treat as fabulous or allegorical, the accounts in history, of prodigious armies being formed, of men who engaged themselves for an unlimited time, under the penalty of immediate death, to obey implicitly the orders of commanders to whom they were not attached either by affection or by interest; that these armies were sometimes led with toilsome expedition over vast tracts of land, sometimes crouded into ships, and obliged to endure tedious, unhealthy, and perilous voyages;

and that the purpose of all this toil and danger was not to obtain any comfort or pleasure, but to be in a situation to encounter other armies; and that those opposite multitudes the individuals of which had no cause to quarrel, no ill-will to each other, continued for hours engaged with patient and obstinate perseverance, while thousands were slain, and thousands crushed and mangled by the diversity of wounds.

We who have from our earliest years had our minds filled with scenes of war of which we have read in the books that we most revere and most admire, who have remarked it in every revolving century, and in every country that has been discovered by navigators, even in the gentle and benign regions of the southern oceans; we who have seen all the intelligence, power and ingenuity of our nation employed in war, who have been accustomed to peruse Gazettes, and have had our friends and relations killed or sent home to us wretchedly maimed; we cannot without a steady effort of reflection be sensible of the improbability that rational creatures should act so irrationally as to unite in deliberate plans, which must certainly produce the direful effects which war is known to do. But I have no doubt that if the project for a perpetual peace which the Abbé de St Pierre sketched, and Rousseau improved, were to take place, the incredibility of war would after the lapse of some ages be universal.

Were there any good produced by war which could in any degree compensate its direful effects; were better men to spring up from the ruins of those who fall in battle, as more beautiful material forms sometimes arise from the ashes of others; or were those who escape from its destruction to have an increase of happiness; in short, were there any great beneficial effect to follow it, the notion of its irrationality would be only the notion of narrow comprehension. But we find that war is followed by no general good whatever. The power, the glory, or the wealth of a very few may be enlarged. But the people in general, upon both sides, after all the sufferings are passed, pursue their ordinary occupations, with no difference from their former state. The evils therefore of war, upon a general view of humanity are as the French say, *à pure perte*, a mere loss without any advantage, unless indeed furnishing subjects for history, poetry, and painting. And although it should be allowed that mankind have gained enjoyment in these respects, I suppose it will not be seriously said, that the misery is overbalanced. At any rate, there is already such a store of subjects, that an addition to them would be dearly purchased by more wars.

I am none of those who would set up their notions against 10 the opinion of the world; on the contrary, I have such a respect for that authority, as to doubt of my own judgment when it opposes that of numbers probably as wise as I am. But when I maintain the irrationality of war, I am not contradicting the opinion, but the practice of the world. For, as I have already observed, its irrationality is generally admitted. Horace calls Hannibal, *demens*, a madman; and Pope gives the same appellation to Alexander the Great and Charles XII:

From Macedonia's madman to the Swede.

How long war will continue to be practised, we have no means of conjecturing. Civilization, which it might have been expected would have abolished it, has only refined its savage rudeness. The irrationality remains, though we have learnt *insanire certa ratione modoque*, to have a method in our madness.

That amiable religion which "proclaims peace on earth," hath not as yet made war to cease. The furious passions of men, modified as they are by moral instruction, still operate with much force; and by a perpetual fallacy, even the conscientious in each contending nation think they may join in war, because they each believe they are repelling an aggressor. Were the mild and humane doctrine of those Christians, who are called Quakers, which Mr Jenyns has lately embellished with his elegant pen, to prevail, human felicity would gain more than we can well conceive. But perhaps it is necessary that mankind in this state of existence, the purpose of which is so mysterious, should ever suffer the woes of war.

To relieve my readers from reflections which they may think too abstract, I shall conclude this paper with a few observations upon actual war. In ancient times when a battle was fought man to man, or as somebody has very well expressed it, was a group of duels, there was an opportunity for individuals to distinguish themselves by vigour and bravery. One who was a *"robustus acri militia*, hardy from keen warfare," could gratify his ambition for fame, by the exercise of his own personal qualities. It was therefore more reasonable then, for individuals to enlist, than it is in modern times; for, a battle now is truly nothing else than a huge conflict of opposite engines worked by men, who are themselves as machines directed by a few; and the event is not so frequently decided by what is actually done, as by accidents happening in the dreadful confusion. It is as if two towns in opposite territories should be set on fire at the same time, and victory should be declared to the inhabitants of that in which the flames were least destructive. We hear much of the conduct of generals; and Addison himself has represented the Duke of Marlborough directing an army in battle, as an "angel riding in a whirlwind and directing the storm." Nevertheless I much doubt if upon many occasions the immediate schemes of a commander have had certain effect; and I believe Sir Callaghan O'Bralachan in Mr Macklin's *Love A la-mode* gives a very just account of modern battle: "There is so much doing every where that we cannot tell what is doing any where."

For Discussion and Writing

1. Why does Boswell say that when he thinks of the irrationality of war (par. 2), he always thinks of the Arsenal of Venice?

2. Reread "On War" and make a list of some of the metaphors Boswell uses. Pick three and explain how they work—what is being compared to what, to what end (that is, what is Boswell trying to explain), and to what effect. Why do you think he thought metaphor would be an effective figure for this essay?

3. **connections** Boswell at one point imagines how war would look to people who have never seen it or known anyone who had lived through it (par. 7). Compare the way this passage works to the way Jonathan Swift makes his subject unfamiliar in "A Modest Proposal" (p. 353). What are Boswell's methods and his purpose? What are Swift's methods and purpose?

4. Share your own thoughts on war. Be, as Boswell says of his own words, both abstract and concrete in explaining your feelings about warfare. It's okay if they are mixed—you should by no means feel that you have to be wholly against it or wholly for it. The idea here is to reflect both philosophically and personally on this important topic.

5. **looking further** Based on knowledge you already have and your own research into current events and the state of the world, what do you imagine Boswell might think if he were able to travel through time and see contemporary war? Might it further confirm his thoughts? Contradict them? Add a new layer of complexity?

WILLIAM F. BUCKLEY JR.

Why Don't We Complain?

William F. Buckley Jr. (1925–2008), born in New York City, was one of the leading voices of conservative politics. Best known as founder and longtime editor of the opinion journal National Review *and host of the PBS political talk show* Firing Line, *Buckley also wrote a syndicated column, contributed to many magazines, and authored over forty fiction and nonfiction books.*

"Why Don't We Complain?" originally appeared in Esquire *in 1960. Buckley's connection of political apathy to failures to act in other parts of life is still timely today. As you read, though, think about all that has happened in America since the writing of this article.*

It was the very last coach and the only empty seat on the entire train, so there was no turning back. The problem was to breathe. Outside the temperature was below freezing. Inside the railroad car, the temperature must have been about 85 degrees. I took off my overcoat, and a few minutes later my jacket, and noticed that the car was flecked with the white shirts of passengers. I soon found my hand moving to loosen my tie. From one end of the car to the other, as we rattled through Westchester County, we sweated; but we did not moan.

I watched the train conductor appear at the head of the car. "Tickets, all tickets, please!" In a more virile age, I thought, the passengers would seize the conductor and strap him down on a seat over the radiator to share the fate of his patrons. He shuffled down the aisle, picking up tickets, punching commutation cards. *No one addressed a word to him.* He approached my seat, and I drew a deep breath of resolution. "Conductor," I began with a considerable edge to my voice. . . . Instantly the doleful eyes of my seatmate turned tiredly from his newspaper to fix me with a resentful stare: what question could be so important as to justify my sibilant intrusion into his stupor? I was shaken by those eyes.

72

I am incapable of making a discreet fuss, so I mumbled a question about what time were we due in Stamford (I didn't even ask whether it would be before or after dehydration could be expected to set in), got my reply, and went back to my newspaper and to wiping my brow.

The conductor had nonchalantly walked down the gauntlet of eighty sweating American freemen, and not one of them had asked him to explain why the passengers in that car had been consigned to suffer. There is nothing to be done when the temperature *outdoors* is 85 degrees, and indoors the air conditioner has broken down; obviously when that happens there is nothing to do, except perhaps curse the day that one was born. But when the temperature outdoors is below freezing, it takes a positive act of will on somebody's part to set the temperature *indoors* at 85. Somewhere a valve was turned too far, a furnace overstoked, a thermostat maladjusted: something that could easily be remedied by turning off the heat and allowing the great outdoors to come indoors. All this is so obvious. What is not obvious is what has happened to the American people.

It isn't just the commuters, whom we have come to visualize as a supine breed who have got onto the trick of suspending their sensory faculties twice a day while they submit to the creeping dissolution of the railroad industry. It isn't just they who have given up trying to rectify irrational vexations. It is the American people everywhere.

A few weeks ago at a large movie theatre I turned to my wife   5
and said, "The picture is out of focus." "Be quiet," she answered. I obeyed. But a few minutes later I raised the point again, with mounting impatience. "It will be all right in a minute," she said apprehensively. (She would rather lose her eyesight than be around when I make one of my infrequent scenes.) I waited. It was *just* out of focus—not glaringly out, but out. My vision is 20–20, and I assume that is the vision, adjusted, of most people in the movie house. So, after hectoring my wife throughout the first reel, I finally prevailed upon her to admit that it *was* off, and very annoying. We then settled down, coming to rest on the presumption that: a) someone connected with the management of the theatre must soon notice the blur and make the correction; or b) that someone seated near the rear of the house would make the complaint in behalf of those of us up front; or c) that—any minute

now—the entire house would explode into catcalls and foot stamping, calling dramatic attention to the irksome distortion. What happened was nothing. The movie ended, as it had begun, just out of focus, and as we trooped out, we stretched our faces in a variety of contortions to accustom the eye to the shock of normal focus.

I think it is safe to say that everybody suffered on that occasion. And I think it is safe to assume that everyone was expecting someone else to take the initiative in going back to speak to the manager. And it is probably true even that if we had supposed the movie would run right through with the blurred image, someone surely would have summoned up the purposive indignation to get up out of his seat and file his complaint.

But notice that no one did. And the reason no one did is because we are all increasingly anxious in America to be unobtrusive, we are reluctant to make our voices heard, hesitant about claiming our rights; we are afraid that our cause is unjust, or that if it is not unjust, that it is ambiguous; or if not even that, that it is too trivial to justify the horrors of a confrontation with Authority; we will sit in an oven or endure a racking headache before undertaking a head-on, I'm-here-to-tell-you complaint. That tendency to passive compliance, to a heedless endurance is something to keep one's eyes on—in sharp focus.

I myself can occasionally summon the courage to complain, but I cannot, as I have intimated, complain softly. My own instinct is so strong to let the thing ride, to forget about it—to expect that someone will take the matter up, when the grievance is collective, in my behalf—that it is only when the provocation is at a very special key, whose vibrations touch simultaneously a complexus of nerves, allergies, and passions, that I catch fire and find the reserves of courage and assertiveness to speak up. When that happens, I get quite carried away. My blood gets hot, my brow wet, I become unbearably and unconscionably sarcastic and bellicose: I am girded for a total showdown.

Why should that be? Why could not I (or anyone else) on 10 that railroad coach have said simply to the conductor, "Sir,"— I take that back: that sounds sarcastic—"Conductor, would you be good enough to turn down the heat? I am extremely hot. In fact, I tend to get hot every time the temperature reaches 85 degr—" Strike that last sentence. Just end it with the simple statement that you are extremely hot, and let the conductor infer the cause.

Every New Year's Eve I resolve to do something about the Milquetoast in me and vow to speak up, calmly, for my rights, and for the betterment of our society, on every appropriate occasion. Entering last New Year's Eve I was fortified in my resolve because that morning at breakfast I had had to ask the waitress three times for a glass of milk. She finally brought it—after I had finished my eggs, which is when I don't want it any more. I did not have the manliness to order her to take the milk back, but settled instead for a cowardly sulk, and ostentatiously refused to drink the milk—though I later paid for it—rather than state plainly to the hostess, as I should have, why I had not drunk it, and would not pay for it.

So by the time the New Year ushered out the Old, riding in on my morning's indignation and stimulated by the gastric juices of resolution that flow so faithfully on New Year's Eve, I rendered my vow. Henceforward I would conquer my shyness, my despicable disposition to supineness. I would speak out like a man against the unnecessary annoyances of our time.

Forty-eight hours later, I was standing in line at the ski-repair store in Pico Peak, Vermont. All I needed, to get on with my skiing, was the loan, for one minute, of a small screwdriver, to tighten a loose binding. Behind the counter in the workshop were two men. One was industriously engaged in servicing the complicated requirements of a young lady at the head of the line, and obviously he would be tied up for quite a while. The other— "Jiggs," his workmate called him—was a middle-aged man, who sat in a chair puffing a pipe, exchanging small talk with his working partner. My pulse began its telltale acceleration. The minutes ticked on. I stared at the idle shopkeeper, hoping to shame him into action, but he was impervious to my telepathic reproof and continued his small talk with his friend, brazenly insensitive to the nervous demands of six good men who were raring to ski.

Suddenly my New Year's Eve resolution struck me. It was now or never. I broke from my place in line and marched to the counter. I was going to control myself. I dug my nails into my palms. My effort was only partially successful:

"If you are not too busy," I said icily, "would you mind handing 15 me a screwdriver?"

Work stopped and everyone turned his eyes on me, and I experienced that mortification I always feel when I am the center of centripetal shafts of curiosity, resentment, perplexity.

But the worst was yet to come. "I am sorry, sir," said Jiggs deferentially, moving the pipe from his mouth. "I am not supposed to move. I have just had a heart attack." That was the signal for a great whirring noise that descended from heaven. We looked, stricken, out the window, and it appeared as though a cyclone had suddenly focused on the snowy courtyard between the shop and the ski lift. Suddenly a gigantic Army helicopter materialized, and hovered down to a landing. Two men jumped out of the plane carrying a stretcher, tore into the ski shop, and lifted the shopkeeper onto the stretcher. Jiggs bade his companion good-by, was whisked out the door, into the plane, up to the heavens, down—we learned—to a nearby Army hospital. I looked up manfully—into a score of man-eating eyes. I put the experience down as a reversal.

As I write this, on an airplane, I have run out of paper and need to reach into my briefcase under my legs for more. I cannot do this until my empty lunch tray is removed from my lap. I arrested the stewardess as she passed empty-handed down the aisle on the way to the kitchen to fetch the lunch trays for the passengers up forward who haven't been served yet. "Would you please take my tray?" "Just a *moment*, sir," she said, and marched on sternly. Shall I tell her that since she is headed for the kitchen *anyway*, it cannot delay the feeding of the other passengers by the two seconds necessary to stash away my empty tray? Or remind her that not fifteen minutes ago she spoke unctuously into the loudspeaker the words undoubtedly devised by the airline's highly paid public-relations counselor: "If there is anything I or Miss French can do for you to make your trip more enjoyable, *please* let us—" I have run out of paper.

I think the observable reluctance of the majority of Americans to assert themselves in minor matters is related to our increased sense of helplessness in an age of technology and centralized political and economic power. For generations, Americans who were too hot, or too cold, got up and did something about it. Now we call the plumber, or the electrician, or the furnace man. The habit of looking after our own needs obviously had something to do with the assertiveness that characterized the American family familiar to readers of American literature. With the technification of life goes our direct responsibility for our material environment, and we are conditioned to adopt a position of helplessness not only as regards the broken air conditioner, but as regards the overheated train. It takes an expert to fix the former, but not the latter: yet these distinctions, as we withdraw into helplessness, tend to fade away.

Our notorious political apathy is a related phenomenon. Every 20 year, whether the Republican or the Democratic Party is in office, more and more power drains away from the individual to feed vast reservoirs in far-off places; and we have less and less say about the shape of events which shape our future. From this aberration of personal power comes the sense of resignation with which we accept the political dispensations of a powerful government whose hold upon us continues to increase.

An editor of a national weekly news magazine told me a few years ago that as few as a dozen letters of protest against an editorial stance of his magazine was enough to convene a plenipotentiary meeting of the board of editors to review policy. "So few people complain, or make their voices heard," he explained to me, "that we assume a dozen letters represent the inarticulated views of thousands of readers." In the past ten years, he said, the volume of mail has noticeably decreased, even though the circulation of his magazine has risen.

When our voices are finally mute, when we have finally suppressed the natural instinct to complain, whether the vexation is trivial or grave, we shall have become automatons, incapable of feeling. When Premier Khrushchev first came to this country late in 1959 he was primed, we are informed, to experience the bitter resentment of the American people against his tyranny, against his persecutions, against the movement which is responsible for the then great number of American deaths in Korea, for billions in taxes every year, and for life everlasting on the brink of disasters; but Khrushchev was pleasantly surprised, and reported back to the Russian people that he had been met with overwhelming cordiality (read: apathy), except, to be sure, for "a few fascists who followed me around with their wretched posters, and should be . . . horsewhipped."

I may be crazy, but I say there would have been lots more posters in a society where train temperatures in the dead of winter are not allowed to climb up to 85 degrees without complaint.

For Discussion and Writing

1. What are Buckley's three examples of situations in which one might complain?

2. What does Buckley argue is the relationship between our failure to complain and our failure to care about politics? How does he attempt to convince us of that relationship?

3. **connections** Compare Buckley's argument about our behavior as citizens with Barbara Lazear Ascher's in "On Compassion" (p. 40). Do they focus on the same kinds of behaviors? How do their differences in subject relate to the differences in their essays?

4. Write an essay in which you reflect on your own political feelings and orientation. What do you care about, and why? How do you demonstrate your beliefs?

5. **looking further** Research one of your political ideals. Where does it come from, historically? How is it relevant in contemporary politics? Are there ways in which this ideal has been realized? Ways in which it has not? Are there things you think government should/could do to move closer to it?

ALAN BURDICK

The Truth about Invasive Species

*Alan Burdick was born in 1965 and grew up in Syracuse, New York.
He is a senior editor at the* New Yorker, *where he writes the "Synthesist" column about technology and nature. He has also written for the* New York Times Magazine, Harper's, GQ, Discover, OnEarth, *and* Best American Science and Nature Writing. *His first nonfiction book,* Out of Eden: An Odyssey of Ecological Invasion *(2005), was a National Book Award finalist and won the Overseas Press Club Award for environmental reporting. His next book,* How Time Flies, *will be published in 2016.*

"The Truth about Invasive Species" first appeared in Discover *in 2005. Like much of Burdick's work, the essay is not simply about a natural phenomenon or technological development; it's also about how we think about such an occurrence and what its real significance is. Watch as you read for the ways in which the essay weaves together the story of the phenomenon that is its subject with an analysis of what it really means.*

I have seen the future, and it lives in Miami.

The suburbs of Miami, to be exact: in the ever-expanding netherworld between the potted plants and subtropical nightlife of South Beach to the east and the tropical plants and deep-rooted wildlife of Everglades National Park to the west.

The future lives in Homestead. So does Todd Hardwick, owner and primary employee of Pesky Critters Nuisance Wildlife Control. Noisome possums and trash-can raccoons are his standard fare, and the money is in alligators, which crawl out of the swamps and into backyards, the two environments being ever more synonymous. But the real fun, and Hardwick's specialty, is catching exotic species. Miami is the through point of the nation's imported animal and plant trade, and virtually everyone in South Florida,

79

including Hardwick, has a neighbor with a backyard menagerie of lucrative critters on hold for resale. With so many unofficial zoos so close together and so little expertise at maintaining them, animals are constantly escaping into the streets and flower beds, and when someone spots, say, a pesky cougar on the lawn, Hardwick gets the call.

Hardwick has caught mountain lions, ostriches, rheas, emus, macaque monkeys—even, once, a bison on the freeway. Mostly the animals are lone escapees, but a number of species— especially reptiles—have gone loose often enough that they've formed free-roaming populations that reproduce amid the imported mango groves and ornamental hedgerows. The naturalized aliens include Cuban tree frogs, various South American anoles, and South Asian pythons and boa constrictors. Hardwick's business card shows a photograph of an Indonesian python he once extracted from a burrow beneath someone's home; it was 22 feet long.

In short, if all the biogeographic barriers in the world were   5 suddenly eliminated—all the impassable gulfs, oceans, and mountain ranges that have historically kept the planet's local native species from moving around and mixing together—the jumbled result would look something like Homestead. Minus the lions and pythons, it's the sort of neighborhood into which we're all slowly moving—or is slowly moving into ours. Colonies of stinging South American fire ants have settled in Texas; the zebra mussel, a pistachio-size mollusk from Europe, carpets the bottom of the Great Lakes. Feral pigs, native to Eurasia and North Africa, now root in the lawns of San Jose, California. Giant Asian carp, introduced in the 1970s to control aquatic weeds, leap unsolicited into fishing boats along the Mississippi River. Escaped pets, sport fish and garden plants run amok, insects that come hidden in the foliage of imported plants, pests that are introduced to control other pests—the invaders are legion, from anywhere, going everywhere.

Nature appears to be entering a new era—the Homogecene, one scientist calls it—wherein the greatest threat to biological diversity is no longer just bulldozers or pesticides but, in a sense, nature itself. The renowned Harvard biologist Edward O. Wilson has claimed that the introduction of alien species is second only to habitat destruction as the leading cause of extinctions worldwide.

A recent NASA report, heralding a novel effort to monitor the progress of alien species via satellite, placed the economic cost of alien species between $100 billion and $200 billion. "Nonindigenous invasive species may pose the single most formidable threat of natural disaster of the 21st century," the report's authors warn. "The threat of invasive species is perhaps our most urgent economic and conservation challenge." Purple loosestrife, that showy Eurasian flower you may have seen advancing along roadsides? Its floral path leads straight to hell.

Or not. Like the outwardly pastoral streets of Homestead, nothing is quite what meets the eye when it comes to alien species. For the past 50 years ecologists have devoted close study to movements of exotic species, in an effort to better understand why they go where they do and the impact they have when they arrive. The results of this unintended natural experiment turn out to be surprising, even to scientists. Nature, it seems, is far more resilient and is run by ecological rules that are far less orderly than expected. Alien species do pose a threat. But their real crime isn't against nature; it's against us and our self-serving ideas of what nature is supposed to be.

The scientific study of invasions dates to 1958, with the publication of *The Ecology of Invasions by Animals and Plants* by the English ecologist Charles Elton. "We must make no mistake," he wrote. "We are seeing one of the great historical convulsions in the world's fauna and flora." Elton and his followers sought to discern underlying patterns of invasion, to forge theories about the hidden structures of ecosystems, and so explain the apparent patterns of invasions. Are some organisms better invaders than others? Why do American gray squirrels seem to be everywhere? Why do certain environments, notably islands like Hawaii, seem especially vulnerable to invasion? Every invasion was a potential case study in why ecosystems do—and don't—remain intact.

As Elton saw it, an ecosystem is analogous to a human community, with a limited number of job openings, or niches. "When an ecologist says, 'There goes a badger,'" Elton wrote, "he should include in his thoughts some definite idea of the animal's place in the community to which it belongs, just as if he had said, 'There goes the vicar.'" The secret ingredient determining the composition of any given ecosystem—who's in, who's out—is competition. Every species, native or alien, must vie for limited niche space, like a game of musical chairs or like mailmen battling over access to a handful of mail slots.

For Elton and many subsequent ecologists, this explained why 10 places like Hawaii were unusually vulnerable to the incursion of alien species. Small ecosystems are simpler—with fewer species, and thus more available niches—and so are more open to new species. Also, the native residents of these small ecosystems— surrounded by fewer species than their counterparts in large continental ecosystems—are evolutionarily less fit to compete against invaders. "The balance of relatively simple communities of plants and animals is more easily upset than that of richer ones," he wrote, "and more vulnerable to invasions." For confirmation, look no further that the average vacant lot or agricultural plot: low in diversity and highly invaded.

Elton was among the first natural scientists to articulate a link between biological diversity—the number and variety of native species in an ecosystem—and ecological health. Greater diversity conveys a degree of "biotic resistance," he argued, which helps preserve the integrity of an ecosystem over time. A natural, undisturbed ecosystem could be thought of as an immunologic system; invasion, its disease. A recent issue of *National Geographic* described ecological invasion as a "green cancer."

The disease metaphor is compelling. There's just one problem: Fifty years of research by invasion biologists around the world has failed to confirm it.

When an alien species enters a new ecosystem, it can alter the environment in a number of ways: by eating native species (in its 50 years on Guam, the Australian brown tree snake has eliminated 9 of 13 native bird species); by spreading disease among them (introduced birds in Hawaii thrive in part because they are far less susceptible to the avian malaria parasite, also an introduced species, than native birds are); or by altering the environment in such a way that favors themselves (like melaleuca, an Australian tree that is spreading through the Everglades in part by changing the frequency and intensity of fires).

What invading species mostly don't do, it turns out, is outcompete native species. Take the case of the American gray squirrel, which was introduced in England in 1876. Dubbed "tree rat" by its detractors, the invader has made a pest of itself in its new land, where it is in the habit of eating flower bulbs and birds' eggs and stripping the bark from young birch trees. In addition, the spread of the gray squirrel has coincided with declining numbers of the Eurasian red squirrel, a native beloved by Brits despite the fact that it is only slightly less destructive than the gray squirrel.

Over the years, the gray squirrel has become an almost iconic 15 example of an invading species outcompeting a native one. But even with fewer than 30,000 red squirrels remaining in England today, there is little hard proof that competition explains the gray squirrel's success or the red squirrel's decline. Scientists have found that the gray is more efficient at foraging in the woods and in backyards. On the other hand, even before the gray's arrival, red squirrel populations in Britain had a periodic tendency to die out. (They were reintroduced to Scotland and Ireland several times during the 19th century.) In addition, it is now known that two-thirds of gray squirrels are silent carriers of a viral skin disease fatal to red squirrels. Domination comes easier to those who can spread a pox. But is that competition?

By and large, superior competitive ability isn't what enables alien species to invade. Likewise, small ecosystems can't be said to be competitively weaker than big ones. Small ecosystems are more vulnerable to extinctions; their member species are fewer in number and have limited refuge, and so are at statistically greater risk of being eliminated by a single event, whether a hurricane or the introduction of a predatory snake. But biological diversity per se—the number of species in an ecosystem—provides no shield against invasions. In a 1999 issue of the journal *Biological Invasions*, Daniel Simberloff, a prominent ecologist at the Institute for Biological Invasions at the University of Tennessee at Knoxville, writes simply, "It seems clear to me that there is no prima facie case for the biotic resistance paradigm."

Indeed, one of the big surprises to invasion biologists is the large number of alien species that any given ecosystem can harbor. South Florida, perhaps the most conspicuously invaded region on the U.S. mainland, is home to at least 300 introduced plant species—about 18 percent of the plant total. In San Francisco Bay, marine ecologists Jim Carlton of the Maritime Studies Program of Williams College and Mystic Seaport and Andrew Cohen of the San Francisco Estuary Institute have discovered more than 250 nonindigenous species. In the classic view of ecosystems, outlined by Elton and later Robert MacArthur and E. O. Wilson in their theory of island biogeography, ecosystems run on a knife's edge: They are tightly structured, without much room for new competitors.

"What invasions have shown is that there are plenty of unused resources," says Ted Grosholz, a marine biologist at the University of California at Davis who for years has monitored the incursion of the European green crab into the bay. "Ecosystems can absorb a lot of new species. I mean, holy cow, look at San Francisco Bay! Who would have thought an ecosystem had that much unused niche space?"

Invasions unfold invisibly. The average person will take alarm at a lion in the street—a large novelty and a personal hazard—but pay less heed to the progress of Asian crabgrass and Cuban tree frogs in the backyard ("Honey, is that a toad?"). Most alien species blend seamlessly into the ecosystems they enter. Like wallflowers, they slip in quietly, hang around the margins, and keep to themselves.

Which isn't to say that a wallflower will necessarily remain a 20 wallflower. The Brazilian pepper tree, introduced into South Florida a century ago, began to spread widely only in the 1950s; it now fills significant portions of the Everglades, in part by exuding a poisonous sap and clearing space for itself. And once an alien species becomes widespread, it is extremely difficult to eliminate.

Still, most invasions do no harm. Even prevalent ones can have surprisingly little impact on their new environments. A review of the history of purple loosestrife by zoologists Heather Hager and Karen McCoy, formerly at the University of Guelph in Ontario, concluded that despite belief to the contrary, there is little or no evidence to suggest that the incursion of the plant has serious ecological consequences. "The direct scientific rationale used to advocate purple loosestrife control does not exist," they write, adding that "aesthetic reasons remain the justification for its control."

Marine environments turn out to be particularly absorbent to—and forgiving of—alien species. Although exotic crabs, sea worms, sponges, clams, and diseases have been introduced around the world for hundreds of years on or in ships (and by many other means), marine biologists have documented not a single example of an invading marine species driving a native marine species extinct, whether by predation, competition, or disease.

"The key question is, what is the impact?" says Grosholz. "What effect does it have? Does it matter? Extinction may not be the only issue. That's the main difference between marine and terrestrial ecosystems. With the Australian brown tree snake in Guam you can point to species and say, 'Look, those things are gone.' With marine species it's not so easy. You can get qualitative shifts in communities if a species falls below a certain population threshold. I'm more concerned about those kinds of changes."

Invasion is not a zero-sum game, with invaders replacing natives at a one-to-one (or a one-to-two, or more) ratio. Rather, and with critical exceptions, it is a sum-sum game, in which ecosystems can accept more and more species. Indeed, in both marine and terrestrial ecosystems, the big surprise is that the incursion of alien species can actually increase, rather than decrease, biodiversity at a local level. This makes sense: If you add many new species and subtract no or only a few native ones, the overall species count goes up.

To put it differently, invasions don't cause ecosystems to col- 25 lapse. That's what Florida illustrates so vividly. If anything, there's more nature running around there than ever before. In small ecosystems like the Everglades or the Hawaiian Islands, where native species are already imperiled by disappearing habitat, invading species may be the final straw. Invasions may radically alter the components of an ecosystem, perhaps to a point at which the ecosystem becomes less valuable, engaging, or useful to humans. But unlike, say, the clear-cutting of a forest or the poisoning of a lake, invasions don't make ecosystems shrink or disappear.

For Discussion and Writing

1. What is the accepted idea about the presence of non-native species that Burdick argues against here?
2. The essay begins by focusing on Homestead, Florida. How does Burdick use Homestead to build his argument?

3. **connections**   Compare the way Burdick employs the metaphor of the invader in "The Truth about Invasive Species" to the way Zora Neale Hurston uses the metaphor of the bags in "How It Feels to Be Colored Me" (p. 188). How does each writer use metaphor to make his or her point?

4. Science is usually assumed to be purely objective, but as we know from the history of science, the field can be shaped by nonscientific assumptions. Write a reflection on a scientific idea about the world that was shaped by ideas about the way the world works. What changed that allowed these ideas to change? Did the science change first, or the way people thought about the world?

5. **looking further**   The power of the metaphor of the invader extends beyond the natural world. In some ways, this is an obvious fact, since the metaphor comes from the world of human behavior. But as you look into the history of reactions to demographic change—to immigration or internal migration—you can see that the trope of the invading horde is applied to situations in ways that can only be considered metaphorical. What do you think of this application? Why do people use it? What are the effects of its use?

NICHOLAS CARR

Is Google Making Us Stupid?

Nicholas Carr was born in 1959 and first gained widespread recognition with his 2003 Harvard Business Review *article "IT Doesn't Matter." He has continued to write about technology, culture, and economics for the* Guardian, *the* Atlantic, *the* New York Times, *the* Wall Street Journal, Wired, *the* New Republic, *the* Financial Times, *and* Technology Review. *He is author of* The Big Switch: Rewiring the World, from Edison to Google *(2008) and* The Shallows: What the Internet Is Doing to Our Brains, *which was nominated for a 2011 Pulitzer Prize. His most recent book,* The Glass Cage, *came out in 2014.*

"Is Google Making Us Stupid?" originally appeared in the Atlantic *in 2008. Carr expanded the article into a book-length exploration of the topic—*The Shallows*—published three years later. As in much of his work, Carr examines the impact of technological innovation, specifically in computing, on the way we live now, asking readers to step out of the fast-running stream of computing progress—from the expansion of information technology to cloud computing to our ever-increasing time spent online—and think about what we're doing and what effects it has. As you read this essay, note the way Carr slows us down and helps us look around.*

"Dave, stop. Stop, will you? Stop, Dave. Will you stop, Dave?" So the supercomputer HAL pleads with the implacable astronaut Dave Bowman in a famous and weirdly poignant scene toward the end of Stanley Kubrick's *2001: A Space Odyssey.* Bowman, having nearly been sent to a deep-space death by the malfunctioning machine, is calmly, coldly disconnecting the memory circuits that control its artificial "brain." "Dave, my mind is going," HAL says, forlornly. "I can feel it. I can feel it."

I can feel it, too. Over the past few years I've had an uncomfortable sense that someone, or something, has been tinkering with my brain, remapping the neural circuitry, reprogramming the

87

memory. My mind isn't going — so far as I can tell — but it's changing. I'm not thinking the way I used to think. I can feel it most strongly when I'm reading. Immersing myself in a book or a lengthy article used to be easy. My mind would get caught up in the narrative or the turns of the argument, and I'd spend hours strolling through long stretches of prose. That's rarely the case anymore. Now my concentration often starts to drift after two or three pages. I get fidgety, lose the thread, begin looking for something else to do. I feel as if I'm always dragging my wayward brain back to the text. The deep reading that used to come naturally has become a struggle.

I think I know what's going on. For more than a decade now, I've been spending a lot of time online, searching and surfing and sometimes adding to the great databases of the Internet. The Web has been a godsend to me as a writer. Research that once required days in the stacks or periodical rooms of libraries can now be done in minutes. A few Google searches, some quick clicks on hyperlinks, and I've got the telltale fact or pithy quote I was after. Even when I'm not working, I'm as likely as not to be foraging in the Web's info-thickets, reading and writing e-mails, scanning headlines and blog posts, watching videos and listening to podcasts, or just tripping from link to link to link. (Unlike footnotes, to which they're sometimes likened, hyperlinks don't merely point to related works; they propel you toward them.)

For me, as for others, the Net is becoming a universal medium, the conduit for most of the information that flows through my eyes and ears and into my mind. The advantages of having immediate access to such an incredibly rich store of information are many, and they've been widely described and duly applauded. "The perfect recall of silicon memory," *Wired*'s Clive Thompson has written, "can be an enormous boon to thinking." But that boon comes at a price. As the media theorist Marshall McLuhan pointed out in the 1960s, media are not just passive channels of information. They supply the stuff of thought, but they also shape the process of thought. And what the Net seems to be doing is chipping away my capacity for concentration and contemplation. My mind now expects to take in information the way the Net distributes it: in a swiftly moving stream of particles. Once I was a scuba diver in the sea of words. Now I zip along the surface like a guy on a Jet Ski.

I'm not the only one. When I mention my troubles with reading   5
to friends and acquaintances—literary types, most of them—
many say they're having similar experiences. The more they use
the Web, the more they have to fight to stay focused on long pieces
of writing. Some of the bloggers I follow have also begun mentioning the phenomenon. Scott Karp, who writes a blog about
online media, recently confessed that he has stopped reading
books altogether. "I was a lit major in college, and used to be [a]
voracious book reader," he wrote. "What happened?" He specu-
lates on the answer: "What if I do all my reading on the Web not
so much because the way I read has changed, i.e., I'm just seeking
convenience, but because the way I THINK has changed?"

Bruce Friedman, who blogs regularly about the use of computers in medicine, also has described how the Internet has altered
his mental habits. "I now have almost totally lost the ability to
read and absorb a longish article on the Web or in print," he wrote
earlier this year. A pathologist who has long been on the faculty of
the University of Michigan Medical School, Friedman elaborated
on his comment in a telephone conversation with me. His thinking, he said, has taken on a "staccato" quality, reflecting the way
he quickly scans short passages of text from many sources online.
"I can't read *War and Peace* anymore," he admitted. "I've lost the
ability to do that. Even a blog post of more than three or four
paragraphs is too much to absorb. I skim it."

Anecdotes alone don't prove much. And we still await the long-
term neurological and psychological experiments that will provide a definitive picture of how Internet use affects cognition. But
a recently published study of online research habits, conducted
by scholars from University College London, suggests that we
may well be in the midst of a sea change in the way we read and
think. As part of the five-year research program, the scholars
examined computer logs documenting the behavior of visitors to
two popular research sites, one operated by the British Library
and one by a U.K. educational consortium, that provide access to
journal articles, e-books, and other sources of written information. They found that people using the sites exhibited "a form of
skimming activity," hopping from one source to another and
rarely returning to any source they'd already visited. They typi-
cally read no more than one or two pages of an article or book
before they would "bounce" out to another site. Sometimes they'd

save a long article, but there's no evidence that they ever went back and actually read it. The authors of the study report:

> It is clear that users are not reading online in the traditional sense; indeed there are signs that new forms of "reading" are emerging as users "power browse" horizontally through titles, contents pages and abstracts going for quick wins. It almost seems that they go online to avoid reading in the traditional sense.

Thanks to the ubiquity of text on the Internet, not to mention the popularity of text-messaging on cell phones, we may well be reading more today than we did in the 1970s or 1980s, when television was our medium of choice. But it's a different kind of reading, and behind it lies a different kind of thinking—perhaps even a new sense of the self. "We are not only *what* we read," says Maryanne Wolf, a developmental psychologist at Tufts University and the author of *Proust and the Squid: The Story and Science of the Reading Brain.* "We are *how* we read." Wolf worries that the style of reading promoted by the Net, a style that puts "efficiency" and "immediacy" above all else, may be weakening our capacity for the kind of deep reading that emerged when an earlier technology, the printing press, made long and complex works of prose commonplace. When we read online, she says, we tend to become "mere decoders of information." Our ability to interpret text, to make the rich mental connections that form when we read deeply and without distraction, remains largely disengaged.

Reading, explains Wolf, is not an instinctive skill for human 10 beings. It's not etched into our genes the way speech is. We have to teach our minds how to translate the symbolic characters we see into the language we understand. And the media or other technologies we use in learning and practicing the craft of reading play an important part in shaping the neural circuits inside our brains. Experiments demonstrate that readers of ideograms, such as the Chinese, develop a mental circuitry for reading that is very different from the circuitry found in those of us whose written language employs an alphabet. The variations extend across many regions of the brain, including those that govern such essential cognitive functions as memory and the interpretation of visual and auditory stimuli. We can expect as well that the circuits woven by our use of the Net will be different from those woven by our reading of books and other printed works.

Sometime in 1882, Friedrich Nietzsche bought a typewriter—a Malling-Hansen Writing Ball, to be precise. His vision was failing, and keeping his eyes focused on a page had become exhausting and painful, often bringing on crushing headaches. He had been forced to curtail his writing, and he feared that he would soon have to give it up. The typewriter rescued him, at least for a time. Once he had mastered touch-typing, he was able to write with his eyes closed, using only the tips of his fingers. Words could once again flow from his mind to the page.

But the machine had a subtler effect on his work. One of Nietzsche's friends, a composer, noticed a change in the style of his writing. His already terse prose had become even tighter, more telegraphic. "Perhaps you will through this instrument even take to a new idiom," the friend wrote in a letter, noting that, in his own work, his "'thoughts' in music and language often depend on the quality of pen and paper."

"You are right," Nietzsche replied, "our writing equipment takes part in the forming of our thoughts." Under the sway of the machine, writes the German media scholar Friedrich A. Kittler, Nietzsche's prose "changed from arguments to aphorisms, from thoughts to puns, from rhetoric to telegram style."

The human brain is almost infinitely malleable. People used to think that our mental meshwork, the dense connections formed among the 100 billion or so neurons inside our skulls, was largely fixed by the time we reached adulthood. But brain researchers have discovered that that's not the case. James Olds, a professor of neuroscience who directs the Krasnow Institute for Advanced Study at George Mason University, says that even the adult mind "is very plastic." Nerve cells routinely break old connections and form new ones. "The brain," according to Olds, "has the ability to reprogram itself on the fly, altering the way it functions."

As we use what the sociologist Daniel Bell has called our "intel-   15 lectual technologies"—the tools that extend our mental rather than our physical capacities—we inevitably begin to take on the qualities of those technologies. The mechanical clock, which came into common use in the 14th century, provides a compelling example. In *Technics and Civilization*, the historian and cultural critic Lewis Mumford described how the clock "disassociated time from human events and helped create the belief in an independent world of mathematically measurable sequences." The "abstract framework of divided time" became "the point of reference for both action and thought."

The clock's methodical ticking helped bring into being the scientific mind and the scientific man. But it also took something away. As the late MIT computer scientist Joseph Weizenbaum observed in his 1976 book, *Computer Power and Human Reason: From Judgment to Calculation*, the conception of the world that emerged from the widespread use of timekeeping instruments "remains an impoverished version of the older one, for it rests on a rejection of those direct experiences that formed the basis for, and indeed constituted, the old reality." In deciding when to eat, to work, to sleep, to rise, we stopped listening to our senses and started obeying the clock.

The process of adapting to new intellectual technologies is reflected in the changing metaphors we use to explain ourselves to ourselves. When the mechanical clock arrived, people began thinking of their brains as operating "like clockwork." Today, in the age of software, we have come to think of them as operating "like computers." But the changes, neuroscience tells us, go much deeper than metaphor. Thanks to our brain's plasticity, the adaptation occurs also at a biological level.

The Internet promises to have particularly far-reaching effects on cognition. In a paper published in 1936, the British mathematician Alan Turing proved that a digital computer, which at the time existed only as a theoretical machine, could be programmed to perform the function of any other information-processing device. And that's what we're seeing today. The Internet, an immeasurably powerful computing system, is subsuming most of our other intellectual technologies. It's becoming our map and our clock, our printing press and our typewriter, our calculator and our telephone, and our radio and TV.

When the Net absorbs a medium, that medium is re-created in the Net's image. It injects the medium's content with hyperlinks, blinking ads, and other digital gewgaws, and it surrounds the content with the content of all the other media it has absorbed. A new e-mail message, for instance, may announce its arrival as we're glancing over the latest headlines at a newspaper's site. The result is to scatter our attention and diffuse our concentration.

The Net's influence doesn't end at the edges of a computer screen, either. As people's minds become attuned to the crazy quilt 20 of Internet media, traditional media have to adapt to the audience's new expectations. Television programs add text crawls and pop-up ads, and magazines and newspapers shorten their articles, introduce capsule summaries, and crowd their pages with easy-to-browse info-snippets. When, in March of this year, the *New York Times* decided to devote the second and third pages of every edition to article abstracts, its design director, Tom Bodkin, explained that the "shortcuts" would give harried readers a quick "taste" of the day's news, sparing them the "less efficient" method of actually turning the pages and reading the articles. Old media have little choice but to play by the new-media rules.

Never has a communications system played so many roles in our lives—or exerted such broad influence over our thoughts—as the Internet does today. Yet, for all that's been written about the Net, there's been little consideration of how, exactly, it's reprogramming us. The Net's intellectual ethic remains obscure.

About the same time that Nietzsche started using his typewriter, an earnest young man named Frederick Winslow Taylor carried a stopwatch into the Midvale Steel plant in Philadelphia and began a historic series of experiments aimed at improving the efficiency of the plant's machinists. With the approval of Midvale's owners, he recruited a group of factory hands, set them to work on various metalworking machines, and recorded and timed their every movement as well as the operations of the machines. By breaking down every job into a sequence of small, discrete steps and then testing different ways of performing each one, Taylor created a set of precise instructions—an "algorithm," we might say today—for how each worker should work. Midvale's employees grumbled about the strict new regime, claiming that it turned them into little more than automatons, but the factory's productivity soared.

More than a hundred years after the invention of the steam engine, the Industrial Revolution had at last found its philosophy and its philosopher. Taylor's tight industrial choreography—his "system," as he liked to call it—was embraced by manufacturers throughout the country and, in time, around the world. Seeking maximum speed, maximum efficiency, and maximum output, factory owners used time-and-motion studies to organize their work and configure the jobs of their workers. The goal, as Taylor defined it in his celebrated 1911 treatise, *The Principles of Scientific Management*, was to identify and adopt, for every job, the "one best method" of work and thereby to effect "the gradual substitution of science for rule of thumb throughout the mechanic arts." Once his system was applied to all acts of manual labor, Taylor assured his followers, it would bring about a restructuring not only of industry but of society, creating a utopia of perfect efficiency. "In the past the man has been first," he declared; "in the future the system must be first."

Taylor's system is still very much with us; it remains the ethic of industrial manufacturing. And now, thanks to the growing power that computer engineers and software coders wield over our intellectual lives, Taylor's ethic is beginning to govern the realm of the mind as well. The Internet is a machine designed for the efficient and automated collection, transmission, and manipulation of information, and its legions of programmers are intent on finding the "one best method"—the perfect algorithm—to carry out every mental movement of what we've come to describe as "knowledge work."

Google's headquarters, in Mountain View, California—the 25 Googleplex—is the Internet's high church, and the religion practiced inside its walls is Taylorism. Google, says its chief executive, Eric Schmidt, is "a company that's founded around the science of measurement," and it is striving to "systematize everything" it does. Drawing on the terabytes of behavioral data it collects through its search engine and other sites, it carries out thousands of experiments a day, according to the *Harvard Business Review*, and it uses the results to refine the algorithms that increasingly control how people find information and extract meaning from it. What Taylor did for the work of the hand, Google is doing for the work of the mind.

The company has declared that its mission is "to organize the world's information and make it universally accessible and useful." It seeks to develop "the perfect search engine," which it defines as something that "understands exactly what you mean and gives you back exactly what you want." In Google's view, information is a kind of commodity, a utilitarian resource that can be mined and processed with industrial efficiency. The more pieces of information we can "access" and the faster we can extract their gist, the more productive we become as thinkers.

Where does it end? Sergey Brin and Larry Page, the gifted young men who founded Google while pursuing doctoral degrees in computer science at Stanford, speak frequently of their desire to turn their search engine into an artificial intelligence, a HAL-like machine that might be connected directly to our brains. "The ultimate search engine is something as smart as people—or smarter," Page said in a speech a few years back. "For us, working on search is a way to work on artificial intelligence." In a 2004 interview with *Newsweek*, Brin said, "Certainly if you had all the world's information directly attached to your brain, or an artificial brain that was smarter than your brain, you'd be better off." Last year, Page told a convention of scientists that Google is "really trying to build artificial intelligence and to do it on a large scale."

Such an ambition is a natural one, even an admirable one, for a pair of math whizzes with vast quantities of cash at their disposal and a small army of computer scientists in their employ. A fundamentally scientific enterprise, Google is motivated by a desire to use technology, in Eric Schmidt's words, "to solve problems that have never been solved before," and artificial intelligence is the hardest problem out there. Why wouldn't Brin and Page want to be the ones to crack it?

Still, their easy assumption that we'd all "be better off" if our brains were supplemented, or even replaced, by an artificial intelligence is unsettling. It suggests a belief that intelligence is the output of a mechanical process, a series of discrete steps that can be isolated, measured, and optimized. In Google's world, the world we enter when we go online, there's little place for the fuzziness of contemplation. Ambiguity is not an opening for insight but a bug to be fixed. The human brain is just an outdated computer that needs a faster processor and a bigger hard drive.

The idea that our minds should operate as high-speed data- 30 processing machines is not only built into the workings of the Internet, it is the network's reigning business model as well. The faster we surf across the Web—the more links we click and pages we view—the more opportunities Google and other companies gain to collect information about us and to feed us advertisements. Most of the proprietors of the commercial Internet have a financial stake in collecting the crumbs of data we leave behind as we flit from link to link—the more crumbs, the better. The last thing these companies want is to encourage leisurely reading or slow, concentrated thought. It's in their economic interest to drive us to distraction.

Maybe I'm just a worrywart. Just as there's a tendency to glorify technological progress, there's a countertendency to expect the worst of every new tool or machine. In Plato's *Phaedrus*, Socrates bemoaned the development of writing. He feared that, as people came to rely on the written word as a substitute for the knowledge they used to carry inside their heads, they would, in the words of one of the dialogue's characters, "cease to exercise their memory and become forgetful." And because they would be able to "receive a quantity of information without proper instruction," they would "be thought very knowledgeable when they are for the most part quite ignorant." They would be "filled with the conceit of wisdom instead of real wisdom." Socrates wasn't wrong—the new technology did often have the effects he feared—but he was shortsighted. He couldn't foresee the many ways that writing and reading would serve to spread information, spur fresh ideas, and expand human knowledge (if not wisdom).

The arrival of Gutenberg's printing press, in the 15th century, set off another round of teeth gnashing. The Italian humanist Hieronimo Squarciafico worried that the easy availability of books would lead to intellectual laziness, making men "less studious," and weakening their minds. Others argued that cheaply printed books and broadsheets would undermine religious authority, demean the work of scholars and scribes, and spread sedition and debauchery. As New York University professor Clay Shirky notes, "Most of the arguments made against the printing press were correct, even prescient." But, again, the doomsayers were unable to imagine the myriad blessings that the printed word would deliver.

So, yes, you should be skeptical of my skepticism. Perhaps those who dismiss critics of the Internet as Luddites or nostalgists will be proved correct, and from our hyperactive, data-stoked minds will spring a golden age of intellectual discovery and universal wisdom. Then again, the Net isn't the alphabet, and although it may replace the printing press, it produces something altogether different. The kind of deep reading that a sequence of printed pages promotes is valuable not just for the knowledge we acquire from the author's words but for the intellectual vibrations those words set off within our own minds. In the quiet spaces opened up by the sustained, undistracted reading of a book, or by any other act of contemplation, for that matter, we make our own associations, draw our own inferences and analogies, foster our own ideas. Deep reading, as Maryanne Wolf argues, is indistinguishable from deep thinking.

If we lose those quiet spaces, or fill them up with "content," we will sacrifice something important not only in our selves but in our culture. In a recent essay, the playwright Richard Foreman eloquently described what's at stake:

> I come from a tradition of Western culture, in which the ideal (my ideal) was the complex, dense and "cathedral-like" structure of the highly educated and articulate personality—a man or woman who carried inside themselves a personally constructed and unique version of the entire heritage of the West. [But now] I see within us all (myself included) the replacement of complex inner density with a new kind of self—evolving under the pressure of information overload and the technology of the "instantly available."

As we are drained of our "inner repertory of dense cultural inheritance," Foreman concluded, we risk turning into "'pancake people'—spread wide and thin as we connect with that vast network of information accessed by the mere touch of a button."

I'm haunted by that scene in *2001*. What makes it so poignant, 35 and so weird, is the computer's emotional response to the disassembly of its mind: its despair as one circuit after another goes dark, its childlike pleading with the astronaut—"I can feel it. I can feel it. I'm afraid"—and its final reversion to what can only be called a state of innocence. HAL's outpouring of feeling contrasts with the emotionlessness that characterizes the human figures in the film, who go about their business with an almost robotic efficiency. Their thoughts and actions feel scripted, as if they're following the steps of an algorithm. In the world of *2001*, people have become so machinelike that the most human character turns out to be a machine. That's the essence of Kubrick's dark prophecy: as we come to rely on computers to mediate our understanding of the world, it is our own intelligence that flattens into artificial intelligence.

For Discussion and Writing

1. What common idea about the effect of our increased access to information is Carr arguing against? If you could phrase the idea as a play on the essay's title, in a declarative sentence, what would it be?

2. Though Carr is writing about a large social phenomenon, he begins with a scene from an old movie and some personal reflection. Why do you think he chose to begin his essay in this way?

3. **connections** Compare Carr's reflections on technology to Verlyn Klinkenborg's thoughts in "Our Vanishing Night" (p. 216). Though they are writing about quite different subjects, both authors are focusing on the effects of things made possible by modern technology. How does each essay treat modernity? What role does each see for technology?

4. A common image in science fiction is the future human with the personal computer taken even more personally—on a special pair of glasses, on the forearm, on a chip inside the brain. This image can be interpreted positively, as one of the fantastic inventions that will extend our capabilities, or negatively, as a frightening invasion of our lives by technology. Write about this, either in an essay imagining these advances and their effects or in a piece of short speculative fiction, and try to include some thoughts about the ultimate value of such innovation. (If you wish, you can also try to incorporate connections back to Carr's subject—that is, the effects of current revolutions in information technology.)

5. **looking further** Keep a log of your activities for several hours while you are doing schoolwork on your computer. How much time do you spend concentrating on one task at a time? How do you use the computer in the service of that task? Conversely, how much time do you multitask or get distracted by social media? How able are you to turn to reading and non-computer-mediated activities? Reflect on your own relationship to information technology, thinking about its effects on the way you work and think.

The Paranoid Style of American Policing

Ta-Nehisi Coates, born in Baltimore, Maryland, in 1975, began his career in journalism at the Washington City Paper *and contributed to the* Village Voice *and* Time *before becoming an editor and national correspondent at the* Atlantic. *In 2015, he received both the National Book Award for Nonfiction for his autobiography,* Between the World and Me *(2015), and a visiting fellowship at the American Library in Paris.*

Coates's essay, "The Paranoid Style of American Policing," was first published in the Atlantic *on December 30, 2015. In it, he addresses the rise in police violence against the black community and the loss of trust that many have in the police as an agent of order and justice. As you read, think about your own interactions with the police—either casual or perhaps more formal. Does what Coates says ring true for your experience?*

When I was around 10 years old, my father confronted a young man who was said to be "crazy." The young man was always too quick to want to fight. A foul in a game of 21 was an insult to his honor. A cross word was cause for a duel, and you never knew what that cross word might be. One day, the young man got into it with one of my older brother's friends. The young man pulled a metal stake out of the ground (there was some work being done nearby) and began swinging it wildly in a threatening manner. My father, my mother, or my older brother—I don't recall which— told the other boy to go inside of our house. My dad then came outside. I don't really remember what my father said to the young man. Perhaps he said something like "Go home," or maybe something like, "Son, it's over." I don't really recall. But what I do recall is that my dad did not shoot and kill the young man.

That wasn't the first time I'd seen my father confront the violence of young people without resorting to killing them. This was not remarkable. When you live in communities like ours—or perhaps any community—mediating violence between young people is part of being an adult. Sometimes the young people are involved in scary behavior—like threatening people with metal objects. And yet the notion that it is permissible, wise, moral, or advisable to kill such a person as a method of de-escalation, to kill because one was afraid, did not really exist among parents in my community.

The same could not be said for those who came from outside of the community.

This weekend, after a Chicago police officer killed her 19-year-old son Quintonio LeGrier, Janet Cooksey struggled to understand the mentality of the people she pays to keep her community safe:

> "What happened to Tasers? Seven times my son was shot," Cooksey said.
>
> "The police are supposed to serve and protect us and yet they take the lives," Cooksey said.
>
> "Where do we get our help?" she asked.

LeGrier had struggled with mental illness. When LeGrier attempted to break down his father's door, his father called the police, who apparently arrived to find the 19-year-old wielding a bat. Interpreting this as a lethal threat, one of the officers shot and killed LeGrier and somehow managed to shoot and kill one of his neighbors, Bettie Jones. Cooksey did not merely have a problem with how the police acted, but with the fact that the police were even called in the first place. "He should have called me," Cooksey said of LeGrier's father.

Instead, the father called the Chicago Police Department. Likely he called them because he invested them with some measure of legitimacy. This is understandable. In America, police officers are agents of the state and thus bound by the social contract in a way that criminals, and even random citizens, are not. Criminals and random citizens are not paid to protect other citizens. Police officers are. By that logic, one might surmise that the police would be better able to mediate conflicts than community members. In Chicago, this appears, very often, not to be the case.

5

It will not do to note that 99 percent of the time the police mediate conflicts without killing people anymore than it will do for a restaurant to note that 99 percent of the time rats don't run through the dining room. Nor will it do to point out that most black citizens are killed by other black citizens, not police officers, anymore than it will do to point out that most American citizens are killed by other American citizens, not terrorists. If officers cannot be expected to act any better than ordinary citizens, why call them in the first place? Why invest them with any more power?

Legitimacy is what is ultimately at stake here. When Cooksey says that her son's father should not have called the police, when she says that they "are supposed to serve and protect us and yet they take the lives," she is saying that police in Chicago are police in name only. This opinion is widely shared. Asked about the possibility of an investigation, Melvin Jones, the brother of Bettie Jones, could muster no confidence. "I already know how that will turn out," he scoffed. "We all know how that will turn out."

Indeed, we probably do. Two days after Jones and LeGrier were killed, a district attorney in Ohio declined to prosecute the two officers who drove up, and within two seconds of arriving, killed the 12-year-old Tamir Rice. No one should be surprised by this. In America, we have decided that it is permissible, that it is wise, that it is moral for the police to de-escalate through killing. A standard which would not have held for my father in West Baltimore, which did not hold for me in Harlem, is reserved for those who have the maximum power—the right to kill on behalf of the state. When police can not adhere to the standards of the neighborhood, of citizens, or of parents, what are they beyond a bigger gun and a sharper sword? By what right do they enforce their will, save force itself?

When policing is delegitimized, when it becomes an occupying force, the community suffers. The neighbor-on-neighbor violence in Chicago, and in black communities around the country, is not an optical illusion. Policing is (one) part of the solution to that violence. But if citizens don't trust officers, then policing can't actually work. And in Chicago, it is very hard to muster reasons for trust.

When Bettie Jones's brother displays zero confidence in an investigation into the killing of his sister, he is not being cynical.

He is shrewdly observing a government that executed a young man and sought to hide that fact from citizens. He is intelligently assessing a local government which, for two decades, ran a torture ring. What we have made of our police departments [in] America, what we have ordered them to do, is a direct challenge to any usable definition of democracy. A state that allows its agents to kill, to beat, to tase, without any real sanction, has ceased to govern and has commenced to simply rule.

For Discussion and Writing

1. Why does Coates begin with a story from his childhood that has nothing directly to do with policing?

2. Coates uses variations on the phrase "it will not do" more than once in this essay. How does he use it? Why does he repeat it? Imagine other phrases he could have used to serve the same purpose; why did he not use those?

3. **connections**   Coates, in "The Paranoid Style of American Policing," and Audre Lorde, in "The Fourth of July" (p. 221), focus on racism in America, but in very different ways. Compare and contrast the two essays in terms of their subjects and their methods. What kinds of stories do Lorde and Coates tell, and to what ends? What kind of evidence does each use? How do the kinds of narratives and evidence fit each author's subject and argument?

4. As Coates writes, "99 percent of the time the police mediate conflicts without killing people" (par. 7). Write a reflection about one or more interactions you have had with the police, from the serious to the casual; how did the interaction(s) make you feel? How do you feel about the police generally? Did the interaction(s) confirm your opinion or change it? (If you've had no direct dealings with a police officer of any kind, write about things you've witnessed or read about.)

5. **looking further**   List Coates's objections to the use of what he deems excessive force by police. Many connect to larger political questions about the nature of the relationship between the state and the citizen. Extrapolate, from these objections, Coates's theory of government. Why does it exist? What is it for? Then, with the help of a little reading, connect this theory to contemporary thinking about government's role in American life.

JUDITH ORTIZ COFER

The Myth of the Latin Woman: I Just Met a Girl Named María

Judith Ortiz Cofer was born in Puerto Rico in 1952 and grew up there and in New Jersey. She is a poet, fiction writer, and autobiographer, and teaches literature and writing at the University of Georgia. In 2010, Cofer was inducted into the Georgia Writers Hall of Fame. Much of her work, such as her novel The Line of the Sun *(1989) and* The Latin Deli: Prose and Poetry *(1993), explores her experiences as a Puerto Rican émigré and a Latina. Her most recent books include a novel,* If I Could Fly *(2011), and three children's books,* Animal Jamboree: Latino Folktales *(2012),* The Poet Upstairs *(2012), and* ¡A bailar! *(2011).*

"The Myth of the Latin Woman: I Just Met a Girl Named María" considers the stereotypes Americans hold about Latinas, and it does so through narrative and reflection. At the end of one of the stories she tells in her essay, dealing with an offensive man, Cofer writes, "My friend complimented me on my cool handling of the situation" (par. 10), then notes that what she really wanted to do was push the man into the pool. Notice, as you read, the ways in which Cofer is able in this essay, as in that incident, to strike a balance between anger and analysis.

On a bus trip to London from Oxford University where I was earning some graduate credits one summer, a young man, obviously fresh from a pub, spotted me and as if struck by inspiration went down on his knees in the aisle. With both hands over his heart he broke into an Irish tenor's rendition of "María" from *West Side Story.* My politely amused fellow passengers gave his lovely voice the round of gentle applause it deserved. Though I was not quite as amused, I managed my version of an English smile: no show of teeth, no extreme contortions of the facial muscles—I was at this time of my life practicing reserve and cool. Oh, that British control, how I coveted it. But María had followed me to London, reminding me of a prime fact of my life: you can leave the Island, master the English language, and travel as far as you can, but if you are a Latina, especially one like me who so obviously belongs to Rita Moreno's gene pool, the Island travels with you.

This is sometimes a very good thing—it may win you that extra minute of someone's attention. But with some people, the same things can make *you* an island—not so much a tropical paradise as an Alcatraz, a place nobody wants to visit. As a Puerto Rican girl growing up in the United States and wanting like most children to "belong," I resented the stereotype that my Hispanic appearance called forth from many people I met.

Our family lived in a large urban center in New Jersey during the sixties, where life was designed as a microcosm of my parents' casas on the island. We spoke in Spanish, we ate Puerto Rican food bought at the bodega, and we practiced strict Catholicism complete with Saturday confession and Sunday mass at a church where our parents were accommodated into a one-hour Spanish mass slot, performed by a Chinese priest trained as a missionary for Latin America.

As a girl I was kept under strict surveillance, since virtue and modesty were, by cultural equation, the same as family honor. As a teenager I was instructed on how to behave as a proper señorita. But it was a conflicting message girls got, since the Puerto Rican mothers also encouraged their daughters to look and act like women and to dress in clothes our Anglo friends and their mothers found too "mature" for our age. It was, and is, cultural, yet I often felt humiliated when I appeared at an American friend's party wearing a dress more suitable to a semiformal than to a playroom birthday celebration. At Puerto Rican festivities, neither the music nor the colors we wore could be too loud. I still experience a vague sense of letdown when I'm invited to a "party" and it turns out to be a marathon conversation in hushed tones rather than a fiesta with salsa, laughter, and dancing—the kind of celebration I remember from my childhood.

I remember Career Day in our high school, when teachers told   5
us to come dressed as if for a job interview. It quickly became obvious that to the barrio girls, "dressing up" sometimes meant wearing ornate jewelry and clothing that would be more appropriate

(by mainstream standards) for the company Christmas party than as daily office attire. That morning I had agonized in front of my closet, trying to figure out what a "career girl" would wear because, essentially, except for Marlo Thomas on TV, I had no models on which to base my decision. I knew how to dress for school: at the Catholic school I attended we all wore uniforms; I knew how to dress for Sunday mass, and I knew what dresses to wear for parties at my relatives' homes. Though I do not recall the precise details of my Career Day outfit, it must have been a composite of the above choices. But I remember a comment my friend (an Italian-American) made in later years that coalesced my impressions of that day. She said that at the business school she was attending the Puerto Rican girls always stood out for wearing "everything at once." She meant, of course, too much jewelry, too many accessories. On that day at school, we were simply made the negative models by the nuns who were themselves not credible fashion experts to any of us. But it was painfully obvious to me that to the others, in their tailored skirts and silk blouses, we must have seemed "hopeless" and "vulgar." Though I now know that most adolescents feel out of step much of the time, I also know that for the Puerto Rican girls of my generation that sense was intensified. The way our teachers and classmates looked at us that day in school was just a taste of the culture clash that awaited us in the real world, where prospective employers and men on the street would often misinterpret our tight skirts and jingling bracelets as a come-on.

Mixed cultural signals have perpetuated certain stereotypes — for example, that of the Hispanic woman as the "Hot Tamale" or sexual firebrand. It is a one-dimensional view that the media have found easy to promote. In their special vocabulary, advertisers have designated "sizzling" and "smoldering" as the adjectives of choice for describing not only the foods but also the women of Latin America. From conversations in my house I recall hearing about the harassment that Puerto Rican women endured in factories where the "boss men" talked to them as if sexual innuendo was all they understood and, worse, often gave them the choice of submitting to advances or being fired.

It is custom, however, not chromosomes, that leads us to choose scarlet over pale pink. As young girls, we were influenced in our decisions about clothes and colors by the women—older sisters and mothers who had grown up on a tropical island where the natural environment was a riot of primary colors, where showing your skin was one way to keep cool as well as to look sexy. Most important of all, on the island, women perhaps felt freer to dress and move more provocatively, since, in most cases, they were protected by the traditions, mores, and laws of a Spanish/Catholic system of morality and machismo whose main rule was: *You may look at my sister, but if you touch her I will kill you.* The extended family and church structure could provide a young woman with a circle of safety in her small pueblo on the island; if a man "wronged" a girl, everyone would close in to save her family honor.

This is what I have gleaned from my discussions as an adult with older Puerto Rican women. They have told me about dressing in their best party clothes on Saturday nights and going to the town's plaza to promenade with their girlfriends in front of the boys they liked. The males were thus given an opportunity to admire the women and to express their admiration in the form of *piropos*: erotically charged street poems they composed on the spot. I have been subjected to a few piropos while visiting the Island, and they can be outrageous, although custom dictates that they must never cross into obscenity. This ritual, as I understand it, also entails a show of studied indifference on the woman's part; if she is "decent," she must not acknowledge the man's impassioned words. So I do understand how things can be lost in translation. When a Puerto Rican girl dressed in her idea of what is attractive meets a man from the mainstream culture who has been trained to react to certain types of clothing as a sexual signal, a clash is likely to take place. The line I first heard based on this aspect of the myth happened when the boy who took me to my first formal dance leaned over to plant a sloppy overeager kiss painfully on my mouth, and when I didn't respond with sufficient passion said in a resentful tone: "I thought you Latin girls were supposed to mature early"—my first instance of being thought of as a fruit or vegetable—I was supposed to *ripen*, not just grow into womanhood like other girls.

It is surprising to some of my professional friends that some people, including those who should know better, still put others "in their place." Though rarer, these incidents are still commonplace in my life. It happened to me most recently during a stay at a very classy metropolitan hotel favored by young professional couples for their weddings. Late one evening after the theater, as I walked toward my room with my new colleague (a woman with whom I was coordinating an arts program), a middle-aged man in a tuxedo, a young girl in satin and lace on his arm, stepped directly into our path. With his champagne glass extended toward me, he exclaimed, "Evita!"

Our way blocked, my companion and I listened as the man 10 half-recited, half-bellowed "Don't Cry for Me, Argentina." When he finished, the young girl said: "How about a round of applause for my daddy?" We complied, hoping this would bring the silly spectacle to a close. I was becoming aware that our little group was attracting the attention of the other guests. "Daddy" must have perceived this too, and he once more barred the way as we tried to walk past him. He began to shout-sing a ditty to the tune of "La Bamba"—except the lyrics were about a girl named María whose exploits all rhymed with her name and gonorrhea. The girl kept saying "Oh, Daddy" and looking at me with pleading eyes. She wanted me to laugh along with the others. My companion and I stood silently waiting for the man to end his offensive song. When he finished, I looked not at him but at his daughter. I advised her calmly never to ask her father what he had done in the army. Then I walked between them and to my room. My friend complimented me on my cool handling of the situation. I confessed to her that I really had wanted to push the jerk into the swimming pool. I knew that this same man—probably a corporate executive, well educated, even worldly by most standards— would not have been likely to regale a white woman with a dirty song in public. He would perhaps have checked his impulse by assuming that she could be somebody's wife or mother, or at least *somebody* who might take offense. But to him, I was just an Evita or a María: merely a character in his cartoon-populated universe.

Because of my education and my proficiency with the English language, I have acquired many mechanisms for dealing with the anger I experience. This was not true for my parents, nor is it true for the many Latin women working at menial jobs who must put up with stereotypes about our ethnic group such as: "They make good domestics." This is another facet of the myth of the Latin woman in the United States. Its origin is simple to deduce. Work as domestics, waitressing, and factory jobs are all that's available

to women with little English and few skills. The myth of the Hispanic menial has been sustained by the same media phenomenon
that made "Mammy" from *Gone with the Wind* America's idea of
the black woman for generations: María, the housemaid or counter girl, is now indelibly etched into the national psyche. The big
and the little screens have presented us with the picture of the
funny Hispanic maid, mispronouncing words and cooking up a
spicy storm in a shiny California kitchen.

This media-engendered image of the Latina in the United
States has been documented by feminist Hispanic scholars, who
claim that such portrayals are partially responsible for the denial
of opportunities for upward mobility among Latinas in the professions. I have a Chicana friend working on a Ph.D. in philosophy at a major university. She says her doctor still shakes his head
in puzzled amazement at all the "big words" she uses. Since I do
not wear my diplomas around my neck for all to see, I too have on
occasion been sent to that "kitchen," where some think I obviously belong.

One such incident that has stayed with me, though I recognize
it as a minor offense, happened on the day of my first public
poetry reading. It took place in Miami in a boat-restaurant where
we were having lunch before the event. I was nervous and excited
as I walked in with my notebook in my hand. An older woman
motioned me to her table. Thinking (foolish me) that she wanted
me to autograph a copy of my brand-new slender volume of verse,
I went over. She ordered a cup of coffee from me, assuming that I
was the waitress. Easy enough to mistake my poems for menus, I
suppose. I know that it wasn't an intentional act of cruelty, yet of
all the good things that happened that day, I remember that scene
most clearly, because it reminded me of what I had to overcome
before anyone would take me seriously. In retrospect I understand that my anger gave my reading fire, that I have almost
always taken doubts in my abilities as a challenge—and that the
result is, most times, a feeling of satisfaction at having won a convert when I see the cold, appraising eyes warm to my words, the
body language change, the smile that indicates that I have opened
some avenue for communication. That day I read to that woman
and her lowered eyes told me that she was embarrassed at her
little faux pas, and when I willed her to look up at me, it was my
victory, and she graciously allowed me to punish her with my full

attention. We shook hands at the end of the reading, and I never saw her again. She has probably forgotten the whole thing but maybe not.

Yet I am one of the lucky ones. My parents made it possible for me to acquire a stronger footing in the mainstream culture by giving me the chance at an education. And books and art have saved me from the harsher forms of ethnic and racial prejudice that many of my Hispanic *compañeras* have had to endure. I travel a lot around the United States, reading from my books of poetry and my novel, and the reception I most often receive is one of positive interest by people who want to know more about my culture. There are, however, thousands of Latinas without the privilege of an education or the entrée into society that I have. For them life is a struggle against the misconceptions perpetuated by the myth of the Latina as whore, domestic, or criminal. We cannot change this by legislating the way people look at us. The transformation, as I see it, has to occur at a much more individual level. My personal goal in my public life is to try to replace the old pervasive stereotypes and myths about Latinas with a much more interesting set of realities. Every time I give a reading, I hope the stories I tell, the dreams and fears I examine in my work, can achieve some universal truth which will get my audience past the particulars of my skin color, my accent, or my clothes.

I once wrote a poem in which I called us Latinas "God's brown   15 daughters." This poem is really a prayer of sorts, offered upward, but also, through the human-to-human channel of art, outward. It is a prayer for communication, and for respect. In it, Latin women pray "in Spanish to an Anglo God / with a Jewish heritage," and they are "fervently hoping / that if not omnipotent, / at least He be bilingual."

For Discussion and Writing

1. What do the incidents on the bus, in the hotel, and at the poetry reading have in common?

2. What are the different kinds of Latinas Cofer says are recognized in mainstream Anglo-American culture? By making explicit her observations of how others classify people like her, what point does she make about classification in general?

3. **connections**   Compare Cofer's feelings about those who react to her based on her ethnicity, and her reactions to them as she relates them

to us, to Nancy Mairs's feelings about those who react to her based on her disability, and her reactions to them, in "On Being a Cripple" (p. 226). How do their feelings compare? How do their reactions compare? Are there any differences? If so, how might they connect to the nature of the characteristics for which each is viewed as different?

4. Write about how you perceive others in certain ways because of something about them — how they look, where they live, what they do for a living. Can we live without these kinds of snap judgments? Can we live with them? Be sure to use specific examples as you write.

5. **looking further**   Do some research into the changing demographic picture of the United States. What is the current racial and ethnic breakdown of the U.S. population? By what year is it predicted that whites will no longer be the majority? Do you think this will affect the way "minorities" are thought of and treated? How, or how not?

DANIEL DEFOE

The Education of Women

Daniel Defoe (c. 1660–1731) was an English merchant, pamphleteer, and one of the earliest novelists. His early career in business proving unsuccessful, Defoe instead pursued a career as a writer of political pamphlets, for which he was imprisoned in 1713. It wasn't until 1719, when he was in his late fifties, that Defoe wrote his most famous work, Robinson Crusoe, *which was followed by a series of novels, including* Moll Flanders, A Journal of the Plague Year *(a fictionalized account of 1665's Great Plague of London), and hundreds of other works short and long.*

"The Education of Women" was written in the same year that saw Robinson Crusoe, *though it covers a very different topic. As you read Defoe's argument in favor of educating women, keep an eye out for the many ways in which he presses his case and the variety of embedded assumptions about women.*

I have often thought of it as one of the most barbarous customs in the world, considering us as a civilized and a Christian country, that we deny the advantages of learning to women. We reproach the sex every day with folly and impertinence; while I am confident, had they the advantages of education equal to us, they would be guilty of less than ourselves.

One would wonder, indeed, how it should happen that women are conversible at all; since they are only beholden to natural parts, for all their knowledge. Their youth is spent to teach them to stitch and sew or make baubles. They are taught to read, indeed, and perhaps to write their names, or so; and that is the height of a woman's education. And I would but ask any who slight the sex for their understanding, what is a man (a gentleman, I mean) good for, that is taught no more? I need not give instances, or examine the character of a gentleman, with a good estate, or a good family, and with tolerable parts; and examine what figure he makes for want of education.

The soul is placed in the body like a rough diamond; and must be polished, or the luster of it will never appear. And 'tis manifest, that as the rational soul distinguishes us from brutes; so education carries on the distinction, and makes some less brutish than others. This is too evident to need any demonstration. But why then should women be denied the benefit of instruction? If knowledge and understanding had been useless additions to the sex, God Almighty would never have given them capacities; for he made nothing needless. Besides, I would ask such, What they can see in ignorance, that they should think it a necessary ornament to a woman? or how much worse is a wise woman than a fool? or what has the woman done to forfeit the privilege of being taught? Does she plague us with her pride and impertinence? Why did we not let her learn, that she might have had more wit? Shall we upbraid women with folly, when 'tis only the error of this inhuman custom, that hindered them from being made wiser?

The capacities of women are supposed to be greater, and their senses quicker than those of the men; and what they might be capable of being bred to, is plain from some instances of female wit, which this age is not without. Which upbraids us with Injustice, and looks as if we denied women the advantages of education, for fear they should vie with the men in their improvements . . .

[They] should be taught all sorts of breeding suitable both to   5
their genius and quality. And in particular, Music and Dancing; which it would be cruelty to bar the sex of, because they are their darlings. But besides this, they should be taught languages, as particularly French and Italian: and I would venture the injury of giving a woman more tongues than one. They should, as a particular study, be taught all the graces of speech, and all the necessary air of conversation; which our common education is so defective in, that I need not expose it. They should be brought to read books, and especially history; and so to read as to make them understand the world, and be able to know and judge of things when they hear of them.

To such whose genius would lead them to it, I would deny no sort of learning; but the chief thing, in general, is to cultivate the understandings of the sex, that they may be capable of all sorts of conversation; that their parts and judgments being improved, they may be as profitable in their conversation as they are pleasant.

Women, in my observation, have little or no difference in them, but as they are or are not distinguished by education. Tempers, indeed, may in some degree influence them, but the main distinguishing part is their Breeding.

The whole sex are generally quick and sharp. I believe, I may be allowed to say, generally so: for you rarely see them lumpish and heavy, when they are children; as boys will often be. If a woman be well bred, and taught the proper management of her natural wit, she proves generally very sensible and retentive.

And, without partiality, a woman of sense and manners is the finest and most delicate part of God's Creation, the glory of Her Maker, and the great instance of His singular regard to man, His darling creature: to whom He gave the best gift either God could bestow or man receive. And 'tis the sordidest piece of folly and ingratitude in the world, to withhold from the sex the due luster which the advantages of education gives to the natural beauty of their minds.

A woman well bred and well taught, furnished with the additional accomplishments of knowledge and behavior, is a creature without comparison. Her society is the emblem of sublimer enjoyments, her person is angelic, and her conversation heavenly. She is all softness and sweetness, peace, love, wit, and delight. She is every way suitable to the sublimest wish, and the man that has such a one to his portion, has nothing to do but to rejoice in her, and be thankful.

On the other hand, Suppose her to be the very same woman, and rob her of the benefit of education, and it follows—

If her temper be good, want of education makes her soft and easy.

Her wit, for want of teaching, makes her impertinent and talkative.

Her knowledge, for want of judgment and experience, makes her fanciful and whimsical.

If her temper be bad, want of breeding makes her worse; and she grows haughty, insolent, and loud.

If she be passionate, want of manners makes her a termagant and a scold, which is much at one with Lunatic.

If she be proud, want of discretion (which still is breeding) makes her conceited, fantastic, and ridiculous.

And from these she degenerates to be turbulent, clamorous, noisy, nasty, the devil!—

should be no difference

The great distinguishing difference, which is seen in the world between men and women, is in their education; and this is manifested by comparing it with the difference between one man or woman, and another.

And herein it is that I take upon me to make such a bold assertion, That all the world are mistaken in their practice about women. For I cannot think that God Almighty ever made them so delicate, so glorious creatures; and furnished them with such charms, so agreeable and so delightful to mankind; with souls capable of the same accomplishments with men: and all, to be only Stewards of our Houses, Cooks, and Slaves.

Not that I am for exalting the female government in the least: but, in short, I would have men take women for companions, and educate them to be fit for it. A woman of sense and breeding will scorn as much to encroach upon the prerogative of man, as a man of sense will scorn to oppress the weakness of the woman. But if the women's souls were refined and improved by teaching, that word would be lost. To say, the weakness of the sex, as to judgment, would be nonsense; for ignorance and folly would be no more to be found among women than men.

I remember a passage, which I heard from a very fine woman. 15 She had wit and capacity enough, an extraordinary shape and face, and a great fortune: but had been cloistered up all her time; and for fear of being stolen, had not had the liberty of being taught the common necessary knowledge of women's affairs. And when she came to converse in the world, her natural wit made her so sensible of the want of education, that she gave this short reflection on herself: "I am ashamed to talk with my very maids," says she, "for I don't know when they do right or wrong. I had more need to go to school, than be married."

I need not enlarge on the loss the defect of education is to the sex; nor argue the benefit of the contrary practice. 'Tis a thing will be more easily granted than remedied. This chapter is but an Essay at the thing: and I refer the Practice to those Happy Days (if ever they shall be) when men shall be wise enough to mend it.

For Discussion and Writing

1. What is Defoe's main argument concerning the education of women? What does he say about it, and what does he say to support his claim?

2. Defoe includes a number of rhetorical questions in this essay. How does he use them, and to what purpose? Identify another rhetorical device he uses here. Where does he use it, and how? What is the effect?

3. **connections**   Read Defoe's essay alongside Virginia Woolf's "Professions for Women" (p. 417). Does Woolf agree with Defoe's ideas about essential female nature? How else can you compare and contrast the two essays' arguments and assumptions about women?

4. Toward the end of the essay, Defoe takes pains to make sure his readers will not think he believes women should be put in charge of anything (par. 14). Write about your reaction to that moment, your sense of where we are today on this question, and where you stand on it. Is this attitude a thing of the past or something you still see around you? Where? Do you agree with it? Can you marshal evidence for its rightness or wrongness? Conversely, do you agree with the idea that the world would actually be a better place if women were in charge? Why, or why not?

5. **looking further**   Do some research on the last issue raised in the previous question. Is there something about women, in their nature (as they are born) or in their socialization (as they are raised), that would make them better or worse heads of state? Look for your answers in psychology, sociology, and the history of female leadership.

JOAN DIDION

On Keeping a Notebook

Joan Didion, a fifth-generation Californian born in 1934, has been an essayist since her undergraduate days. Known for a reflexive, self-conscious, yet cool style and a sharp political eye, Didion has, in essays and novels, carved out a unique place in American letters. Best known for her essay collections Slouching Towards Bethlehem *(1968) and* The White Album *(1979), her novels, including* Play It as It Lays *(1970) and* The Last Thing He Wanted *(1996), are also widely read. Her latest book,* Blue Nights *(2011), is a memoir about her life with her late daughter, aging, and parenthood.*

In "On Keeping a Notebook," Didion writes about writing, or about the work that she does prior to the writing of her published prose. As you read, think about whether her notebook keeping is entirely in the service of preparation for her writing or if it is also about other things and, if so, how these other goals might connect to her work.

"'That woman Estelle,'" the note reads, "'is partly the reason why George Sharp and I are separated today.' *Dirty crepe-de-Chine wrapper, hotel bar, Wilmington RR, 9:45 A.M. August Monday morning.*"

Since the note is in my notebook, it presumably has some meaning to me. I study it for a long while. At first I have only the most general notion of what I was doing on an August Monday morning in the bar of the hotel across from the Pennsylvania Railroad station in Wilmington, Delaware (waiting for a train? missing one? 1960? 1961? why Wilmington?), but I do remember being there. The woman in the dirty crepe-de-Chine wrapper had come down from her room for a beer, and the bartender had heard before the reason why George Sharp and she were separated today. "Sure," he said, and went on mopping the floor. "You told me." At the other end of the bar is a girl. She is talking, pointedly, not to the man beside her but to a cat lying in the triangle of sunlight cast through the open door. She is wearing a plaid silk dress from Peck & Peck, and the hem is coming down.

Here is what it is: the girl has been on the Eastern Shore, and now she is going back to the city, leaving the man beside her, and all she can see ahead are the viscous summer sidewalks and the 3 A.M. long-distance calls that will make her lie awake and then sleep drugged through all the steaming mornings left in August (1960? 1961?). Because she must go directly from the train to lunch in New York, she wishes that she had a safety pin for the hem of the plaid silk dress, and she also wishes that she could forget about the hem and the lunch and stay in the cool bar that smells of disinfectant and malt and make friends with the woman in the crepe-de-Chine wrapper. She is afflicted by a little self-pity, and she wants to compare Estelles. That is what that was all about.

Why did I write it down? In order to remember, of course, but exactly what was it I wanted to remember? How much of it actually happened? Did any of it? Why do I keep a notebook at all? It is easy to deceive oneself on all those scores. The impulse to write things down is a peculiarly compulsive one, inexplicable to those who do not share it, useful only accidentally, only secondarily, in the way that any compulsion tries to justify itself. I suppose that it begins or does not begin in the cradle. Although I have felt compelled to write things down since I was five years old, I doubt that my daughter ever will, for she is a singularly blessed and accepting child, delighted with life exactly as life presents itself to her, unafraid to go to sleep and unafraid to wake up. Keepers of private notebooks are a different breed altogether, lonely and resistant rearrangers of things, anxious malcontents, children afflicted apparently at birth with some presentiment of loss.

My first notebook was a Big Five tablet, given to me by my 5 mother with the sensible suggestion that I stop whining and learn to amuse myself by writing down my thoughts. She returned the tablet to me a few years ago; the first entry is an account of a woman who believed herself to be freezing to death in the Arctic night, only to find, when day broke, that she had stumbled onto the Sahara Desert, where she would die of the heat before lunch. I have no idea what turn of a five-year-old's mind could have prompted so insistently "ironic" and exotic a story, but it does reveal a certain predilection for the extreme which has dogged me into adult life; perhaps if I were analytically inclined I would find it a truer story than any I might have told about Donald Johnson's birthday party or the day my cousin Brenda put Kitty Litter in the aquarium.

So the point of my keeping a notebook has never been, nor is it now, to have an accurate factual record of what I have been doing or thinking. That would be a different impulse entirely, an instinct for reality which I sometimes envy but do not possess. At no point have I ever been able successfully to keep a diary; my approach to daily life ranges from the grossly negligent to the merely absent, and on those few occasions when I have tried dutifully to record a day's events, boredom has so overcome me that the results are mysterious at best. What is this business about "shopping, typing piece, dinner with E, depressed"? Shopping for what? Typing what piece? Who is E? Was this "E" depressed, or was I depressed? Who cares?

In fact I have abandoned altogether that kind of pointless entry; instead I tell what some would call lies. "That's simply not true," the members of my family frequently tell me when they come up against my memory of a shared event. "The party was *not* for you, the spider was not a black widow, *it wasn't that way at all.*" Very likely they are right, for not only have I always had trouble distinguishing between what happened and what merely might have happened, but I remain unconvinced that the distinction, for my purposes, matters. The cracked crab that I recall having for lunch the day my father came home from Detroit in 1945 must certainly be embroidery, worked into the day's pattern to lend verisimilitude; I was ten years old and would not now remember the cracked crab. The day's events did not turn on cracked crab. And yet it is precisely that fictitious crab that makes me see the afternoon all over again, a home movie run all too often, the father bearing gifts, the child weeping, an exercise in family love and guilt. Or that is what it was to me. Similarly, perhaps it never did snow that August in Vermont; perhaps there never were flurries in the night wind, and maybe no one else felt the ground hardening and summer already dead even as we pretended to bask in it, but that was how it felt to me, and it might as well have snowed, could have snowed, did snow.

How it felt to me: that is getting closer to the truth about a notebook. I sometimes delude myself about why I keep a notebook, imagine that some thrifty virtue derives from preserving everything observed. See enough and write it down, I tell myself, and then some morning when the world seems drained of wonder, some day when I am only going through the motions of doing what I am supposed to do, which is write—on that bankrupt morning I will simply open my notebook and there it will all be, a forgotten account with accumulated interest, paid passage back to the world out there: dialogue overheard in hotels and elevators and at the hatcheck counter in Pavillon (one middle-aged man shows his hat check to another and says, "That's my old football number"); impressions of Bettina Aptheker and Benjamin Sonnenberg and Teddy ("Mr. Acapulco") Stauffer; careful aperçus[1] about tennis burns and failed fashion models and Greek shipping heiresses, one of whom taught me a significant lesson (a lesson I could have learned from F. Scott Fitzgerald, but perhaps we all must meet the very rich for ourselves) by asking, when I arrived to interview her in her orchid-filled sitting room on the second day of a paralyzing New York blizzard, whether it was snowing outside.

I imagine, in other words, that the notebook is about other people. But of course it is not. I have no real business with what one stranger said to another at the hat-check counter in Pavillon; in fact I suspect that the line "That's my old football number" touched not my own imagination at all, but merely some memory of something once read, probably "The Eighty-Yard Run." Nor is my concern with a woman in a dirty crepe-de-Chine wrapper in a Wilmington bar. My stake is always, of course, in the unmentioned girl in the plaid silk dress. *Remember what it was to be me*: that is always the point.

It is a difficult point to admit. We are brought up in the ethic 10 that others, any others, all others, are by definition more interesting than ourselves; taught to be diffident, just this side of self-effacing. ("You're the least important person in the room and don't forget it," Jessica Mitford's governess would hiss in her ear on the advent of any social occasion; I copied that into my notebook because it is only recently that I have been able to enter a room without hearing some such phrase in my inner ear.) Only the very young and the very old may recount their dreams at breakfast, dwell upon self, interrupt with memories of beach picnics and favorite Liberty lawn dresses and the rainbow trout in a creek near Colorado Springs. The rest of us are expected, rightly,

---

1. aperçus: Insights (French). [Ed.]

to affect absorption in other people's favorite dresses, other people's trout.

And so we do. But our notebooks give us away, for however dutifully we record what we see around us, the common denominator of all we see is always, transparently, shamelessly, the implacable "I." We are not talking here about the kind of notebook that is patently for public consumption, a structural conceit for binding together a series of graceful *pensées*;[2] we are talking about something private, about bits of the mind's string too short to use, an indiscriminate and erratic assemblage with meaning only for its maker.

And sometimes even the maker has difficulty with the meaning. There does not seem to be, for example, any point in my knowing for the rest of my life that, during 1964, 720 tons of soot fell on every square mile of New York City, yet there it is in my notebook labeled "FACT." Nor do I really need to remember that Ambrose Bierce liked to spell Leland Stanford's name "£eland $tanford" or that "smart women almost always wear black in Cuba," a fashion hint without much potential for practical application. And does not the relevance of these notes seem marginal at best?:

> In the basement museum of the Inyo County Courthouse in Independence, California, sign pinned to a mandarin coat: "This MANDARIN COAT was often worn by Mrs. Minnie S. Brooks when giving lectures on her TEAPOT COLLECTION."

> Redhead getting out of car in front of Beverly Wilshire Hotel, chinchilla stole, Vuitton bags with tags reading:

> > MRS LOU FOX
> > HOTEL SAHARA
> > VEGAS

Well, perhaps not entirely marginal. As a matter of fact, Mrs. Minnie S. Brooks and her MANDARIN COAT pull me back into my own childhood, for although I never knew Mrs. Brooks and did not visit Inyo County until I was thirty, I grew up in just such a world, in houses cluttered with Indian relics and bits of gold ore and ambergris and the souvenirs my Aunt Mercy Farnsworth brought back from the Orient. It is a long way from that world to Mrs. Lou Fox's world, where we all live now, and is it not just as well to remember that? Might not Mrs. Minnie S. Brooks help me

2. **pensées:** Thoughts, reflections (French). [Ed.]

to remember what I am? Might not Mrs. Lou Fox help me to
remember what I am not?

But sometimes the point is harder to discern. What exactly did
I have in mind when I noted down that it cost the father of someone I know $650 a month to light the place on the Hudson in
which he lived before the Crash? What use was I planning to
make of this line by Jimmy Hoffa: "I may have my faults, but
being wrong ain't one of them"? And although I think it interesting to know where the girls who travel with the Syndicate have
their hair done when they find themselves on the West Coast, will
I ever make suitable use of it? Might I not be better off just passing it on to John O'Hara? What is a recipe for sauerkraut doing in
my notebook? What kind of magpie keeps this notebook? "*He was
born the night the Titanic went down.*" That seems a nice enough
line, and I even recall who said it, but is it not really a better line
in life than it could ever be in fiction?

But of course that is exactly it: not that I should ever use the   15
line, but that I should remember the woman who said it and the
afternoon I heard it. We were on her terrace by the sea, and we
were finishing the wine left from lunch, trying to get what sun
there was, a California winter sun. The woman whose husband
was born the night the Titanic went down wanted to rent her
house, wanted to go back to her children in Paris. I remember
wishing that I could afford the house, which cost $1,000 a month.
"Someday you will," she said lazily. "Someday it all comes." There
in the sun on her terrace it seemed easy to believe in someday, but
later I had a low-grade afternoon hangover and ran over a black
snake on the way to the supermarket and was flooded with inexplicable fear when I heard the checkout clerk explaining to the
man ahead of me why she was finally divorcing her husband. "He
left me no choice," she said over and over as she punched the register. "He has a little seven-month-old baby by her, he left me no
choice." I would like to believe that my dread then was for the
human condition, but of course it was for me, because I wanted a
baby and did not then have one and because I wanted to own the
house that cost $1,000 a month to rent and because I had a
hangover.

It all comes back. Perhaps it is difficult to see the value in having one's self back in that kind of mood, but I do see it; I think we

are well advised to keep on nodding terms with the people we used to be whether we find them attractive company or not. Otherwise they turn up unannounced and surprise us, come hammering on the mind's door at 4 A.M. of a bad night and demand to know who deserted them, who betrayed them, who is going to make amends. We forget all too soon the things we thought we could never forget. We forget the loves and the betrayals alike, forget what we whispered and what we screamed, forget who we were. I have already lost touch with a couple of people I used to be; one of them, a seventeen-year-old, presents little threat, although it would be of some interest to me to know again what it feels like to sit on a river levee drinking vodka-and-orange-juice and listening to Les Paul and Mary Ford and their echoes sing "How High the Moon" on the car radio. (You see I still have the scenes, but I no longer perceive myself among those present, no longer could even improvise the dialogue.) The other one, a twenty-three-year-old, bothers me more. She was always a good deal of trouble, and I suspect she will reappear when I least want to see her, skirts too long, shy to the point of aggravation, always the injured party, full of recriminations and little hurts and stories I do not want to hear again, at once saddening me and angering me with her vulnerability and ignorance, an apparition all the more insistent for being so long banished.

It is a good idea, then, to keep in touch, and I suppose that keeping in touch is what notebooks are all about. And we are all on our own when it comes to keeping those lines open to ourselves: your notebook will never help me, nor mine you. "So what's new in the whiskey business?" What could that possibly mean to you? To me it means a blonde in a Pucci bathing suit sitting with a couple of fat men by the pool at the Beverly Hills Hotel. Another man approaches, and they all regard one another in silence for a while. "So what's new in the whiskey business?" one of the fat men finally says by way of welcome, and the blonde stands up, arches one foot and dips it in the pool, looking all the while at the cabaña where Baby Pignatari is talking on the telephone. That is all there is to that, except that several years later I saw the blonde coming out of Saks Fifth Avenue in New York with her California complexion and a voluminous mink coat. In the harsh wind that day she looked old and irrevocably tired to me, and even the skins in the mink coat were not worked the way they were doing them that year, not the way she would have wanted them done, and there is the point of the story. For a while after that I did not like to look in the mirror, and my eyes would skim the newspapers and pick out only the deaths, the cancer victims, the premature coronaries, the suicides, and I stopped riding the Lexington Avenue IRT because I noticed for the first time that all the strangers I had seen for years—the man with the seeing-eye dog, the spinster who read the classified pages every day, the fat girl who always got off with me at Grand Central—looked older than they once had.

It all comes back. Even that recipe for sauerkraut: even that brings it back. I was on Fire Island when I first made that sauerkraut, and it was raining, and we drank a lot of bourbon and ate the sauerkraut and went to bed at ten, and I listened to the rain and the Atlantic and felt safe. I made the sauerkraut again last night and it did not make me feel any safer, but that is, as they say, another story.

For Discussion and Writing

1. What are the reasons that Didion keeps a notebook? What are reasons that other people might keep them that are not her reasons?

2. Didion is known as a master stylist. Find five sentences you think are stylish—unusual, or well constructed, or somehow striking. What makes them each good? Imagine how another writer might have written them—what would be different? What would be missing?

3. **connections** Read Didion's essay alongside E. B. White's "Once More to the Lake" (p. 404). Both essays are concerned with aging, with the past, and with memory. In what ways are the methods by which Didion and White recollect and re-create the past similar? How do they differ? What do you make of the comparison, in terms of the difference between the two authors' writing styles, or projects, or implicit beliefs about the nature of selfhood and memory?

4. Are you on "nodding terms" with the person you used to be, to borrow Didion's line (par. 16)? Pick a time in your life, a few to many years ago, and reflect on your relationship to the person you were then. What kinds of things about that time do you remember, from the small to the large? Do you remember how they made you feel or what you thought about them? Do the events you remember and the reactions you remember tell you something about who you were then? Do you find that person "attractive company"?

5. **looking further** Do some research into Joan Didion's career, looking closely at the collection this essay was published in (*Slouching Towards Bethlehem*) or more broadly at the range of work—essays, novels, memoir—she has written. How do you think the ideas about writing and life Didion describes in "On Keeping a Notebook" are reflected in this work?

FREDERICK DOUGLASS

Learning to Read and Write

Frederick Douglass was born a slave in 1818 in Maryland. He learned to read and write, escaped to New York, and became a leader in the abo-litionist movement. He engaged in speaking tours and edited North Star, *a newspaper named for the one guide escaping Southern slaves could rely on to find their way to freedom. Douglass is best known for his autobiography,* Narrative of the Life of Frederick Douglass *(1845), from which "Learning to Read and Write" is excerpted. In this selection, Douglass tells the story of his coming to literacy. As you read, keep your eye on the ways in which Douglass describes the world opening up for him as he learns his letters and the range of emotions this process evokes in him.*

I lived in Master Hugh's family about seven years. During this time, I succeeded in learning to read and write. In accomplishing this, I was compelled to resort to various stratagems. I had no regular teacher. My mistress, who had kindly commenced to instruct me, had, in compliance with the advice and direction of her husband, not only ceased to instruct, but had set her face against my being instructed by any one else. It is due, however, to my mistress to say of her, that she did not adopt this course of treatment immediately. She at first lacked the depravity indis-pensable to shutting me up in mental darkness. It was at least necessary for her to have some training in the exercise of irre-sponsible power, to make her equal to the task of treating me as though I were a brute.

My mistress was, as I have said, a kind and tender-hearted woman; and in the simplicity of her soul she commenced, when I first went to live with her, to treat me as she supposed one human being ought to treat another. In entering upon the duties of a slaveholder, she did not seem to perceive that I sustained to her the relation of a mere chattel, and that for her to treat me as a human being was not only wrong, but dangerously so. Slavery proved as injurious to her as it did to me. When I went there, she was a pious, warm, and tender-hearted woman. There was no sorrow or suffering for which she had not a tear. She had bread for the hungry, clothes for the naked, and comfort for every mourner that came within her reach. Slavery soon proved its ability to divest her of these heavenly qualities. Under its influence, the tender heart became stone, and the lamb-like disposition gave way to one of tiger-like fierceness. The first step in her downward course was in her ceasing to instruct me. She now commenced to practice her husband's precepts. She finally became even more violent in her opposition than her husband himself. She was not satisfied with simply doing as well as he had commanded; she seemed anxious to do better. Nothing seemed to make her more angry than to see me with a newspaper. She seemed to think that here lay the danger. I have had her rush at me with a face made all up of fury, and snatch from me a newspaper, in a manner that fully revealed her apprehension. She was an apt woman; and a little experience soon demonstrated, to her satisfaction, that education and slavery were incompatible with each other.

From this time I was most narrowly watched. If I was in a separate room any considerable length of time, I was sure to be suspected of having a book, and was at once called to give an account of myself. All this, however, was too late. The first step had been taken. Mistress, in teaching me the alphabet, had given me the *inch*, and no precaution could prevent me from taking the *ell*.

The plan which I adopted, and the one by which I was most successful, was that of making friends of all the little white boys whom I met in the street. As many of these as I could, I converted into teachers. With their kindly aid, obtained at different times and in different places, I finally succeeded in learning to read. When I was sent of errands, I always took my book with me, and by going one part of my errand quickly, I found time to get a lesson before my return. I used also to carry bread with me, enough of which was always in the house, and to which I was always welcome; for I was much better off in this regard than many of the poor white children in our neighborhood. This bread I used to bestow upon the hungry little urchins, who, in return, would give me that more valuable bread of knowledge. I am strongly tempted to give the names of two or three of those little boys, as a testimonial of the gratitude and affection I bear them; but prudence forbids:—not that it would injure me, but it might embarrass them; for it is almost an unpardonable offence to teach slaves to read in this Christian country. It is enough to say of the dear little fellows, that they lived on Philpot Street, very near Durgin and Bailey's ship-yard. I used to talk this matter of slavery over with them. I would sometimes say to them, I wished I could be as free as they would be when they got to be men. "You will be free as soon as you are twenty-one, *but I am a slave for life!* Have not I as good a right to be free as you have?" These words used to trouble them; they would express for me the liveliest sympathy, and console me with the hope that something would occur by which I might be free.

I was now about twelve years old, and the thought of being *a*   5 *slave for life* began to bear heavily upon my heart. Just about this time, I got hold of a book entitled "The Columbian Orator." Every opportunity I got, I used to read this book. Among much of other interesting matter, I found in it a dialogue between a master and his slave. The slave was represented as having run away from his master three times. The dialogue represented the conversation which took place between them, when the slave was retaken the third time. In this dialogue, the whole argument in behalf of slavery was brought forward by the master, all of which was disposed of by the slave. The slave was made to say some very smart as well as impressive things in reply to his master—things which had the desired though unexpected effect; for the conversation resulted in the voluntary emancipation of the slave on the part of the master.

In the same book, I met with one of Sheridan's mighty speeches on and in behalf of Catholic emancipation. These were choice documents to me. I read them over and over again with unabated interest. They gave tongue to interesting thoughts of my own soul, which had frequently lashed through my mind, and died away for want of utterance. The moral which I gained from the dialogue was the power of truth over the conscience of even a slaveholder. What I got from Sheridan was a bold denunciation of slavery, and a powerful vindication of human rights. The reading of these documents enabled me to utter my thoughts, and to meet the arguments brought forward to sustain slavery; but while they relieved me of one difficulty, they brought on another even more painful than the one of which I was relieved. The more I read, the more I was led to abhor and detest my enslavers. I could regard them in no other light than a band of successful robbers, who had left their homes, and gone to Africa, and stolen us from our homes, and in a strange land reduced us to slavery. I loathed them as being the meanest as well as the most wicked of men. As I read and contemplated the subject, behold! that very discontentment which Master Hugh had predicted would follow my learning to read had already come, to torment and sting my soul to unutterable anguish. As I writhed under it, I would at times feel that learning to read had been a curse rather than a blessing. It had given me a view of my wretched condition, without the remedy. It opened my eyes to the horrible pit, but to no ladder upon which to get out. In moments of agony, I envied my fellow-slaves for their stupidity. I have often wished myself a beast. I preferred the condition of the meanest reptile to my own. Any thing, no matter what, to get rid of thinking! It was this everlasting thinking of my condition that tormented me. There was no getting rid of it. It was pressed upon me by every object within sight or hearing, animate or inanimate. The silver trump of freedom had roused my soul to eternal wakefulness. Freedom now appeared, to disappear no more forever. It was heard in every sound, and seen in every thing. It was ever present to torment me with a sense of my wretched condition. I saw nothing without seeing it, I heard nothing without hearing it, and felt nothing without feeling it. It looked from every star, it smiled in every calm, breathed in every wind, and moved in every storm.

I often found myself regretting my own existence, and wishing myself dead; and but for the hope of being free, I have no doubt but that I should have killed myself, or done something for which I should have been killed. While in this state of mind, I was eager to hear any one speak of slavery. I was a ready listener. Every little while, I could hear something about the abolitionists. It was some time before I found what the word meant. It was always used in such connections as to make it an interesting word to me. If a slave ran away and succeeded in getting clear, or if a slave killed his master, set fire to a barn, or did any thing very wrong in the mind of a slaveholder, it was spoken of as the fruit of *abolition*. Hearing the word in this connection very often, I set about learning what it meant. The dictionary afforded me little or no help. I found it was "the act of abolishing"; but then I did not know what was to be abolished. Here I was perplexed. I did not dare to ask any one about its meaning, for I was satisfied that it was something they wanted me to know very little about. After a patient waiting, I got one of our city papers, containing an account of the number of petitions from the north, praying for the abolition of slavery in the District of Columbia, and of the slave trade between the States. From this time I understood the words *abolition* and *abolitionist*, and always drew near when that word was spoken, expecting to hear something of importance to myself and fellow-slaves. The light broke in upon me by degrees. I went one day down on the wharf of Mr. Waters; and seeing two Irishmen unloading a scow of stone, I went, unasked, and helped them. When we had finished, one of them came to me and asked me if I were a slave. I told him I was. He asked, "Are ye a slave for life?" I told him that I was. The good Irishman seemed to be deeply affected by the statement. He said to the other that it was a pity so fine a little fellow as myself should be a slave for life. He said it was a shame to hold me. They both advised me to run away to the north; that I should find friends there, and that I should be free. I pretended not to be interested in what they said, and treated them as if I did not understand them; for I feared they might be treacherous. White men have been known to encourage slaves to escape, and then, to get the reward, catch them and return them to their masters. I was afraid that these seemingly good men might use me so; but I nevertheless remembered their advice, and from that time I resolved to run away. I looked forward to a time at which it would be safe for me to escape. I was too young to think of doing so immediately; besides, I wished to learn how to write, as I might have occasion to write my own pass. I consoled myself with the hope that I should one day find a good chance. Meanwhile, I would learn to write.

The idea as to how I might learn to write was suggested to me by being in Durgin and Bailey's ship-yard, and frequently seeing the ship carpenters, after hewing, and getting a piece of timber ready for use, write on the timber the name of that part of the ship for which it was intended. When a piece of timber was intended for the larboard side, it would be marked thus—"L." When a piece was for the starboard side, it would be marked thus—"S." A piece for the larboard side forward, would be marked thus—"L. F." When a piece was for starboard side forward, it would be marked thus—"S. F." For larboard aft, it would be marked thus—"L. A." For starboard aft, it would be marked thus—"S. A." I soon learned the names of these letters, and for what they were intended when placed upon a piece of timber in the ship-yard. I immediately commenced copying them, and in a short time was able to make the four letters named. After that, when I met with any boy who I knew could write, I would tell him I could write as well as he. The next word would be, "I don't believe you. Let me see you try it." I would then make the letters which I had been so fortunate as to learn, and ask him to beat that. In this way I got a good many lessons in writing, which it is quite possible I should never have gotten in any other way. During this time, my copy-book was the board fence, brick wall, and pavement; my pen and ink was a lump of chalk. With these, I learned mainly how to write. I then commenced and continued copying the Italics in Webster's Spelling Book, until I could make them all without looking on the book. By this time, my little Master Thomas had gone to school, and learned how to write, and had written over a number of copy-books. These had been brought home, and shown to some of our near neighbors, and then laid aside. My mistress used to go to class meeting at the Wilk Street meetinghouse every Monday afternoon, and leave me to take care of the house. When left thus, I used to spend the time in writing in the spaces left in Master Thomas's copy-book, copying what he had written. I continued to do this until I could write a hand very similar to that of Master Thomas. Thus, after a long, tedious effort for years, I finally succeeded in learning how to write.

For Discussion and Writing

1. List the different ways Douglass taught himself to read and write. List also some other things he learns.
2. The main focus of this passage is the process by which Douglass began to become literate. Who else in the passage undergoes a "learning" process, and what are the results?
3. **connections** Douglass teaches himself to read and write in a society that condemns literacy for people like him; the education and the society Malcolm X describes in "Learning to Read" (p. 240) are very different. How are they similar?

4. Douglass's education is presented as both pleasurable and painful, opening up new worlds to him at the same time as it helps him to understand painful facts. Describe something you have learned—a new subject, a new fact about the world—that has been similarly double-edged for you.

5. **looking further**   A common topic of conversation among educators concerns the ultimate goal of learning. One version of this conversation is about the tension between instrumentalist goals—you learn to prepare yourself to do certain things, such as a particular job—and the goal of knowledge for its own sake. Read up on this debate and think about what Douglass has to say about education in that light. How does this distinction make sense in his situation? What do you think about the distinction in this context and in itself?

BRIAN DOYLE

Joyas Voladores

Brian Doyle was born in 1956 in New York City. He was an editor at U.S. Catholic magazine *and a writer at* Boston College Magazine *before becoming the editor of the University of Portland's* Portland Magazine. *He is the author of a number of books, including* Saints Passionate & Peculiar *(2002),* Credo *(1999), and* Two Voices *(1996), and his essays have been published in the* American Scholar, *the* Atlantic Monthly, Orion, Commonweal, Georgia Review, Brevity, *and* Harper's, *among other periodicals.*

"Joyas Voladores" is a short, finely crafted piece of what these days is often called creative nonfiction. As you read, admiring the creativity and craft, don't forget to notice that the essay is talking to you, the reader, asking you to do certain things, telling you certain things.

Consider the hummingbird for a long moment. A hummingbird's heart beats ten times a second. A hummingbird's heart is the size of a pencil eraser. A hummingbird's heart is a lot of the humming-bird. *Joyas voladores,* flying jewels, the first white explorers in the Americas called them, and the white men had never seen such creatures, for hummingbirds came into the world only in the Americas, nowhere else in the universe, more than three hundred species of them whirring and zooming and nectaring in hummer time zones nine times removed from ours, their hearts hammering faster than we could clearly hear if we pressed our elephantine ears to their infinitesimal chests.

Each one visits a thousand flowers a day. They can dive at sixty miles an hour. They can fly backwards. They can fly more than five hundred miles without pausing to rest. But when they rest they come close to death: on frigid nights, or when they are starving, they retreat into torpor, their metabolic rate slowing to a fifteenth of their normal sleep rate, their hearts sludging nearly to a halt, barely beating, and if they are not soon warmed, if they do not soon find that which is sweet, their hearts grow cold, and they cease to be. Consider for a moment those hummingbirds who did not open their eyes again today, this very day, in the Americas: bearded helmet-crests and booted racket-tails, violet-tailed sylphs and violet-capped wood-nymphs, crimson topazes and purple-crowned fairies, red-tailed comets and amethyst wood-stars, rainbow-bearded thornbills and glittering-bellied emeralds, velvet-purple coronets and golden-bellied star-frontlets, fiery-tailed awlbills and Andean hillstars, spatuletails and pufflegs, each the most amazing thing you have never seen, each thunderous wild heart the size of an infant's fingernail, each mad heart silent, a brilliant music stilled.

Hummingbirds, like all flying birds but more so, have incredible enormous immense ferocious metabolisms. To drive those metabolisms they have race-car hearts that eat oxygen at an eye-popping rate. Their hearts are built of thinner, leaner fibers than ours. Their arteries are stiffer and more taut. They have more mitochondria in their heart muscles—anything to gulp more oxygen. Their hearts are stripped to the skin for the war against gravity and inertia, the mad search for food, the insane idea of flight. The price of their ambition is a life closer to death; they suffer heart attacks and aneurysms and ruptures more than any other living creature. It's expensive to fly. You burn out. You fry the machine. You melt the engine. Every creature on earth has approximately two billion heartbeats to spend in a lifetime. You can spend them slowly, like a tortoise, and live to be two hundred years old, or you can spend them fast, like a hummingbird, and live to be two years old.

The biggest heart in the world is inside the blue whale. It weighs more than seven tons. It's as big as a room. It *is* a room, with four chambers. A child could walk around in it, head high, bending only to step through the valves. The valves are as big as the swinging doors in a saloon. This house of a heart drives a creature a hundred feet long. When this creature is born it is twenty feet long and weighs four tons. It is waaaaay bigger than your car. It drinks a hundred gallons of milk from its mama every day and gains two hundred pounds a day and when it is seven or eight years old it endures an unimaginable puberty and then it essentially disappears from human ken, for next to nothing is known of the mating habits, travel patterns, diet, social life, language, social structure, diseases, spirituality, wars, stories, despairs, and arts of the blue whale. There are perhaps ten thousand blue whales in the world, living in every ocean on earth, and of the largest mammal who ever lived we know nearly nothing. But we know this: the animals with the largest hearts in the world generally travel in pairs, and their penetrating moaning cries, their piercing yearning tongue, can be heard underwater for miles and miles.

Mammals and birds have hearts with four chambers. Reptiles 5 and turtles have hearts with three chambers. Fish have hearts with two chambers. Insects and mollusks have hearts with one chamber. Worms have hearts with one chamber, although they may have as many as eleven single-chambered hearts. Unicellular bacteria have no hearts at all; but even they have fluid eternally in motion, washing from one side of the cell to the other, swirling and whirling. No living being is without interior liquid motion. We all churn inside.

So much held in a heart in a lifetime. So much held in a heart in a day, an hour, a moment. We are utterly open with no one, in the end—not mother and father, not wife or husband, not lover, not child, not friend. We open windows to each but we live alone in the house of the heart. Perhaps we must. Perhaps we could not bear to be so naked, for fear of a constantly harrowed heart. When young we think there will come one person who will savor and sustain us always; when we are older we know this is the dream of a child, that all hearts finally are bruised and scarred, scored and torn, repaired by time and will, patched by force of character, yet fragile and rickety forevermore, no matter how ferocious the defense and how many bricks you bring to the wall. You can brick up your heart as stout and tight and hard and cold and impregnable as you possibly can and down it comes in an instant, felled by a woman's second glance, a child's apple breath, the shatter of glass in the road, the words *I have something to tell you*, a cat with a broken spine dragging itself into the forest to die, the brush of your mother's papery ancient hand in the thicket of your hair, the memory of your father's voice early in the morning echoing from the kitchen where he is making pancakes for his children.

For Discussion and Writing

1. What is the chief metaphor in "Joyas Voladores"?
2. How would you describe Doyle's style in this essay? Is it more matter-of-fact or more literary? Answer with specific examples, and consider also the effects of these choices.
3. **connections** Read "Joyas Voladores" next to E. B. White's "Once More to the Lake" (p. 404). What themes do they share? What reflections does each author make on these themes?
4. Doyle's descriptions of different animals' hearts and habits are masterful. Break one or two of them down and explain what it is that makes them models of this kind of writing. What choices does he make? What are their effects? (If stuck, imagine other ways he could have described them—for example, "Whale hearts are really big.")
5. **looking further** "Joyas Voladores" leaves two ostensibly opposite impressions: one, that animal life can be observed, named, and understood, as in paragraph 2; two, that animal life is mysterious to us, as in paragraph 4. What does it mean to think of the world of nonhuman animals in the first way? What does it mean to think about it in the second way? What does it mean to think in each of these ways about humans?

BARBARA EHRENREICH

Serving in Florida

Born in 1941 and raised in Butte, Montana, Barbara Ehrenreich earned a doctorate in biology before devoting herself to writing about culture and politics. She has written extensively on social class, work, gender, and politics in columns and in books, including The Worst Years of Our Lives: Irreverent Notes on a Decade of Greed *(1990),* Blood Rites: The Origins and History of the Passions for War *(1997),* Nickel and Dimed: On (Not) Getting By in America *(2001),* Bright-Sided: How the Relentless Promotion of Positive Thinking Has Undermined America *(2009), and her newest book,* Living with a Wild God: A Nonbeliever's Search for the Truth about Everything *(2014).*

"Serving in Florida" comes from Nickel and Dimed. *In the book, Ehrenreich recounts her experiences trying to live on the income earned working a number of low-paying jobs. While these stories are engrossing, that is not the only reason they are in the book. As you read the stories in "Serving in Florida," keep an eye out for the ways in which Ehrenreich uses these stories to make a number of points about contemporary American life.*

I could drift along like this, in some dreamy proletarian idyll, except for two things. One is management. If I have kept this subject to the margins so far it is because I still flinch to think that I spent all those weeks under the surveillance of men (and later women) whose job it was to monitor my behavior for signs of sloth, theft, drug abuse, or worse. Not that managers and especially "assistant managers" in low-wage settings like this are exactly the class enemy. Mostly, in the restaurant business, they are former cooks still capable of pinch-hitting in the kitchen, just as in hotels they are likely to be former clerks, and paid a salary of only about $400 a week. But everyone knows they have crossed over to the other side, which is, crudely put, corporate as opposed to human. Cooks want to prepare tasty meals, servers want to serve them graciously, but managers are there for only one reason—to make sure that money is made for some theoretical entity, the corporation, which exists far away in Chicago or New York, if a corporation can be said to have a physical existence at all. Reflecting on her career, Gail tells me ruefully that she swore, years ago, never to work for a corporation again. "They don't cut you no slack. You give and you give and they take."

Managers can sit—for hours at a time if they want—but it's their job to see that no one else ever does, even when there's nothing to do, and this is why, for servers, slow times can be as exhausting as rushes. You start dragging out each little chore because if the manager on duty catches you in an idle moment he will give you something far nastier to do. So I wipe, I clean, I consolidate catsup bottles and recheck the cheesecake supply, even tour the tables to make sure the customer evaluation forms are all standing perkily in their places—wondering all the time how many calories I burn in these strictly theatrical exercises. In desperation, I even take the desserts out of their glass display case and freshen them up with whipped cream and bright new maraschino cherries; anything to look busy. When, on a particularly dead afternoon, Stu finds me glancing at a *USA Today* a customer has left behind, he assigns me to vacuum the entire floor with the broken vacuum cleaner, which has a handle only two feet long, and the only way to do that without incurring orthopedic damage is to proceed from spot to spot on your knees.

On my first Friday at Hearthside there is a "mandatory meeting for all restaurant employees," which I attend, eager for insight into our overall marketing strategy and the niche (your basic Ohio cuisine with a tropical twist?) we aim to inhabit. But there is no "we" at this meeting. Phillip, our top manager except for an occasional "consultant" sent out by corporate headquarters, opens it with a sneer: "The break room—it's disgusting. Butts in the ashtrays, newspapers lying around, crumbs." This windowless little room, which also houses the time clock for the entire hotel, is where we stash our bags and civilian clothes and take our half-hour meal breaks. But a break room is not a right, he tells us, it can be taken away. We should also know that the lockers in the break room and whatever is in them can be searched at any time. Then comes gossip; there has been gossip; gossip (which seems to mean employees talking among themselves) must stop. Off-duty employees are henceforth barred from eating at the restaurant, because "other servers gather around them and gossip." When Phillip has exhausted his agenda of rebukes, Joan complains about the condition of the ladies' room and I throw in my two bits about the vacuum cleaner. But I don't see any backup coming from my fellow servers, each of whom has slipped into her own personal funk; Gail, my role model, stares sorrowfully at a point six inches from her nose. The meeting ends when Andy, one of the cooks, gets up, muttering about breaking up his day off for this almighty bullshit.

Just four days later we are suddenly summoned into the kitchen at 3:30 P.M., even though there are live tables on the floor. We all—about ten of us—stand around Phillip, who announces grimly that there has been a report of some "drug activity" on the night shift and that, as a result, we are now to be a "drug-free" workplace, meaning that all new hires will be tested and possibly also current employees on a random basis. I am glad that this part of the kitchen is so dark because I find myself blushing as hard as if I had been caught toking up in the ladies' room myself: I haven't been treated this way—lined up in the corridor, threatened with locker searches, peppered with carelessly aimed accusations—since at least junior high school. Back on the floor, Joan cracks, "Next they'll be telling us we can't have *sex* on the job." When I ask Stu what happened to inspire the crackdown, he just mutters about "management decisions" and takes the opportunity to upbraid Gail and me for being too generous with the rolls. From now on there's to be only one per customer and it goes out with the dinner, not with the salad. He's also been riding the cooks, prompting Andy to come out of the kitchen and observe— with the serenity of a man whose customary implement is a butcher knife—that "Stu has a death wish today."

Later in the evening, the gossip crystallizes around the theory   5 that Stu is himself the drug culprit, that he uses the restaurant phone to order up marijuana and sends one of the late servers out to fetch it for him. The server was caught and she may have ratted out Stu, at least enough to cast some suspicion on him, thus accounting for his pissy behavior. Who knows? Personally, I'm ready to believe anything bad about Stu, who serves no evident function and presumes too much on our common ethnicity, sidling up to me one night to engage in a little nativism directed at the Haitian immigrants: "I feel like I'm the foreigner here. They're taking over the country." Still later that evening, the drug in question escalates to crack. Lionel, the busboy, entertains us for the rest of the shift by standing just behind Stu's back and sucking deliriously on a imaginary joint or maybe a pipe.

The other problem, in addition to the less-than-nurturing management style, is that this job shows no sign of being financially viable. You might imagine, from a comfortable distance, that people who live, year in and year out, on $6 to $10 an hour have discovered some survival stratagems unknown to the middle class. But no. It's not hard to get my coworkers talking about their living situations, because housing, in almost every case, is the principal source of disruption in their lives, the first thing they fill you in on when they arrive for their shifts. After a week, I have compiled the following survey:

> Gail is sharing a room in a well-known downtown flophouse for $250 a week. Her roommate, a male friend, has begun hitting on her, driving her nuts, but the rent would be impossible alone.

> Claude, the Haitian cook, is desperate to get out of the two-room apartment he shares with his girlfriend and two other, unrelated people. As far as I can determine, the other Haitian men live in similarly crowded situations.

> Annette, a twenty-year-old server who is six months pregnant and abandoned by her boyfriend, lives with her mother, a postal clerk.

> Marianne, who is a breakfast server, and her boyfriend are paying $170 a week for a one-person trailer.

> Billy, who at $10 an hour is the wealthiest of us, lives in the trailer he owns, paying only the $400-a-month lot fee.

> The other white cook, Andy, lives on his dry-docked boat, which, as far as I can tell from his loving descriptions, can't be more than twenty feet long. He offers to take me out on it once it's repaired, but the offer comes with inquiries as to my marital status, so I do not follow up on it.

> Tina, another server, and her husband are paying $60 a night for a room in the Days Inn. This is because they have no car and the Days Inn is in walking distance of the Hearthside. When Marianne is tossed out of her trailer for subletting (which is against trailer park rules), she leaves her boyfriend and moves in with Tina and her husband.

> Joan, who had fooled me with her numerous and tasteful outfits (hostesses wear their own clothes), lives in a van parked behind a shopping

center at night and showers in Tina's motel room. The clothes are from thrift shops.[1]

It strikes me, in my middle-class solipsism, that there is gross improvidence in some of these arrangements. When Gail and I are wrapping silverware in napkins—the only task for which we are permitted to sit—she tells me she is thinking of escaping from her roommate by moving into the Days Inn herself. I am astounded: how she can even think of paying $40 to $60 a day? But if I was afraid of sounding like a social worker, I have come out just sounding like a fool. She squints at me in disbelief: "And where am I supposed to get a month's rent and a month's deposit for an apartment?" I'd been feeling pretty smug about my $500 efficiency, but of course it was made possible only by the $1,300 I had allotted myself for start-up costs when I began my low-wage life: $1,000 for the first month's rent and deposit, $100 for initial groceries and cash in my pocket, $200 stuffed away for emergencies. In poverty, as in certain propositions in physics, starting conditions are everything.

There are no secret economies that nourish the poor; on the contrary, there are a host of special costs. If you can't put up the two months' rent you need to secure an apartment, you end up paying through the nose for a room by the week. If you have only a room, with a hot plate at best, you can't save by cooking up huge lentil stews that can be frozen for the week ahead. You eat fast food or the hot dogs and Styrofoam cups of soup that can be microwaved in a convenience store. If you have no money for health insurance—and the Hearthside's niggardly plan kicks in only after three months—you go without routine care or prescription drugs and end up paying the price. Gail, for example, was doing fine, healthwise anyway, until she ran out of money for estrogen pills. She is supposed to be on the company health plan by now, but they claim to have lost her application form and to be beginning the paperwork all over again. So she spends $9 a pop for pills to control the migraines she wouldn't have, she insists,

1. I could find no statistics on the number of employed people living in cars or vans, but according to a 1997 report of the National Coalition for the Homeless, "Myths and Facts about Homelessness," nearly one-fifth of all homeless people (in twenty-nine cities across the nation) are employed in full- or part-time jobs. [Ehrenreich's note.]

if her estrogen supplements were covered. Similarly, Marianne's boyfriend lost his job as a roofer because he missed so much time after getting a cut on his foot for which he couldn't afford the prescribed antibiotic.

My own situation, when I sit down to assess it after two weeks of work, would not be much better if this were my actual life. The seductive thing about waitressing is that you don't have to wait for payday to feel a few bills in your pocket, and my tips usually cover meals and gas, plus something left over to stuff into the kitchen drawer I use as a bank. But as the tourist business slows in the summer heat, I sometimes leave work with only $20 in tips (the gross is higher, but servers share about 15 percent of their tips with the busboys and bartenders). With wages included, this amounts to about the minimum wage of $5.15 an hour. The sum in the drawer is piling up but at the present rate of accumulation will be more than $100 short of my rent when the end of the month comes around. Nor can I see any expenses to cut. True, I haven't gone the lentil stew route yet, but that's because I don't have a large cooking pot, potholders, or a ladle to stir with (which would cost a total of about $30 at Kmart, somewhat less at a thrift store), not to mention onions, carrots, and the indispensable bay leaf. I do make my lunch almost every day—usually some slow-burning, high-protein combo like frozen chicken patties with melted cheese on top and canned pinto beans on the side. Dinner is at the Hearthside, which offers its employees a choice of BLT, fish sandwich, or hamburger for only $2. The burger lasts longest, especially if it's heaped with gut-puckering jalapeños, but by midnight my stomach is growling again.

So unless I want to start using my car as a residence, I have to 10 find a second or an alternative job. I call all the hotels I'd filled out housekeeping applications at weeks ago—the Hyatt, Holiday Inn, Econo Lodge, HoJo's, Best Western, plus a half dozen locally run guest houses. Nothing. Then I start making the rounds again, wasting whole mornings waiting for some assistant manger to show up, even dipping into places so creepy that the front-desk clerk greets you from behind bullet-proof glass and sells pints of liquor over the counter. But either someone has exposed my real-life housekeeping habits—which are, shall we say, mellow—or I am at the wrong end of some infallible ethnic equation: most, but by no means all, of the working housekeepers I see on my job searches are African Americans, Spanish-speaking, or refugees from the Central European post-Communist world, while servers are almost invariably white and monolingually English-speaking. When I finally get a positive response, I have been identified once again as server material. Jerry's—again, not the real name— which is part of a well-known national chain and physically attached here to another budget hotel, is ready to use me at once. The prospect is both exciting and terrifying because, with about the same number of tables and counter seats, Jerry's attracts three or four times the volume of customers as the gloomy old Hearthside.

Picture a fat person's hell, and I don't mean a place with no food. Instead there is everything you might eat if eating had no bodily consequences—the cheese fries, the chicken-fried steaks, the fudge-laden desserts—only here every bit must be paid for, one way or another, in human discomfort. The kitchen is a cavern, a stomach leading to the lower intestine that is the garbage and dishwashing area, from which issue bizarre smells combining the edible and the offal: creamy carrion, pizza barf, and that unique and enigmatic Jerry's scent, citrus fart. The floor is slick with spills, forcing us to walk through the kitchen with tiny steps, like Susan McDougal in leg irons. Sinks everywhere are clogged with scraps of lettuce, decomposing lemon wedges, water-logged toast crusts. Put your hand down on any counter and you risk being stuck to it by the film of ancient syrup spills, and this is unfortunate because hands are utensils here, used for scooping up lettuce onto the salad plates, lifting out pie slices, and even moving hash browns from one plate to another. The regulation poster in the single unisex rest room admonishes us to wash our hands thoroughly, and even offers instructions for doing so, but there is always some vital substance missing—soap, paper towels, toilet paper—and I never found all three at once. You learn to stuff your pockets with napkins before going in there, and too bad about the customers, who must eat, although they don't realize it, almost literally out of our hands.

The break room summarizes the whole situation: there is none, because there are no breaks at Jerry's. For six to eight hours in a row, you never sit except to pee. Actually, there are three folding chairs at a table immediately adjacent to the bathroom, but hardly anyone ever sits in this, the very rectum of the gastroarchitectural system. Rather, the function of the peri-toilet area is to house the ashtrays in which servers and dishwashers leave their cigarettes burning at all times, like votive candles, so they don't have to waste time lighting up again when they dash back here for a puff. Almost everyone smokes as if their pulmonary well-being depended on it—the multinational mélange of cooks; the dishwashers, who are all Czechs here; the servers, who are American natives—creating an atmosphere in which oxygen is only an occasional pollutant. My first morning at Jerry's, when the hypoglycemic shakes set in, I complain to one of my fellow servers that I don't understand how she can go so long without food. "Well, I don't understand how *you* can go so long without a cigarette," she responds in a tone of reproach. Because work is what you do for others; smoking is what you do for yourself. I don't know why the antismoking crusaders have never grasped the element of defiant self-nurturance that makes the habit so endearing to its victims—as if, in the American workplace, the only thing people have to call their own is the tumors they are nourishing and the spare moments they devote to feeding them.

Now, the Industrial Revolution is not an easy transition, especially, in my experience, when you have to zip through it in just a couple of days. I have gone from craft work straight into the factory, from the air-conditioned morgue of the Hearthside directly into the flames. Customers arrive in human waves, sometimes disgorged fifty at a time from their tour buses, puckish and whiny. Instead of two "girls" on the floor at once, there can be as many as six of us running around in our brilliant pink-and-orange Hawaiian shirts. Conversations, either with customers or with fellow employees, seldom last more than twenty seconds at a time. On my first day, in fact, I am hurt by my sister servers' coldness. My mentor for the day is a supremely competent, emotionally uninflected twenty-three-year-old, and the others, who gossip a little among themselves about the real reason someone is out sick today and the size of the bail bond someone else has had to pay, ignore me completely. On my second day, I find out why. "Well, it's good to see *you* again," one of them says in greeting. "Hardly anyone comes back after the first day." I feel powerfully vindicated—a survivor—but it would take a long time, probably months, before I could hope to be accepted into this sorority.

I start out with the beautiful, heroic idea of handling the two jobs at once, and for two days I almost do it: working the breakfast/lunch shift at Jerry's from 8:00 till 2:00, arriving at the Hearthside a few minutes late, at 2:10, and attempting to hold out until 10:00. In the few minutes I have between jobs, I pick up a spicy chicken sandwich at the Wendy's drive-through window, gobble it down in the car, and change from khaki slacks to black, from Hawaiian to rust-colored polo. There is a problem, though. When, during the 3:00–4:00 o'clock dead time, I finally sit down to wrap silver, my flesh seems to bond to the seat. I try to refuel with a purloined cup of clam chowder, as I've seen Gail and Joan do dozens of times, but Stu catches me and hisses "No *eating!*" although there's not a customer around to be offended by the sight of food making contact with a server's lips. So I tell Gail I'm going to quit, and she hugs me and says she might just follow me to Jerry's herself.

But the chances of this are minuscule. She has left the flop-   15 house and her annoying roommate and is back to living in her truck. But, guess what, she reports to me excitedly later that evening. Phillip has given her permission to park overnight in the hotel parking lot, as long as she keeps out of sight, and the parking lot should be totally safe since it's patrolled by a hotel security guard! With the Hearthside offering benefits like that, how could anyone think of leaving? This must be Phillip's theory, anyway. He accepts my resignation with a shrug, his main concern being that I return my two polo shirts and aprons.

Gail would have triumphed at Jerry's, I'm sure, but for me it's a crash course in exhaustion management. Years ago, the kindly fry cook who trained me to waitress at a Los Angeles truck stop used to say: Never make an unnecessary trip; if you don't have to walk fast, walk slow; if you don't have to walk, stand. But at Jerry's the effort of distinguishing necessary from unnecessary and urgent from whenever would itself be too much of an energy drain. The only thing to do is to treat each shift as a one-time-only emergency: you've got fifty starving people out there, lying scattered on the battlefield, so get out there and feed them! Forget that you will have to do this again tomorrow, forget that you will have to be alert enough to dodge the drunks on the drive home tonight — just burn, burn, burn! Ideally, at some point you enter what servers call a "rhythm" and psychologists term a "flow state," where

signals pass from the sense organs directly to the muscles, bypass-
ing the cerebral cortex, and a Zen-like emptiness sets in. I'm on a
2:00–10:00 P.M. shift now, and a male server from the morning
shift tells me about the time he "pulled a triple"—three shifts in a
row, all the way around the clock—and then got off and had a
drink and met this girl, and maybe he shouldn't tell me this, but
they had sex right then and there and it was like *beautiful*. . . .

For Discussion and Writing

1. Why is Ehrenreich working as a waitress?

2. Ehrenreich builds her argument about the difficulties of living on
   minimum or near-minimum wage through her use of examples. Her
   argument is well constructed and her examples plentiful, but the
   effectiveness of many of her examples comes from their being part
   of a story. By looking closely at one of the stories she tells about her
   experiences and the experiences of the men and women she works
   with, describe how Ehrenreich embeds examples in stories about
   individuals.

3. **connections**   Lars Eighner's "On Dumpster Diving" (p. 146) makes
   most of its readers rethink homelessness. Similarly, Ehrenreich's
   piece makes us rethink employment: contrary to what many comfortable middle- or upper-class people might think, it is clear from
   "Serving in Florida" that employed people can be homeless or at least
   in a precarious financial position. With regard to the way in which
   these pieces make us rethink ways of life, how are Ehrenreich's and
   Eighner's pieces similar? How are they different?

4. One of the key points of comparison between "Serving in Florida" and
   Lars Eighner's "On Dumpster Diving" (p. 146) is the position of the
   writer in relation to the life he or she is describing. It is also a point of
   contrast, as Eighner was homeless when he wrote his book, while
   Ehrenreich was only living as a wage worker in order to write her
   book. Write a dialogue between the two writers in which they discuss
   this difference. Might Eighner challenge Ehrenreich? Or praise her?
   How might she defend herself?

5. **looking further**   The first sentence of "Serving in Florida" includes
   the term *proletarian*. Outside of Roman law, the term is best known
   from its appearance in Marxist theory. Do a little research on Marxist
   political theory. Though Ehrenreich doesn't discuss larger economic
   systems, there is certainly a critique of capitalism here. Do you think
   this critique is informed by Marxist thought? Do you agree with the
   implicit critique of capitalism Ehrenreich makes here? Based on your
   limited research, do you agree with the explicit critique Marx made?

LARS EIGHNER

On Dumpster Diving

Born in Texas in 1948, Lars Eighner became famous with the publication of his memoir Travels with Lizbeth: Three Years on the Road and on the Streets *(1993). The memoir of his (and his dog's) homelessness,* Travels with Lizbeth, *was a great success but was not enough to keep Eighner and Lizbeth off the streets. Eventually with the support of friends, new housing was found for them, but Lizbeth died in 1998. Eighner continues to write fiction, essays, and erotica and has a new dog named Wilma.*

"On Dumpster Diving" is the essay that led to the writing of what was to become the rest of Travels with Lizbeth. *In it Eighner explains one aspect of his life during the three hard years that are the subject of his memoir—the process of feeding himself from the refuse of others. The clear-eyed way in which he describes this process and the manner in which he situates it in the larger culture make this essay worthy of careful reading.*

Long before I began Dumpster diving I was impressed with Dumpsters, enough so that I wrote the Merriam-Webster research service to discover what I could about the word "Dumpster." I learned from them that "Dumpster" is a proprietary word belonging to the Dempster Dumpster company.

Since then I have dutifully capitalized the word although it was lowercased in almost all of the citations Merriam-Webster photocopied for me. Dempster's word is too apt. I have never heard these things called anything but Dumpsters. I do not know anyone who knows the generic name for these objects. From time to time, however, I hear a wino or hobo give some corrupted credit to the original and call them Dipsy Dumpsters.

I began Dumpster diving about a year before I became homeless. I prefer the term "scavenging" and use the word "scrounging" when I mean to be obscure. I have heard people, evidently meaning to be polite, using the word "foraging," but I prefer to reserve that

146

word for gathering nuts and berries and such which I do also
according to the season and the opportunity. "Dumpster diving"
seems to me to be a little too cute and, in my case, inaccurate
because I lack the athletic ability to lower myself into the Dumpsters as the true divers do, much to their increased profit.

I like the frankness of the word "scavenging," which I can   5
hardly think of without picturing a big black snail on an aquarium wall. I live from the refuse of others. I am a scavenger. I think
it a sound and honorable niche, although if I could I would naturally prefer to live the comfortable consumer life, perhaps—and
only perhaps—as a slightly less wasteful consumer owing to what
I have learned as a scavenger.

While my dog Lizbeth and I were still living in the house on
Avenue B in Austin, as my savings ran out, I put almost all my
sporadic income into rent. The necessities of daily life I began
to extract from Dumpsters. Yes, we ate from Dumpsters. Except
for jeans, all my clothes came from Dumpsters. Boom boxes,
candles, bedding, toilet paper, medicine, books, a typewriter, a
virgin male love doll, change sometimes amounting to many dollars: I acquired many things from the Dumpsters.

I have learned much as a scavenger. I mean to put some of
what I have learned down here, beginning with the practical art
of Dumpster diving and proceeding to the abstract.

What is safe to eat?

After all, the finding of objects is becoming something of an
urban art. Even respectable employed people will sometimes find
something tempting sticking out of a Dumpster or standing
beside one. Quite a number of people, not all of them of the bohemian type, are willing to brag that they found this or that piece in
the trash. But eating from Dumpsters is the thing that separates
the dilettanti from the professionals.

Eating safely from the Dumpsters involves three principles: 10
using the senses and common sense to evaluate the condition of
the found materials, knowing the Dumpsters of a given area and
checking them regularly, and seeking always to answer the question "Why was this discarded?"

Perhaps everyone who has a kitchen and a regular supply of
groceries has, at one time or another, made a sandwich and eaten
half of it before discovering mold on the bread or got a mouthful
of milk before realizing the milk had turned. Nothing of the sort

is likely to happen to a Dumpster diver because he is constantly reminded that most food is discarded for a reason. Yet a lot of perfectly good food can be found in Dumpsters.

Canned goods, for example, turn up fairly often in the Dumpsters I frequent. All except the most phobic people would be willing to eat from a can even if it came from a Dumpster. Canned goods are among the safest of foods to be found in Dumpsters, but are not utterly foolproof.

Although very rare with modern canning methods, botulism is a possibility. Most other forms of food poisoning seldom do lasting harm to a healthy person. But botulism is almost certainly fatal and often the first symptom is death. Except for carbonated beverages, all canned goods should contain a slight vacuum and suck air when first punctured. Bulging, rusty, dented cans and cans that spew when punctured should be avoided, especially when the contents are not very acidic or syrupy.

Heat can break down the botulin, but this requires much more cooking than most people do to canned goods. To the extent that botulism occurs at all, of course, it can occur in cans on pantry shelves as well as in cans from Dumpsters. Need I say that home-canned goods found in Dumpsters are simply too risky to be recommended.

From time to time one of my companions, aware of the source 15 of my provisions, will ask, "Do you think these crackers are really safe to eat?" For some reason it is most often the crackers they ask about.

This question always makes me angry. Of course I would not offer my companion anything I had doubts about. But more than that I wonder why he cannot evaluate the condition of the crackers for himself. I have no special knowledge and I have been wrong before. Since he knows where the food comes from, it seems to me he ought to assume some of the responsibility for deciding what he will put in his mouth.

For myself I have few qualms about dry foods such as crackers, cookies, cereal, chips, and pasta if they are free of visible contaminates and still dry and crisp. Most often such things are found in the original packaging, which is not so much a positive sign as it is the absence of a negative one.

Raw fruits and vegetables with intact skins seem perfectly safe to me, excluding of course the obviously rotten. Many are discarded for minor imperfections which can be pared away. Leafy vegetables, grapes, cauliflower, broccoli, and similar things may be contaminated by liquids and may be impractical to wash.

Candy, especially hard candy, is usually safe if it has not drawn ants. Chocolate is often discarded only because it has become discolored as the cocoa butter de-emulsified. Candying after all is one method of food preservation because pathogens do not like very sugary substances.

All of these foods might be found in any Dumpster and can be evaluated with some confidence largely on the basis of appearance. Beyond these are foods which cannot be correctly evaluated without additional information. 20

more food

I began scavenging by pulling pizzas out of the Dumpster behind a pizza delivery shop. In general prepared food requires caution, but in this case I knew when the shop closed and went to the Dumpster as soon as the last of the help left.

Such shops often get prank orders, called "bogus." Because help seldom stays long at these places pizzas are often made with the wrong topping, refused on delivery for being cold, or baked incorrectly. The products to be discarded are boxed up because inventory is kept by counting boxes: a boxed pizza can be written off; an unboxed pizza does not exist.

I never placed a bogus order to increase the supply of pizzas and I believe no one else was scavenging in this Dumpster. But the people in the shop became suspicious and began to retain their garbage in the shop overnight.

While it lasted I had a steady supply of fresh, sometimes warm pizza. Because I knew the Dumpster I knew the source of the pizza, and because I visited the Dumpster regularly I knew what was fresh and what was yesterday's.

The area I frequent is inhabited by many affluent college students. I am not here by chance; the Dumpsters in this area are 25 very rich. Students throw out many good things, including food. In particular they tend to throw everything out when they move at the end of a semester, before and after breaks, and around midterm when many of them despair of college. So I find it advantageous to keep an eye on the academic calendar.

The students throw food away around the breaks because they do not know whether it has spoiled or will spoil before they return. A typical discard is a half jar of peanut butter. In fact nonorganic *protein*

[peanut butter does not require refrigeration and is unlikely to spoil in any reasonable time. The student does not know that, and since it is Daddy's money, the student decides not to take a chance.

Opened containers require caution and some attention to the question "Why was this discarded?" But in the case of discards from student apartments, the answer may be that the item was discarded through carelessness, ignorance, or wastefulness. This can sometimes be deduced when the item is found with many others, including some that are obviously perfectly good.

Some students, and others, approach defrosting a freezer by chucking out the whole lot. Not only do the circumstances of such a find tell the story, but also the mass of frozen goods stays cold for a long time and items may be found still frozen or freshly thawed. *This guy knows a lot for being homeless*

Yogurt, cheese, and sour cream are items that are often thrown out while they are still good. Occasionally I find a cheese with a spot of mold, which of course I just pare off, and because it is obvious why such a cheese was discarded, I treat it with less suspicion than an apparently perfect cheese found in similar circumstances. Yogurt is often discarded, still sealed, only because the expiration date on the carton had passed. This is one of my favorite finds because yogurt will keep for several days, even in warm weather.

Food

Students throw out canned goods and staples at the end of 30 semesters and when they give up college at midterm. Drugs, pornography, spirits, and the like are often discarded when parents are expected—Dad's day, for example. And spirits also turn up after big party weekends, presumably discarded by the newly reformed. Wine and spirits, of course, keep perfectly well even once opened.

My test for carbonated soft drinks is whether they still fizz vigorously. Many juices or other beverages are too acid or too syrupy to cause much concern provided they are not visibly contaminated. Liquids, however, require some care.

One hot day I found a large jug of Pat O'Brien's Hurricane mix. The jug had been opened, but it was still ice cold. I drank three large glasses before it became apparent to me that someone had added the rum to the mix, and not a little rum. I never tasted the rum and by the time I began to feel the effects I had already ingested a very large quantity of the beverage. Some divers would have considered this a boon, but being suddenly and thoroughly intoxicated in a public place in the early afternoon is not my idea of a good time.

I have heard of people maliciously contaminating discarded food and even handouts, but mostly I have heard of this from people with vivid imaginations who have had no experience with the Dumpsters themselves. Just before the pizza shop stopped discarding its garbage at night, jalapeños began showing up on most of the discarded pizzas. If indeed this was meant to discourage me it was a wasted effort because I am native Texan.

For myself, I avoid game, poultry, pork, and egg-based foods whether I find them raw or cooked. I seldom have the means to cook what I find, but when I do I avail myself of plentiful supplies of beef which is often in very good condition. I suppose fish becomes disagreeable before it becomes dangerous. The dog is happy to have any such thing that is past its prime and, in fact, does not recognize fish as food until it is quite strong.

Home leftovers, as opposed to surpluses from restaurants, are 35 very often bad. Evidently, especially among students, there is a common type of personality that carefully wraps up even the smallest leftover and shoves it into the back of the refrigerator for six months or so before discarding it. Characteristic of this type are the reused jars and margarine tubs which house the remains.

I avoid ethnic foods I am unfamiliar with. If I do not know what it is supposed to look like when it is good, I cannot be certain I will be able to tell if it is bad.

No matter how careful I am I still get dysentery at least once a month, oftener in warm weather. I do not want to paint too romantic a picture. Dumpster diving has serious drawbacks as a way of life.

I learned to scavenge gradually, on my own. Since then I have initiated several companions into the trade. I have learned that there is a predictable series of stages a person goes through in learning to scavenge.

At first the new scavenger is filled with disgust and self-loathing. He is ashamed of being seen and may lurk around, trying to duck behind things, or he may try to dive at night.

(In fact, most people instinctively look away from a scavenger. 40 By skulking around, the novice calls attention to himself and arouses suspicion. Diving at night is ineffective and needlessly messy.)

Every grain of rice seems to be a maggot. Everything seems to stink. He can wipe the egg yolk off the found can, but he cannot erase the stigma of eating garbage out of his mind.

That stage passes with experience. The scavenger finds a pair of running shoes that fit and look and smell brand new. He finds a pocket calculator in perfect working order. He finds pristine ice cream, still frozen, more than he can eat or keep. He begins to understand: people do throw away perfectly good stuff, a lot of perfectly good stuff.

At this stage, Dumpster shyness begins to dissipate. The diver, after all, has the last laugh. He is finding all manner of good things which are his for the taking. Those who disparage his profession are the fools, not he.

He may begin to hang onto some perfectly good things for which he has neither a use nor a market. Then he begins to take note of the things which are not perfectly good but are nearly so. He mates a Walkman with broken earphones and one that is missing a battery cover. He picks up things which he can repair.

At this stage he may become lost and never recover. Dumpsters 45 are full of things of some potential value to someone and also of things which never have much intrinsic value but are interesting. All the Dumpster divers I have known come to the point of trying to acquire everything they touch. Why not take it, they reason, since it is all free.

This is, of course, hopeless. Most divers come to realize that they must restrict themselves to items of relatively immediate utility. But in some cases the diver simply cannot control himself. I have met several of these pack-rat types. Their ideas of the values of various pieces of junk verge on the psychotic. Every bit of glass may be a diamond, they think, and all that glistens, gold.

I tend to gain weight when I am scavenging. Partly this is because I always find far more pizza and doughnuts than water-packed tuna, nonfat yogurt, and fresh vegetables. Also I have not developed much faith in the reliability of Dumpsters as a food source, although it has been proven to me many times. I tend to eat as if I have no idea where my next meal is coming from. But mostly I just hate to see food go to waste and so I eat much more than I should. Something like this drives the obsession to collect junk.

As for collecting objects, I usually restrict myself to collecting one kind of small object at a time, such as pocket calculators, sunglasses, or campaign buttons. To live on the street I must anticipate my needs to a certain extent: I must pick up and save warm bedding I find in August because it will not be found in Dumpsters in November. But even if I had a home with extensive storage space I could not save everything that might be valuable in some contingency. *I tj his Dvmpster*

I have proprietary feelings about my Dumpsters. As I have suggested, it is no accident that I scavenge from Dumpsters where good finds are common. But my limited experience with Dumpsters in other areas suggests to me that it is the population of competitors rather than the affluence of the dumpers that most affects the feasibility of survival by scavenging. The large number of competitors is what puts me off the idea of trying to scavenge in places like Los Angeles.

Curiously, I do not mind my direct competition, other scaven- 50
gers, so much as I hate the can scroungers.

People scrounge cans because they have to have a little cash. I have tried scrounging cans with an able-bodied companion. Afoot a can scrounger simply cannot make more than a few dollars a day. One can extract the necessities of life from the Dumpsters directly with far less effort than would be required to accumulate the equivalent value in cans.

Can scroungers, then, are people who *must* have small amounts of cash. These are drug addicts and winos, mostly the latter because the amounts of cash are so small.

Spirits and drugs do, like all other commodities, turn up in Dumpsters and the scavenger will from time to time have a half bottle of a rather good wine with his dinner. But the wino cannot survive on these occasional finds; he must have his daily dose to stave off the DTs. All the cans he can carry will buy about three bottles of Wild Irish Rose.

I do not begrudge them the cans, but can scroungers tend to tear up the Dumpsters, mixing the contents and littering the area. They become so specialized that they can see only cans. They earn my contempt by passing up change, canned goods, and readily hockable items.

There are precious few courtesies among scavengers. But it is 55
a common practice to set aside surplus items: pairs of shoes,

clate

clothing, canned goods, and such. A true scavenger hates to see good stuff go to waste and what he cannot use he leaves in good condition in plain sight.

Can scroungers lay waste to everything in their path and will stir one of a pair of good shoes to the bottom of a Dumpster, to be lost or ruined in the muck. Can scroungers will even go through individual garbage cans, something I have never seen a scavenger do.

personal garbage

Individual garbage cans are set out on the public easement only on garbage days. On other days going through them requires trespassing close to a dwelling. Going through individual garbage cans without scattering litter is almost impossible. Litter is likely to reduce the public's tolerance of scavenging. Individual garbage cans are simply not as productive as Dumpsters; people in houses and duplexes do not move as often and for some reason do not tend to discard as much useful material. Moreover, the time required to go through one garbage can that serves one household is not much less than the time required to go through a Dumpster that contains the refuse of twenty apartments.

But my strongest reservation about going through individual garbage cans is that this seems to me a very personal kind of invasion to which I would object if I were a householder. Although many things in Dumpsters are obviously meant never to come to light, a Dumpster is somehow less personal.

I avoid trying to draw conclusions about the people who dump in the Dumpsters I frequent. I think it would be unethical to do so, although I know many people will find the idea of scavenger ethics too funny for words.

Dumpsters contain bank statements, bills, correspondence, 60 and other documents, just as anyone might expect. But there are also less obvious sources of information. Pill bottles, for example. The labels on pill bottles contain the name of the patient, the name of the doctor, and the name of the drug. AIDS drugs and antipsychotic medicines, to name but two groups, are specific and are seldom prescribed for any other disorders. The plastic compacts for birth control pills usually have complete label information.

Despite all of this sensitive information, I have had only one apartment resident object to my going through the Dumpster. In that case it turned out the resident was a university athlete who was taking bets and who was afraid I would turn up his wager slips.

Occasionally a find tells a story. I once found a small paper bag containing some unused condoms, several partial tubes of flavored sexual lubricant, a partially used compact of birth control pills, and the torn pieces of a picture of a young man. Clearly she was through with him and planning to give up sex altogether.

Dumpster things are often sad—abandoned teddy bears, shredded wedding books, despaired-of sales kits. I find many pets lying in state in Dumpsters. Although I hope to get off the streets so that Lizbeth can have a long and comfortable old age, I know this hope is not very realistic. So I suppose when her time comes she too will go into a Dumpster. I will have no better place for her. And after all, for most of her life her livelihood has come from the Dumpster. When she finds something I think is safe that has been spilled from the Dumpster I let her have it. She already knows the route around the best Dumpsters. I like to think that if she survives me she will have a chance of evading the dog catcher and of finding her sustenance on the route.

Silly vanities also come to rest in the Dumpsters. I am a rather accomplished needleworker. I get a lot of materials from the Dumpsters. Evidently sorority girls, hoping to impress someone, perhaps themselves, with their mastery of a womanly art, buy a lot of embroider-by-number kits, work a few stitches horribly, and eventually discard the whole mess. I pull out their stitches, turn the canvas over, and work an original design. Do not think I refrain from chuckling as I make original gifts from these kits.

I find diaries and journals. I have often thought of compil- 65 ing a book of literary found objects. And perhaps I will one day. But what I find is hopelessly commonplace and bad without being, even unconsciously, camp. College students also discard their papers. I am horrified to discover the kind of paper which now merits an A in an undergraduate course. I am grateful, however, for the number of good books and magazines the students throw out.

In the area I know best I have never discovered vermin in the Dumpsters, but there are two kinds of kitty surprise. One is alley cats which I meet as they leap, claws first, out of Dumpsters. This is especially thrilling when I have Lizbeth in tow. The other kind of kitty surprise is a plastic garbage bag filled with some ponderous, amorphous mass. This always proves to be used cat litter.

City bees harvest doughnut glaze and this makes the Dumpster at the doughnut shop more interesting. My faith in the instinctive wisdom of animals is always shaken whenever I see Lizbeth attempt to catch a bee in her mouth, which she does whenever bees are present. Evidently some birds find Dumpsters profitable, for birdie surprise is almost as common as kitty surprise of the first kind. In hunting season all kinds of small game turn up in Dumpsters, some of it, sadly, not entirely dead. Curiously, summer and winter, maggots are uncommon.

The worst of the living and near-living hazards of the Dumpsters are the fire ants. The food that they claim is not much of a loss, but they are vicious and aggressive. It is very easy to brush against some surface of the Dumpster and pick up half a dozen or more fire ants, usually in some sensitive area such as the underarm. One advantage of bringing Lizbeth along as I make Dumpster rounds is that, for obvious reasons, she is very alert to ground-based fire ants. When Lizbeth recognizes the signs of fire ant infestation around our feet she does the Dance of the Zillion Fire Ants. I have learned not to ignore this warning from Lizbeth, whether I perceive the tiny ants or not, but to remove ourselves at Lizbeth's first pas de bourrée.[1] All the more so because the ants are the worst in the months I wear flip-flops, if I have them.

(Perhaps someone will misunderstand the above. Lizbeth does the Dance of the Zillion Fire Ants when she recognizes more fire ants than she cares to eat, not when she is being bitten. Since I have learned to react promptly, she does not get bitten at all. It is the isolated patrol of fire ants that falls in Lizbeth's range that deserves pity. Lizbeth finds them quite tasty.)

By far the best way to go through a Dumpster is to lower yourself into it. Most of the good stuff tends to settle at the bottom because it is usually weightier than the rubbish. My more athletic companions have often demonstrated to me that they can extract much good material from a Dumpster I have already been over.

To those psychologically or physically unprepared to enter a Dumpster, I recommend a stout stick, preferably with some barb or hook at one end. The hook can be used to grab plastic garbage

70

---

1. **pas de bourrée:** A ballet step (French). [Ed.]

bags. When I find canned goods or other objects loose at the bottom of a Dumpster I usually can roll them into a small bag that I can then hoist up. Much Dumpster diving is a matter of experience for which nothing will do except practice.

Dumpster diving is outdoor work, often surprisingly pleasant. It is not entirely predictable; things of interest turn up every day and some days there are finds of great value. I am always very pleased when I can turn up exactly the thing I most wanted to find. Yet in spite of the element of chance, scavenging more than most other pursuits tends to yield returns in some proportion to the effort and intelligence brought to bear. It is very sweet to turn up a few dollars in change from a Dumpster that has just been gone over by a wino.

The land is now covered with cities. The cities are full of Dumpsters. I think of scavenging as a modern form of self-reliance. In any event, after ten years of government service, where everything is geared to the lowest common denominator, I find work that rewards initiative and effort refreshing. Certainly I would be happy to have a sinecure again, but I am not heartbroken not to have one anymore.

I find from the experience of scavenging two rather deep lessons. The first is to take what I can use and let the rest go by. I have come to think that there is no value in the abstract. A thing I cannot use or make useful, perhaps by trading, has no value however fine or rare it may be. I mean useful in a broad sense — so, for example, some art I would think useful and valuable, but other art might be otherwise for me.

I was shocked to realize that some things are not worth acquir- 75
ing, but now I think it is so. Some material things are white elephants that eat up the possessor's substance.

The second lesson is of the transience of material being. This has not quite converted me to a dualist, but it has made some headway in that direction. I do not suppose that ideas are immortal, but certainly mental things are longer-lived than other material things.

Once I was the sort of person who invests material objects with sentimental value. Now I no longer have those things, but I have the sentiments yet.

Many times in my travels I have lost everything but the clothes I was wearing and Lizbeth. The things I find in Dumpsters, the

love letters and ragdolls of so many lives, remind me of this lesson. Now I hardly pick up a thing without envisioning the time I
will cast it away. This I think is a healthy state of mind. Almost
everything I have now has already been cast out at least once,
proving that what I own is valueless to someone.

Anyway, I find my desire to grab for the gaudy bauble has been
largely sated. I think this is an attitude I share with the very
wealthy—we both know there is plenty more where what we have
came from. Between us are the rat-race millions who have confounded their selves with the objects they grasp and who nightly
scavenge the cable channels looking for they know not what.

I am sorry for them.   80

For Discussion and Writing

1. Eighner is careful to offer definitions of the key terms he uses. List
   those key terms and their definitions.

2. Summarize Eighner's analysis of the practical stages through which a
   beginning Dumpster diver goes. What does his analysis tell us about
   the larger experience of having to scavenge for food? What does his
   writing style tell you about his views on his way of life?

3. **connections**   Read William F. Buckley Jr.'s "Why Don't We Complain?" (p. 72) alongside Eighner's essay. Compare the two essayists'
   attitudes about their daily lives. Compare their lives, using the evidence presented in their essays. Who sees his life as more difficult?
   Who complains more? What do you make of the differences between
   their lives and their attitudes toward them?

4. How does reading Eighner make you feel about your own material
   values? How do you relate to Dumpster diving and to what he calls the
   "grab for the gaudy bauble" (par. 79)?

5. **looking further**   "On Dumpster Diving" is a classic example of the
   rhetorical mode known as process analysis. Eighner takes readers
   through all of the things involved in Dumpster diving, sharing descriptive details and step-by-step accounts. Rarely does he step back and
   talk about what living in this way has taught him about how the larger
   world works. Do you think his close attention to the process of
   Dumpster diving helps him make a larger argument about how the
   world is or should be, or do you think it obscures any larger point he
   might want to press? Further, do you think his attention to the process is less effective as an exposé because it makes something that
   could be seen as the degrading result of larger forces seem more
   acceptable?

STEPHANIE ERICSSON

The Ways We Lie

A screenwriter and advertising copywriter, Stephanie Ericsson, born in 1953 and raised in San Francisco, is also an author of self-help books, including Companion through the Darkness: Inner Dialogues on Grief *(1993). "The Ways We Lie" originally appeared in the* Utne Reader. *Consider, as you read, how Ericsson breaks down the activity of lying into the different kinds of lies we tell but also manages to pull together the different sections of her essay to make a larger point about the role lying plays in our lives and our culture.*

The bank called today and I told them my deposit was in the mail, even though I hadn't written a check yet. It'd been a rough day. The baby I'm pregnant with decided to do aerobics on my lungs for two hours, our three-year-old daughter painted the living-room couch with lipstick, the IRS put me on hold for an hour, and I was late to a business meeting because I was tired.

I told my client that traffic had been bad. When my partner came home, his haggard face told me his day hadn't gone any better than mine, so when he asked, "How was your day?" I said, "Oh, fine," knowing that one more straw might break his back. A friend called and wanted to take me to lunch. I said I was busy. Four lies in the course of a day, none of which I felt the least bit guilty about.

We lie. We all do. We exaggerate, we minimize, we avoid confrontation, we spare people's feelings, we conveniently forget, we keep secrets, we justify lying to the big-guy institutions. Like most people, I indulge in small falsehoods and still think of myself as an honest person. Sure I lie, but it doesn't hurt anything. Or does it?

I once tried going a whole week without telling a lie, and it was paralyzing. I discovered that telling the truth all the time is nearly impossible. It means living with some serious consequences: the

159

bank charges me $60 in overdraft fees, my partner keels over when I tell him about my travails, my client fires me for telling her I didn't feel like being on time, and my friend takes it personally when I say I'm not hungry. There must be some merit to lying.

But if I justify lying, what makes me any different from slick politicians or the corporate robbers who raided the S&L industry? Saying it's okay to lie one way and not another is hedging. I cannot seem to escape the voice deep inside me that tells me: when someone lies, someone loses. 5

What far-reaching consequences will I, or others, pay as a result of my lie? Will someone's trust be destroyed? Will someone else pay *my* penance because I ducked out? We must consider the *meaning of our actions*. Deception, lies, capital crimes, and misdemeanors all carry meanings. *Webster's* definition of *lie* is specific:

1. a false statement or action especially made with the intent to deceive;
2. anything that gives or is meant to give a false impression.

A definition like this implies that there are many, many ways to tell a lie. Here are just a few.

THE WHITE LIE

A man who won't lie to a woman has very little consideration for her feelings. — BERGEN EVANS

The white lie assumes that the truth will cause more damage than a simple, harmless untruth. Telling a friend he looks great when he looks like hell can be based on a decision that the friend needs a compliment more than a frank opinion. But, in effect, it is the liar deciding what is best for the lied to. Ultimately, it is a vote of no confidence. It is an act of subtle arrogance for anyone to decide what is best for someone else.

Yet not all circumstances are quite so cut-and-dried. Take, for instance, the sergeant in Vietnam who knew one of his men was killed in action but listed him as missing so that the man's family would receive indefinite compensation instead of the lump-sum pittance the military gives widows and children. His intent was honorable. Yet for twenty years this family kept their hopes alive, unable to move on to a new life.

FAÇADES

Et tu, Brute?—CAESAR

We all put up façades to one degree or another. When I put on a   10
suit to go to see a client, I feel as though I am putting on another face, obeying the expectation that serious businesspeople wear suits rather than sweatpants. But I'm a writer. Normally, I get up, get the kid off to school, and sit at my computer in my pajamas until four in the afternoon. When I answer the phone, the caller thinks I'm wearing a suit (though the UPS man knows better).

But façades can be destructive because they are used to seduce others into an illusion. For instance, I recently realized that a former friend was a liar. He presented himself with all the right looks and the right words and offered lots of new consciousness theories, fabulous books to read, and fascinating insights. Then I did some business with him, and the time came for him to pay me. He turned out to be all talk and no walk. I heard a plethora of reasonable excuses, including in-depth descriptions of the big break around the corner. In six months of work, I saw less than a hundred bucks. When I confronted him, he raised both eyebrows and tried to convince me that I'd heard him wrong, that he'd made no commitment to me. A simple investigation into his past revealed a crowded graveyard of disenchanted former friends.

IGNORING THE PLAIN FACTS

Well, you must understand that Father Porter is only human.
—A MASSACHUSETTS PRIEST

In the '60s, the Catholic Church in Massachusetts began hearing complaints that Father James Porter was sexually molesting children. Rather than relieving him of his duties, the ecclesiastical authorities simply moved him from one parish to another between 1960 and 1967, actually providing him with a fresh supply of unsuspecting families and innocent children to abuse. After treatment in 1967 for pedophilia, he went back to work, this time in Minnesota. The new diocese was aware of Father Porter's obsession with children, but they needed priests and recklessly believed treatment had cured him. More children were abused until he was relieved of his duties a year later. By his own admission, Porter may have abused as many as a hundred children.

Ignoring the facts may not in and of itself be a form of lying, but consider the context of this situation. If a lie is *a false action done with the intent to deceive*, then the Catholic Church's conscious covering for Porter created irreparable consequences. The church became a co-perpetrator with Porter.

DEFLECTING

When you have no basis for an argument, abuse the plaintiff.
　　　　　　　　　　　　　　　　　　　—CICERO

I've discovered that I can keep anyone from seeing the true me by being selectively blatant. I set a precedent of being up-front about intimate issues, but I never bring up the things I truly want to hide; I just let people assume I'm revealing everything. It's an effective way of hiding.

Any good liar knows that the way to perpetuate an untruth is to deflect attention from it. When Clarence Thomas exploded with accusations that the Senate hearings were a "high-tech lynching," he simply switched the focus from a highly charged subject to a radioactive subject. Rather than defending himself, he took the offensive and accused the country of racism. It was a brilliant maneuver. Racism is now politically incorrect in official circles— unlike sexual harassment, which still rewards those who can get away with it.

Some of the most skilled deflectors are passive-aggressive people who, when accused of inappropriate behavior, refuse to respond to the accusations. This you-don't-exist stance infuriates the accuser, who, understandably, screams something obscene out of frustration. The trap is sprung and the act of deflection successful, because now the passive-aggressive person can indignantly say, "Who can talk to someone as unreasonable as you?" The real issue is forgotten and the sins of the original victim become the focus. Feeling guilty of name-calling, the victim is fully tamed and crawls into a hole, ashamed. I have watched this fighting technique work thousands of times in disputes between men and women, and what I've learned is that the real culprit is not necessarily the one who swears the loudest.

OMISSION

The cruelest lies are often told in silence. — R. L. STEVENSON

Omission involves telling most of the truth minus one or two key facts whose absence changes the story completely. You break a pair of glasses that are guaranteed under normal use and get a new pair, without mentioning that the first pair broke during a rowdy game of basketball. Who hasn't tried something like that? But what about omission of information that could make a difference in how a person lives his or her life?

For instance, one day I found out that rabbinical legends tell of another woman in the Garden of Eden before Eve. I was stunned. The omission of the Sumerian goddess Lilith from Genesis—as well as her demonization by ancient misogynists as an embodiment of female evil—felt like spiritual robbery. I felt like I'd just found out my mother was really my stepmother. To take seriously the tradition that Adam was created out of the same mud as his equal counterpart, Lilith, redefines all of Judeo-Christian history.

Some renegade Catholic feminists introduced me to a view of Lilith that had been suppressed during the many centuries when this strong goddess was seen only as a spirit of evil. Lilith was a proud goddess who defied Adam's need to control her, attempted negotiations, and when this failed, said adios and left the Garden of Eden.

This omission of Lilith from the Bible was a patriarchal strat- 20 egy to keep women weak. Omitting the strong-woman archetype of Lilith from Western religions and starting the story with Eve the Rib has helped keep Christian and Jewish women believing they were the lesser sex for thousands of years.

STEREOTYPES AND CLICHÉS

I do not believe in a -ism m- Ferris- buelker

Where opinion does not exist, the status quo becomes stereotyped and all originality is discouraged. — BERTRAND RUSSELL

Stereotype and cliché serve a purpose as a form of shorthand. Our need for vast amounts of information in nanoseconds has made the stereotype vital to modern communication. Unfortunately, it often shuts down original thinking, giving those hungry for the truth a candy bar of misinformation instead of a balanced meal. The stereotype explains a situation with just enough truth to seem unquestionable.

All the "isms" — racism, sexism, ageism, et al. — are founded on and fueled by the stereotype and the cliché, which are lies of exaggeration, omission, and ignorance. They are always dangerous. They take a single tree and make it a landscape. They destroy curiosity. They close minds and separate people. The single mother on welfare is assumed to be cheating. Any black male could tell you how much of his identity is obliterated daily by stereotypes. Fat people, ugly people, beautiful people, old people, large-breasted women, short men, the mentally ill, and the homeless all could tell you how much more they are like us than we want to think. I once admitted to a group of people that I had a mouth like a truck driver. Much to my surprise, a man stood up and said, "I'm a truck driver, and I never cuss." Needless to say, I was humbled.

GROUPTHINK

Who is more foolish, the child afraid of the dark, or the man afraid of the light? — MAURICE FREEHILL

Irving Janis, in *Victims of Group Think*, defines this sort of lie as a psychological phenomenon within decision-making groups in which loyalty to the group has become more important than any other value, with the result that dissent and the appraisal of alternatives are suppressed. If you've ever worked on a committee or in a corporation, you've encountered groupthink. It requires a combination of other forms of lying—ignoring facts, selective memory, omission, and denial, to name a few.

The textbook example of groupthink came on December 7, 1941. From as early as the fall of 1941, the warnings came in, one after another, that Japan was preparing for a massive military operation. The navy command in Hawaii assumed Pearl Harbor was invulnerable—the Japanese weren't stupid enough to attack the United States' most important base. On the other hand, racist stereotypes said the Japanese weren't smart enough to invent a torpedo effective in less than 60 feet of water (the fleet was docked in 30 feet); after all, US technology hadn't been able to do it.

On Friday, December 5, normal weekend leave was granted to all the commanders at Pearl Harbor, even though the Japanese consulate in Hawaii was busy burning papers. Within the tight, good-ole-boy cohesiveness of the US command in Hawaii, the myth of invulnerability stayed well entrenched. No one in the group considered the alternatives. The rest is history.

OUT-AND-OUT LIES

The only form of lying that is beyond reproach is lying for its own sake. — OSCAR WILDE

Of all the ways to lie, I like this one the best, probably because I get tired of trying to figure out the real meanings behind things. At least I can trust the bald-faced lie. I once asked my five-year-old nephew, "Who broke the fence?" (I had seen him do it.) He answered, "The murderers." Who could argue?

At least when this sort of lie is told it can be easily confronted. As the person who is lied to, I know where I stand. The bald-faced lie doesn't toy with my perceptions—it argues with them. It doesn't try to refashion reality, it tries to refute it. *Read my lips. . . .* No sleight of hand. No guessing. If this were the only form of lying, there would be no such things as floating anxiety or the adult-children-of-alcoholics movement.

DISMISSAL

Pay no attention to that man behind the curtain!
I am the Great Oz! — THE WIZARD OF OZ

Dismissal is perhaps the slipperiest of all lies. Dismissing feelings, perceptions, or even the raw facts of a situation ranks as a kind of lie that can do as much damage to a person as any other kind of lie.

The roots of many mental disorders can be traced back to the dismissal of reality. Imagine that a person is told from the time she is a tot that her perceptions are inaccurate. *"Mommy, I'm scared."* "No you're not, darling." *"I don't like that man next door, he makes me feel icky."* "Johnny, that's a terrible thing to say, of course you like him. You go over there right now and be nice to him."

I've often mused over the idea that madness is actually a sane reaction to an insane world. Psychologist R. D. Laing supports this hypothesis in *Sanity, Madness and the Family*, an account of his investigation into the families of schizophrenics. The common thread that ran through all of the families he studied was a deliberate, staunch dismissal of the patient's perceptions from a very early age. Each of the patients started out with an accurate grasp of reality, which, through meticulous and methodical dismissal, was demolished until the only reality the patient could trust was catatonia.

Dismissal runs the gamut. Mild dismissal can be quite handy for forgiving the foibles of others in our day-to-day lives. Toddlers who have just learned to manipulate their parents' attention sometimes are dismissed out of necessity. Absolute attention from the parents would require so much energy that no one would get to eat dinner. But we must be careful and attentive about how far we take our "necessary" dismissals. Dismissal is a dangerous tool, because it's nothing less than a lie.

DELUSION

We lie loudest when we lie to ourselves. — ERIC HOFFER

I could write the book on this one. Delusion, a cousin of dismissal, is the tendency to see excuses as facts. It's a powerful lying tool because it filters out information that contradicts what we want to believe. Alcoholics who believe that the problems in their lives are legitimate reasons for drinking rather than results of the drinking offer the classic example of deluded thinking. Delusion uses the mind's ability to see things in myriad ways to support what it wants to be the truth.

But delusion is also a survival mechanism we all use. If we were to fully contemplate the consequences of our stockpiles of nuclear weapons or global warming, we could hardly function on a day-to-day level. We don't want to incorporate that much reality into our lives because to do so would be paralyzing.

Delusion acts as an adhesive to keep the status quo intact. It shamelessly employs dismissal, omission, and amnesia, among other sorts of lies. Its most cunning defense is that it cannot see itself.

> *The liar's punishment [. . .] is that he cannot believe anyone else.*
> —GEORGE BERNARD SHAW

These are only a few of the ways we lie. Or are lied to. As I said earlier, it's not easy to entirely eliminate lies from our lives. No matter how pious we may try to be, we will still embellish, hedge, and omit to lubricate the daily machinery of living. But there is a world of difference between telling functional lies and living a lie. Martin Buber once said, "The lie is the spirit committing treason against itself." Our acceptance of lies becomes a cultural cancer that eventually shrouds and reorders reality until moral garbage becomes as invisible to us as water is to a fish.

How much do we tolerate before we become sick and tired of being sick and tired? When will we stand up and declare our *right* to trust? When do we stop accepting that the real truth is in the fine print? Whose lips do we read this year when we vote for president? When will we stop being so reticent about making judgments? When do we stop turning over our personal power and responsibility to liars?

Maybe if I don't tell the bank the check's in the mail I'll be less tolerant of the lies told me every day. A country song I once heard said it all for me: "You've got to stand for something or you'll fall for anything."

For Discussion and Writing

1. What are the different kinds of lies Ericsson catalogs?
2. How many kinds of lies does Ericsson describe? How does the number of kinds of lies help her make her larger point about lying?
3. **connections** What might Ericsson have to say about what William F. Buckley Jr. describes in "Why Don't We Complain?" (p. 72).
4. Imagine a day in which you told no lies of any kind. Write a narrative telling the story of that day and the consequences of your total honesty.
5. **looking further** Is there, as Ericsson writes, "a world of difference between telling functional lies and living a lie" (par. 35)? Regardless of your opinion of Ericsson's claim, write a counterargument to that claim. What is the strongest argument you can come up with against untruth? How can you use it to counter her argument? Where does your counterargument come from—that is, on what moral or ethical system or belief does it depend?

MALCOLM GLADWELL

Small Change: Why the Revolution Will Not Be Tweeted

Born in England in 1963 and raised there and in Ontario, Canada, Malcolm Gladwell is a staff writer for the New Yorker *and author of* The Tipping Point: How Little Things Make a Big Difference *(2000),* Blink: The Power of Thinking without Thinking *(2005),* Outliers: The Story of Success *(2008),* What the Dog Saw: And Other Adventures *(2009), and* David and Goliath: Underdogs, Misfits, and the Art of Battling Giants *(2014).*

Gladwell's work usually takes the broad view, looking for explanations for cultural phenomena so widespread that they are often overlooked as things not needing or susceptible to explanation. Here, in "Small Change: Why the Revolution Will Not Be Tweeted," he takes on a phenomenon that is far from unnoticed—the development of social media—and a possible effect of its growth: the recent spate of revolutionary movements. However, Gladwell uses many of the same techniques and ways of thinking to make his argument. As you read, keep an eye out for the ways in which he makes connections.

At four-thirty in the afternoon on Monday, February 1, 1960, four college students sat down at the lunch counter at the Woolworth's in downtown Greensboro, North Carolina. They were freshmen at North Carolina A. & T., a black college a mile or so away.

"I'd like a cup of coffee, please," one of the four, Ezell Blair, said to the waitress.

"We don't serve Negroes here," she replied.

The Woolworth's lunch counter was a long L-shaped bar that could seat sixty-six people, with a standup snack bar at one end. The seats were for whites. The snack bar was for blacks. Another employee, a black woman who worked at the steam table, approached the students and tried to warn them away. "You're acting stupid, ignorant!" she said. They didn't move. Around five-thirty, the front doors to the store were locked. The four still didn't move. Finally, they left by a side door. Outside, a small crowd had gathered, including a photographer from the Greensboro *Record*. "I'll be back tomorrow with A. & T. College," one of the students said.

By next morning, the protest had grown to twenty-seven men   5 and four women, most from the same dormitory as the original four. The men were dressed in suits and ties. The students had brought their schoolwork, and studied as they sat at the counter. On Wednesday, students from Greensboro's "Negro" secondary school, Dudley High, joined in, and the number of protesters swelled to eighty. By Thursday, the protesters numbered three hundred, including three white women, from the Greensboro campus of the University of North Carolina. By Saturday, the sit-in had reached six hundred. People spilled out onto the street. White teenagers waved Confederate flags. Someone threw a firecracker. At noon, the A. & T. football team arrived. "Here comes the wrecking crew," one of the white students shouted.

By the following Monday, sit-ins had spread to Winston-Salem, twenty-five miles away, and Durham, fifty miles away. The day after that, students at Fayetteville State Teachers College and at Johnson C. Smith College, in Charlotte, joined in, followed on Wednesday by students at St. Augustine's College and Shaw University, in Raleigh. On Thursday and Friday, the protest crossed state lines, surfacing in Hampton and Portsmouth, Virginia, in Rock Hill, South Carolina, and in Chattanooga, Tennessee. By the end of the month, there were sit-ins throughout the South, as far west as Texas. "I asked every student I met what the first day of the sitdowns had been like on his campus," the political theorist Michael Walzer wrote in *Dissent*. "The answer was always the same: 'It was like a fever. Everyone wanted to go.'" Some seventy thousand students eventually took part. Thousands were arrested and untold thousands more radicalized. These events in the early sixties became a civil-rights war that engulfed the South for the rest of the decade—and it happened without e-mail, texting, Facebook, or Twitter.

The world, we are told, is in the midst of a revolution. The new tools of social media have reinvented social activism. With Facebook and Twitter and the like, the traditional relationship between political authority and popular will has been upended, making it easier for the powerless to collaborate, coordinate, and give voice to their concerns. When ten thousand protesters took to the streets in Moldova in the spring of 2009 to protest against their country's Communist government, the action was dubbed the Twitter Revolution, because of the means by which the demonstrators had been brought together. A few months after that, when student protests rocked Tehran, the State Department took the unusual step of asking Twitter to suspend scheduled maintenance of its Web site, because the Administration didn't want such a critical organizing tool out of service at the height of the demonstrations. "Without Twitter the people of Iran would not have felt empowered and confident to stand up for freedom and democracy," Mark Pfeifle, a former national-security adviser, later wrote, calling for Twitter to be nominated for the Nobel Peace Prize. Where activists were once defined by their causes, they are now defined by their tools. Facebook warriors go online to push for change. "You are the best hope for us all," James K. Glassman, a former senior State Department official, told a crowd of cyber activists at a recent conference sponsored by Facebook, A. T. & T., Howcast, MTV, and Google. Sites like Facebook, Glassman said, "give the U.S. a significant competitive advantage over terrorists. Some time ago, I said that Al Qaeda was 'eating our lunch on the Internet.' That is no longer the case. Al Qaeda is stuck in Web 1.0. The Internet is now about interactivity and conversation."

These are strong, and puzzling, claims. Why does it matter who is eating whose lunch on the Internet? Are people who log on to their Facebook page really the best hope for us all? As for Moldova's so-called Twitter Revolution, Evgeny Morozov, a scholar at Stanford who has been the most persistent of digital evangelism's critics, points out that Twitter had scant internal significance in Moldova, a country where very few Twitter accounts exist. Nor does it seem to have been a revolution, not least because the protests—as Anne Applebaum suggested in the *Washington Post*—may well have been a bit of stagecraft cooked up by the government. (In a country paranoid about Romanian revanchism,[1] the protesters flew a Romanian flag over the Parliament building.) In the Iranian case, meanwhile, the people tweeting about

1. **revanchism** (from the French: *revanche*, "revenge"): A political policy of a nation or an ethnic group, intended to regain lost territory or standing. [Ed.]

the demonstrations were almost all in the West. "It is time to get Twitter's role in the events in Iran right," Golnaz Esfandiari wrote, this past summer, in *Foreign Policy*. "Simply put: There was no Twitter Revolution inside Iran." The cadre of prominent bloggers, like Andrew Sullivan, who championed the role of social media in Iran, Esfandiari continued, misunderstood the situation. "Western journalists who couldn't reach—or didn't bother reaching?—people on the ground in Iran simply scrolled through the English-language tweets post with tag #iranelection," she wrote. "Through it all, no one seemed to wonder why people trying to coordinate protests in Iran would be writing in any language other than Farsi."

Some of this grandiosity is to be expected. Innovators tend to be solipsists. They often want to cram every stray fact and experience into their new model. As the historian Robert Darnton has written, "The marvels of communication technology in the present have produced a false consciousness about the past—even a sense that communication has no history, or had nothing of importance to consider before the days of television and the Internet." But there is something else at work here, in the outsized enthusiasm for social media. Fifty years after one of the most extraordinary episodes of social upheaval in American history, we seem to have forgotten what activism is.

Greensboro in the early nineteen-sixties was the kind of place where racial insubordination was routinely met with violence. The four students who first sat down at the lunch counter were terrified. "I suppose if anyone had come up behind me and yelled 'Boo,' I think I would have fallen off my seat," one of them said later. On the first day, the store manager notified the police chief, who immediately sent two officers to the store. On the third day, a gang of white toughs showed up at the lunch counter and stood ostentatiously behind the protesters, ominously muttering epithets such as "burr-head nigger." A local Ku Klux Klan leader made an appearance. On Saturday, as tensions grew, someone called in a bomb threat, and the entire store had to be evacuated.

The dangers were even clearer in the Mississippi Freedom Summer Project of 1964, another of the sentinel campaigns of the civil-rights movement. The Student Nonviolent Coordinating Committee recruited hundreds of Northern, largely white unpaid volunteers to run Freedom Schools, register black voters, and raise civil-rights awareness in the Deep South. "No one should go *anywhere* alone, but certainly not in an automobile and certainly not at night," they were instructed. Within days of arriving in Mississippi, three volunteers—Michael Schwerner, James Chaney, and Andrew Goodman—were kidnapped and killed, and, during the rest of the summer, thirty-seven black churches were set on fire and dozens of safe houses were bombed; volunteers were beaten, shot at, arrested, and trailed by pickup trucks full of armed men. A quarter of those in the program dropped out. Activism that challenges the status quo—that attacks deeply rooted problems—is not for the faint of heart.

What makes people capable of this kind of activism? The Stanford sociologist Doug McAdam compared the Freedom Summer dropouts with the participants who stayed, and discovered that the key difference wasn't, as might be expected, ideological fervor. "*All* of the applicants—participants and withdrawals alike— emerge as highly committed, articulate supporters of the goals and values of the summer program," he concluded. What mattered more was an applicant's degree of personal connection to the civil-rights movement. All the volunteers were required to provide a list of personal contacts—the people they wanted kept apprised of their activities—and participants were far more likely than dropouts to have close friends who were also going to Mississippi. High-risk activism, McAdam concluded, is a "strong-tie" phenomenon.

This pattern shows up again and again. One study of the Red Brigades, the Italian terrorist group of the nineteen-seventies, found that seventy percent of recruits had at least one good friend already in the organization. The same is true of the men who joined the mujahideen in Afghanistan. Even revolutionary actions that look spontaneous, like the demonstrations in East Germany that led to the fall of the Berlin Wall, are, at core, strong-tie phenomena. The opposition movement in East Germany consisted of several hundred groups, each with roughly a dozen members. Each group was in limited contact with the others: at the time, only thirteen percent of East Germans even had a phone. All they knew was that on Monday nights, outside St. Nicholas Church in downtown Leipzig, people gathered to voice their anger at the state. And the primary determinant of who showed up was "critical friends"—the more friends you had who were critical of the regime the more likely you were to join the protest.

So one crucial fact about the four freshmen at the Greensboro lunch counter—David Richmond, Franklin McCain, Ezell Blair, and Joseph McNeil—was their relationship with one another. McNeil was a roommate of Blair's in A. & T.'s Scott Hall dormitory. Richmond roomed with McCain one floor up, and Blair, Richmond, and McCain had all gone to Dudley High School. The four would smuggle beer into the dorm and talk late into the night in Blair and McNeil's room. They would all have remembered the murder of Emmett Till in 1955, the Montgomery bus boycott that same year, and the showdown in Little Rock in 1957. It was McNeil who brought up the idea of a sit-in at Woolworth's. They'd discussed it for nearly a month. Then McNeil came into the dorm room and asked the others if they were ready. There was a pause, and McCain said, in a way that works only with people who talk late into the night with one another, "Are you guys chicken or not?" Ezell Blair worked up the courage the next day to ask for a cup of coffee because he was flanked by his roommate and two good friends from high school.

The kind of activism associated with social media isn't like this 15 at all. The platforms of social media are built around weak ties. Twitter is a way of following (or being followed by) people you may never have met. Facebook is a tool for efficiently managing your acquaintances, for keeping up with the people you would not otherwise be able to stay in touch with. That's why you can have a thousand "friends" on Facebook, as you never could in real life.

This is in many ways a wonderful thing. There is strength in weak ties, as the sociologist Mark Granovetter has observed. Our acquaintances—not our friends—are our greatest source of new ideas and information. The Internet lets us exploit the power of these kinds of distant connections with marvellous efficiency. It's terrific at the diffusion of innovation, interdisciplinary collaboration, seamlessly matching up buyers and sellers, and the logistical functions of the dating world. But weak ties seldom lead to high-risk activism.

In a new book called *The Dragonfly Effect: Quick, Effective, and Powerful Ways to Use Social Media to Drive Social Change*, the business consultant Andy Smith and the Stanford Business

School professor Jennifer Aaker tell the story of Sameer Bhatia, a young Silicon Valley entrepreneur who came down with acute myelogenous leukemia. It's a perfect illustration of social media's strengths. Bhatia needed a bone-marrow transplant, but he could not find a match among his relatives and friends. The odds were best with a donor of his ethnicity, and there were few South Asians in the national bone-marrow database. So Bhatia's business partner sent out an e-mail explaining Bhatia's plight to more than four hundred of their acquaintances, who forwarded the e-mail to their personal contacts; Facebook pages and YouTube videos were devoted to the Help Sameer campaign. Eventually, nearly twenty-five thousand new people were registered in the bone-marrow database, and Bhatia found a match.

But how did the campaign get so many people to sign up? By not asking too much of them. That's the only way you can get someone you don't really know to do something on your behalf. You can get thousands of people to sign up for a donor registry, because doing so is pretty easy. You have to send in a cheek swab and—in the highly unlikely event that your bone marrow is a good match for someone in need—spend a few hours at the hospital. Donating bone marrow isn't a trivial matter. But it doesn't involve financial or personal risk; it doesn't mean spending a summer being chased by armed men in pickup trucks. It doesn't require that you confront socially entrenched norms and practices. In fact, it's the kind of commitment that will bring only social acknowledgment and praise.

The evangelists of social media don't understand this distinction; they seem to believe that a Facebook friend is the same as a real friend and that signing up for a donor registry in Silicon Valley today is activism in the same sense as sitting at a segregated lunch counter in Greensboro in 1960. "Social networks are particularly effective at increasing motivation," Aaker and Smith write. But that's not true. Social networks are effective at increasing *participation*—by lessening the level of motivation that participation requires. The Facebook page of the Save Darfur Coalition has 1,282,339 members, who have donated an average of nine cents apiece. The next biggest Darfur charity on Facebook has 22,073 members, who have donated an average of thirty-five cents. Help Save Darfur has 2,797 members, who have given, on average, fifteen cents. A spokesperson for the Save

Darfur Coalition told *Newsweek*, "We wouldn't necessarily gauge someone's value to the advocacy movement based on what they've given. This is a powerful mechanism to engage this critical population. They inform their community, attend events, volunteer. It's not something you can measure by looking at a ledger." In other words, Facebook activism succeeds not by motivating people to make a real sacrifice but by motivating them to do the things that people do when they are not motivated enough to make a real sacrifice. We are a long way from the lunch counters of Greensboro.

The students who joined the sit-ins across the South during the 20 winter of 1960 described the movement as a "fever." But the civil-rights movement was more like a military campaign than like a contagion. In the late nineteen-fifties, there had been sixteen sit-ins in various cities throughout the South, fifteen of which were formally organized by civil-rights organizations like the NAACP and CORE. Possible locations for activism were scouted. Plans were drawn up. Movement activists held training sessions and retreats for would-be protesters. The Greensboro Four were a product of this groundwork: all were members of the NAACP Youth Council. They had close ties with the head of the local NAACP chapter. They had been briefed on the earlier wave of sit-ins in Durham, and had been part of a series of movement meetings in activist churches. When the sit-in movement spread from Greensboro throughout the South, it did not spread indiscriminately. It spread to those cities which had preexisting "movement centers"—a core of dedicated and trained activists ready to turn the "fever" into action.

The civil-rights movement was high-risk activism. It was also, crucially, strategic activism: a challenge to the establishment mounted with precision and discipline. The NAACP was a centralized organization, run from New York according to highly formalized operating procedures. At the Southern Christian Leadership Conference, Martin Luther King, Jr., was the unquestioned authority. At the center of the movement was the black church, which had, as Aldon D. Morris points out in his superb 1984 study, "The Origins of the Civil Rights Movement," a carefully demarcated division of labor, with various standing committees and disciplined groups. "Each group was task-oriented and coordinated its activities through authority structures," Morris writes. "Individuals were held accountable for their assigned duties, and important conflicts were resolved by the minister, who usually exercised ultimate authority over the congregation."

This is the second crucial distinction between traditional activism and its online variant: social media are not about this kind of hierarchical organization. Facebook and the like are tools for building *networks*, which are the opposite, in structure and character, of hierarchies. Unlike hierarchies, with their rules and procedures, networks aren't controlled by a single central authority. Decisions are made through consensus, and the ties that bind people to the group are loose.

This structure makes networks enormously resilient and adaptable in low-risk situations. Wikipedia is a perfect example. It doesn't have an editor, sitting in New York, who directs and corrects each entry. The effort of putting together each entry is self-organized. If every entry in Wikipedia were to be erased tomorrow, the content would swiftly be restored, because that's what happens when a network of thousands spontaneously devote their time to a task.

There are many things, though, that networks don't do well. Car companies sensibly use a network to organize their hundreds of suppliers, but not to design their cars. No one believes that the articulation of a coherent design philosophy is best handled by a sprawling, leaderless organizational system. Because networks don't have a centralized leadership structure and clear lines of authority, they have real difficulty reaching consensus and setting goals. They can't think strategically; they are chronically prone to conflict and error. How do you make difficult choices about tactics or strategy or philosophical direction when everyone has an equal say?

The Palestine Liberation Organization originated as a network, and the international-relations scholars Mette Eilstrup-Sangiovanni and Calvert Jones argue in a recent essay in *International Security* that this is why it ran into such trouble as it grew: "Structural features typical of networks—the absence of central authority, the unchecked autonomy of rival groups, and the inability to arbitrate quarrels through formal mechanisms—made the P.L.O. excessively vulnerable to outside manipulation and internal strife."

In Germany in the nineteen-seventies, they go on, "the far more unified and successful left-wing terrorists tended to organize hierarchically, with professional management and clear divisions of labor. They were concentrated geographically in universities, where they could establish central leadership, trust, and camaraderie through regular, face-to-face meetings." They seldom betrayed their comrades in arms during police interrogations. Their counterparts on the right were organized as decentralized networks, and had no such discipline. These groups were regularly infiltrated, and members, once arrested, easily gave up their comrades. Similarly, Al Qaeda was most dangerous when it was a unified hierarchy. Now that it has dissipated into a network, it has proved far less effective.

The drawbacks of networks scarcely matter if the network isn't interested in systemic change—if it just wants to frighten or humiliate or make a splash—or if it doesn't need to think strategically. But if you're taking on a powerful and organized establishment you have to be a hierarchy. The Montgomery bus boycott required the participation of tens of thousands of people who depended on public transit to get to and from work each day. It lasted a *year*. In order to persuade those people to stay true to the cause, the boycott's organizers tasked each local black church with maintaining morale, and put together a free alternative private carpool service, with forty-eight dispatchers and forty-two pickup stations. Even the White Citizens Council, King later said, conceded that the carpool system moved with "military precision." By the time King came to Birmingham, for the climactic showdown with Police Commissioner Eugene (Bull) Connor, he had a budget of a million dollars, and a hundred full-time staff members on the ground, divided into operational units. The operation itself was divided into steadily escalating phases, mapped out in advance. Support was maintained through consecutive mass meetings rotating from church to church around the city.

Boycotts and sit-ins and nonviolent confrontations—which were the weapons of choice for the civil-rights movement—are high-risk strategies. They leave little room for conflict and error. The moment even one protester deviates from the script and responds to provocation, the moral legitimacy of the entire protest is compromised. Enthusiasts for social media would no doubt have us believe that King's task in Birmingham would have been made infinitely easier had he been able to communicate with his followers through Facebook, and contented himself with tweets from a Birmingham jail. But networks are messy: think of the ceaseless pattern of correction and revision, amendment and debate, that characterizes Wikipedia. If Martin Luther King, Jr., had tried to do a wiki-boycott in Montgomery, he would have been steamrollered by the white power structure. And of what use would a digital communication tool be in a town where ninety-eight percent of the black community could be reached every Sunday morning at church? The things that King needed in Birmingham—discipline and strategy—were things that online social media cannot provide.

The bible of the social-media movement is Clay Shirky's *Here Comes Everybody*. Shirky, who teaches at New York University, sets out to demonstrate the organizing power of the Internet, and he begins with the story of Evan, who worked on Wall Street, and his friend Ivanna, after she left her smart phone, an expensive Sidekick, on the back seat of a New York City taxicab. The telephone company transferred the data on Ivanna's lost phone to a new phone, whereupon she and Evan discovered that the Sidekick was now in the hands of a teenager from Queens, who was using it to take photographs of herself and her friends.

When Evan e-mailed the teenager, Sasha, asking for the phone 30 back, she replied that his "white ass" didn't deserve to have it back. Miffed, he set up a Web page with her picture and a description of what had happened. He forwarded the link to his friends, and they forwarded it to their friends. Someone found the MySpace page of Sasha's boyfriend, and a link to it found its way onto the site. Someone found her address online and took a video of her home while driving by; Evan posted the video on the site. The story was picked up by the news filter Digg. Evan was now up to ten e-mails a minute. He created a bulletin board for his readers to share their stories, but it crashed under the weight of responses. Evan and Ivanna went to the police, but the police filed the report under "lost," rather than "stolen," which essentially closed the case. "By this point millions of readers were watching," Shirky writes, "and dozens of mainstream news outlets had covered the story." Bowing to the pressure, the NYPD reclassified the item as "stolen." Sasha was arrested, and Evan got his friend's Sidekick back.

Shirky's argument is that this is the kind of thing that could never have happened in the pre-Internet age—and he's right. Evan could never have tracked down Sasha. The story of the Sidekick would never have been publicized. An army of people could never have been assembled to wage this fight. The police wouldn't have bowed to the pressure of a lone person who had misplaced something as trivial as a cell phone. The story, to Shirky, illustrates "the ease and speed with which a group can be mobilized for the right kind of cause" in the Internet age.

Shirky considers this model of activism an upgrade. But it is simply a form of organizing which favors the weak-tie connections that give us access to information over the strong-tie connections that help us persevere in the face of danger. It shifts our energies from organizations that promote strategic and disciplined activity and toward those which promote resilience and adaptability. It makes it easier for activists to express themselves, and harder for that expression to have any impact. The instruments of social media are well suited to making the existing social order more efficient. They are not a natural enemy of the status quo. If you are of the opinion that all the world needs is a little buffing around the edges, this should not trouble you. But if you think that there are still lunch counters out there that need integrating it ought to give you pause.

Shirky ends the story of the lost Sidekick by asking, portentously, "What happens next?"—no doubt imagining future waves of digital protesters. But he has already answered the question. What happens next is more of the same. A networked, weak-tie world is good at things like helping Wall Streeters get phones back from teenage girls. *Viva la revolución.*

For Discussion and Writing

1. What idea about social media is Gladwell arguing against?
2. The most important comparison Gladwell makes here is between revolutionary moments pre- and post-Internet. How does he use this comparison not only to make his point but also to structure his essay? Imagine other ways in which he could have structured it. How would they have differed? Would they have been less effective?

3. **connections**   Compare Gladwell on social media to Nicholas Carr, in "Is Google Making Us Stupid?" (p. 87), on the Internet. In connection to what nontechnological phenomenon does each discuss his technological topic? What does each have to say about the connection? Ultimately, how does each essay reconsider the nature of both elements of the connection?

4. Reconsider Gladwell's argument from the point of view of someone who believes in the possibility of social media–enabled revolutions. Make your argument both in response to Gladwell's points and examples and with your own. What evidence or proof or logical point supports the case for Twitter revolutions?

5. **looking further**   Gladwell wrote this essay before Occupy Wall Street. Research the Occupy movement, describe social media's role(s), and consider whether including Occupy, if Gladwell had written this essay after its inception, would bolster or undermine his argument.

CRISTINA HENRÍQUEZ

Lunch

Cristina Henríquez is an award-winning American author. She has published three books, including, most recently, The Book of Unknown Americas *(2014), which was a* New York Times *Notable Book and was nominated for the Andrew Carnegie Medal for Excellence in Fiction. Henríquez has also published both stories and essays in the* New Yorker, *the* Atlantic, *and* Ploughshares, *and her work has been anthologized in several collections.*

"Lunch" appeared in the September 2007 issue of the New Yorker *as one of a group of essays about food and family. As you read it, pay attention to the way a story about a meal is really about family and much more.*

This is odd

In Panama, family dinners happen at lunchtime. At least, in my family they did. This was something I learned as a young girl when we took summer vacations to the country where my father had lived until, with two worn suitcases and a student visa in hand, he left to study chemical engineering at the University of Delaware. There was never any discussion of alternative destinations, and I looked forward to the trips because of how different everything seemed from the United States and how, year after year, so much in Panama remained the same.

We stayed at my grandparents' house, a two-story building not far from Panama City's financial district with twisted pink columns like candy and a wavy red clay roof like the ruffled edge of lasagna. In the morning, I would lie in the small bedroom I shared with my brother and sister—a circulating fan perched on a wooden chair, hens in the back yard cawing, sunlight pouring in through the gauzy curtains—and inhale the sharp smell of garlic as it wafted through the house, the signal that my grandmother had already begun her lunch preparations. I would wander out in my nightgown and flip-flops to find her in a thin housecoat and a

182

baseball cap, hunched over the stove, stirring a gigantic pot of the meal she made every day: *sancocho*.

Sancocho is a traditional Latin American soup, and my grandmother crafted her version out of yucca, *ñame, otoe, culantro,* garlic, oregano, a stumpy cob of corn, chicken feet, a chicken neck, and chicken meat. Alongside it, she served plantains and rice that she cooked in a cast-aluminum *paila*, intentionally burning the grains at the bottom in hot oil.

Two aunts, two uncles, six cousins, and at least a dozen friends so intimate that we called them family also lived in Panama City, so every day my grandmother set two tables—one in the kitchen and one in the adjacent dining room—in case anyone should stop by. She dressed the tables with her best silverware, plastic placemats, plastic tablecloths, plastic napkin holders, plastic toothpick dispensers, drinking glasses emblazoned with worn World Cup decals, and salt shakers cut with dry rice to keep the salt from clumping in the humid air. She filled the glasses with water or Coca-Cola and covered them with coasters to keep the flies at bay. At every place setting, she turned melamine bowls, like miniature igloos, over packed mounds of rice on matching plates.

It was a boisterous time of day, with everyone talking across rooms, reaching for food, and laughing. It seemed all the more so because, until my Spanish improved, in high school, to me the noise was just that—noise—rising up around me like puffs of smoke. My grandfather removed his work shirt and cufflinks, and ate in a white ribbed tank, grinning underneath his silver mustache, regaling everyone with the news of the day and tales of politics, all of which I heard secondhand, translated by my mother. My grandmother went from one table to the other, making sure everyone was fed.

Much of this was the sort of thing we might have done at home in the United States, of course. My mother cooked dishes like pepper steak, Shake 'n Bake chicken, and spaghetti; we set the table, laid out silverware, ate rapaciously, and, with five people in the house, had our share of spirited conversation. But at home those activities were a cue to start winding down for the evening—to finish our homework, watch something on television, put on our pajamas. In Panama, it was still the middle of the day. By the time dinner rolled around, no one sat together at the table. We were expected to fend for ourselves.

sucks when this happens

My grandfather died five years ago, and since then our lunchtime ceremony has never quite been the same. My grandmother moved into my aunt's house, on the opposite side of the city. She cooks in a different kitchen now, and no one comes home for lunch anymore, because it's too far from people's jobs.

good time with Gram

The last time I visited was also the first time I had travelled to Panama by myself. My grandmother and I sat together in the midday heat and shared Chinese food, the leftovers from my dinner at a restaurant the night before. The dog, who was our only companion, stretched out under the table, cooling his belly against the floor. I warmed two plates of mixed vegetables and tofu in the microwave and slid one in front of my grandmother. She studied it for a long time. Finally, she speared the tofu with a fork and tentatively put it to her lips. When she tasted it, she grimaced.

For Discussion and Writing

1. Where did the author live at the time the essay begins? Where does the lunch of the title happen?

2. This essay is quite brief but also quite rich and vivid. This is so in part because of the author's use of detail and imagery. Make a list of the different kinds of details and sensory images used in the essay. Then break the list down by what the details pertain to—the food itself, or the table and eating of the food, or clothing, or people. What effects do the details make possible? What do they tell us about the different things they illustrate?

3. **connections**   Read Henríquez's essay with Audre Lorde's "The Fourth of July" (p. 221). How can you compare and contrast the significance of food and the occasions for eating it in the two essays? To what larger social issues does eating connect in each?

4. Write about something from your own memories of food—from your own home, or visits to friends or relatives. Can you think of times when food was important and different from what you or others you know normally ate? What stands out? The food? The way it was served and eaten? If you don't remember anything like this, write about how food was prepared and eaten in your childhood. What did it mean? What does it mean to you now?

5. **looking further**   Read up on the cultural meaning of food and rituals surrounding eating. Anthropology is a good place to start. What are the most important things about food across cultures? What are the important differences between cultures?

LANGSTON HUGHES

Salvation

Born in 1902 in Joplin, Missouri, Langston Hughes became a major figure in the Harlem Renaissance, a flowering of African American literature, art, music, and scholarship in the 1920s and 1930s. He was first and foremost a poet, incorporating the vernacular of the streets and the rhythms of the jazz clubs into his voice. He was also a playwright, a fiction writer, an essayist, and an autobiographer. In "Salvation" we can see the skills with which Hughes created imaginative literature; here, in nonfiction, he both tells the story of an important point in his life and makes his readers think about significant ideas, doing so poetically and with great economy and expressiveness. As you read, keep the essay's title in the back of your head, and think about why Hughes might have chosen it.

I was saved from sin when I was going on thirteen. But not really saved. It happened like this. There was a big revival at my Auntie Reed's church. Every night for weeks there had been much preaching, singing, praying, and shouting, and some very hardened sinners had been brought to Christ, and the membership of the church had grown by leaps and bounds. Then just before the revival ended, they held a special meeting for children, "to bring the young lambs to the fold." My aunt spoke of it for days ahead. That night I was escorted to the front row and placed on the mourners' bench with all the other young sinners, who had not yet been brought to Jesus.

My aunt told me that when you were saved you saw a light, and something happened to you inside! And Jesus came into your life! And God was with you from then on! She said you could see and hear and feel Jesus in your soul. I believed her. I had heard a great many old people say the same thing and it seemed to me they ought to know. So I sat there calmly in the hot, crowded church, waiting for Jesus to come to me.

185

The preacher preached a wonderful rhythmical sermon, all moans and shouts and lonely cries and dire pictures of hell, and then he sang a song about the ninety and nine safe in the fold, but one little lamb was left out in the cold. Then he said: "Won't you come? Won't you come to Jesus? Young lambs, won't you come?" And he held out his arms to all us young sinners there on the mourners' bench. And the little girls cried. And some of them jumped up and went to Jesus right away. But most of us just sat there.

A great many old people came and knelt around us and prayed, old women with jet-black faces and braided hair, old men with work-gnarled hands. And the church sang a song about the lower lights are burning, some poor sinners to be saved. And the whole building rocked with prayer and song.

Still I kept waiting to *see* Jesus.   5

Finally all the young people had gone to the altar and were saved, but one boy and me. He was a rounder's son named Westley. Westley and I were surrounded by sisters and deacons praying. It was very hot in the church, and getting late now. Finally Westley said to me in a whisper: "God damn! I'm tired o' sitting here. Let's get up and be saved." So he got up and was saved.

Then I was left all alone on the mourners' bench. My aunt came and knelt at my knees and cried, while prayers and songs swirled all around me in the little church. The whole congregation prayed for me alone, in a mighty wail of moans and voices. And I kept waiting serenely for Jesus, waiting, waiting—but he didn't come. I wanted to see him, but nothing happened to me. Nothing! I wanted something to happen to me, but nothing happened.

I heard the songs and the minister saying: "Why don't you come? My dear child, why don't you come to Jesus? Jesus is wait-ing for you. He wants you. Why don't you come? Sister Reed, what is this child's name?"

"Langston," my aunt sobbed.

"Langston, why don't you come? Why don't you come and be   10 saved? Oh, Lamb of God! Why don't you come?"

Now it was really getting late. I began to be ashamed of myself, holding everything up so long. I began to wonder what God thought about Westley, who certainly hadn't seen Jesus either, but who was now sitting proudly on the platform, swinging his knick-erbockered legs and grinning down at me, surrounded by deacons and old women on their knees praying. God had not struck Westley dead for taking his name in vain or for lying in the temple. So I decided that maybe to save further trouble, I'd better lie, too, and say that Jesus had come, and get up and be saved.

So I got up.

Suddenly the whole room broke into a sea of shouting, as they saw me rise. Waves of rejoicing swept the place. Women leaped in the air. My aunt threw her arms around me. The minister took me by the hand and led me to the platform.

When things quieted down, in a hushed silence, punctuated by a few ecstatic "Amens," all the new young lambs were blessed in the name of God. Then joyous singing filled the room.

That night, for the last time in my life but one—for I was a big   15
boy twelve years old—I cried. I cried, in bed alone, and couldn't stop. I buried my head under the quilts, but my aunt heard me. She woke up and told my uncle I was crying because the Holy Ghost had come into my life, and because I had seen Jesus. But I was really crying because I couldn't bear to tell her that I had lied, that I had deceived everybody in the church, and I hadn't seen Jesus, and that now I didn't believe there was a Jesus any more, since he didn't come to help me.

For Discussion and Writing

1. Why does Hughes cry that night?
2. Hughes's story is told very briefly; how does that brevity make it more powerful? How might a longer version have been less affecting?
3. **connections**   Compare the feeling the young Hughes has when he is the last child on the bench to the feeling George Orwell has when the crowd follows him in "Shooting an Elephant" (p. 272). What are the effects of being watched on each?
4. Write about a time when you felt your family held certain expectations for you. Was it a positive experience, a negative one, or both? Why?
5. **looking further**   There are people today who profess what some refer to as secular religion. Research this topic, then describe it. If you could speak to the twelve-year-old Langston Hughes, or to the adult Hughes who wrote "Salvation," what might you say to him about it? How would you relate it to the experience he writes about?

ZORA NEALE HURSTON

How It Feels to Be
Colored Me

*Born in 1891 in rural Alabama and raised in Florida, Zora Neale
Hurston arrived in New York at the height of the Harlem Renaissance,
a flowering of African American literature, art, music, and scholarship
in the 1920s and 1930s, and became an active participant, writing stories and coauthoring a play with Langston Hughes. Her interest in the
folk culture of the South, influenced by her studies with noted anthro-
pologist Franz Boas, led to her return to Florida to study her native
community and, eventually, to the work for which she is best known,
the novel* Their Eyes Were Watching God *(1937). When reading "How
It Feels to Be Colored Me," it is interesting to think about Hurston's
statements about race and identity—such as her image of people of different races as different-colored bags stuffed with similar contents—in
the context of this anthropological training.*

I am colored but I offer nothing in the way of extenuating circumstances except the fact that I am the only Negro in the United
States whose grandfather on the mother's side was *not* an Indian
chief.

I remember the very day that I became colored. Up to my thir-
teenth year I lived in the little Negro town of Eatonville, Florida.
It is exclusively a colored town. The only white people I knew
passed through the town going to or coming from Orlando. The
native whites rode dusty horses, the Northern tourists chugged
down the sandy village road in automobiles. The town knew the
Southerners and never stopped cane chewing when they passed.
But the Northerners were something else again. They were peered
at cautiously from behind curtains by the timid. The more ven-
turesome would come out on the porch to watch them go past
and got just as much pleasure out of the tourists as the tourists
got out of the village.

The front porch might seem a daring place for the rest of the town, but it was a gallery seat for me. My favorite place was atop the gate-post. Proscenium box for a born first-nighter. Not only did I enjoy the show, but I didn't mind the actors knowing that I liked it. I usually spoke to them in passing. I'd wave at them and when they returned my salute, I would say something like this: "Howdy-do-well-I-thank-you-where-you-goin'?" Usually automobile or the horse paused at this, and after a queer exchange of compliments, I would probably "go a piece of the way" with them, as we say in farthest Florida. If one of my family happened to come to the front in time to see me, of course negotiations would be rudely broken off. But even so, it is clear that I was the first "welcome-to-our-state" Floridian, and I hope the Miami Chamber of Commerce will please take notice.

During this period, white people differed from colored to me only in that they rode through town and never lived there. They liked to hear me "speak pieces" and sing and wanted to see me dance the parse-me-la, and gave me generously of their small silver for doing these things, which seemed strange to me for I wanted to do them so much that I needed bribing to stop. Only they didn't know it. The colored people gave no dimes. They deplored any joyful tendencies in me, but I was their Zora nevertheless. I belonged to them, to the nearby hotels, to the county—everybody's Zora.

But changes came in the family when I was thirteen, and I was sent to school in Jacksonville. I left Eatonville, the town of the oleanders, as Zora. When I disembarked from the river-boat at Jacksonville, she was no more. It seemed that I had suffered a sea change. I was not Zora of Orange County any more, I was now a little colored girl. I found it out in certain ways. In my heart as well as in the mirror, I became a fast brown—warranted not to rub nor run.

But I am not tragically colored. There is no great sorrow dammed up in my soul, nor lurking behind my eyes. I do not mind at all. I do not belong to the sobbing school of Negrohood who hold that nature somehow has given them a lowdown dirty deal and whose feelings are all hurt about it. Even in the helter-skelter skirmish that is my life, I have seen that the world is to the strong regardless of a little pigmentation more or less. No, I do not weep at the world—I am too busy sharpening my oyster knife.

Someone is always at my elbow reminding me that I am the granddaughter of slaves. It fails to register depression with me. Slavery is sixty years in the past. The operation was successful and the patient is doing well, thank you. The terrible struggle that made me an American out of a potential slave said "On the line!" The Reconstruction said "Get set!"; and the generation before said "Go!" I am off to a flying start and I must not halt in the stretch to look behind and weep. Slavery is the price I paid for civilization, and the choice was not with me. It is a bully adventure and worth all that I have paid through my ancestors for it. No one on earth ever had a greater chance for glory. The world to be won and nothing to be lost. It is thrilling to think—to know that for any act of mine, I shall get twice as much praise or twice as much blame. It is quite exciting to hold the center of the national stage, with the spectators not knowing whether to laugh or to weep.

The position of my white neighbor is much more difficult. No brown specter pulls up a chair beside me when I sit down to eat. No dark ghost thrusts its leg against mine in bed. The game of keeping what one has is never so exciting as the game of getting.

I do not always feel colored. Even now I often achieve the unconscious Zora of Eatonville before the Hegira.[1] I feel most colored when I am thrown against a sharp white background.

For instance at Barnard. "Beside the waters of the Hudson" I feel my race. Among the thousand white persons, I am a dark rock surged upon, and overswept, but through it all, I remain myself. When covered by the waters, I am; and the ebb but reveals me again.

Sometimes it is the other way around. A white person is set down in our midst, but the contrast is just as sharp for me. For instance, when I sit in the drafty basement that is The New World Cabaret with a white person, my color comes. We enter chatting about any little nothing that we have in common and are seated by the jazz waiters. In the abrupt way that jazz orchestras have, this one plunges into a number. It loses no time in circumlocutions, but gets right down to business. It constricts the thorax and splits the heart with its tempo and narcotic harmonies. This

1. **Hegira:** A flight to escape danger. [Ed.]

orchestra grows rambunctious, rears on its hind legs and attacks the tonal veil with primitive fury, rending it, clawing it until it breaks through to the jungle beyond. I follow those heathen— follow them exultingly. I dance wildly inside myself; I yell within, I whoop; I shake my assegai[2] above my head, I hurl it true to the mark yeeeeooww! I am in the jungle and living in the jungle way. My face is painted red and yellow and my body is painted blue. My pulse is throbbing like a war drum. I want to slaughter something—give pain, give death to what, I do not know. But the piece ends. The men of the orchestra wipe their lips and rest their fingers. I creep back slowly to the veneer we call civilization with the last tone and find the white friend sitting motionless in his seat, smoking calmly.

"Good music they have here," he remarks, drumming the table with his fingertips.

Music. The great blobs of purple and red emotion have not touched him. He has only heard what I felt. He is far away and I see him but dimly across the ocean and the continent that have fallen between us. He is so pale with his whiteness then and I am so colored.

At certain times I have no race, I am me. When I set my hat at a certain angle and saunter down Seventh Avenue, Harlem City, feeling as snooty as the lions in front of the Forty-Second Street Library, for instance. So far as my feelings are concerned, Peggy Hopkins Joyce on the Boule Mich with her gorgeous raiment, stately carriage, knees knocking together in a most aristocratic manner, has nothing on me. The cosmic Zora emerges. I belong to no race nor time. I am the eternal feminine with its string of beads.

I have no separate feeling about being an American citizen and   15 colored. I am merely a fragment of the Great Soul that surges within the boundaries. My country, right or wrong.

Sometimes, I feel discriminated against, but it does not make me angry. It merely astonishes me. How can any deny themselves the pleasure of my company? It's beyond me.

But in the main, I feel like a brown bag of miscellany propped against a wall. Against a wall in company with other bags, white,

2. assegai: A spear. [Ed.]

red, and yellow. Pour out the contents, and there is discovered a jumble of small things priceless and worthless. A first-water diamond, an empty spool, bits of broken glass, lengths of string, a key to a door long since crumbled away, a rusty knife-blade, old shoes saved for a road that never was and never will be, a nail bent under the weight of things too heavy for any nail, a dried flower or two still a little fragrant. In your hand is the brown bag. On the ground before you is the jumble it held—so much like the jumble in the bags, could they be emptied, that all might be dumped in a single heap and the bags refilled without altering the content of any greatly. A bit of colored glass more or less would not matter. Perhaps that is how the Great Stuffer of Bags filled them in the first place—who knows?

For Discussion and Writing

1. What point is Hurston trying to make in her first paragraph? *Is* she "the only Negro in the United States whose grandfather on the mother's side was *not* an Indian chief"?

2. Consider Hurston's use of imagination in her descriptions of the white neighbor, her experience at the jazz club, and in the final paragraph. How does she use specific details to ground these flights of imagination? How does she use these imaginative moments to make her points?

3. **connections**   Name an African American writer in this book whom you think Hurston might include in what she calls "the sobbing school of Negrohood" (par. 6). How might he or she answer Hurston's criticism?

4. How do you respond to the conception of race with which Hurston ends her essay? Does it agree with how you understand race?

5. **looking further**   Hurston's reference to "the Great Stuffer of Bags" is not meant to be a serious engagement with religion, but it can be taken as more than a throwaway line. Think (and maybe do a little research) about how conceptions of race have been tied to larger systems of belief, both religious and secular. How have different ideas about the nature of race depended on varying systems of belief about how human beings came to be? Why and in what ways are they different from each other? What do you believe, and why?

THOMAS JEFFERSON

The Declaration of Independence

Born in 1743 in the British colony that is now the state of Virginia, Thomas Jefferson, descendant of one of the first families of Virginia, went on to become a founding father of the nation born out of thirteen united colonies. In addition to being the primary writer of the Declaration of Independence, Jefferson was governor of Virginia, vice president, president (from 1801 to 1809), and founder of the University of Virginia.

The Declaration is more than a historical document. It is a clear and effective piece of writing. We present both an early version and the final document. As you read, note the choices that were made in its writing, in particular the revisions evident in the final draft.

DRAFT OF THE DECLARATION OF INDEPENDENCE

A Declaration of the Representatives
of the UNITED STATES OF AMERICA,
in General Congress Assembled.

When in the course of human events it becomes necessary for a people to advance from that subordination in which they have hitherto remained, & to assume among the powers of the earth the equal & independant station to which the laws of nature & of nature's god entitle them, a decent respect to the opinions of mankind requires that they should declare the causes which impel them to the change.

We hold these truths to be sacred & undeniable; that all men are created equal & independant, that from that equal creation they derive rights inherent & inalienable, among which are the preservation of life, & liberty, & the spirit of happiness; that to secure these ends, governments are instituted among men, deriving their just powers from the consent of the governed; that whenever any form of government shall become destructive of these ends, it is the right of the people to alter or to abolish it, & to institute new government, laying its foundation on such principles & organizing its powers in such form, as to them shall seem most likely to effect their safety & happiness. prudence indeed will dictate that governments long established should not be changed for light & transient causes: and accordingly all experience hath shewn that mankind are more disposed to suffer while evils are sufferable, than to right themselves by abolishing the forms to which they are accustomed. but when a long train of abuses & usurpations, begun at a distinguished period, & pursuing invariably the same object, evinces a design to subject them to arbitrary power, it is their right, it is their duty, to throw off such government & to provide new guards for their future security. such has been the patient sufferance of these colonies; & such is now the necessity which constrains them to expunge their former systems of government. The history of his present majesty, is a history of unremitting injuries and usurpations, among which no one fact stands single or solitary to contradict the uniform tenor of the rest, all of which have in direct object the establishment of an absolute tyranny over these states. to prove this, let facts be submitted to a candid world, for the truth of which we pledge a faith yet unsullied by falsehood.

he has refused his assent to laws the most wholesome and necessary for the public good:

he has forbidden his governors to pass laws of immediate & pressing importance, unless suspended in their operation till his assent should be obtained: and when so suspended, he has neglected utterly to attend to them:

he has refused to pass other laws for the accommodation of large districts of people unless those people would relinquish the right of representation, a right inestimable to them, & formidable to tyrants alone:

he has dissolved Representative houses repeatedly & continually, for opposing with manly firmness his invasions on the rights of the people:

he has refused for a long space of time to cause others to be elected, whereby the legislative powers, incapable of annihilation, have returned to the people at large for their exercise, the state remaining in the mean time exposed to all the dangers of invasion from without, &, convulsions within:

he has suffered the administration of justice totally to cease in some of these colonies, refusing his assent to laws for establishing judiciary powers:

he has made our judges dependant on his will alone, for the tenure of their offices, and amount of their salaries:
he has erected a multitude of new offices by a self-assumed power, & sent hither swarms of officers to harrass our people & eat out their substance: he has kept among us in times of peace standing armies & ships of war:
he has affected to render the military, independent of & superior to the civil power:
he has combined with others to subject us to a jurisdiction foreign to our constitutions and unacknowledged by our laws; giving his assent to their pretended acts of legislation, for quartering large bodies of armed troops among us:
for protecting them by a mock-trial from punishment for any murders they should commit on the inhabitants of these states;
for cutting off our trade with all parts of the world;
for imposing taxes on us without our consent;
for depriving us of the benefits of trial by jury
he has endeavored to prevent the population of these states; for that purpose obstructing the laws for naturalization of foreigners; refusing to pass others to encourage their migrations hither; & raising the conditions of new appropriations of lands;
for transporting us beyond seas to be tried for pretended offences;
for taking away our charters & altering fundamentally the forms of our governments;
for suspending our own legislatures & declaring themselves invested with power to legislate for us in all cases whatsoever;
he has abdicated government here, withdrawing his governors, & declaring us out of his allegiance & protection:
he has plundered our seas, ravaged our coasts, burnt our towns & destroyed the lives of our people:
he is at this time transporting large armies of foreign mercenaries to compleat the works of death, desolation & tyranny, already begun with circumstances of cruelty & perfidy unworthy the head of a civilized nation:
he has endeavored to bring on the inhabitants of our frontiers the merciless Indian savages, whose known rule of warfare is an undistinguished destruction of all ages, sexes, & conditions of existence:
he has incited treasonable insurrections of our fellow-citizens, with the allurements of forfeiture & confiscation of our property:
he has waged cruel war against human nature itself, violating its most sacred rights of life & liberty in the persons of a distant people who never offended him, captivating & carrying them into slavery in another hemisphere, or to incur miserable death in their transportation thither. this piratical warfare, the opprobrium of *infidel* powers, is the warfare of the CHRISTIAN king of Great Britain, determined to keep open a market where MEN should be bought & sold; he has prostituted his negative for

suppressing every legislative attempt to prohibit or to restrain this exe-
crable commerce: and that this assemblage of horrors might want no fact
of distinguished die, he is now exciting those very people to rise in arms
among us, and to purchase that liberty of which *he* has deprived them, by
murdering the people upon whom *he* also obtruded them; thus paying off
former crimes committed against the *liberties* of one people, with crimes
which he urges them to commit against the *lives* of another.

in every stage of these oppressions we have petitioned for redress
in the most humble terms; our repeated petitions have been
answered by repeated injury. a prince whose character is thus
marked by every act which may define a tyrant, is unfit to be the
ruler of a people who mean to be free. future ages will scarce
believe that the hardiness of one man, adventured within the
short compass of twelve years only, on so many acts of tyranny
without a mask, over a people fostered & fixed in principles of
liberty.

Nor have we been wanting in attentions to our British brethren. we have warned them from time to time of attempts by their
legislature to extend a jurisdiction over these our states. we have
reminded them of the circumstances of our emigration & settlement here, no one of which could warrant so strange a preten-
sion: that these were effected at the expence of our own blood &
treasure, unassisted by the wealth or the strength of Great Britain: that in constituting indeed our several forms of government,
we had adopted one common king, thereby laying a foundation
for perpetual league & amity with them; but that submission to
their [Parliament, was no Part of our Constitution, nor ever in
Idea, if History may be] credited: and we appealed to their native
justice & magnanimity, as to the ties of our common kindred to
disavow these usurpations which were likely to interrupt our correspondence & connection. they too have been deaf to the voice
of justice & of consanguinity, & when occasions have been given
them, by the regular course of their laws, of removing from their
councils the disturbers of our harmony, they have by their free
election re-established them in power. at this very time too they are
permitting their chief magistrate to send over not only soldiers of
our common blood, but Scotch & foreign mercenaries to invade &
deluge us in blood. these facts have given the last stab to agonizing affection, and manly spirit bids us to renounce for ever these
unfeeling brethren. we must endeavor to forget our former love

for them, and to hold them as we hold the rest of mankind, enemies in war, in peace friends. we might have been a free & a great people together; but a communication of grandeur & of freedom it seems is below their dignity. be it so, since they will have it: the road to glory & happiness is open to us too; we will climb it in a separate state, and acquiesce in the necessity which pronounces our everlasting Adieu!

We therefore the representatives of the United States of America in General Congress assembled do, in the name & by authority of the good people of these states, reject and renounce all allegiance & subjection to the kings of Great Britain & all others who may hereafter claim by, through, or under them; we utterly dissolve & break off all political connection which may have heretofore subsisted between us & the people or parliament of Great Britain; and finally we do assert and declare these colonies to be free and independant states, and that as free & independant states they shall hereafter have power to levy war, conclude peace, contract alliances, establish commerce, & to do all other acts and things which independant states may of right do. And for the support of this declaration we mutually pledge to each other our lives, our fortunes, & our sacred honor.

THE DECLARATION OF INDEPENDENCE

In Congress, July 4, 1776
The Unanimous Declaration of the
Thirteen United States of America

When in the Course of human events it becomes necessary for   5
one people to dissolve the political bands which have connected them with another, and to assume among the powers of the earth, the separate and equal station to which the Laws of Nature and of Nature's God entitle them, a decent respect to the opinions of mankind requires that they should declare the causes which impel them to the separation.

We hold these truths to be self-evident, that all men are created equal, that they are endowed by their Creator with certain unalienable Rights, that among these are Life, Liberty, and the pursuit of Happiness. That to secure these rights, Governments are instituted among Men, deriving their just powers from the consent of the governed. That whenever any Form of Government becomes destructive of these ends, it is the Right of the People to alter or to abolish it, and to institute new Government, laying its foundation on such principles and organizing its powers in such form, as to them shall seem most likely to effect their Safety and Happiness. Prudence, indeed, will dictate that Governments long established should not be changed for light and transient causes; and accordingly all experience hath shewn that mankind are more disposed to suffer, while evils are sufferable, than right themselves by abolishing the forms to which they are accustomed. But when a long train of abuses and usurpations, pursuing invariably the same Object evinces a design to reduce them under absolute Despotism, it is their right, it is their duty, to throw off such Government, and to provide new Guards for their future security. Such has been the patient sufferance of these Colonies; and such is now the necessity which constrains them to alter their former Systems of Government. The history of the present King of Great Britain is a history of repeated injuries and usurpations, all having in direct object the establishment of an absolute Tyranny over these States. To prove this, let Facts be submitted to a candid world.

He has refused his Assent to Laws, the most wholesome and necessary for the public good.

He has forbidden his Government to pass laws of immediate and pressing importance, unless suspended in their operation till his Assent should be obtained; and when so suspended, he has utterly neglected to attend to them.

He has refused to pass other Laws for the accommodation of large districts of people, unless those people would relinquish the right of Representation in the Legislature, a right inestimable to them and formidable to tyrants only.

He has called together legislative bodies at places unusual, 10 uncomfortable, and distant from the depository of their Public Records, for the sole purpose of fatiguing them into compliance with his measures.

He has dissolved Representative Houses repeatedly, for opposing with manly firmness his invasions on the rights of the people.

He has refused for a long time, after such dissolutions, to cause others to be elected; whereby the Legislative Powers, incapable of

Annihilation, have returned to the People at large for their exercise; the State remaining in the mean time exposed to all the dangers of invasion from without, and convulsions within.

He has endeavored to prevent the population of these States; for that purpose obstructing the Laws for Naturalization of Foreigners; refusing to pass others to encourage their migration hither, and raising the conditions of new Appropriations of Lands.

He has obstructed the Administration of Justice, by refusing his Assent to Laws for establishing Judiciary Powers.

He has made Judges dependent on his Will alone, for the tenure   15
of their offices, and the amount and payment of their salaries.

He has erected a multitude of New Offices, and sent hither swarms of Officers to harass our people, and eat out their substance.

He has kept among us, in times of peace, Standing Armies without the Consent of our legislatures.

He has affected to render the Military independent of and superior to the Civil Power.

He has combined with others to subject us to a jurisdiction foreign to our constitution, and unacknowledged by our laws; giving his Assent to their Acts of pretended Legislation: For quartering large bodies of armed troops among us: For protecting them, by a mock Trial, from punishment for any Murders which they should commit on the Inhabitants of these States: For cutting off our Trade with all parts of the world: For imposing Taxes on us without our Consent: For depriving us in many cases, of the benefits of Trial by Jury: For transporting us beyond Seas to be tried for pretended offenses: for abolishing the free System of English Laws in a neighboring Province, establishing therein an Arbitrary government, and enlarging its Boundaries so as to render it at once an example and fit instrument for introducing the same absolute rule into these Colonies: For taking away our Charters, abolishing our most valuable Laws and altering fundamentally the Forms of our Governments: For suspending our own Legislatures, and declaring themselves invested with power to legislate for us in all cases whatsoever.

He has abdicated Government here, by declaring us out of his   20
Protection and waging War against us.

He has plundered our seas, ravaged our Coasts, burnt our towns, and destroyed the lives of our people.

He is at this time transporting large Armies of foreign Mercenaries to complete the works of death, desolation and tyranny, already begun with circumstances of Cruelty & Perfidy scarcely paralleled in the most barbarous ages, and totally unworthy the Head of a civilized nation.

He has constrained our fellow Citizens taken Captive on the high Seas to bear Arms against their Country, to become the executioners of their friends and Brethren, or to fall themselves by their Hands.

He has excited domestic insurrections amongst us, and has endeavored to bring on the inhabitants of our frontiers, the merciless Indian Savages, whose known rule of warfare, is an undistinguished destruction of all ages, sexes, and conditions.

In every stage of these Oppressions We have Petitioned for 25 Redress in the most humble terms: Our repeated Petitions have been answered only by repeated injury. A Prince, whose character is thus marked by every act which may define a Tyrant, is unfit to be the ruler of a free people.

Nor have We been wanting in attention to our British brethren. We have warned them from time to time of attempts by their legislature to extend an unwarrantable jurisdiction over us. We have reminded them of the circumstances of our emigration and settlement here. We have appealed to their native justice and magnanimity, and we have conjured them by the ties of our common kindred to disavow these usurpations, which would inevitably interrupt our connections and correspondence. They too have been deaf to the voice of justice and of consanguinity. We must, therefore, acquiesce in the necessity, which denounces our Separation, and hold them, as we hold the rest of mankind, Enemies in War, in Peace Friends.

We, THEREFORE the Representatives of the UNITED STATES OF AMERICA, in General Congress, Assembled, appealing to the Supreme Judge of the world for the rectitude of our intentions, do, in the Name, and by Authority of the good People of these Colonies, solemnly publish and declare, That these United Colonies are, and of Right ought to be FREE AND INDEPENDENT STATES; that they are Absolved from all Allegiance to the British Crown, and that all political connection between them and the State of Great Britain, is and ought to be totally dissolved; and that as Free and Independent States, they have full Power to levy War, conclude Peace, contract Alliances, establish Commerce, and to do all other Acts and Things which Independent States may of right do. And for the support of this Declaration, with a firm reliance on the protection of Divine Providence, we mutually pledge to each other our Lives, our Fortunes, and our sacred Honor.

For Discussion and Writing

1. How many examples of wrongs done by the Crown to the colonies are offered here? What is the effect of this list?

2. In small groups, compile lists of all of the differences between the first and second drafts of the Declaration. Write up a summary of these changes and an analysis of how they make the final document more effective.

3. **connections**   Compare the Declaration and George Orwell's "Shooting an Elephant" (p. 272). How do these two condemnations of the British Empire differ?

4. Think about America today. From your personal experience and observations, discuss how it meets the promise of the opening of the Declaration's second paragraph, and how it does not.

5. **looking further**   One of the stated rationales behind American intervention in the affairs of other nations, historically, has been the idea that other peoples want to live under the same kind of system of government that the Declaration helped establish in the United States. Keeping in mind the many, far-flung places where this dynamic has played out (and doing some research if you need to), which elements of the Declaration might have appealed to these peoples? Which elements might be more problematic?

CAMDEN JOY

Surviving Sinatra

Camden Joy is the pen name Tom Adelman first used in the mid-1990s for his New York City postering projects and pamphlets. His work, which blurs the lines between fiction, music criticism, and memoir, has appeared in periodicals such as the Boston Phoenix, *the* Village Voice, *and* McSweeney's *and on public radio's* This American Life. *He is the author of five novels and novellas—including* The Last Rock Star Book or Liz Phair: A Rant *(1998)—and* Lost Joy *(2002), a collection of stories, pamphlets, and posters. Recently, Adelman has authored two books on baseball under his own name.*

"Surviving Sinatra" first appeared on public radio's This American Life *before being included in Joy's collection of short stories,* Lost Joy. *In it, he describes the danger of combining Frank Sinatra with Turkish kebabs.*

Recently a roomful of people were almost killed by Frank Sinatra.

The scene was a Turkish kabob house in lower Manhattan. This is my neighborhood hang-out; the sort of place where only the employees are permitted to smoke, and the walls are amply coated in grease. I go there because so do a lot of others, Muslim cabbies on their breaks, fashion students from Kyoto, elegant immigrants from Teheran, techno gals in floor-length flares and techno boys in ball caps with bent-down brims.

So there we all were the other day, eating grilled lamb and deep-fried balls of chick peas off styrofoam plates with plastic forks and knives, when suddenly we heard a new sound—a television! Now many of you have already seen televisions, and most of us had too, but the surprise of it in my local kabob-ery was that thus far we'd only heard Turkish radio. So with all due respect we turned to look at it, as tradition tells you to do whenever anyone switches on a television in your presence.

There was a black and white movie. There was a man twitching on a train. There was a woman wearing pearls and a great deal of mascara, hairspray, and lipstick. There was Janet Leigh. And there was Frank Sinatra.

There are moments in a crowd when America makes so much 5
sense, when you want to scream BRING ME YOUR TIRED, YOUR POOR, YOUR HUNGRY, AND LET'S ALL DIG FRANK SINATRA. I mean to say, this was one such moment.

So all of us fell silent, as again custom holds is the courteous thing to do when a television plays in a public setting, and through the steam of onions browning in olive oil we watched *The Manchurian Candidate.*

Now I have always wondered why you can never go into a place and hear my favorite Sinatra albums, his sad albums like *No One Cares* or *In the Wee Small Hours*, and instead you only hear songs like "New York, New York." Well, there's a reason, and it's the same reason restaurants have to be careful when his movies are on TV—it's a possible Health Code Violation: you can die from Sinatra.

In the movie, Sinatra is coming apart. He sets a cigarette between his lips, and it falls into his scotch and water. He looks around, embarrassed. Only Janet Leigh is watching. He tries to light a match, drops it, manages to light one—but his hands shake too badly and the match goes out. He asks Janet Leigh whether she minds if he smokes and their eyes meet and they fall in love. She tells him she doesn't mind at all, please do. He tries to light one up again, looks like he's going to vomit, bursts out of his chair, knocks over his drink, and runs.

There in the Turkish kabob house, our mouths were full of babaghannush and hummus and chopped beef and baby lamb . . . but all of us had stopped chewing. We were too struck by what we were seeing: a man we all recognized—that famous widow's peak, that trim waist, those eyebrows drifting up there on his forehead like lost rainclouds—was on the television about to break down.

People will tell you Sinatra and Elvis Presley were similiar tal- 10
ents in that they both sang and acted well; but the fact is, there's no picture Elvis ever shot which didn't obligate him to do songs, whereas Sinatra made most of his movies without singing. In

fact, in the movie we were all watching, he was about as far from bursting into song as anybody can be.

Sinatra has tried to flee the woman but she follows him. She is clever and gorgeous. Her eyes are dark as Turkish coffee and her voice like baklava. She asks him where his home is. He can't look at her. He seems to be thinking: *She doesn't know what she's doing.* His voice catches on every syllable as he tells her he's in the army. His eyelids flutter. He sucks on the cigarette she has lit for him. Some part of him is dying to get out of the conversation but that part of him is losing the battle. Softly he asks Janet Leigh for her name, in such a way that it's clear her name is the one thing he's always had to know. But he's even more confused by her answer. He sighs, apparently at everything—the magnitude of life, of conversations, the sheer difficulty of what names we should call one another.

We all know people who hate Frank Sinatra for all sorts of reasons, mostly for how he treats other human beings in so-called real life, and they dismiss the undeniable beauty of his talent because of his undeniably sick soul. I wonder if these people had been in the Turkish kabob house with us what they would think seeing this scene, in which Janet Leigh, acting entirely on our behalf, reaches out to save this fragile bird-boned boy. As with his best albums, Sinatra doesn't seem to be going from any script. There aren't printed-up lyrics and dialogue for this kind of thing. This isn't acting; it's the real stuff. He is standing before us, letting his feelings utterly overwhelm him. It's scary. Perhaps Frank Sinatra is a bad person but he defines the word "presence." In this scene, he says almost nothing, he exhales and sweats and looks away, and yet Janet Leigh, who does all the talking, seems barely alive by comparison.

It's time I mention what else was happening in our Turkish kabob house and that was that all of us—employees, bike messengers, cabbies—felt Sinatra's confusion so completely that we ourselves were about to cry . . . we would have been crying, that is, if our throats weren't clogged up with Turkish cuisine. Sinatra can barely talk. We could barely breathe.

On the television, Janet Leigh starts to tell Sinatra who she is, then she stops, instead tells him her address, tells him the apartment number, her phone number. She gently asks him if he can remember it. His larynx closes up as he tells her, yes. You aren't sure how to take this response because he still can't look at her. Janet Leigh repeats the phone number and he turns even further from her, shakes his head slightly, closes his eyes in weariness.

In that moment, finally, after attentively watching this, the 15 whole group of us in the kabob-ery began to cough. Most everyone was choking back tears but by this time many of us were choking on shish kebab too, great wads of barbecued meat stuck somewhere mid-swallow. We were gagging into napkins, downing our sodas, poking ourselves in the ribs, crossing our hands at our throats. The look of serious injury was on everybody's face and then, abruptly, just like that, it was gone. We were okay, we would be fine. We looked up at the television. Sinatra, our would-be killer, was breathing easier too.

For Discussion and Writing

1. How does Sinatra almost kill a roomful of people, as described in this essay?

2. The author makes ample use of irony in this essay. Make a list of its appearances. How does the author use it? What are its effects, in the moments of use and for the essay as a whole?

3. **connections**   Think about this essay in the light of Joan Didion's "On Keeping a Notebook" (p. 116). While "Surviving Sinatra" is about a movie being watched in a crowded restaurant and "On Keeping a Notebook" is about the author's use of a notebook, the two essays share similar perspectives. In what ways does "Surviving Sinatra" reflect what Didion says her notebook is about? What does this essay tell us about its author?

4. Think of a moment when you have been deeply affected by a work of art—a movie, or book, or song, or work of visual art. Describe that moment, and the surroundings, and try to re-create how that moment felt. What might the moment and the feeling tell you about yourself? About art?

5. **looking further**   The movie that figures in the story Joy tells in this essay is *The Manchurian Candidate*. It is an interesting work in the history of film and in the history of American culture. Read up on *The Manchurian Candidate*. What makes it interesting artistically, and in terms of its production and reception? What makes it interesting in terms of the historical era in which it was made?

JAMAICA KINCAID

The Ugly Tourist

Jamaica Kincaid was born Elaine Potter Richardson in Antigua in 1949 and raised there until she left for New York when she was seventeen. Working as a domestic, she returned to school, earned her high school and college degrees, and returned to New York to write, where under her new name she eventually became a staff writer for the New Yorker. *She is the author of fifteen books of poetry, fiction, and nonfiction about her Caribbean home, her family, and gardening, among other topics, including* At the Bottom of the River *(1983),* Annie John *(1985),* Lucy *(1990),* The Autobiography of My Mother *(1996),* My Brother *(1997), and* See Now Then *(2013).*

"The Ugly Tourist," which originally appeared in Harper's *in 1988, became the opening chapter of* A Small Place. *The editor of the* New Yorker *rejected the essay as "too angry," and when the full book appeared many of the reviews agreed. However, many did not, finding the book's tone appropriate to its subject. As you read, put yourself in the shoes of these editors and reviewers. Would you have accepted "The Ugly Tourist" for publication? What kind of review would you have given it?*

no indent

The thing you have always suspected about yourself the minute you become a tourist is true: a tourist is an ugly human being. You are not an ugly person all the time; you are not an ugly person ordinarily; you are not an ugly person day to day. From day to day, you are a nice person. From day to day, all the people who are supposed to love you on the whole do. From day to day, as you walk down a busy street in the large and modern and prosperous city in which you work and live, dismayed, puzzled (a cliché, but only a cliché can explain you) at how alone you feel in this crowd, how awful it is to go unnoticed, how awful it is to go unloved, even as you are surrounded by more people than you could possibly get to know in a lifetime that lasted for millennia, and then out of the corner of your eye you see someone looking at you and

First paragraph

206

absolute pleasure is written all over that person's face, and then
you realise that you are not as revolting a presence as you think
you are (for that look just told you so). And so, ordinarily, you are
a nice person, an attractive person, a person capable of drawing to
yourself the affection of other people (people just like you), a person at home in your own skin (sort of; I mean, in a way; I mean,
your dismay and puzzlement are natural to you, because people
like you just seem to be like that, and so many of the things people
like you find admirable about yourselves—the things you think
about, the things you think really define you—seem rooted in
these feelings): a person at home in your own house (and all
its nice house things), with its nice back yard (and its nice backyard things), at home on your street, your church, in community
activities, your job, at home with your family, your relatives, your
friends—you are a whole person. But one day, when you are sitting somewhere, alone in that crowd, and that awful feeling of
displacedness comes over you, and really, as an ordinary person
you are not well equipped to look too far inward and set yourself
aright, because being ordinary is already so taxing, and being
ordinary takes all you have out of you, and though the words "I
must get away" do not actually pass across your lips, you make a
leap from being that nice blob just sitting like a boob in your
amniotic sac of the modern experience to being a person visiting
heaps of death and ruin and feeling alive and inspired at the sight
of it; to being a person lying on some faraway beach, your stilled
body stinking and glistening in the sand, looking like something
first forgotten, then remembered, then not important enough to
go back for; to being a person marvelling at the harmony (ordinarily, what you would say is the backwardness) and the union
these other people (and they are other people) have with nature.
And you look at the things they can do with a piece of ordinary
cloth, the things they fashion out of cheap, vulgarly colored (to
you) twine, the way they squat down over a hole they have made
in the ground, the hole itself is something to marvel at, and since
you are being an ugly person this ugly but joyful thought will
swell inside you: their ancestors were not clever in the way yours
were and not ruthless in the way yours were, for then would it not
be you who would be in harmony with nature and backwards in
that charming way? An ugly thing, that is what you are when you
become a tourist, an ugly, empty thing, a stupid thing, a piece of

rubbish pausing here and there to gaze at this and taste that, and it will never occur to you that the people who inhabit the place in which you have just passed cannot stand you, that behind their closed doors they laugh at your strangeness (you do not look the way they look); the physical sight of you does not please them; you have bad manners (it is their custom to eat their food with their hands; you try eating their way, you look silly; you try eating the way you always eat, you look silly); they do not like the way you speak (you have an accent); they collapse helpless from laughter, mimicking the way they imagine you must look as you carry out some everyday bodily function. They do not like you. *They do not like me!* That thought never actually occurs to you. Still, you feel a little uneasy. Still, you feel a little foolish. Still, you feel a little out of place. But the banality of your own life is very real to you; it drove you to this extreme, spending your days and your nights in the company of people who despise you, people you do not like really, people you would not want to have as your actual neighbour. And so you must devote yourself to puzzling out how much of what you are told is really, really true (Is ground-up bottle glass in peanut sauce really a delicacy around here, or will it do just what you think ground-up bottle glass will do? Is this rare, multicoloured, snout-mouthed fish really an aphrodisiac, or will it cause you to fall asleep permanently?). Oh, the hard work all of this is, and is it any wonder, then, that on your return home you feel the need of a long rest, so that you can recover from your life as a tourist?

That the native does not like the tourist is not hard to explain. For every native of every place is a potential tourist, and every tourist is a native of somewhere. Every native everywhere lives a life of overwhelming and crushing banality and boredom and desperation and depression, and every deed, good and bad, is an attempt to forget this. Every native would like to find a way out, every native would like a rest, every native would like a tour. But some natives—most natives in the world—cannot go anywhere. They are too poor. They are too poor to go anywhere. They are too poor to escape the reality of their lives; and they are too poor to live properly in the place where they live, which is the very place you, the tourist, want to go—so when the natives see you, the tourist, they envy you, they envy your ability to leave your own banality and boredom, they envy your ability to turn their own banality and boredom into a source of pleasure for yourself.

For Discussion and Writing

1. What does Kincaid argue is wrong with how tourists think of natives?

2. In addition to its brevity, what is notable about "The Ugly Tourist" is the length of its first paragraph. What is the effect of reading such a long paragraph? Why do you think Kincaid chose to write it that way?

3. **connections**   Read Kincaid's essay next to Barbara Ehrenreich's "Serving in Florida" (p. 136). How are both about tourism? How are both about class? What can the differences between the two tell us about each?

4. Write about a trip you have taken; it can be to another town or state, or even another part of your town—it doesn't have to be to another country. How did it feel to be a tourist? Did anything in your experience relate to Kincaid's description of tourism? Alternatively, write about a time when you have felt like a native in the presence of people from elsewhere visiting your home.

5. **looking further**   Kincaid argues that it is a recognition of the "banality and boredom" (par. 2) of their lives that leads people to visit other parts of the world. Imagine a counterargument to Kincaid's. Are there other reasons to want to see the rest of the world? How would you compare them to the one Kincaid assumes?

STEPHEN KING

Reading to Write

Stephen King was born in 1947 in Portland, Maine, and raised in Maine, Wisconsin, Indiana, and Connecticut. He has authored dozens of novels of horror, suspense, and science fiction, nine collections' worth of short stories, and five books of nonfiction; many of his novels and stories have been made into films, including Carrie *(1976),* The Shining *(1980),* Stand by Me *(1986),* Misery *(1990),* The Shawshank Redemption *(1994), and* The Green Mile *(1999). While often thought of as a genre writer—someone who writes the kinds of popular stories (like horror or science fiction, in his case) that are not quite considered literary fiction—his work has increasingly been met with critical praise.*

"Reading to Write" is taken from King's book On Writing: A Memoir of the Craft *(2000). In it, this amazingly prolific writer gives advice about writing that ends up being as much about how to use one's time as it is about specific recommended activities. As you read, see if you can extract an underlying philosophy of life from King's essay.*

To be good at anything

If you want to be a writer, you must do two things above all others: read a lot and write a lot. There's no way around these two things that I'm aware of, no shortcut.

I'm a slow reader, but I usually get through seventy or eighty books a year, mostly fiction. I don't read in order to study the craft; I read because I like to read. It's what I do at night, kicked back in my blue chair. Similarly, I don't read fiction to study the art of fiction, but simply because I like stories. Yet there is a learning process going on. Every book you pick up has its own lesson or lessons, and quite often the bad books have more to teach than the good ones.

When I was in the eighth grade, I happened upon a paperback novel by Murray Leinster, a science fiction pulp writer who did most of his work during the forties and fifties, when magazines like *Amazing Stories* paid a penny a word. I had read other books by Mr. Leinster, enough to know that the quality of his writing

210

was uneven. This particular tale, which was about mining in the asteroid belt, was one of his less successful efforts. Only that's too kind. It was terrible, actually, a story populated by paper-thin characters and driven by outlandish plot developments. Worst of all (or so it seemed to me at the time), Leinster had fallen in love with the word *zestful*. Characters watched the approach of ore-bearing asteroids with *zestful smiles*. Characters sat down to supper aboard their mining ship with *zestful anticipation*. Near the end of the book, the hero swept the large-breasted, blonde heroine into a *zestful embrace*. For me, it was the literary equivalent of a smallpox vaccination: I have never, so far as I know, used the word *zestful* in a novel or a story. God willing, I never will.

Asteroid Miners (which wasn't the title, but that's close enough) was an important book in my life as a reader. Almost everyone can remember losing his/or her virginity, and most writers can remember the first book he/she put down thinking: *I can do better than this. Hell, I am doing better than this!* What could be more encouraging to the struggling writer than to realize his/her work is unquestionably better than that of someone who actually got paid for his/her stuff?

One learns most clearly what not to do by reading bad prose—one novel like *Asteroid Miners* (or *Valley of the Dolls, Flowers in the Attic*, and *The Bridges of Madison County*, to name just a few) is worth a semester at a good writing school, even with the superstar guest lecturers thrown in.

Good writing, on the other hand, teaches the learning writer about style, graceful narration, plot development, the creation of believable characters, and truth-telling. A novel like *The Grapes of Wrath* may fill a new writer with feelings of despair and good old-fashioned jealousy—"I'll never be able to write anything that good, not if I live to be a thousand"—but such feelings can also serve as a spur, goading the writer to work harder and aim higher. Being swept away by a combination of great story and great writing—of being flattened, in fact—is part of every writer's necessary formation. You cannot hope to sweep someone else away by the force of your writing until it has been done to you.

So we read to experience the mediocre and the outright rotten; such experience helps us to recognize those things when they begin to creep into our own work, and to steer clear of them. We also read in order to measure ourselves against the good and the great, to get a sense of all that can be done. And we read in order to experience different styles.

You may find yourself adopting a style you find particularly exciting, and there's nothing wrong with that. When I read Ray Bradbury as a kid, I wrote like Ray Bradbury—everything green and wondrous and seen through a lens smeared with the grease of nostalgia. When I read James M. Cain, everything I wrote came out clipped and stripped and hard-boiled. When I read Lovecraft, my prose became luxurious and Byzantine. I wrote stories in my teenage years where all these styles merged, creating a kind of hilarious stew. This sort of stylistic blending is a necessary part of developing one's own style, but it doesn't occur in a vacuum. You have to read widely, constantly refining (and redefining) your own work as you do so. It's hard for me to believe that people who read very little (or not at all in some cases) should presume to write and expect people to like what they have written, but I know it's true. If I had a nickel for every person who ever told me he/she wanted to become a writer but "didn't have time to read," I could buy myself a pretty good steak dinner. Can I be blunt on this subject? If you don't have time to read, you don't have the time (or the tools) to write. Simple as that.

Reading is the creative center of a writer's life. I take a book with me everywhere I go, and find there are all sorts of opportunities to dip in. The trick is to teach yourself to read in small sips as well as in long swallows. Waiting rooms were made for books— of course! But so are theater lobbies before the show, long and boring checkout lines, and everyone's favorite, the john. You can even read while you're driving, thanks to the audiobook revolution. Of the books I read each year, anywhere from six to a dozen are on tape. As for all the wonderful radio you will be missing, come on—how many times can you listen to Deep Purple sing "Highway Star"?

Reading at meals is considered rude in polite society, but if you 10 expect to succeed as a writer, rudeness should be the second-to-least of your concerns. The least of all should be polite society and what it expects. If you intend to write as truthfully as you can, your days as a member of polite society are numbered, anyway.

Where else can you read? There's always the treadmill, or whatever you use down at the local health club to get aerobic. I try to spend an hour doing that every day, and I think I'd go mad without a good novel to keep me company. Most exercise facilities (at home as well as outside it) are now equipped with TVs, but TV—while working out or anywhere else—really is about the last thing an aspiring writer needs. If you feel you must have the news analyst blowhards on CNN while you exercise, or the stock market blowhards on MSNBC, or the sports blowhards on ESPN, it's time for you to question how serious you really are about becoming a writer. You must be prepared to do some serious turning inward toward the life of the imagination, and that means, I'm afraid, that Geraldo, Keith Olbermann, and Jay Leno must go. Reading takes time, and the glass teat takes too much of it.

Once weaned from the ephemeral craving for TV, most people will find they enjoy the time they spend reading. I'd like to suggest that turning off that endlessly quacking box is apt to improve the quality of your life as well as the quality of your writing. And how much of a sacrifice are we talking about here? How many *Frasier* and *ER* reruns does it take to make one American life complete? How many Richard Simmons infomercials? How many whiteboy/fatboy Beltway insiders on CNN? Oh man, don't get me started. Jerry-Springer-Dr.-Dre-Judge-Judy-Jerry-Falwell-Donny-and-Marie, I rest my case.

When my son Owen was seven or so, he fell in love with Bruce Springsteen's E Street Band, particularly with Clarence Clemons, the band's burly sax player. Owen decided he wanted to learn to play like Clarence. My wife and I were amused and delighted by this ambition. We were also hopeful, as any parent would be, that our kid would turn out to be talented, perhaps even some sort of prodigy. We got Owen a tenor saxophone for Christmas and lessons with Gordon Bowie, one of the local music men. Then we crossed our fingers and hoped for the best.

Seven months later I suggested to my wife that it was time to discontinue the sax lessons, if Owen concurred. Owen did, and with palpable relief—he hadn't wanted to say it himself, especially not after asking for the sax in the first place, but seven months had been long enough for him to realize that, while he might love Clarence Clemons's big sound, the saxophone was simply not for him—God had not given him that particular talent.

I knew, not because Owen stopped practicing, but because he 15 was practicing only during the periods Mr. Bowie had set for him: half an hour after school four days a week, plus an hour on the weekends. Owen mastered the scales and the notes—nothing wrong with his memory, his lungs, or his eye-hand coordination—but we never heard him taking off, surprising himself with something new, blissing himself out. And as soon as his practice time was over, it was back into the case with the horn, and there it stayed until the next lesson or practice time. What this suggested to me was that when it came to the sax and my son, there was never going to be any real playtime; it was all going to be rehearsal. That's no good. If there's no joy in it, it's just no good. It's best to go on to some other area, where the deposits of talent may be richer and the fun quotient higher.

Talent renders the whole idea of rehearsal meaningless; when you find something at which you are talented, you do it (whatever *it* is) until your fingers bleed or your eyes are ready to fall out of your head. Even when no one is listening (or reading, or watching), every outing is a bravura performance, because you as the creator are happy. Perhaps even ecstatic. That goes for reading and writing as well as for playing a musical instrument, hitting a baseball, or running the four-forty. The sort of strenuous reading and writing program I advocate—four to six hours a day, every day—will not seem strenuous if you really enjoy doing these things and have an aptitude for them; in fact, you may be following such a program already. If you feel you need permission to do all the reading and writing your little heart desires, however, consider it hereby granted by yours truly.

The real importance of reading is that it creates an ease and intimacy with the process of writing; one comes to the country of the writer with one's papers and identification pretty much in order. Constant reading will pull you into a place (a mind-set, if you like the phrase) where you can write eagerly and without self-consciousness. It also offers you a constantly growing knowledge of what has been done and what hasn't, what is trite and what is fresh, what works and what just lies there dying (or dead) on the page. The more you read, the less apt you are to make a fool of yourself with your pen or word processor.

For Discussion and Writing

1. Why does King say that people who want to be writers should read?
2. "Reading to Write" might not seem to be literature—it's nonfiction and informational rather than creative—but it is well written. Make

some observations about the way it is written—King's word choices, the kinds of voice he uses, the kinds of stories he tells—and consider what you might learn, as a budding writer, from reading it.

3. **connections** Compare King's essay to Sherman Alexie's "The Joy of Reading and Writing: Superman and Me" (p. 22). In some ways, these essays are very different: one is a reflection by a writer on what learning to be a writer meant to him growing up where he did, the other an offering of advice on one important part of learning to write. In what ways are they similar? Are there points of comparison between their authors' motivations? Between the ways they pursue their shared goal? Between the ways they feel about pursuing it?

4. Write a piece inspired by King's essay. It can be about writing, if you are passionate about that, or about some other pursuit—academic, creative, or neither. Try to include elements inspired by King's essay: tell a story or two about yourself, offer observations about something important to that pursuit (maybe one that others might overlook), and convey the sense of dedication that King conveys in "Reading to Write."

5. **looking further** In urging aspiring writers to turn off their tele visions when exercising so they might use that time for reading, King calls TV "the glass teat" (par. 11). Write a response informed by research on contemporary television which argues that writers have something to learn from television. How might you argue that TV is not a glass teat but a source of information about the world, as well as a place where good writing can also be found?

VERLYN KLINKENBORG

Our Vanishing Night

Most city skies have become virtually empty of stars

Born in 1952 in Colorado and raised in Iowa and California, Verlyn Klinkenborg has a Ph.D. in English from Princeton University and has taught literature and creative writing at a number of colleges and universities. He is on the editorial board of the New York Times *and is the author of* Making Hay *(1986),* The Last Fine Time *(1991), and* The Rural Life *(2003). He has written for the* New Yorker, National Geographic, Harper's, *and many other magazines.*

"Our Vanishing Night," which first appeared in National Geographic, *shows Klinkenborg doing more than writing about the rural life he has captured so evocatively in his pieces for the* New York Times. *As you read, observe how he deftly incorporates history and science into his writing.*

If humans were truly at home under the light of the moon and stars, we would go in darkness happily, the midnight world as visible to us as it is to the vast number of nocturnal species on this planet. Instead, we are diurnal creatures, with eyes adapted to living in the sun's light. This is a basic evolutionary fact, even though most of us don't think of ourselves as diurnal beings any more than we think of ourselves as primates or mammals or Earthlings. Yet it's the only way to explain what we've done to the night: we've engineered it to receive us by filling it with light.

This kind of engineering is no different than damming a river. Its benefits come with consequences—called light pollution— whose effects scientists are only now beginning to study. Light pollution is largely the result of bad lighting design, which allows artificial light to shine outward and upward into the sky, where it's not wanted, instead of focusing it downward, where it is. Ill-designed lighting washes out the darkness of night and radically alters the light levels—and light rhythms—to which many forms

216

of life, including ourselves, have adapted. Wherever human light spills into the natural world, some aspect of life—migration, reproduction, feeding—is affected.

For most of human history, the phrase "light pollution" would have made no sense. Imagine walking toward London on a moon-lit night around 1800, when it was Earth's most populous city. Nearly a million people lived there, making do, as they always had, with candles and rushlights and torches and lanterns. Only a few houses were lit by gas, and there would be no public gaslights in the streets or squares for another seven years. From a few miles away, you would have been as likely to *smell* London as to see its dim collective glow.

Now most of humanity lives under intersecting domes of reflected, refracted light, of scattering rays from overlit cities and suburbs, from light-flooded highways and factories. Nearly all of nighttime Europe is a nebula of light, as is most of the United States and all of Japan. In the south Atlantic the glow from a single fishing fleet—squid fishermen luring their prey with metal halide lamps—can be seen from space, burning brighter, in fact, than Buenos Aires or Rio de Janeiro.

In most cities the sky looks as though it has been emptied of 5 stars, leaving behind a vacant haze that mirrors our fear of the dark and resembles the urban glow of dystopian science fiction. We've grown so used to this pervasive orange haze that the orig-inal glory of an unlit night—dark enough for the planet Venus to throw shadows on Earth—is wholly beyond our experience, beyond memory almost. And yet above the city's pale ceiling lies the rest of the universe, utterly undiminished by the light we waste—a bright shoal of stars and planets and galaxies, shining in seemingly infinite darkness.

We've lit up the night as if it were an unoccupied country, when nothing could be further from the truth. Among mammals alone, the number of nocturnal species is astonishing. Light is a powerful biological force, and on many species it acts as a magnet, a process being studied by researchers such as Travis Longcore and Catherine Rich, co-founders of the Los Angeles–based Urban Wildlands Group. The effect is so powerful that scientists speak of songbirds and seabirds being "captured" by searchlights on land or by the light from gas flares on marine oil platforms, circling and circling in the thousands until they drop. Migrating at night, birds are apt to collide with brightly lit tall buildings; immature birds on their first journey suffer disproportionately.

Insects, of course, cluster around streetlights, and feeding at those insect clusters is now ingrained in the lives of many bat species. In some Swiss valleys the European lesser horseshoe bat began to vanish after streetlights were installed, perhaps because those valleys were suddenly filled with light-feeding pipistrelle bats. Other nocturnal mammals—including desert rodents, fruit bats, opossums, and badgers—forage more cautiously under the permanent full moon of light pollution because they've become easier targets for predators.

Some birds—blackbirds and nightingales, among others— sing at unnatural hours in the presence of artificial light. Scientists have determined that long artificial days—and artificially short nights—induce early breeding in a wide range of birds. And because a longer day allows for longer feeding, it can also affect migration schedules. One population of Bewick's swans wintering in England put on fat more rapidly than usual, priming them to begin their Siberian migration early. The problem, of course, is that migration, like most other aspects of bird behavior, is a precisely timed biological behavior. Leaving early may mean arriving too soon for nesting conditions to be right.

Nesting sea turtles, which show a natural predisposition for dark beaches, find fewer and fewer of them to nest on. Their hatchlings, which gravitate toward the brighter, more reflective sea horizon, find themselves confused by artificial lighting behind the beach. In Florida alone, hatchling losses number in the hundreds of thousands every year. Frogs and toads living near brightly lit highways suffer nocturnal light levels that are as much as a million times brighter than normal, throwing nearly every aspect of their behavior out of joint, including their nighttime breeding choruses.

Of all the pollutions we face, light pollution is perhaps the most 10 easily remedied. Simple changes in lighting design and installation yield immediate changes in the amount of light spilled into the atmosphere and, often, immediate energy savings.

It was once thought that light pollution only affected astronomers, who need to see the night sky in all its glorious clarity. And, in fact, some of the earliest civic efforts to control light pollution—in Flagstaff, Arizona, half a century ago—were made to protect the view from Lowell Observatory, which sits high above that city. Flagstaff has tightened its regulations since then, and in 2001 it was declared the first International Dark Sky City. By now the effort to control light pollution has spread around the globe. More and more cities and even entire countries, such as the Czech Republic, have committed themselves to reducing unwanted glare.

Unlike astronomers, most of us may not need an undiminished view of the night sky for our work, but like most other creatures we do need darkness. Darkness is as essential to our biological welfare, to our internal clockwork, as light itself. The regular oscillation of waking and sleep in our lives—one of our circadian rhythms—is nothing less than a biological expression of the regular oscillation of light on Earth. So fundamental are these rhythms to our being that altering them is like altering gravity.

For the past century or so, we've been performing an open-ended experiment on ourselves, extending the day, shortening the night, and short-circuiting the human body's sensitive response to light. The consequences of our bright new world are more readily perceptible in less adaptable creatures living in the peripheral glow of our prosperity. But for humans, too, light pollution may take a biological toll. At least one new study has suggested a direct correlation between higher rates of breast cancer in women and the nighttime brightness of their neighborhoods.

In the end, humans are no less trapped by light pollution than the frogs in a pond near a brightly lit highway. Living in a glare of our own making, we have cut ourselves off from our evolutionary and cultural patrimony—the light of the stars and the rhythms of day and night. In a very real sense, light pollution causes us to lose sight of our true place in the universe, to forget the scale of our being, which is best measured against the dimensions of a deep night with the Milky Way—the edge of our galaxy—arching overhead.

For Discussion and Writing

1. "We've lit up the night as if it were an unoccupied country, when nothing could be further from the truth," Klinkenborg writes (par. 6). How have we done this? By what is the night occupied?

2. Klinkenborg makes an argument in "Our Vanishing Night," but he does so through the use of precise, evocative descriptions. Often these

descriptions are of phenomena readers may not have known about or realized. How do these kinds of descriptions help Klinkenborg to make his argument?

3. **connections** In "Small Change: Why the Revolution Will Not Be Tweeted" (p. 169), Malcolm Gladwell is pessimistic about the potential of current social movements (or at least those rooted in social media) to bring about real change. Does "Our Vanishing Night" believe in the possibility of change? Does it consider the differences between individual action and social movements in bringing about change?

4. Klinkenborg describes the shortening of the night and lighting up of the night sky as an experiment we've been performing on ourselves. Think about your own life in these terms, about the amount of sleep you get and the amount of night light you experience. Do you think the modern experiment with light pollution has had effects on you?

5. **looking further** Doing some research, think about light pollution and other ways in which humans have changed the planet we live on. Follow your thinking and see where it takes you: How does the way we have changed other things compare to this? Have we changed any things for the better? Is it our place to worry about the effect of the way we live? What will the planet look like in a hundred years? In a thousand?

AUDRE LORDE

The Fourth of July

Audre Lorde (1934–1992) was a poet and nonfiction writer. Born in New York City to Caribbean immigrants, Lorde trained and worked as a librarian and became a widely published poet in the 1960s, when she also became politically active. Her poetry collections include The First Cities *(1968)*, Cables to Rage *(1970), and* The Black Unicorn *(1978); her other books were memoir and political and social theory, including* The Cancer Journals *(1980) and* Zami: A New Spelling of My Name *(1982).*

"The Fourth of July" is a beautifully spare yet forceful piece of writing. In it, readers can see the anger that spurred much of Lorde's writing, whether about racism, as in this essay, or about sexism or homophobia, but they can also see the control with which Lorde expressed her ideas and the honesty with which she implicated herself and her family in her writing.

The first time I went to Washington, D.C., was on the edge of the summer when I was supposed to stop being a child. At least that's what they said to us all at graduation from the eighth grade. My sister Phyllis graduated at the same time from high school. I don't know what she was supposed to stop being. But as graduation presents for us both, the whole family took a Fourth of July trip to Washington, D.C., the fabled and famous capital of our country.

It was the first time I'd ever been on a railroad train during the day. When I was little, and we used to go to the Connecticut shore, we always went at night on the milk train, because it was cheaper.

Preparations were in the air around our house before school was even over. We packed for a week. There were two very large suitcases that my father carried, and a box filled with food. In fact, my first trip to Washington was a mobile feast; I started eating as

221

soon as we were comfortably ensconced in our seats, and did not stop until somewhere after Philadelphia. I remember it was Philadelphia because I was disappointed not to have passed by the Liberty Bell.

My mother had roasted two chickens and cut them up into dainty bite-size pieces. She packed slices of brown bread and butter and green pepper and carrot sticks. There were little violently yellow iced cakes with scalloped edges called "marigolds," that came from Cushman's Bakery. There was a spice bun and rockcakes from Newton's, the West Indian bakery across Lenox Avenue from St. Mark's School, and iced tea in a wrapped mayonnaise jar. There were sweet pickles for us and dill pickles for my father, and peaches with the fuzz still on them, individually wrapped to keep them from bruising. And, for neatness, there were piles of napkins and a little tin box with a washcloth dampened with rosewater and glycerine for wiping sticky mouths.

I wanted to eat in the dining car because I had read all about 5 them, but my mother reminded me for the umpteenth time that dining car food always cost too much money and besides, you never could tell whose hands had been playing all over that food, nor where those same hands had been just before. My mother never mentioned that black people were not allowed into railroad dining cars headed south in 1947. As usual, whatever my mother did not like and could not change, she ignored. Perhaps it would go away, deprived of her attention.

I learned later that Phyllis's high school senior class trip had been to Washington, but the nuns had given her back her deposit in private, explaining to her that the class, all of whom were white, except Phyllis, would be staying in a hotel where Phyllis "would not be happy," meaning, Daddy explained to her, also in private, that they did not rent rooms to Negroes. "We will take you to Washington, ourselves," my father had avowed, "and not just for an overnight in some measly fleabag hotel."

American racism was a new and crushing reality that my parents had to deal with every day of their lives once they came to this country. They handled it as a private woe. My mother and father believed that they could best protect their children from the realities of race in America and the fact of American racism by never giving them name, much less discussing their nature. We were told we must never trust white people, but *why* was never explained, nor the nature of their ill will. Like so many other vital pieces of information in my childhood, I was supposed to know without being told. It always seemed like a very strange injunction coming from my mother, who looked so much like one of those people we were never supposed to trust. But something always warned me not to ask my mother why she wasn't white, and why Auntie Lillah and Auntie Etta weren't, even though they were all that same problematic color so different from my father and me, even from my sisters, who were somewhere in-between.

In Washington, D.C., we had one large room with two double beds and an extra cot for me. It was a back-street hotel that belonged to a friend of my father's who was in real estate, and I spent the whole next day after Mass squinting up at the Lincoln Memorial where Marian Anderson had sung after the D.A.R. refused to allow her to sing in their auditorium because she was black. Or because she was "Colored," my father said as he told us the story. Except that what he probably said was "Negro," because for his times, my father was quite progressive.

I was squinting because I was in that silent agony that characterized all of my childhood summers, from the time school let out in June to the end of July, brought about by my dilated and vulnerable eyes exposed to the summer brightness.

I viewed Julys through an agonizing corolla of dazzling white-   10
ness and I always hated the Fourth of July, even before I came to realize the travesty such a celebration was for black people in this country.

My parents did not approve of sunglasses, nor of their expense.

I spent the afternoon squinting up at monuments to freedom and past presidencies and democracy, and wondering why the light and heat were both so much stronger in Washington, D.C., than back home in New York City. Even the pavement on the streets was a shade lighter in color than back home.

Late that Washington afternoon my family and I walked back down Pennsylvania Avenue. We were a proper caravan, mother bright and father brown, the three of us girls step-standards in-between. Moved by our historical surroundings and the heat of early evening, my father decreed yet another treat. He had a great sense of history, a flair for the quietly dramatic and the sense of specialness of an occasion and a trip.

"Shall we stop and have a little something to cool off, Lin?"
Two blocks away from our hotel, the family stopped for a dish   15
of vanilla ice cream at a Breyer's ice cream and soda fountain.
Indoors, the soda fountain was dim and fan-cooled, deliciously
relieving to my scorched eyes.

Corded and crisp and pinafored, the five of us seated ourselves
one by one at the counter. There was I between my mother and
father, and my two sisters on the other side of my mother. We
settled ourselves along the white mottled marble counter, and
when the waitress spoke at first no one understood what she was
saying, and so the five of us just sat there.

The waitress moved along the line of us closer to my father and
spoke again. "I said I kin give you to take out, but you can't eat
here. Sorry." Then she dropped her eyes looking very embarrassed,
and suddenly we heard what it was she was saying all at the same
time, loud and clear.

Straight-backed and indignant, one by one, my family and I
got down from the counter stools and turned around and marched
out of the store, quiet and outraged, as if we had never been black
before. No one would answer my emphatic questions with anything other than a guilty silence. "But we hadn't done anything!"
This wasn't right or fair! Hadn't I written poems about Bataan
and freedom and democracy for all?

My parents wouldn't speak of this injustice, not because they
had contributed to it, but because they felt they should have
anticipated it and avoided it. This made me even angrier. My fury
was not going to be acknowledged by a like fury. Even my two
sisters copied my parents' pretense that nothing unusual and
anti-American had occurred. I was left to write my angry letter to
the president of the United States all by myself, although my
father did promise I could type it out on the office typewriter next
week, after I showed it to him in my copybook diary.

The waitress was white, and the counter was white, and the ice   20
cream I never ate in Washington, D.C., that summer I left childhood was white, and the white heat and the white pavement and
the white stone monuments of my first Washington summer
made me sick to my stomach for the whole rest of that trip and it
wasn't much of a graduation present after all.

For Discussion and Writing

1. What adjective does Lorde use six times in the essay's one-sentence final paragraph? Why do you think she chose to use it so many times?

2. Though Lorde says that the story she tells here really happened to her, it is as carefully constructed as any short story. One aspect of story construction she pays special attention to is setting things up in such a way that the dramatic moment will have its greatest impact. What is the dramatic moment in "The Fourth of July"? How does Lorde tell the story in a way that makes that moment especially effective?

3. **connections**   Jamaica Kincaid's "The Ugly Tourist" (p. 206) is in many ways quite different from Lorde's essay, from its narrative voice to its setting. But both essays are about tourists and race. Compare and contrast these two essays: What are their concerns? How do they explore them? How do they use point of view, scene and setting, and narrative to get their points across? Finally, how are their topics related? Is there any way in which one could be made to speak to the other?

4. Reflect on Lorde's use of irony in this essay. On one level, irony is simply when you say one thing but mean another, or when people in a narrative perceive a situation one way while readers know they're wrong; on another, deeper level, irony is about how things in the world are widely said to be one way when in fact they are not that way at all. How does Lorde use the surface ironies available to narrative — the ways in which things aren't what they seem — to write about the deeper ironies of American society?

5. **looking further**   What might Audre Lorde have to say about this childhood experience if she were still alive today? How might the election of Barack Obama as president have changed the way she looked back on this visit to Washington, D.C.? Imagine her possible reactions, and not just in a "things sure have changed" kind of way; try to consider ways in which her reactions might be mixed and even contradictory.

NANCY MAIRS

On Being a Cripple

Born in 1943 in Long Beach, California, and raised north of Boston, Massachusetts, Nancy Mairs is a poet, essayist, and teacher. She has written memoirs and personal essays about women's issues, disability, and death in contemporary culture. In "On Being a Cripple," Mairs demonstrates the power of writing that confronts social issues through personal narrative as well as impersonal analysis. Starting with her blunt title, the piece offers an extended consideration of how we choose to name disability, and how that definition affects how we think about it. "I am not a disease," she writes (par. 23). Note other powerful moments in her essay when these two strands cross.

sounds familiar

> *To escape is nothing. Not to escape is nothing.* — LOUISE BOGAN

The other day I was thinking of writing an essay on being a cripple. I was thinking hard in one of the stalls of the women's room in my office building, as I was shoving my shirt into my jeans and tugging up my zipper. Preoccupied, I flushed, picked up my book bag, took my cane down from the hook, and unlatched the door. So many movements unbalanced me, and as I pulled the door open I fell over backward, landing fully clothed on the toilet seat with my legs splayed in front of me: the old beetle-on-its-back routine. Saturday afternoon, the building deserted, I was free to laugh aloud as I wriggled back to my feet, my voice bouncing off the yellowish tiles from all directions. Had anyone been there with me, I'd have been still and faint and hot with chagrin. I decided that it was high time to write the essay.

First, the matter of semantics. I am a cripple. I choose this word to name me. I choose from among several possibilities, the most common of which are "handicapped" and "disabled." I made the choice a number of years ago, without thinking, unaware of my motives for doing so. Even now, I'm not sure what those motives are, but I recognize that they are complex and not entirely

226

flattering. People—crippled or not—wince at the word "cripple," as they do not at "handicapped" or "disabled." Perhaps I want them to wince. I want them to see me as a tough customer, one to whom the fates/gods/viruses have not been kind, but who can face the brutal truth of her existence squarely. As a cripple, I swagger.

But, to be fair to myself, a certain amount of honesty underlies my choice. "Cripple" seems to me a clean word, straightforward and precise. It has an honorable history, having made its first appearance in the Lindisfarne Gospel in the tenth century. As a lover of words, I like the accuracy with which it describes my condition: I have lost the full use of my limbs. "Disabled," by contrast, suggests any incapacity, physical or mental. And I certainly don't like "handicapped," which implies that I have deliberately been put at a disadvantage, by whom I can't imagine (my God is not a Handicapper General), in order to equalize chances in the great race of life. These words seem to me to be moving away from my condition, to be widening the gap between word and reality. Most remote is the recently coined euphemism "differently abled," which partakes of the same semantic hopefulness that transformed countries from "undeveloped" to "underdeveloped," then to "less developed," and finally to "developing" nations. People have continued to starve in those countries during the shift. Some realities do not obey the dictates of language.

Mine is one of them. Whatever you call me, I remain crippled. But I don't care what you call me, so long as it isn't "differently abled," which strikes me as pure verbal garbage designed, by its ability to describe anyone, to describe no one. I subscribe to George Orwell's thesis that "the slovenliness of our language makes it easier for us to have foolish thoughts." And I refuse to participate in the degeneration of the language to the extent that I deny that I have lost anything in the course of this calamitous disease; I refuse to pretend that the only differences between you and me are the various ordinary ones that distinguish any one person from another. But call me "disabled" or "handicapped" if you like. I have long since grown accustomed to them; and if they are vague, at least they hint at the truth. Moreover, I use them myself. Society is no readier to accept crippledness than to accept death, war, sex, sweat, or wrinkles. I would never refer to another person as a cripple. It is the word I use to name only myself.

I haven't always been crippled, a fact for which I am soundly 5
grateful. To be whole of limb is, I know from experience, infinitely
more pleasant and useful than to be crippled; and if that knowledge leaves one open to bitterness at my loss, the physical soundness I once enjoyed (though I did not enjoy it half enough) is well
worth the occasional stab of regret. Though never any good at
sports, I was a normally active child and young adult. I climbed
trees, played hopscotch, jumped rope, skated, swam, rode my
bicycle, sailed. I despised team sports, spending some of the
wretchedest afternoons of my life, sweaty and humiliated, behind
a field-hockey stick and under a basketball hoop. I tramped alone
for miles along the bridle paths that webbed the woods behind
the house I grew up in. I swayed through countless dim hours in
the arms of one man or another under the scattered shot of light
from mirrored balls, and gyrated through countless more as Tab
Hunter and Johnny Mathis gave way to the Rolling Stones,
Creedence Clearwater Revival, Cream. I walked down the aisle.
I pushed baby carriages, changed tires in the rain, marched for
peace.

When I was twenty-eight I started to trip and drop things. What
at first seemed my natural clumsiness soon became too pronounced to shrug off. I consulted a neurologist, who told me that
I had a brain tumor. A battery of tests, increasingly disagreeable,
revealed no tumor. About a year and a half later I developed a
blurred spot in one eye. I had, at last, the episodes "disseminated
in space and time" requisite for a diagnosis: multiple sclerosis. I
have never been sorry for the doctor's initial misdiagnosis, however. For almost a week, until the negative results of the tests were
in, I thought that I was going to die right away. Every day for the
past nearly ten years, then, has been a kind of gift. I accept all
gifts.

Multiple sclerosis is a chronic degenerative disease of the
central nervous system, in which the myelin that sheathes the
nerves is somehow eaten away and scar tissue forms in its place,
interrupting the nerves' signals. During its course, which is unpredictable and uncontrollable, one may lose vision, hearing, speech,
the ability to walk, control of bladder and/or bowels, strength in
any or all extremities, sensitivity to touch, vibration, and/or pain,
potency, coordination of movements—the list of possibilities
is lengthy and, yes, horrifying. One may also lose one's sense of

humor. That's the easiest to lose and the hardest to survive without.

In the past ten years, I have sustained some of these losses. Characteristic of MS are sudden attacks, called exacerbations, followed by remissions, and these I have not had. Instead, my disease has been slowly progressive. My left leg is now so weak that I walk with the aid of a brace and a cane; and for distances I use an Amigo, a variation on the electric wheelchair that looks rather like an electrified kiddie car. I no longer have much use of my left hand. Now my right side is weakening as well. I still have the blurred spot in my right eye. Overall, though, I've been lucky so far. My world has, of necessity, been circumscribed by my losses, but the terrain left me has been ample enough for me to continue many of the activities that absorb me: writing, teaching, raising children and cats and plants and snakes, reading, speaking publicly about MS and depression, even playing bridge with people patient and honorable enough to let me scatter cards every which way without sneaking a peek.

Lest I begin to sound like Pollyanna, however, let me say that I don't like having MS. I hate it. My life holds realities—harsh ones, some of them—that no right-minded human being ought to accept without grumbling. One of them is fatigue. I know of no one with MS who does not complain of bone-weariness; in a disease that presents an astonishing variety of symptoms, fatigue seems to be a common factor. I wake up in the morning feeling the way most people do at the end of a bad day, and I take it from there. As a result, I spend a lot of time *in extremis* and, impatient with limitation, I tend to ignore my fatigue until my body breaks down in some way and forces rest. Then I miss picnics, dinner parties, poetry readings, the brief visits of old friends from out of town. The offspring of a puritanical tradition of exceptional venerability, I cannot view these lapses without shame. My life often seems a series of small failures to do as I ought.

I lead, on the whole, an ordinary life, probably rather like the   10 one I would have led had I not had MS. I am lucky that my predilections were already solitary, sedentary, and bookish—unlike the world-famous French cellist I have read about, or the young woman I talked with one long afternoon who wanted only to be a jockey. I had just begun graduate school when I found out something was wrong with me, and I have remained, interminably, a graduate student. Perhaps I would not have if I'd thought I had the stamina to return to a full-time job as a technical editor; but I've enjoyed my studies.

In addition to studying, I teach writing courses. I also teach medical students how to give neurological examinations. I pick up freelance editing jobs here and there. I have raised a foster son and sent him into the world, where he has made me two grand-babies, and I am still escorting my daughter and son through adolescence. I go to Mass every Saturday. I am a superb, if messy, cook. I am also an enthusiastic laundress, capable of sorting a hamper full of clothes into five subtly differentiated piles, but a terrible housekeeper. I can do italic writing and, in an emergency, bathe an oil-soaked cat. I play a fiendish game of Scrabble. When I have the time and the money, I like to sit on my front steps with my husband drinking Amaretto and smoking a cigar, as we imagine our counterparts in Leningrad and make sure that the sun gets down once more behind the sharp childish scrawl of the Tucson Mountains.

This lively plenty has its bleak complement, of course, in all the things I can no longer do. I will never run again, except in dreams, and one day I may have to write that I will never walk again. I like to go camping, but I can't follow George and the children along the trails that wander out of a campsite through the desert or into the mountains. In fact, even on the level I've learned never to check the weather or try to hold a coherent conversation: I need all my attention for my wayward feet. Of late, I have begun to catch myself wondering how people can propel themselves without canes. With only one usable hand, I have to select my clothing with care not so much for style as for ease of ingress and egress, and even so, dressing can be laborious. I can no longer do fine stitchery, pick up babies, play the piano, braid my hair. I am immobilized by acute attacks of depression, which may or may not be physiologically related to MS but are certainly its logical concomitant.

These two elements, the plenty and the privation, are never pure, nor are the delight and wretchedness that accompany them. Almost every pickle that I get into as a result of my weakness and clumsiness—and I get into plenty—is funny as well as maddening and sometimes painful. I recall one May afternoon when a friend and I were going out for a drink after finishing up at school.

As we were climbing into opposite sides of my car, chatting, I tripped and fell, flat and hard, onto the asphalt parking lot, my abrupt departure interrupting him in mid-sentence. "Where'd you go?" he called as he came around the back of the car to find me hauling myself up by the door frame. "Are you all right?" Yes, I told him, I was fine, just a bit rattly, and we drove off to find a shady patio and some beer. When I got home an hour or so later, my daughter greeted me with "What have you done to yourself?" I looked down. One elbow of my white turtleneck with the green froggies, one knee of my white trousers, one white kneesock were bloodsoaked. We peeled off the clothes and inspected the damage, which was nasty enough but not alarming. That part wasn't funny: the abrasions took a long time to heal, and one got a little infected. Even so, when I think of my friend talking earnestly, suddenly, to the hot thin air while I dropped from his view as though through a trap door, I find the image as silly as something from a Marx Brothers movie.

I may find it easier than other cripples to amuse myself because I live propped by the acceptance and the assistance and, sometimes, the amusement of those around me. Grocery clerks tear my checks out of my checkbook for me, and sales clerks find chairs to put into dressing rooms when I want to try on clothes. The people I work with make sure I teach at times when I am least likely to be fatigued, in places I can get to, with the materials I need. My students, with one anonymous exception (in an end-of-the-semester evaluation), have been unperturbed by my disability. Some even like it. One was immensely cheered by the information that I paint my own fingernails; she decided, she told me, that if I could go to such trouble over fine details, she could keep on writing essays. I suppose I became some sort of bright-fingered muse. She wrote good essays, too.

The most important struts in the framework of my existence, 15 of course, are my husband and children. Dismayingly few marriages survive the MS test, and why should they? Most twenty-two- and nineteen-year-olds, like George and me, can vow in clear conscience, after a childhood of chicken pox and summer colds, to keep one another in sickness and in health so long as they both shall live. Not many are equipped for catastrophe: the dismay, the depression, the extra work, the boredom that a degenerative disease can insinuate into a relationship. And our society, with

its emphasis on fun and its association of fun with physical performance, offers little encouragement for a whole spouse to stay
with a crippled partner. Children experience similar stresses
when faced with a crippled parent, and they are more helpless,
since parents and children can't usually get divorced. They hate,
of course, to be different from their peers, and the child whose
mother is tacking down the aisle of a school auditorium packed
with proud parents like a Cape Cod dinghy in a stiff breeze jolly
well stands out in a crowd. Deprived of legal divorce, the child
can at least deny the mother's disability, even her existence, forgetting to tell her about recitals and PTA meetings, refusing to
accompany her to stores or church or the movies, never inviting
friends to the house. Many do.

But I've been limping along for ten years now, and so far
George and the children are still at my left elbow, holding tight.
Anne and Matthew vacuum floors and dust furniture and haul
trash and rake up dog droppings and button my cuffs and bake
lasagna and Toll House cookies with just enough grumbling so I
know that they don't have brain fever. And far from hiding me,
they're forever dragging me by racks of fancy clothes or through
teeming school corridors, or welcoming gaggles of friends while
I'm wandering through the house in Anne's filmy pink babydoll
pajamas. George generally calls before he brings someone home,
but he does just as many dumb thankless chores as the children.
And they all yell at me, laugh at some of my jokes, write me funny
letters when we're apart—in short, treat me as an ordinary
human being for whom they have some use. I think they like me.
Unless they're faking. . . .

Faking. There's the rub. Tugging at the fringes of my consciousness always is the terror that people are kind to me only because
I'm a cripple. My mother almost shattered me once, with that
instinct mothers have—blind, I think, in this case, but unerring
nonetheless—for striking blows along the fault-lines of their children's hearts, by telling me, in an attack on my selfishness, "We all
have to make allowances for you, of course, because of the way
you are." From the distance of a couple of years, I have to admit
that I haven't any idea just what she meant, and I'm not sure that
she knew either. She was awfully angry. But at the time, as the
words thudded home, I felt my worst fear, suddenly realized. I
could bear being called selfish: I am. But I couldn't bear the

corroboration that those around me were doing in fact what I'd always suspected them of doing, professing fondness while silently putting up with me because of the way I am. A cripple. I've been a little cracked ever since.

Along with this fear that people are secretly accepting shoddy goods comes a relentless pressure to please—to prove myself worth the burdens I impose, I guess, or to build a substantial account of goodwill against which I may write drafts in times of need. Part of the pressure arises from social expectations. In our society, anyone who deviates from the norm had better find some way to compensate. Like fat people, who are expected to be jolly, cripples must bear their lot meekly and cheerfully. A grumpy cripple isn't playing by the rules. And much of pressure is self-generated. Early on I vowed that, if I had to have MS, by God I was going to do it well. This is a class act, ladies and gentlemen. No tears, no recriminations, no faint-heartedness.

One way and another, then, I wind up feeling like Tiny Tim, peering over the edge of the table at the Christmas goose, waving my crutch, piping down God's blessing on us all. Only sometimes I don't want to play Tiny Tim. I'd rather be Caliban, a most scurvy monster. Fortunately, at home no one much cares whether I'm a good cripple or a bad cripple as long as I make vichyssoise with fair regularity. One evening several years ago, Anne was reading at the dining-room table while I cooked dinner. As I opened a can of tomatoes, the can slipped in my left hand and juice spattered me and the counter with bloody spots. Fatigued and infuriated, I bellowed, "I'm so sick of being crippled!" Anne glanced at me over the top of her book. "There now," she said, "do you feel better?" "Yes," I said, "yes, I do." She went back to her reading. I felt better. That's about all the attention my scurviness ever gets.

Because I hate being crippled, I sometimes hate myself for being a cripple. Over the years I have come to expect—even accept—attacks of violent self-loathing. Luckily, in general our society no longer connects deformity and disease directly with evil (though a charismatic once told me that I have MS because a devil is in me) and so I'm allowed to move largely at will, even among small children. But I'm not sure that this revision of attitude has been particularly helpful. Physical imperfection, even freed of moral disapprobation, still defies and violates the ideal, especially for women, whose confinement in their bodies as objects of desire is far from over. Each age, of course, has its ideal, and I doubt that ours is any better or worse than any other. Today's ideal woman, who lives on the glossy pages of dozens of magazines, seems to be between the ages of eighteen and twenty-five; her hair has body, her teeth flash white, her breath smells minty, her underarms are dry; she has a career but is still a fabulous cook, especially of meals that take less than twenty minutes to prepare; she does not ordinarily appear to have a husband or children; she is trim and deeply tanned; she jogs, swims, plays tennis, rides a bicycle, sails, but does not bowl; she travels widely, even to out-of-the-way places like Finland and Samoa, always in the company of the ideal man, who possesses a nearly identical set of characteristics. There are a few exceptions. Though usually white and often blonde, she may be black, Hispanic, Asian, or Native American, so long as she is unusually sleek. She may be old, provided she is selling a laxative or is Lauren Bacall. If she is selling a detergent, she may be married and have a flock of strikingly messy children. But she is never a cripple.

Like many women I know, I have always had an uneasy relationship with my body. I was not a popular child, largely, I think now, because I was peculiar: intelligent, intense, moody, shy, given to unexpected actions and inexplicable notions and emotions. But as I entered adolescence, I believed myself unpopular because I was homely: my breasts too flat, my mouth too wide, my hips too narrow, my clothing never quite right in fit or style. I was not, in fact, particularly ugly, old photographs inform me, though I was well off the ideal; but I carried this sense of self-alienation with me into adulthood, where it regenerated in response to the depredations of MS. Even with my brace I walk with a limp so pronounced that, seeing myself on the videotape of a television program on the disabled, I couldn't believe that anything but an inchworm could make progress humping along like that. My shoulders droop and my pelvis thrusts forward as I try to balance myself upright, throwing my frame into a bony S. As a result of contractures, one shoulder is higher than the other and I carry one arm bent in front of me, the fingers curled into a claw. My left arm and leg have wasted into pipestems, and I try always to keep them covered. When I think about how my body must look to others, especially to men, to whom I have been trained to display myself, I feel ludicrous, even loathsome.

At my age, however, I don't spend much time thinking about my appearance. The burning egocentricity of adolescence, which assures one that all the world is looking all the time, has passed, thank God, and I'm generally too caught up in what I'm doing to step back, as I used to, and watch myself as though upon a stage. I'm also too old to believe in the accuracy of self-image. I know that I'm not a hideous crone, that in fact, when I'm rested, well dressed, and well made up, I look fine. The self-loathing I feel is neither physically nor intellectually substantial. What I hate is not me but a disease.

I am not a disease.

And a disease is not—at least not singlehandedly—going to determine who I am, though at first it seemed to be going to. Adjusting to a chronic incurable illness, I have moved through a process similar to that outlined by Elisabeth Kübler-Ross in *On Death and Dying*. The major difference—and it is far more significant than most people recognize—is that I can't be sure of the outcome, as the terminally ill cancer patient can. Research studies indicate that, with proper medical care, I may achieve a "normal" life span. And in our society, with its vision of death as the ultimate evil, worse even than decrepitude, the response to such news is, "Oh well, at least you're not going to die." Are there worse things than dying? I think that there may be.

I think of two women I know, both with MS, both enough older than I to have served me as models. One took to her bed several years ago and has been there ever since. Although she can sit in a high-backed wheelchair, because she is incontinent she refuses to go out at all, even though incontinence pants, which are readily available at any pharmacy, could protect her from embarrassment. Instead, she stays at home and insists that her husband, a small quiet man, a retired civil servant, stay there with her except for a quick weekly foray to the supermarket. The other woman, whose illness was diagnosed when she was eighteen, a nursing student engaged to a young doctor, finished her training, married her doctor, accompanied him to Germany when he was in the service, bore three sons and a daughter, now grown and gone. When she can, she travels with her husband; she plays bridge, embroiders, swims regularly; she works, like me, as a symptomatic-patient instructor of medical students in neurology. Guess which woman I hope to be.

At the beginning, I thought about having MS almost incessantly and because of the unpredictable course of the disease, my thoughts were always terrified. Each night I'd get into bed wondering whether I'd get out again the next morning, whether I'd be able to see, to speak, to hold a pen between my fingers. Knowing that the day might come when I'd be physically incapable of killing myself, I thought perhaps I ought to do so right away, while I still had the strength. Gradually I came to understand that the Nancy who might one day lie inert under a bedsheet, arms and legs paralyzed, unable to feed or bathe herself, unable to reach out for a gun, a bottle of pills, was not the Nancy I was at present, and that I could not presume to make decisions for that future Nancy, who might well not want in the least to die. Now the only provision I've made for the future Nancy is that when the time comes—and it is likely to come in the form of pneumonia, friend to the weak and the old—I am not to be treated with machines and medications. If she is unable to communicate by then, I hope she will be satisfied with these terms.

Thinking all the time about having MS grew tiresome and intrusive, especially in the large and tragic mode in which I was accustomed to considering my plight. Months and even years went by without catastrophe (at least without one related to MS), and really I was awfully busy, what with George and children and snakes and students and poems, and I hadn't the time, let alone the inclination, to devote myself to being a disease. Too, the richer my life became, the funnier it seemed, as though there were some connection between largesse and laughter, and so my tragic stance began to waver until, even with the aid of a brace and a cane, I couldn't hold it for very long at a time.

After several years I was satisfied with my adjustment. I had suffered my grief and fury and terror, I thought, but now I was at ease with my lot. Then one summer day I set out with George and the children across the desert for a vacation in California. Part way to Yuma I became aware that my right leg felt funny. "I think I've had an exacerbation," I told George. "What shall we do?" he asked. "I think we'd better get the hell to California," I said, "because I don't know whether I'll ever make it again." So we went on to San Diego and then to Orange, up the Pacific Coast Highway to Santa Cruz, across to Yosemite, down to Sequoia and Joshua Tree, and so back over the desert to home. It was a fine two-week trip, filled with friends and fair weather, and I wouldn't have missed it for the world, though I did in fact make it back to California two years later. Nor would there have been any point in missing it, since in MS, once the symptoms have appeared, the neurological damage has been done, and there's no way to predict or prevent that damage.

The incident spoiled my self-satisfaction, however. It renewed my grief and fury and terror, and I learned that one never finishes adjusting to MS. I don't know now why I thought one would. One does not, after all, finish adjusting to life, and MS is simply a fact of my life—not my favorite fact, of course—but as ordinary as my nose and my tropical fish and my yellow Mazda station wagon. It may at any time get worse, but no amount of worry, or anticipation can prepare me for a new loss. My life is a lesson in losses. I learn one at a time.

And I had best be patient in the learning, since I'll have to do it like it or not. As any rock fan knows, you can't always get what you want. Particularly when you have MS. You can't, for example, get cured. In recent years researchers and the organizations that fund research have started to pay MS some attention even though it isn't fatal; perhaps they have begun to see that life is something other than a quantitative phenomenon, that one may be very much alive for a very long time in a life that isn't worth living. The researchers have made some progress toward understanding the mechanism of the disease: it may well be an autoimmune reaction triggered by a slow-acting virus. But they are nowhere near its prevention, control, or cure. And most of us want to be cured. Some, unable to accept incurability, grasp at one treatment after another, no matter how bizarre: megavitamin therapy, gluten-free diet, injections of cobra venom, hypothermal suits, lymphocytopharesis, hyperbaric chambers. Many treatments are probably harmless enough, but none are curative.

The absence of a cure often makes MS patients bitter toward their doctors. Doctors are, after all, the priests of modern society, the new shamans, whose business is to heal, and many an MS patient roves from one to another, searching for the "good" doctor who will make him well. Doctors too think of themselves as healers, and for this reason many have trouble dealing with MS patients, whose disease in its intransigence defeats their aims and mocks their skills. Too few doctors, it is true, treat their patients as whole human beings, but the reverse is also true. I have always tried to be gentle with my doctors, who often have more at stake in terms of ego than I do. I may be frustrated, maddened, depressed by the incurability of my disease, but I am not diminished by it, and they are. When I push myself up from my seat in the waiting room and stumble toward them, I incarnate the limitation of their powers. The least I can do is refuse to press on their tenderest spots.

This gentleness is part of the reason that I'm not sorry to be a cripple. I didn't have it before. Perhaps I'd have developed it anyway—how could I know such a thing?—and I wish I had more of it, but I'm glad of what I have. It has opened and enriched my life enormously, this sense that my frailty and need must be mirrored in others, that in searching for and shaping a stable core in a life wrenched by change and loss, change and loss, I must recognize the same process, under individual conditions, in the lives around me. I do not deprecate such knowledge, however I've come by it.

All the same, if a cure were found, would I take it? In a minute. I may be a cripple, but I'm only occasionally a loony and never a saint. Anyway, in my brand of theology God doesn't give bonus points for a limp. I'd take a cure; I just don't need one. A friend who also has MS startled me once by asking, "Do you ever say to yourself, 'Why me, Lord?'" "No, Michael, I don't," I told him, "because whenever I try, the only response I can think of is 'Why not?'" If I could make a cosmic deal, who would I put in my place? What in my life would I give up in exchange for sound limbs and a thrilling rush of energy? No one. Nothing. I might as well do the job myself. Now that I'm getting the hang of it.

For Discussion and Writing

1. Make two lists, one of Mairs's talents and one of the activities her MS makes difficult or impossible.

2. "As a cripple, I swagger," Mairs writes (par. 2). What does this mean? More generally, what is Mairs saying about her MS in this essay? How does this use of the word *cripple* help her say it?

3. **connections**   Mairs rejects the labels "handicapped" and "disabled," preferring "crippled," even though many see it as offensive. Compare Mairs's attention to words in this essay to Gloria Anzaldúa's in "How to Tame a Wild Tongue" (p. 27). What power does Anzaldúa see words having? What can words do and undo? Are there moments when

Anzaldúa harnesses that power for herself in ways analogous to what Mairs does in "On Being a Cripple"?

4. Think about the way others see you and the way you see yourself. How would you correct their perception of you if it were possible?

5. **looking further** Read up on Franklin Delano Roosevelt's physical disability. While some attitudes and laws have changed since the 1940s, do you think they have changed enough that if he were president today, he could (or would) act differently about his disability? Make an argument based on evidence including current laws and current politicians.

Learning to Read

*Malcolm Little, born in Omaha, Nebraska, in 1925, was reborn
Malcolm X in his twenties while imprisoned for burglary. (He considered "Little" a slave name and chose the "X" to signify his lost African
tribal name.) His conversion to Islam under the Nation of Islam and
his rigorous self-education led him to a life of political activism marked
by hatred, violence, and hope. For a time, as the foremost spokesman of
the Nation of Islam, Malcolm preached a separatist philosophy with
racist rhetoric; on breaking with the Nation of Islam and converting to
orthodox Islam after a pilgrimage to Mecca, Malcolm again changed
his name (to El-Hajj Malik El-Shabazz) and philosophy, moving closer
to the integrationist goals of the mainstream civil rights movement.
Not quite a year later, he was assassinated.*

"Learning to Read" is an excerpt from The Autobiography of
Malcolm X *(1965), which was written by Alex Haley from interviews
completed shortly before Malcolm's death. While this work was ghostwrit-
ten, Malcolm's fierce intelligence and passion are evident; it is easier to
miss the sometimes surprising moments of humor, but look for them
because they give a fuller sense of the man.*

It was because of my letters that I happened to stumble upon
starting to acquire some kind of a homemade education.

I became increasingly frustrated at not being able to express
what I wanted to convey in letters that I wrote, especially those to
Mr. Elijah Muhammad. In the street, I had been the most articulate hustler out there—I had commanded attention when I said
something. But now, trying to write simple English, I not only
wasn't articulate, I wasn't even functional. How would I sound
writing in slang, the way I would *say* it, something such as "Look,
daddy, let me pull your coat about a cat, Elijah Muhammad—"

Many who today hear me somewhere in person, or on television, or those who read something I've said, will think I went to

240

school far beyond the eighth grade. This impression is due entirely to my prison studies.

It had really begun back in the Charlestown Prison, when Bimbi first made me feel envy of his stock of knowledge. Bimbi had always taken charge of any conversation he was in, and I had tried to emulate him. But every book I picked up had few sentences which didn't contain anywhere from one to nearly all of the words that might as well have been in Chinese. When I just skipped those words, of course, I really ended up with little idea of what the book said. So I had come to the Norfolk Prison Colony still going through only book-reading motions. Pretty soon, I would have quit even these motions, unless I had received the motivation that I did.

I saw that the best thing I could do was get hold of a dictio-   5
nary—to study, to learn some words. I was lucky enough to reason also that I should try to improve my penmanship. It was sad. I couldn't even write in a straight line. It was both ideas together that moved me to request a dictionary along with some tablets and pencils from the Norfolk Prison Colony school.

I spent two days just riffling uncertainly through the dictionary's pages. I'd never realized so many words existed! I didn't know *which* words I needed to learn. Finally, just to start some kind of action, I began copying.

In my slow, painstaking, ragged handwriting, I copied into my tablet everything printed on that first page, down to the punctuation marks.

I believe it took me a day. Then, aloud, I read back, to myself, everything I'd written on the tablet. Over and over, aloud, to myself, I read my own handwriting.

I woke up the next morning, thinking about those words—immensely proud to realize that not only had I written so much at one time, but I'd written words that I never knew were in the world. Moreover, with a little effort, I also could remember what many of these words meant. I reviewed the words whose meanings I didn't remember. Funny thing, from the dictionary first page right now, that "aardvark" springs to my mind. The dictionary had a picture of it, a long-tailed, long-eared, burrowing African mammal, which lives off termites caught by sticking out its tongue as an anteater does for ants.

I was so fascinated that I went on—I copied the dictionary's   10
next page. And the same experience came when I studied that.

With every succeeding page, I also learned of people and places and events from history. Actually the dictionary is like a miniature encyclopedia. Finally the dictionary's A section had filled a whole tablet—and I went on into the B's. That was the way I started copying what eventually became the entire dictionary. It went a lot faster after so much practice helped me to pick up handwriting speed. Between what I wrote in my tablet, and writing letters, during the rest of my time in prison I would guess I wrote a million words.

I suppose it was inevitable that as my word-base broadened, I could for the first time pick up a book and read and now begin to understand what the book was saying. Anyone who has read a great deal can imagine the new world that opened. Let me tell you something: from then until I left that prison, in every free moment I had, if I was not reading in the library, I was reading on my bunk. You couldn't have gotten me out of books with a wedge. Between Mr. Muhammad's teachings, my correspondence, my visitors— usually Ella and Reginald—and my reading of books, months passed without my even thinking about being imprisoned. In fact, up to then, I never had been so truly free in my life.

The Norfolk Prison Colony's library was in the school building. A variety of classes was taught there by instructors who came from such places as Harvard and Boston universities. The weekly debates between inmate teams were also held in the school building. You would be astonished to know how worked up convict debaters and audiences would get over subjects like "Should Babies Be Fed Milk?"

Available on the prison library's shelves were books on just about every general subject. Much of the big private collection that Parkhurst had willed to the prison was still in crates and boxes in the back of the library—thousands of old books. Some of them looked ancient: covers faded, old-time parchment-looking binding. Parkhurst, I've mentioned, seemed to have been principally interested in history and religion. He had the money and the special interest to have a lot of books that you wouldn't have in general circulation. Any college library would have been lucky to get that collection.

As you can imagine, especially in a prison where there was heavy emphasis on rehabilitation, an inmate was smiled upon if he demonstrated an unusually intense interest in books. There was a sizable number of well-read inmates, especially the popular

debaters. Some were said by many to be practically walking ency-
clopedias. They were almost celebrities. No university would ask
any student to devour literature as I did when this new world
opened to me, of being able to read and *understand*.

I read more in my room than in the library itself. An inmate   15
who was known to read a lot could check out more than the permitted maximum number of books. I preferred reading in the
total isolation of my own room.

When I had progressed to really serious reading, every night at
about ten P.M. I would be outraged with the "lights out." It always
seemed to catch me right in the middle of something engrossing.

Fortunately, right outside my door was a corridor light that
cast a glow into my room. The glow was enough to read by, once
my eyes adjusted to it. So when "lights out" came, I would sit on
the floor where I could continue reading in that glow.

At one-hour intervals the night guards paced past every room.
Each time I heard the approaching footsteps, I jumped into bed
and feigned sleep. And as soon as the guard passed, I got back out
of bed onto the floor area of that light-glow, where I would read
for another fifty-eight minutes— until the guard approached
again. That went on until three or four every morning. Three or
four hours of sleep a night was enough for me. Often in the years
in the streets I had slept less than that.

The teachings of Mr. Muhammad stressed how history had
been "whitened"—when white men had written history books,
the black man simply had been left out. Mr. Muhammad couldn't
have said anything that would have struck me much harder. I had
never forgotten how when my class, me and all of those whites,
had studied seventh-grade United States history back in Mason,
the history of the Negro had been covered in one paragraph, and
the teacher had gotten a big laugh with his joke, "Negroes' feet
are so big that when they walk, they leave a hole in the ground."

This is one reason why Mr. Muhammad's teachings spread so   20
swiftly all over the United States, among *all* Negroes, whether or
not they became followers of Mr. Muhammad. The teachings ring
true—to every Negro. You can hardly show me a black adult in
America—or a white one, for that matter—who knows from the
history books anything like the truth about the black man's role.
In my own case, once I heard of the "glorious history of the black

man," I took special pains to hunt in the library for books that would inform me on details about black history.

I can remember accurately the very first set of books that really impressed me. I have since bought that set of books and have it at home for my children to read as they grow up. It's called *Wonders of the World*. It's full of pictures of archeological finds, statues that depict, usually, non-European people.

I found books like Will Durant's *Story of Civilization*. I read H. G. Wells' *Outline of History*. *Souls of Black Folk* by W. E. B. Du Bois gave me a glimpse into the black people's history before they came to this country. Carter G. Woodson's *Negro History* opened my eyes about black empires before the black slave was brought to the United States, and the early Negro struggles for freedom.

J. A. Rogers' three volumes of *Sex and Race* told about race-mixing before Christ's time; about Aesop being a black man who told fables; about Egypt's Pharaohs; about the great Coptic Christian Empires; about Ethiopia, the earth's oldest continuous black civilization, as China is the oldest continuous civilization.

Mr. Muhammad's teaching about how the white man had been created led me to *Findings in Genetics* by Gregor Mendel. (The dictionary's G section was where I had learned what "genetics" meant.) I really studied this book by the Austrian monk. Reading it over and over, especially certain sections, helped me to understand that if you started with a black man, a white man could be produced; but starting with a white man, you never could produce a black man—because the white gene is recessive. And since no one disputes that there was but one Original Man, the conclusion is clear.

During the last year or so, in the *New York Times*, Arnold 25 Toynbee used the word "bleached" in describing the white man. (His words were: "White (i.e., bleached) human beings of North European origin. . . .") Toynbee also referred to the European geographic area as only a peninsula of Asia. He said there is no such thing as Europe. And if you look at the globe, you will see for yourself that America is only an extension of Asia. (But at the same time Toynbee is among those who have helped to bleach history. He has written that Africa was the only continent that produced no history. He won't write that again. Every day now, the truth is coming to light.)

I never will forget how shocked I was when I began reading about slavery's total horror. It made such an impact upon me that it later became one of my favorite subjects when I became a minister of Mr. Muhammad's. The world's most monstrous crime, the sin and the blood on the white man's hands, are almost impossible to believe. Books like the one by Frederick Olmstead opened my eyes to the horrors suffered when the slave was landed in the United States. The European woman, Fannie Kimball, who had married a Southern white slaveowner, described how human beings were degraded. Of course I read *Uncle Tom's Cabin*. In fact, I believe that's the only novel I have ever read since I started serious reading.

Parkhurst's collection also contained some bound pamphlets of the Abolitionist Anti-Slavery Society of New England. I read descriptions of atrocities, saw those illustrations of black slave women tied up and flogged with whips; of black mothers watching their babies being dragged off, never to be seen by their mothers again; of dogs after slaves, and of the fugitive slave catchers, evil white men with whips and clubs and chains and guns. I read about the slave preacher Nat Turner, who put the fear of God into the white slavemaster. Nat Turner wasn't going around preaching pie-in-the-sky and "non-violent" freedom for the black man. There in Virginia one night in 1831, Nat and seven other slaves started out at his master's home and through the night they went from one plantation "big house" to the next, killing, until by the next morning 57 white people were dead and Nat had about 70 slaves following him. White people, terrified for their lives, fled from their homes, locked themselves up in public buildings, hid in the woods, and some even left the state. A small army of soldiers took two months to catch and hang Nat Turner. Somewhere I have read where Nat Turner's example is said to have inspired John Brown to invade Virginia and attack Harper's Ferry nearly thirty years later, with thirteen white men and five Negroes.

I read Herodotus, "the father of History," or, rather, I read about him. And I read the histories of various nations, which opened my eyes gradually, then wider and wider, to how the whole world's white men had indeed acted like devils, pillaging and raping and bleeding and draining the whole world's non-white people. I remember, for instance, books such as Will Durant's story of Oriental civilization, and Mahatma Gandhi's accounts of the struggle to drive the British out of India.

Book after book showed me how the white man had brought upon the world's black, brown, red, and yellow peoples every variety of the sufferings of exploitation. I saw how since the sixteenth century, the so-called "Christian trader" white man began to ply the seas in his lust for Asian and African empires, and plunder, and power. I read, I saw, how the white man never has gone among the non-white peoples bearing the Cross in the true manner and spirit of Christ's teachings—meek, humble, and Christ-like.

I perceived, as I read, how the collective white man had been actually nothing but a piratical opportunist who used Faustian machinations to make his own Christianity his initial wedge in criminal conquests. First, always "religiously," he branded "heathen" and "pagan" labels upon ancient non-white cultures and civilizations. The stage thus set, he then turned upon his non-white victims his weapons of war. 30

I read how, entering India—half a *billion* deeply religious brown people—the British white man, by 1759, through promises, trickery, and manipulations, controlled much of India through Great Britain's East India Company. The parasitical British administration kept tentacling out to half of the subcontinent. In 1857, some of the desperate people of India finally mutinied—and, excepting the African slave trade, nowhere has history recorded any more unnecessary bestial and ruthless human carnage than the British suppression of the non-white Indian people.

Over 115 million African blacks—close to the 1930s population of the United States—were murdered or enslaved during the slave trade. And I read how when the slave market was glutted, the cannibalistic white powers of Europe next carved up, as their colonies, the richest areas of the black continent. And Europe's chancelleries for the next century played a chess game of naked exploitation and power from Cape Horn to Cairo.

Ten guards and the warden couldn't have torn me out of those books. Not even Elijah Muhammad could have been more eloquent than those books were in providing indisputable proof that the collective white man had acted like a devil in virtually every contact he had with the world's collective non-white man. I listen today to the radio, and watch television, and read the headlines about the collective white man's fear and tension concerning China. When the white man professes ignorance about why the Chinese hate him so, my mind can't help flashing back to what I read, there in prison, about how the blood forebears of this same white man raped China at a time when China was trusting and helpless. Those original white "Christian traders" sent into China millions of pounds of opium. By 1839, so many of the Chinese were addicts that China's desperate government destroyed twenty thousand chests of opium. The first Opium War was promptly declared by the white man. Imagine! Declaring *war* upon someone who objects to being narcotized! The Chinese were severely beaten, with Chinese-invented gunpowder.

The Treaty of Nanking made China pay the British white man for the destroyed opium; forced open China's major ports to British trade; forced China to abandon Hong Kong; fixed China's import tariffs so low that cheap British articles soon flooded in, maiming China's industrial development.

After a second Opium War, the Tientsin Treaties legalized the ravaging opium trade, legalized a British-French-American control of China's customs. China tried delaying that Treaty's ratification; Peking was looted and burned.

"Kill the foreign white devils!" was the 1901 Chinese war cry in the Boxer Rebellion. Losing again, this time the Chinese were driven from Peking's choicest areas. The vicious, arrogant white man put up the famous signs, "Chinese and dogs not allowed."

Red China after World War II closed its doors to the Western white world. Massive Chinese agricultural, scientific, and industrial efforts are described in a book that *Life* magazine recently published. Some observers inside Red China have reported that the world never has known such a hate-white campaign as is now going on in this non-white country where, present birth-rates continuing, in fifty more years Chinese will be half the earth's population. And it seems that some Chinese chickens will soon come home to roost, with China's recent successful nuclear tests.

Let us face reality. We can see in the United Nations a new world order being shaped, along color lines — an alliance among the non-white nations. America's U.N. Ambassador Adlai Stevenson complained not long ago that in the United Nations "a skin game" was being played. He was right. He was facing reality. A "skin game" *is* being played. But Ambassador Stevenson sounded like Jesse James accusing the marshal of carrying a gun. Because who in the world's history ever has played a worse "skin game" than the white man?

* * *

Mr. Muhammad, to whom I was writing daily, had no idea of what a new world had opened up to me through my efforts to document his teachings in books.

When I discovered philosophy, I tried to touch all the land- 40 marks of philosophical development. Gradually, I read most of the old philosophers, Occidental and Oriental. The Oriental philosophers were the ones I came to prefer; finally, my impression was that most Occidental philosophy had largely been borrowed from the Oriental thinkers. Socrates, for instance, traveled in Egypt. Some sources even say that Socrates was initiated into some of the Egyptian mysteries. Obviously Socrates got some of his wisdom among the East's wise men.

I have often reflected upon the new vistas that reading opened to me. I knew right there in prison that reading had changed forever the course of my life. As I see it today, the ability to read awoke inside me some long dormant craving to be mentally alive. I certainly wasn't seeking any degree, the way a college confers a status symbol upon its students. My homemade education gave me, with every additional book that I read, a little bit more sensitivity to the deafness, dumbness, and blindness that was afflicting the black race in America. Not long ago, an English writer telephoned me from London, asking questions. One was, "What's your alma mater?" I told him, "Books." You will never catch me with a free fifteen minutes in which I'm not studying something I feel might be able to help the black man.

Yesterday I spoke in London, and both ways on the plane across the Atlantic I was studying a document about how the United Nations proposes to insure the human rights of the oppressed minorities of the world. The American black man is the world's most shameful case of minority oppression. What makes the black man think of himself as only an internal United States issue is just a catch-phrase, two words, "civil rights." How is the black man going to get "civil rights" before first he wins his *human* rights? If the American black man will start thinking about his *human* rights, and then start thinking of himself as part of one of the world's great peoples, he will see he has a case for the United Nations.

I can't think of a better case! Four hundred years of black blood and sweat invested here in America, and the white man still has the black man begging for what every immigrant fresh off the ship can take for granted the minute he walks down the gang-plank.

But I'm digressing. I told the Englishman that my alma mater was books, a good library. Every time I catch a plane, I have with me a book that I want to read—and that's a lot of books these days. If I weren't out here every day battling the white man, I could spend the rest of my life reading, just satisfying my curiosity—because you can hardly mention anything I'm not curious about. I don't think anybody ever got more out of going to prison than I did. In fact, prison enabled me to study far more intensively than I would have if my life had gone differently and I had attended some college. I imagine that one of the biggest troubles with colleges is there are too many distractions, too much panty-raiding, fraternities, and boola-boola and all of that. Where else but in a prison could I have attacked my ignorance by being able to study intensely sometimes as much as fifteen hours a day?

For Discussion and Writing

1. How did the process by which Malcolm learned to read differ from the typical way people learn to read?

2. In "Learning to Read," Malcolm tells us that he learned to read by teaching himself. What else did he teach himself while he taught himself to read?

3. **connections** What are the parallels between the ways Malcolm and Frederick Douglass, in "Learning to Read and Write" (p. 125), learned to read? What are the parallels and differences in the things they learned from their reading?

4. Though Malcolm changed many of his views after the time covered in this portion of his autobiography, the project of recovering African history remained important to him and remains important to this day to many African Americans. How do you react to his claims about African history?

5. **looking further** Do some research into the literacy rate in the United States today. How would you characterize the situation? What do you think are the causes and ramifications of illiteracy? What might Malcolm X have to say about it?

JOHN MCPHEE

The Search for Marvin Gardens

John McPhee is a Pulitzer Prize–winning American writer and one of the early practitioners of creative nonfiction, or fact-based writing that adapts techniques normally thought of as belonging to the writing of fiction. In addition to writing regularly for the New Yorker *since 1965 and producing twenty-nine books on a wide range of subjects from sports to science to farming (many originating in material first written for the* New Yorker*), McPhee has taught writing at Princeton University since 1974. His most well-known books include his biography of basketball player and future U.S. senator Bill Bradley, and* Annals of the Former World, *a collection of five books, four previously published, on the subject of geology.*

"The Search for Marvin Gardens" is one of the more creative and formally difficult works McPhee has written. As you read this essay, keep an eye on form—on the way he constructs the narratives, on the way he connects them and cuts them up—and think about the effects of putting this piece of writing together in this unusual way.

Go. I roll the dice—a six and a two. Through the air I move my token, the flatiron, to Vermont Avenue, where dog packs range.

The dogs are moving (some are limping) through ruins, rubble, fire damage, open garbage. Doorways are gone. Lath is visible in the crumbling walls of the buildings. The street sparkles with shattered glass. I have never seen, anywhere, so many broken windows. A sign— "Slow, Children at Play"—has been bent backward by an automobile. At the lighthouse, the dogs turn up Pacific and disappear. George Meade, Army engineer, built the lighthouse—brick upon brick, six hundred thousand bricks, to reach up high enough to throw a beam twenty miles over the sea. Meade, seven years later, saved the Union at Gettysburg.

* * *

I buy Vermont Avenue for $100. My opponent is a tall, shadowy figure, across from me, but I know him well, and I know his game like a favorite tune. If he can, he will always go for the quick kill. And when it is foolish to go for the quick kill he will be foolish. On the whole, though, he is a master assessor of percentages. It is a mistake to underestimate him. His eleven carries his top hat to St. Charles Place, which he buys for $140.

The sidewalks of St. Charles Place have been cracked to shards by through-growing weeds. There are no buildings. Mansions, hotels once stood here. A few street lamps now drop cones of light on broken glass and vacant space behind a chain-link fence that some great machine has in places bent to the ground. Five plane trees—in full summer leaf, flecking the light—are all that live on St. Charles Place.

Block upon block, gradually, we are cancelling each other out—in the blues, the lavenders, the oranges, the greens. My opponent follows a plan of his own devising. I use the Horn-blower & Weeks opening and the Zuricher defense. The first game draws tight, will soon finish. In 1971, a group of people in Racine, Wisconsin, played for seven hundred and sixty-eight hours. A game begun a month later in Danville, California, lasted eight hundred and twenty hours. These are official records, and they stun us. We have been playing for eight minutes. It amazes us that Monopoly is thought of as a long game. It is possible to play to a complete, absolute, and final conclusion in less than fifteen minutes, all within the rules as written. My opponent and I have done so thousands of times. No wonder we are sitting across from each other now in this best-of-seven series for the international singles championship of the world.

On Illinois Avenue, three men lean out from second-story windows. A girl is coming down the street. She wears dungarees and a bright-red shirt, has ample breasts and a Hadendoan Afro, a black halo, two feet in diameter. Ice rattles in the glasses in the hands of the men.

"Hey, sister!"

"Come on up!"

She looks up, looks from one to another to the other, looks them flat in the eye.

"What for?" she says, and she walks on.   10

I buy Illinois for $240. It solidifies my chances, for I already own Kentucky and Indiana. My opponent pales. If he had landed first on Illinois, the game would have been over then and there, for he has houses built on Boardwalk and Park Place, we share the railroads equally, and we have cancelled each other everywhere else. We never trade.

In 1852, R.B. Osborne, an immigrant Englishman, civil engineer, surveyed the route of a railroad line that would run from Camden to Absecon Island, in New Jersey, traversing the state from the Delaware River to the barrier beaches of the sea. He then sketched in the plan of a "bathing village" that would surround the eastern terminus of the line. His pen flew glibly, framing and naming spacious avenues parallel to the shore—Mediterranean, Baltic, Oriental, Ventnor—and narrower transsecting avenues: North Carolina, Pennsylvania, Vermont, Connecticut, States, Virginia, Tennessee, New York, Kentucky, Indiana, Illinois. The place as a whole had no name, so when he had completed the plan Osborne wrote in large letters over the ocean, "Atlantic City." No one ever challenged the name, or the names of Osborne's streets. Monopoly was invented in the early nineteen-thirties by Charles B. Darrow, but Darrow was only transliterating what Osborne had created. The railroads, crucial to any player, were the making of Atlantic City. After the rails were down, houses and hotels burgeoned from Mediterranean and Baltic to New York and Kentucky. Properties— building lots—sold for as little as six dollars apiece and as much as a thousand dollars. The original investors in the railroads and the real estate called themselves the Camden & Atlantic Land Company. Reverently, I repeat their names: Dwight Bell, William Coffin, John DaCosta, Daniel Deal, William Fleming, Andrew Hay, Joseph Porter, Jonathan Pitney, Samuel Richards— founders, fathers, forerunners, archetypical masters of the quick kill.

My opponent and I are now in a deep situation of classical Monopoly. The torsion is almost perfect—Boardwalk and Park

Place versus the brilliant reds. His cash position is weak, though, and if I escape him now he may fade. I land on Luxury Tax, contiguous to but in sanctuary from his power. I have four houses on Indiana. He lands there. He concedes.

Indiana Avenue was the address of the Brighton Hotel, gone now. The Brighton was exclusive—a word that no longer has retail value in the city. If you arrived by automobile and tried to register at the Brighton, you were sent away. Brighton-class people came in private railroad cars. Brighton-class people had other private railroad cars for their horses—dawn rides on the firm sand at water's edge, skirts flying. Colonel Anthony J. Drexel Biddle—the sort of name that would constrict throats in Philadelphia—lived, much of the year, in the Brighton.

Colonel Sanders' fried chicken is on Kentucky Avenue. So is 15 Clifton's Club Harlem, with the Sepia Revue and the Sepia Follies, featuring the Honey Bees, the Fashions, and the Lords.

My opponent and I, many years ago, played 2,428 games of Monopoly in a single season. He was then a recent graduate of the Harvard Law School, and he was working for a downtown firm, looking up law. Two people we knew—one from Chase Manhattan, the other from Morgan, Stanley—tried to get into the game, but after a few rounds we found that they were not in the conversation and we sent them home. Monopoly should always be *mano a mano* anyway. My opponent won 1,199 games, and so did I. Thirty were ties. He was called into the Army, and we stopped just there. Now, in Game 2 of the series, I go immediately to jail, and again to jail while my opponent seines property. He is dumbfoundingly lucky. He wins in twelve minutes.

Visiting hours are daily; eleven to two; Sunday, eleven to one; evenings, six to nine. "NO MINORS, NO FOOD, Immediate Family Only Allowed in Jail." All this above a blue steel door in a blue cement wall in the windowless interior of the basement of the city hall. The desk sergeant sits opposite the door to the jail. In a cigar box in front of him are pills in every color, a banquet of fruit salad an inch and a half deep—leapers, co-pilots, footballs, truck drivers, peanuts, blue angels, yellow jackets, redbirds, rainbows. Near the desk are two soldiers, waiting to go through the blue door. They are about eighteen years old. One of them is trying hard to light a cigarette. His wrists are in steel cuffs. A military policeman waits, too. He is a year or so older than the soldiers, taller, studious in appearance, gentle, fat. On a bench against a wall sits a good-looking girl in slacks. The blue door rattles, swings heavily open. A turnkey stands in the doorway. "Don't you guys kill yourselves back there now," says the sergeant to the soldiers.

"One kid, he overdosed himself about ten and a half hours ago," says the M.P.

The M.P., the soldiers, the turnkey, and the girl on the bench are white. The sergeant is black. "If you take off the handcuffs, take off the belts," says the sergeant to the M.P. "I don't want them hanging themselves back there." The door shuts and its tumblers move. When it opens again, five minutes later, a young white man in sandals and dungarees and a blue polo shirt emerges. His hair is in a ponytail. He has no beard. He grins at the good-looking girl. She rises, joins him. The sergeant hands him a manila envelope. From it he removes his belt and a small notebook. He borrows a pencil, makes an entry in the notebook. He is out of jail, free. What did he do? He offended Atlantic City in some way. He spent a night in the jail. In the nineteen-thirties, men visiting Atlantic City went to jail, directly to jail, did not pass Go, for appearing in topless bathing suits on the beach. A city statute requiring all men to wear full-length bathing suits was not seriously challenged until 1937, and the first year in which a man could legally go bare-chested on the beach was 1940.

Game 3. After seventeen minutes, I am ready to begin construction on overpriced and sluggish Pacific, North Carolina, and Pennsylvania. Nothing else being open, opponent concedes. 20

The physical profile of streets perpendicular to the shore is something like a playground slide. It begins in the high skyline of Boardwalk hotels, plummets into warrens of "side-avenue" motels, crosses Pacific, slopes through church missions, convalescent homes, burlesque houses, rooming houses, and liquor stores, crosses Atlantic, and runs level through the bombed-out ghetto as far—Baltic, Mediterranean—as the eye can see. North Carolina Avenue, for example, is flanked at its beach end by the

Chalfonte and the Haddon Hall (908 rooms, air-conditioned), where, according to one biographer, John Philip Sousa (1854–1932) first played when he was twenty-two, insisting, even then, that everyone call him by his entire name. Behind these big hotels, motels—Barbizon, Catalina—crouch. Between Pacific and Atlantic is an occasional house from 1910—wooden porch, wooden mullions, old yellow paint—and two churches, a package store, a strip show, a dealer in fruits and vegetables. Then, beyond Atlantic Avenue, North Carolina moves on into the vast ghetto, the bulk of the city, and it looks like Metz in 1919, Cologne in 1944. Nothing has actually exploded. It is not bomb damage. It is deep and complex decay. Roofs are off. Bricks are scattered in the street. People sit on porches, six deep, at nine on a Monday morning. When they go off to wait in unemployment lines, they wait sometimes two hours. Between Mediterranean and Baltic runs a chain-link fence, enclosing rubble. A patrol car sits idling by the curb. In the back seat is a German shepherd. A sign on the fence says, "Beware of Bad Dogs."

Mediterranean and Baltic are the principal avenues of the ghetto. Dogs are everywhere. A pack of seven passes me. Block after block, there are three-story brick row houses. Whole segments of them are abandoned, a thousand broken windows. Some parts are intact, occupied. A mattress lies in the street, soaking in a pool of water. Wet stuffing is coming out of the mattress. A postman is having a rye and a beer in the Plantation Bar at nine-fifteen in the morning. I ask him idly if he knows where Marvin Gardens is. He does not. "HOOKED AND NEED HELP? CONTACT N.A.R.C.O." "REVIVAL NOW GOING ON, CONDUCTED BY REVEREND H. HENDERSON OF TEXAS." These are signboards on Mediterranean and Baltic. The second one is upside down and leans against a boarded-up window of the Faith Temple Church of God in Christ. There is an old peeling poster on a warehouse wall showing a figure in an electric chair. "The Black Panther Manifesto" is the title of the poster, and its message is, or was, that "the fascists have already decided in advance to murder Chairman Bobby Seale in the electric chair." I pass an old woman who carries a bucket. She wears blue sneakers, worn through. Her feet spill out. She wears red socks, rolled at the knees. A white handkerchief, spread over her head, is knotted at the corners. Does she know where Marvin Gardens is? "I sure don't know," she says, setting down the bucket.

"I sure don't know. I've heard of it somewhere, but I just can't say where." I walk on, through a block of shattered glass. The glass crunches underfoot like coarse sand. I remember when I first came here—a long train ride from Trenton, long ago, games of poker in the train—to play basketball against Atlantic City. We were half black, they were all black. We scored forty points, they scored eighty, or something like it. What I remember most is that they had glass backboards—glittering, pendent, expensive glass backboards, a rarity then in high schools, even in colleges, the only ones we played on all year.

I turn on Pennsylvania, and start back toward the sea. The windows of the Hotel Astoria, on Pennsylvania near Baltic, are boarded up. A sheet of unpainted plywood is the door, and in it is a triangular peephole that now frames an eye. The plywood door opens. A man answers my question. Rooms there are six, seven, and ten dollars a week. I thank him for the information and move on, emerging from the ghetto at the Catholic Daughters of America Women's Guest House, between Atlantic and Pacific. Between Pacific and the Boardwalk are the blinking vacancy signs of the Aristocrat and Colton Manor motels. Pennsylvania terminates at the Sheraton-Seaside—thirty-two dollars a day, ocean corner. I take a walk on the Boardwalk and into the Holiday Inn (twenty-three stories). A guest is registering. "You reserved for Wednesday, and this is Monday," the clerk tells him. "But that's all right. We have *plenty* of rooms." The clerk is very young, female, and has soft brown hair that hangs below her waist. Her superior kicks her.

He is a middle-aged man with red spiderwebs in his face. He is jacketed and tied. He takes her aside. "Don't say 'plenty,' " he says. "Say 'You are fortunate, sir. We have rooms available.' "

The face of the young woman turns sour. "We have all the rooms you need," she says to the customer, and, to her superior, "How's that?"

Game 4. My opponent's luck has become abrasive. He has Boardwalk and Park Place, and has sealed the board.

Darrow was a plumber. He was, specifically, a radiator repairman who lived in Germantown, Pennsylvania. His first Monopoly board was a sheet of linoleum. On it he placed houses and hotels that he had carved from blocks of wood. The game he thus invented was brilliantly conceived, for it was an uncannily exact reflection of the business milieu at large. In its depth, range, and subtlety, in its luck-skill ratio, in its sense of infrastructure and socio-economic parameters, in its philosophical characteristics, it reached to the profundity of the financial community. It was as scientific as the stock market. It suggested the manner and means through which an underdeveloped world had been developed. It was chess at Wall Street level. "Advance token to the nearest Railroad and pay owner twice the rental to which he is otherwise entitled. If Railroad is unowned, you may buy it from the Bank. Get out of Jail, free. Advance token to nearest utility. If unowned, you may buy it from Bank. If owned, throw dice and pay owner a total ten times the amount thrown. You are assessed for street repairs: $40 per house, $115 per hotel. Pay poor tax of $15. Go to Jail. Go directly to Jail. Do not pass Go. Do not collect $200."

The turnkey opens the blue door. The turnkey is known to the inmates as Sidney K. Above his desk are ten closed-circuit-TV screens—assorted viewpoints of the jail. There are three cell-blocks—men, women, juvenile boys. Six days is the average stay. Showers twice a week. The steel doors and the equipment that operates them were made in San Antonio. The prisoners sleep on bunks of butcher block. There are no mattresses. There are three prisoners to a cell. In winter, it is cold in here. Prisoners burn newspapers to keep warm. Cell corners are black with smudge. The jail is three years old. The men's block echoes with chatter. The man in the cell nearest Sidney K. is pacing. His shirt is covered with broad stains of blood. The block for juvenile boys is, by contrast, utterly silent—empty corridor, empty cells. There is only one prisoner. He is small and black and appears to be thirteen. He says he is sixteen and that he has been alone in here for three days.
"Why are you here? What did you do?"
"I hit a jitney driver." 30

The series stands at three all. We have split the fifth and sixth games. We are scrambling for property. Around the board we fairly fly. We move so fast because we do our own banking and search our own deeds. My opponent grows tense.

* * *

Ventnor Avenue, a street of delicatessens and doctors' offices, is leafy with plane trees and hydrangeas, the city flower. Water Works is on the mainland. The water comes over in submarine pipes. Electric Company gets power from across the state, on the Delaware River, in Deepwater. States Avenue, now a wasteland like St. Charles, once had gardens running down the middle of the street, a horse-drawn trolley, private homes. States Avenue was as exclusive as the Brighton. Only an apartment house, a small motel, and the All Wars Memorial Building—monadnocks spaced widely apart—stand along States Avenue now. Pawnshops, convalescent homes, and the Paradise Soul Saving Station are on Virginia Avenue. The soul-saving station is pink, orange, and yellow. In the windows flanking the door of the Virginia Money Loan Office are Nikons, Polaroids, Yashicas, Sony TVs, Underwood typewriters, Singer sewing machines, and pictures of Christ. On the far side of town, beside a single track and locked up most of the time, is the new railroad station, a small hut made of glazed firebrick, all that is left of the lines that built the city. An authentic phrenologist works on New York Avenue close to Frank's Extra Dry Bar and a church where the sermon today is "Death in the Pot." The church is of pink brick, has blue and amber windows and two red doors. St. James Place, narrow and twisting, is lined with boarding houses that have wooden porches on each of three stories, suggesting a New Orleans made of salt-bleached pine. In a vacant lot on Tennessee is a white Ford station wagon stripped to the chassis. The windows are smashed. A plastic Clorox bottle sits on the driver's seat. The wind has pressed newspaper against the chain-link fence around the lot. Atlantic Avenue, the city's principal thoroughfare, could be seventeen American Main Streets placed end to end—discount vitamins and Vienna Corset shops, movie theatres, shoe stores, and funeral homes. The Boardwalk is made of yellow pine and Douglas fir, soaked in pentachlorophenol. Downbeach, it reaches far beyond the city. Signs everywhere—on windows, lampposts, trash baskets—proclaim "Bienvenue Canadiens!" The salt air is full of Canadian French. In the Claridge Hotel, on Park Place, I ask a clerk if she knows where Marvin Gardens is. She says, "Is it a floral shop?" I ask a cabdriver, parked outside. He says, "Never heard of it." Park Place is one block long, Pacific to Boardwalk. On the roof of the Claridge is the Solarium, the highest point in town—panoramic view of the ocean, the bay, the saltwater ghetto. I look down at the rooftops of the side-avenue motels and into swimming pools. There are hundreds of people around the rooftop pools, sunbathing, reading—many more people than are on the beach. Walls, windows, and a block of sky are all that is visible from these pools—no sand, no sea. The pools are craters, and with the people around them they are counter-sunk into the motels.

The seventh, and final, game is ten minutes old and I have hotels on Oriental, Vermont, and Connecticut. I have Tennessee and St. James. I have North Carolina and Pacific. I have Board-walk, Atlantic, Ventnor, Illinois, Indiana. My fingers are forming a "V." I have mortgaged most of these properties in order to pay for others, and I have mortgaged the others to pay for the hotels. I have seven dollars. I will pay off the mortgages and build my reserves with income from the three hotels. My cash position may be low, but I feel like a rocket in an underground silo. Meanwhile, if I could just go to jail for a time I could pause there, wait there, until my opponent, in his inescapable rounds, pays the rates of my hotels. Jail, at times, is the strategic place to be. I roll boxcars from the Reading and move the flatiron to Community Chest. "Go to Jail. Go directly to Jail."

The prisoners, of course, have no pens and no pencils. They take paper napkins, roll them tight as crayons, char the ends with matches, and write on the walls. The things they write are not entirely idiomatic; for example, "In God We Trust." All is in car-bon. Time is required in the writing. "Only humanity could know of such pain." "God So Loved the World." "There is no greater pain than life itself." In the women's block now, there are six blacks, giggling, and a white asleep in red shoes. She is drunk. The others are pushers, prostitutes, an auto thief, a burglar caught with pistol in purse. A sixteen-year-old accused of murder was in here last week. These words are written on the wall of a now empty cell: "Laying here I see two bunks about six inches thick, not counting the one I'm laying on, which is hard as brick. No cushion for my back. No pillow for my head. Just a couple scratchy blankets which is best to use it's said. I wake up in the morning so shivery and cold, waiting and waiting till I am told the food is coming. It's on its way. It's not worth waiting for, but I eat it anyway. I know one thing when they set me free I'm gonna be good if it kills me."

How many years must a game be played to produce an Anthony 35 J. Drexel Biddle and chestnut geldings on the beach? About half a century was the original answer, from the first railroad to Biddle at his peak. Biddle, at his peak, hit an Atlantic City streetcar conductor with his fist, laid him out with one punch. This increased Biddle's legend. He did not go to jail. While John Philip Sousa led his band along the boardwalk playing "The Stars and Stripes Forever" and Jack Dempsey ran up and down in training for his fight with Gene Tunney, the city crossed the high curve of its parabola. Al Capone held conventions here—upstairs with his sleeves rolled, apportioning among his lieutenant governors the states of the Eastern seaboard. The natural history of an American resort proceeds from Indians to French Canadians via Biddles and Capones. French Canadians, whatever they may be at home, are Visigoths here. Bienvenue Visigoths!

My opponent plods along incredibly well. He has got his fourth railroad, and patiently, unbelievably, he has picked up my potential winners until he has blocked me everywhere but Marvin Gardens. He has avoided, in the fifty-dollar zoning, my increasingly petty hotels. His cash flow swells. His railroads are costing me two hundred dollars a minute. He is building hotels on States, Virginia, and St. Charles. He has temporarily reversed the current. With the yellow monopolies and my blue monopolies, I could probably defeat his lavenders and his railroads. I have Atlantic and Ventnor. I need Marvin Gardens. My only hope is Marvin Gardens.

There is a plaque at Boardwalk and Park Place, and on it in relief is the leonine profile of a man who looks like an officer in a metropolitan bank—"Charles B. Darrow, 1889–1967, inventor of the game of Monopoly." "Darrow," I address him, aloud. "Where is Marvin Gardens?" There is, of course, no answer. Bronze, impassive, Darrow looks south down the Boardwalk. "Mr. Darrow, please, where is Marvin Gardens?" Nothing. Not a sign. He just looks south down the Boardwalk.

* * *

My opponent accepts the trophy with his natural ease, and I make, from notes, remarks that are even less graceful than his.

Marvin Gardens is the one color-block Monopoly property that is not in Atlantic City. It is a suburb within a suburb, secluded. It is a planned compound of seventy-two handsome houses set on curvilinear private streets under yews and cedars, poplars and willows. The compound was built around 1920, in Margate, New Jersey, and consists of solid buildings of stucco, brick, and wood, with slate roofs, tile roofs, multi-mullioned porches, Giraldic towers, and Spanish grilles. Marvin Gardens, the ultimate outwash of Monopoly, is a citadel and sanctuary of the middle class. "We're heavily patrolled by police here. We don't take no chances. Me? I'm living here nine years. I paid seventeen thousand dollars and I've been offered thirty. Number one, I don't want to move. Number two, I don't need the money. I have four bedrooms, two and a half baths, front den, back den. No basement. The Atlantic is down there. Six feet down and you float. A lot of people have a hard time finding this place. People that lived in Atlantic City all their life don't know how to find it. They don't know where the hell they're going. They just know it's south, down the Boardwalk."

For Discussion and Writing

1. What is this essay's subject? Does it have more than one? If so, what are they?
2. While McPhee is known as a progenitor of creative nonfiction, his work is not usually quite as creative as this essay is. What makes it so creative, and so difficult? Describe a number of the things McPhee does in this essay that diverge from more traditional, mainstream nonfiction magazine writing. What are the effects of these techniques on readers?
3. **connections** Like McPhee, Joan Didion is thought of as one of the writers who contributed to the new journalism, a new kind of nonfiction writing developed in the 1960s. Compare "The Search for Marvin Gardens" with Didion's "On Keeping a Notebook" (p. 116). What do you notice in common between the two essays? Do they share specific methods for relating facts or events? Do they share ways of positioning the author in relation to the story the author tells? Are there ways in which their subjects or styles differ?

4. Do you know the history of your town or city? Reflect on your answer. How do you know the past of the place you live, if you do? If you don't, why do you think that is? Do you think you should?

5. **looking further**   Pick a favorite pastime—a board game, a sport, even the playing of a musical instrument—and research its history. What did you find that you didn't expect? What did you find that illuminated your chosen pastime? Also reflect on the act of research: how did you get to the interesting, illuminating, or surprising information? Finally, reflect on the results of your research: will your time spent on this activity change at all now that you know what you know?

LYDIA MILLET

Victor's Hall

Lydia Millet is an American writer of novels, short stories, and essays. She has shown remarkable productivity and versatility over the course of a twenty-year career, during which she has had ten novels and one short story collection published. The subjects of her fiction range from politics to pornography to the threat of nuclear annihilation, but all exhibit her dark humor and restrained yet powerful prose. Millet's recent trilogy, How the Dead Dream *(2008),* Ghost Lights *(2011), and* Magnificence *(2012), represents an important contribution to environmental literature. Her latest novel is* Sweet Lamb of Heaven *(2016). In addition to producing a new book-length work every two years, Millet is staff writer for the conservationist nonprofit Center for Biological Diversity in Tucson, Arizona.*

Many of Millet's novels exhibit a tendency to include fantastic elements—events and situations that are not realistic but rather would seem to be more at home in a fantasy or science fiction novel. While nothing in this essay is fictional, let alone fantastic, keep an eye out as you read for the feelings people sometimes get when reading fantastic fiction, feelings of wonder, uneasiness, of being unsure whether they are in a dream or awake. Ask yourself: How does Millet evoke these feelings? What use might Millet's own feelings be to her, as a writer, in developing this essay?

On the outskirts of this city stands a fake-medieval castle with an elk statue atop its battlements. In the courtyard is a bronze relief of a man shouldering his rifle—one C. J. McElroy, a Texan who founded both this International Wildlife Museum in 1988 and, before that, in the early 1970s, Safari Club International, the trophy hunters' group that's headquartered here.

The wildlife museum contains, like its more pedigreed natural-history cousins in cities like New York and Washington, dioramas composed of the stuffed bodies of animals posed in sculpted woodlands or prairies with painted backdrops. These dioramas—as the scholar Donna Haraway has shown—have roots as colonial-era gardens of Eden in miniature. Some are very beautiful, too, with sublime and tragic qualities that captivate adults and children alike. And the dioramas have more to recommend them than the McElroy Hall, where hundreds of disembodied heads, many from animals shot by the museum's founder, are lined up in long rows on knotty pine walls. The room is a monument to the scale of these kills. (Mr. McElroy reportedly took more than 100 safaris on six continents; his obituary says he claimed 425 trophies in the safari club's record book.)

More than the dioramas, it's this old-school trophy chamber—a victor's hall of imperial conquest, plunder and braggadocio—that seems to lay bare the museum's core. Giraffes soar toward the high ceiling while a polar bear and black bear stand on hind legs, paws raised, faces frozen in fearsome roars. In the middle, great cats are penned, one from each famous species in a phantom Ark. But most overwhelming are the heads, protruding from the walls all around. If I weren't familiar with the bizarre conventions of taxidermy—if I were a child, for example—these gentle, doe-eyed faces on chopped necks would certainly haunt me.

Amateurishness is evident throughout the museum, where I spotted interpretive plaques with typos like "threateneing" and "achidna" (for echidna, an egg-laying mammal). An icy penguin scene claims that emperor and Adélie penguins are deemed species of "least concern" by the International Union for the Conservation of Nature when in fact the organization has classified both as "near threatened" since 2012. And in the Conservation Room I saw no mention of climate change, likely to become the biggest threat to conservation in the coming century.

Whatever charms this place has, I realized as I ambled through   5 the rooms—and it does have charms, half-hidden in the moth-eaten seams, the demure pathos of an extinct passenger pigeon—its amateurishness is crucial to them. The amateur is a form of American authenticity, and museums like this embody a deeply resonant utopianism that plays to our culture's love of the homespun.

Here we can fulfill our craving for childlike wonder unfettered by the chains of reason or responsibility; the amateur institution reassures us, in a country increasingly hostile to scientific expertise and even to education, that expertise is not required. How comforting it is that when we gaze upon, say, the sleek and waddling forms of penguins, we don't have to read below the glass case about their uncertain future. Even for me, a conservationist, there was something liberating about looking at those tubby, flightless birds and forgetting, just for a moment, the wrongs we did them yesterday and will repeat tomorrow.

Behind this surface of poor spelling, outdated information and missing science lies the power of big money and big politics. Safari Club International is no N.R.A. leviathan; it claims a mere 50,000 members and in 2014 reported revenues of about $24 million, more than half from its annual convention. (The museum draws some 70,000 visitors a year.) But its members have included prominent leaders like Gen. H. Norman Schwarzkopf and the first President Bush, whose son presented himself as down home and authentic, just as this minor cultural outpost in Tucson does.

Trophy hunters are not Everyman. These world-traveling endangered-species shooters are a far cry from the hunters who spend weekends in the American outback near their suburban or rural homes. In the 1970s, Safari Club International asked the federal government to approve its import of 1,125 not-yet-killed trophies of 40 endangered species, including gorillas, orangutans and tigers, according to the Humane Society of the United States.

The club still promotes the "Big Five" African safaris of the colonial great white hunters of yesteryear; even today the richest of the rich can kill the "big five" (leopard, Cape buffalo, elephant, lion and rhino). In Namibia, for instance, you can bag a rhino—but only if you find you have $350,000 burning a hole in your pocket. The Dallas Safari Club recently auctioned a permit to kill a black rhino and as recently as this January attempted to sell a permit to hunt an elephant.

The Safari Club International has worked the legal system 10 hard to try to keep polar bears—threatened primarily by climate change, but also by hunting—on the list of creatures people can import as trophies after shooting. It sued the federal government because native Alaskans, who traditionally hunted to survive, were given preference for polar-bear hunting permits over out-of-state trophy seekers. The list is long, but the point is brief: none of the group's expensive back-room campaigns are mentioned on the museum's halls.

None of its actions are presented to this visiting public. Instead, we see only once-lovely animals made lovely anew with fiberglass forms and chemicals, glowing in their amber-lit pastoral scenes as though eternally on the brink of reanimation. They seem to wish for no higher honor than to be beheld by us—and surely their grace and nobility suggest our own.

Yet something is missing. As we wander among the skin-covered forms, something lurks in the alcoves: our hosts. They seem to be invisible. Who really dwells in this castle, moving at night among the dusty and the dead? Beneath these forests of antlers, beneath the hundreds of pairs of gleaming glass eyes, a dark fairy tale remains to be decoded if we wish to know what unseen hand has stilled these living beasts and made them ghosts.

For Discussion and Writing

1. This essay originally appeared on the *New York Times* op-ed page under the title "Stuffed Animals with an Agenda." What do you think Millet meant by that?

2. As the headnote attests, Lydia Millet is primarily a writer of fiction. In fact, taxidermy plays an important part in one of her novels. Can you detect any elements of her writing in this essay that might also be used in a novel or short story? Are there any parts of the essay that seem unlikely to appear in fiction?

3. **connections**   In "Shooting an Elephant" (p. 272), George Orwell describes an up-close encounter with the imperialistic influences that Millet touches on in her essay. How might the Europeans in Orwell's essay have perceived the museum Millet visited? How would Millet likely feel about Orwell's shooting of the elephant?

4. How do you feel about trophy hunting? What do you think about it in relation to sport hunting or hunting for food? Is it the same? If you consider them different, are the differences significant? Why?

5. **looking further**   Toward the end of the nineteenth century in Europe, there was a craze for anthropomorphic taxidermy. Do a little reading into this practice. What were the different variations? Why do you think people did it? How do you feel about it? Can you think of any contemporary analogues?

Two Ways to Belong in America

Born in 1940 and raised in Calcutta, India, Bharati Mukherjee immi-grated to the United States in 1961 and earned an M.F.A. and a Ph.D. in literature. Mukherjee is the author of several novels, including Tiger's Daughter *(1972),* Jasmine *(1989),* Desirable Daughters *(2002), and* The Tree Bride *(2004). She has also written short story collections, such as* The Middleman and Other Stories *(1988). She is a professor emerita at the University of California, Berkeley.*

"Two Ways to Belong in America" first appeared in the New York Times. *It was written to address a movement in Congress to take away government benefits from resident aliens. Like her fiction, though, it is about the issues that confront immigrants in America.*

This is a tale of two sisters from Calcutta, Mira and Bharati, who have lived in the United States for some 35 years, but who find themselves on different sides in the current debate over the status of immigrants. I am an American citizen and she is not. I am moved that thousands of long-term residents are finally taking the oath of citizenship. She is not.

Mira arrived in Detroit in 1960 to study child psychology and pre-school education. I followed her a year later to study creative writing at the University of Iowa. When we left India, we were almost identical in appearance and attitude. We dressed alike, in saris; we expressed identical views on politics, social issues, love, and marriage in the same Calcutta convent-school accent. We would endure our two years in America, secure our degrees, then return to India to marry the grooms of our father's choosing.

Instead, Mira married an Indian student in 1962 who was get-ting his business administration degree at Wayne State Univer-sity. They soon acquired the labor certifications necessary for the green card of hassle-free residence and employment.

Mira still lives in Detroit, works in the Southfield, Mich., school system, and has become nationally recognized for her contributions in the fields of pre-school education and parent-teacher relationships. After 36 years as a legal immigrant in this country, she clings passionately to her Indian citizenship and hopes to go home to India when she retires.

In Iowa City in 1963, I married a fellow student, an American 5 of Canadian parentage. Because of the accident of his North Dakota birth, I bypassed labor-certification requirements and the race-related "quota" system that favored the applicant's country of origin over his or her merit. I was prepared for (and even welcomed) the emotional strain that came with marrying outside my ethnic community. In 33 years of marriage, we have lived in every part of North America. By choosing a husband who was not my father's selection, I was opting for fluidity, self-invention, blue jeans, and T-shirts, and renouncing 3,000 years (at least) of caste-observant, "pure culture" marriage in the Mukherjee family. My books have often been read as unapologetic (and in some quarters overenthusiastic) texts for cultural and psychological "mongrelization." It's a word I celebrate.

Mira and I have stayed sisterly close by phone. In our regular Sunday morning conversations, we are unguardedly affectionate. I am her only blood relative on this continent. We expect to see each other through the looming crises of aging and ill health without being asked. Long before Vice President Gore's "Citizenship U.S.A." drive, we'd had our polite arguments over the ethics of retaining an overseas citizenship while expecting the permanent protection and economic benefits that come with living and working in America.

Like well-raised sisters, we never said what was really on our minds, but we probably pitied one another. She, for the lack of structure in my life, the erasure of Indianness, the absence of an unvarying daily core. I, for the narrowness of her perspective, her uninvolvement with the mythic depths or the superficial pop culture of this society. But, now, with the scapegoatings of "aliens" (documented or illegal) on the increase, and the targeting of long-term legal immigrants like Mira for new scrutiny and new self-consciousness, she and I find ourselves unable to maintain the same polite discretion. We were always unacknowledged adversaries, and we are now, more than ever, sisters.

"I feel used," Mira raged on the phone the other night. "I feel manipulated and discarded. This is such an unfair way to treat a person who was invited to stay and work here because of her talent. My employer went to the I.N.S. and petitioned for the labor certification. For over 30 years, I've invested my creativity and professional skills into the improvement of *this* country's preschool system. I've obeyed all the rules, I've paid my taxes, I love my work, I love my students, I love the friends I've made. How dare America now change its rules in midstream? If America wants to make new rules curtailing benefits of legal immigrants, they should apply only to immigrants who arrive after those rules are already in place."

To my ears, it sounded like the description of a long-enduring, comfortable yet loveless marriage, without risk or recklessness. Have we the right to demand, and to expect, that we be loved? (That, to me, is the subtext of the arguments by immigration advocates.) My sister is an expatriate, professionally generous and creative, socially courteous and gracious, and that's as far as her Americanization can go. She is here to maintain an identity, not to transform it.

I asked her if she would follow the example of others who have   10 decided to become citizens because of the anti-immigration bills in Congress. And here, she surprised me. "If America wants to play the manipulative game, I'll play it, too," she snapped. "I'll become a U.S. citizen for now, then change back to India when I'm ready to go home. I feel some kind of irrational attachment to India that I don't to America. Until all this hysteria against legal immigrants, I was totally happy. Having my green card meant I could visit any place in the world I wanted to and then come back to a job that's satisfying and that I do very well."

In one family, from two sisters alike as peas in a pod, there could not be a wider divergence of immigrant experience. America spoke to me—I married it—I embraced the demotion from expatriate aristocrat to immigrant nobody, surrendering those thousands of years of "pure culture," the saris, the delightfully accented English. She retained them all. Which of us is the freak?

Mira's voice, I realize, is the voice not just of the immigrant South Asian community but of an immigrant community of the millions who have stayed rooted in one job, one city, one house, one ancestral culture, one cuisine, for the entirety of their productive years.

She speaks for greater numbers than I possibly can. Only the fluency of her English and the anger, rather than fear, born of confidence from her education, differentiate her from the seamstresses, the domestics, the technicians, the shop owners, the millions of hard-working but effectively silenced documented immigrants as well as their less fortunate "illegal" brothers and sisters.

Nearly 20 years ago, when I was living in my husband's ancestral homeland of Canada, I was always well-employed but never allowed to feel part of the local Quebec or larger Canadian society. Then, through a Green Paper that invited a national referendum on the unwanted side effects of "nontraditional" immigration, the government officially turned against its immigrant communities, particularly those from South Asia.

I felt then the same sense of betrayal that Mira feels now. I will never forget the pain of that sudden turning, and the casual racist outbursts the Green Paper elicited. That sense of betrayal had its desired effect and drove me, and thousands like me, from the country.

Mira and I differ, however, in the ways in which we hope to   15
interact with the country that we have chosen to live in. She is happier to live in America as expatriate Indian than as an immigrant American. I need to feel like a part of the community I have adopted (as I tried to feel in Canada as well). I need to put roots down, to vote and make the difference that I can. The price that the immigrant willingly pays, and that the exile avoids, is the trauma of self-transformation.

For Discussion and Writing

1. Make a list of specific qualities, behaviors, and beliefs for each of the two sisters. What similarities and differences are evident?

2. Mukherjee spends much of this essay comparing herself to her sister. What larger comparison does this analysis support?

3. **connections** Mukherjee's essay contains a lot of background information (about politics and history), which she skillfully weaves into the story she tells about herself and her sister. Compare the way she weaves together these two strands of the narrative with the methods employed by John McPhee in "The Search for Marvin Gardens" (p. 250).

TWO WAYS TO BELONG IN AMERICA 271

4. Think of a sibling or friend with whom you disagree vehemently over some issue or idea. Describe your arguments about it. Are they "polite," as Mukherjee says hers are with her sister?

5. **looking further** Mukherjee quotes her sister as describing her own allegiance to her native culture as "some kind of irrational attachment" (par. 10). Would you describe it as irrational, as some critics of multiculturalism do? Or do you find it a natural result of her identity, as advocates of multiculturalism do? Research multiculturalism and discuss "Two Ways to Belong in America" in the light of multiculturalism as both demographic fact and political philosophy.

GEORGE ORWELL

Shooting an Elephant

Born in India in 1903, Eric Blair was the son of an English civil ser-
vant in the British Raj, the rule of India by the British, as was his father.
Educated in England, Blair was an imperial policeman in India for
five years but resigned and returned to England to pursue his dream
of becoming a writer, complete with a pen name, George Orwell. Known
best for his novels Animal Farm *(1945) and* 1984 *(1949), Orwell's*
political concerns were expressed in nonfiction as well, in works such
as his chronicle of life among the poor, Down and Out in Paris and
London *(1933). Because of his stands against economic injustice and*
totalitarianism, Orwell remains an influential figure, as the adjectiviza-
tion of his pen name shows— Orwellian *has entered the vernacular as*
a term to describe the violence done to language and common sense by
totalitarianism. "Shooting an Elephant" tells the story of a moment
early in Orwell's life when his sense of injustice surfaced. As you read,
watch for the ways in which Orwell uses the tools of narrative writing
to dramatize the moment.

In Moulmein, in Lower Burma, I was hated by large numbers of
people—the only time in my life that I have been important
enough for this to happen to me. I was sub-divisional police officer
of the town, and in an aimless, petty kind of way anti-European
feeling was very bitter. No one had the guts to raise a riot, but if a
European woman went through the bazaars alone somebody
would probably spit betel juice over her dress. As a police officer I
was an obvious target and was baited whenever it seemed safe to
do so. When a nimble Burman tripped me up on the football field
and the referee (another Burman) looked the other way, the
crowd yelled with hideous laughter. This happened more than
once. In the end the sneering yellow faces of young men that met
me everywhere, the insults hooted after me when I was at a safe
distance, got badly on my nerves. The young Buddhist priests
were the worst of all. There were several thousands of them in the

town and none of them seemed to have anything to do except stand on street corners and jeer at Europeans.

All this was perplexing and upsetting. For at that time I had already made up my mind that imperialism was an evil thing and the sooner I chucked up my job and got out of it the better. Theoretically—and secretly, of course—I was all for the Burmese and all against their oppressors, the British. As for the job I was doing, I hated it more bitterly than I can perhaps make clear. In a job like that you see the dirty work of Empire at close quarters. The wretched prisoners huddling in the stinking cages of the lock-ups, the grey, cowed faces of the long-term convicts, the scarred buttocks of the men who had been flogged with bamboos—all these oppressed me with an intolerable sense of guilt. But I could get nothing into perspective. I was young and ill-educated and I had had to think out my problems in the utter silence that is imposed on every Englishman in the East. I did not even know that the British Empire is dying, still less did I know that it is a great deal better than the younger empires that are going to supplant it. All I knew was that I was stuck between my hatred of the empire I served and my rage against the evil-spirited little beasts who tried to make my job impossible. With one part of my mind I thought of the British Raj as an unbreakable tyranny, as something clamped down, in *saecula saeculorum* upon the will of prostrate peoples; with another part I thought that the greatest joy in the world would be to drive a bayonet into a Buddhist priest's guts. Feelings like these are the normal by-products of imperialism; ask any Anglo-Indian official, if you can catch him off duty.

One day something happened which in a roundabout way was enlightening. It was a tiny incident in itself, but it gave me a better glimpse than I had had before of the real nature of imperialism—the real motives for which despotic governments act. Early one morning the sub-inspector at a police station the other end of the town rang me up on the phone and said that an elephant was ravaging the bazaar. Would I please come and do something about it? I did not know what I could do, but I wanted to see what was happening and I got on to a pony and started out. I took my rifle, an old .44 Winchester and much too small to kill an elephant, but I thought the noise might be useful *in terrorem*. Various Burmans stopped me on the way and told me about the elephant's doings. It was not, of course, a wild elephant, but a tame one which had gone "must." It had been chained up, as tame elephants always are when their attack of "must" is due, but on the previous night it had broken its chain and escaped. Its mahout, the only person who could manage it when it was in that state, had set out in pursuit, but had taken the wrong direction and was now twelve hours' journey away, and in the morning the elephant had suddenly reappeared in the town. The Burmese population had no weapons and were quite helpless against it. It had already destroyed somebody's bamboo hut, killed a cow and raided some fruit-stalls and devoured the stock; also it had met the municipal rubbish van and, when the driver jumped out and took to his heels, had turned the van over and inflicted violences upon it.

The Burmese sub-inspector and some Indian constables were waiting for me in the quarter where the elephant had been seen. It was a very poor quarter, a labyrinth of squalid bamboo huts, thatched with palm-leaf, winding all over a steep hillside. I remember that it was a cloudy, stuffy morning at the beginning of the rains. We began questioning the people as to where the elephant had gone and, as usual, failed to get any definite information. That is invariably the case in the East; a story always sounds clear enough at a distance, but the nearer you get to the scene of events the vaguer it becomes. Some of the people said that the elephant had gone in one direction, some said that he had gone in another, some professed not even to have heard of any elephant. I had almost made up my mind that the whole story was a pack of lies, when we heard yells a little distance away. There was a loud, scandalized cry of "Go away, child! Go away this instant!" and an old woman with a switch in her hand came round the corner of a hut, violently shooing away a crowd of naked children. Some more women followed, clicking their tongues and exclaiming; evidently there was something that the children ought not to have seen. I rounded the hut and saw a man's dead body sprawling in the mud. He was an Indian, a black Dravidian coolie, almost naked, and he could not have been dead many minutes. The people said that the elephant had come suddenly upon him round the corner of the hut, caught him with its trunk, put its foot on his back and ground him into the earth. This was the rainy season and the ground was soft, and his face had scored a trench a foot deep and a couple of yards long. He was lying on his belly with arms crucified and head sharply twisted to one side. His face was coated with mud, the eyes wide open, the teeth bared and grinning with an expression of unendurable agony. (Never tell me, by the way, that the dead look peaceful. Most of the corpses I have seen looked devilish.) The friction of the great beast's foot had stripped the skin from his back as neatly as one skins a rabbit. As soon as I saw the dead man I sent an orderly to a friend's house nearby to borrow an elephant rifle. I had already sent back the pony, not wanting it to go mad with fright and throw me if it smelt the elephant.

The orderly came back in a few minutes with a rifle and five   5 cartridges, and meanwhile some Burmans had arrived and told us that the elephant was in the paddy fields below, only a few hundred yards away. As I started forward practically the whole population of the quarter flocked out of the houses and followed me. They had seen the rifle and were all shouting excitedly that I was going to shoot the elephant. They had not shown much interest in the elephant when he was merely ravaging their homes, but it was different now that he was going to be shot. It was a bit of fun to them, as it would be to an English crowd; besides they wanted the meat. It made me vaguely uneasy. I had no intention of shooting the elephant—I had merely sent for the rifle to defend myself if necessary—and it is always unnerving to have a crowd following you. I marched down the hill, looking and feeling a fool, with the rifle over my shoulder and an ever-growing army of people jostling at my heels. At the bottom, when you got away from the huts, there was a metalled road and beyond that a miry waste of paddy fields a thousand yards across, not yet ploughed but soggy from the first rains and dotted with coarse grass. The elephant was standing eight yards from the road, his left side towards us. He took not the slightest notice of the crowd's approach. He was tearing up bunches of grass, beating them against his knees to clean them and stuffing them into his mouth.

I had halted on the road. As soon as I saw the elephant I knew with perfect certainty that I ought not to shoot him. It is a serious matter to shoot a working elephant—it is comparable to destroying a huge and costly piece of machinery—and obviously one ought not to do it if it can possibly be avoided. And at that distance, peacefully eating, the elephant looked no more dangerous than a cow. I thought then and I think now that his attack of "must" was already passing off; in which case he would merely wander harmlessly about until the mahout came back and caught him. Moreover, I did not in the least want to shoot him. I decided that I would watch him for a little while to make sure that he did not turn savage again, and then go home.

But at that moment I glanced round at the crowd that had followed me. It was an immense crowd, two thousand at the least and growing every minute. It blocked the road for a long distance on either side. I looked at the sea of yellow faces above the garish clothes—faces all happy and excited over this bit of fun, all certain that the elephant was going to be shot. They were watching me as they would watch a conjurer about to perform a trick. They did not like me, but with the magical rifle in my hands I was momentarily worth watching. And suddenly I realized that I should have to shoot the elephant after all. The people expected it of me and I had got to do it; I could feel their two thousand wills pressing me forward, irresistibly. And it was at this moment, as I stood there with the rifle in my hands, that I first grasped the hollowness, the futility of the white man's dominion in the East. Here was I, the white man with his gun, standing in front of the unarmed native crowd—seemingly the leading actor of the piece; but in reality I was only an absurd puppet pushed to and fro by the will of those yellow faces behind. I perceived in this moment that when the white man turns tyrant it is his own freedom that he destroys. He becomes a sort of hollow, posing dummy, the conventionalized figure of a sahib. For it is the condition of his rule that he shall spend his life in trying to impress the "natives," and so in every crisis he has got to do what the "natives" expect of him. He wears a mask, and his face grows to fit it. I had got to shoot the elephant. I had committed myself to doing it when I sent for the rifle. A sahib has got to act like a sahib; he has got to appear resolute, to know his own mind and do definite things. To come all that way, rifle in hand, with two thousand people marching at my heels, and then to trail feebly away, having done nothing—no, that was impossible. The crowd would laugh at me. And my whole life, every white man's life in the East, was one long struggle not to be laughed at.

But I did not want to shoot the elephant. I watched him beating his bunch of grass against his knees, with that preoccupied grandmotherly air that elephants have. It seemed to me that it would be murder to shoot him. At that age I was not squeamish about killing animals, but I had never shot an elephant and never wanted to. (Somehow it always seems worse to kill a *large* animal.) Besides, there was the beast's owner to be considered. Alive, the elephant was worth at least a hundred pounds; dead, he would only be worth the value of his tusks, five pounds, possibly. But I had got to act quickly. I turned to some experienced-looking Burmans who had been there when we arrived, and asked them how the elephant had been behaving. They all said the same thing: he took no notice of you if you left him alone, but he might charge if you went too close to him.

It was perfectly clear to me what I ought to do. I ought to walk up to within, say, twenty-five yards of the elephant and test his behavior. If he charged, I could shoot; if he took no notice of me, it would be safe to leave him until the mahout came back. But also I knew that I was going to do no such thing. I was a poor shot with a rifle and the ground was soft mud into which one would sink at every step. If the elephant charged and I missed him, I should have about as much chance as a toad under a steam-roller. But even then I was not thinking particularly of my own skin, only of the watchful yellow faces behind. For at that moment, with the crowd watching me, I was not afraid in the ordinary sense, as I would have been if I had been alone. A white man mustn't be frightened in front of "natives"; and so, in general, he isn't frightened. The sole thought in my mind was that if anything went wrong those two thousand Burmans would see me pursued, caught, trampled on and reduced to a grinning corpse like that Indian up the hill. And if that happened it was quite probable that some of them would laugh. That would never do. There was only one alternative. I shoved the cartridges into the magazine and lay down on the road to get a better aim.

The crowd grew very still, and a deep, low, happy sigh, as of 10 people who see the theater curtain go up at last, breathed from innumerable throats. They were going to have their bit of fun after all. The rifle was a beautiful German thing with cross-hair sights. I did not then know that in shooting an elephant one would shoot to cut an imaginary bar running from ear-hole to ear-hole. I ought, therefore, as the elephant was sideways on, to have aimed straight at his ear-hole; actually I aimed several inches in front of this, thinking the brain would be further forward.

When I pulled the trigger I did not hear the bang or feel the kick—one never does when a shot goes home—but I heard the devilish roar of glee that went up from the crowd. In that instant, in too short a time, one would have thought, even for the bullet to get there, a mysterious, terrible change had come over the elephant. He neither stirred nor fell, but every line of his body had altered. He looked suddenly stricken, shrunken, immensely old, as though the frightful impact of the bullet had paralyzed him without knocking him down. At last, after what seemed a long time—it might have been five seconds, I dare say—he sagged flabbily to his knees. His mouth slobbered. An enormous senility seemed to have settled upon him. One could have imagined him thousands of years old. I fired again into the same spot. At the second shot he did not collapse but climbed with desperate slowness to his feet and stood weakly upright, with legs sagging and head drooping. I fired a third time. That was the shot that did for him. You could see the agony of it jolt his whole body and knock the last remnant of strength from his legs. But in falling he seemed for a moment to rise, for as his hind legs collapsed beneath him he seemed to tower upward like a huge rock toppling, his trunk reaching skywards like a tree. He trumpeted, for the first and only time. And then down he came, his belly towards me, with a crash that seemed to shake the ground even where I lay.

I got up. The Burmans were already racing past me across the mud. It was obvious that the elephant would never rise again, but he was not dead. He was breathing very rhythmically with long rattling gasps, his great mound of a side painfully rising and falling. His mouth was wide open—I could see far down into caverns of pale pink throat. I waited a long time for him to die, but his breathing did not weaken. Finally I fired my two remaining shots into the spot where I thought his heart must be. The thick blood welled out of him like red velvet, but still he did not die. His body did not even jerk when the shots hit him, the tortured breathing continued without a pause. He was dying, very slowly and in great agony, but in some world remote from me where not even a bullet could damage him further. I felt that I had got to put an end to that dreadful noise. It seemed dreadful to see the great beast lying there, powerless to move and yet powerless to die, and not even to be able to finish him. I sent back for my small rifle and poured shot after shot into his heart and down his throat. They seemed to make no impression. The tortured gasps continued as steadily as the ticking of a clock.

In the end I could not stand it any longer and went away. I heard later that it took him half an hour to die. Burmans were bringing dahs and baskets even before I left, and I was told they had stripped his body almost to the bones by the afternoon.

Afterwards, of course, there were endless discussions about the shooting of the elephant. The owner was furious, but he was only an Indian and could do nothing. Besides, legally I had done the right thing, for a mad elephant has to be killed, like a mad dog, if its owner fails to control it. Among the Europeans opinion was divided. The older men said I was right, the younger men said it was a damn shame to shoot an elephant for killing a coolie, because an elephant was worth more than any damn Coringhee coolie. And afterwards I was very glad that the coolie had been killed; it put me legally in the right and it gave me a sufficient pretext for shooting the elephant. I often wondered whether any of the others grasped that I had done it solely to avoid looking a fool.

For Discussion and Writing

1. Why does Orwell shoot the elephant?
2. Orwell uses the anecdote of his shooting an elephant to illustrate his feelings about imperialism. What are those feelings, and how does the anecdote illustrate them?
3. **connections**   Read Orwell's essay against a very different one— Jonathan Swift's "A Modest Proposal" (p. 353). These pieces are deeply political, yet in very different ways, both in terms of the points they make and the ways in which they make them. How do these differences relate to each other? Do the strategies serve the messages?
4. What would you have done if you had been in Orwell's place? Why?
5. **looking further**   Research the historical situation out of which Orwell was writing. Though we are now said to be in a postcolonial age, situations like the one Orwell describes still exist in the world. Can you imagine a similar story being told from somewhere in today's world? Where? Describe this second situation and compare it to Orwell's. Can the exact same story be told? How might it differ?

PLATO

The Allegory of the Cave

Plato was born in 428 BCE in Athens, Greece. He is known as a student of Socrates and teacher of Aristotle. Most of what we know about Socrates, in fact, comes from Plato's writings, many of which are constructed as philosophical dialogues between Socrates and his students. Plato is best known for the Republic, *a work of political philosophy based in metaphysics (which examines the nature of reality), ethics (the study of right conduct), and epistemology (the study of knowledge itself); as in his other works, he is not concerned only with how we should act but also with how we know, who we are, and what is true.*

"The Allegory of the Cave," taken from the Republic, *demonstrates this mixture of concerns in Plato's work. (An allegory is a representation—a story or image—that dramatizes abstract ideas.) As you read, note the ways in which his thoughts about politics are grounded in his understanding of the nature of human experience and knowledge.*

And now, I said, let me show in a figure how far our nature is enlightened or unenlightened:—Behold! human beings living in an underground den, which has a mouth open towards the light and reaching all along the den; here they have been from their childhood, and have their legs and necks chained so that they cannot move, and can only see before them, being prevented by the chains from turning round their heads. Above and behind them a fire is blazing at a distance, and between the fire and the prisoners there is a raised way; and you will see, if you look, a low wall built along the way, like the screen which marionette players have in front of them, over which they show the puppets.

I see.

And do you see, I said, men passing along the wall carrying all sorts of vessels, and statues and figures of animals made of wood and stone and various materials, which appear over the wall? Some of them are talking, others silent.

You have shown me a strange image, and they are strange prisoners.

Like ourselves, I replied; and they see only their own shadows,   5
or the shadows of one another, which the fire throws on the opposite wall of the cave?

True, he said; how could they see anything but the shadows if they were never allowed to move their heads?

And of the objects which are being carried in like manner they would only see the shadows?

Yes, he said.

And if they were able to converse with one another, would they not suppose that they were naming what was actually before them?

Very true.   10

And suppose further that the prison had an echo which came from the other side, would they not be sure to fancy when one of the passers-by spoke that the voice which they heard came from the passing shadow?

No question, he replied.

To them, I said, the truth would be literally nothing but the shadows of the images.

That is certain.

And now look again, and see what will naturally follow if the   15
prisoners are released and disabused of their error. At first, when any of them is liberated and compelled suddenly to stand up and turn his neck round and walk and look towards the light, he will suffer sharp pains; the glare will distress him, and he will be unable to see the realities of which in his former state he had seen the shadows; and then conceive someone saying to him, that what he saw before was an illusion, but that now, when he is approaching nearer to being and his eye is turned towards more real existence, he has a clearer vision — what will be his reply? And you may further imagine that his instructor is pointing to the objects as they pass and requiring him to name them, — will he not be perplexed? Will he not fancy that the shadows which he formerly saw are truer than the objects which are now shown to him?

Far truer.

And if he is compelled to look straight at the light, will he not have a pain in his eyes which will make him turn away to take refuge in the objects of vision which he can see, and which he will conceive to be in reality clearer than the things which are now being shown to him?

True, he said.

And suppose once more, that he is reluctantly dragged up a steep and rugged ascent, and held fast until he is forced into the presence of the sun himself, is he not likely to be pained and irritated? When he approaches the light his eyes will be dazzled, and he will not be able to see anything at all of what are now called realities.

Not all in a moment, he said.   20

He will require to grow accustomed to the sight of the upper world. And first he will see the shadows best, next the reflections of men and other objects in the water, and then the objects themselves; then he will gaze upon the light of the moon and the stars and the spangled heaven; and he will see the sky and the stars by night better than the sun or the light of the sun by day?

Certainly.

Last of all he will be able to see the sun, and not mere reflections of him in the water, but he will see him in his own proper place, and not in another; and he will contemplate him as he is.

Certainly.

He will then proceed to argue that this is he who gives the sea- 25
son and the years, and is the guardian of all that is in the visible world, and in a certain way the cause of all things which he and his fellows have been accustomed to behold?

Clearly, he said, he would first see the sun and then reason about him.

And when he remembered his old habitation, and the wisdom of the den and his fellow prisoners, do you not suppose that he would felicitate himself on the change, and pity them?

Certainly, he would.

And if they were in the habit of conferring honors among themselves on those who were quickest to observe the passing shadows and to remark which of them went before, and which followed after, and which were together; and who were therefore best able to draw conclusions as to the future, do you think that he would care for such honors and glories, or envy the possessors of them? Would he not say with Homer,

Better to be the poor servant of a poor master,

and to endure anything, rather than think as they do and live after their manner?

Yes, he said, I think that he would rather suffer anything than 30 entertain these false notions and live in this miserable manner.

Imagine once more, I said, such an one coming suddenly out of the sun to be replaced in his old situation; would he not be certain to have his eyes full of darkness?

To be sure, he said.

And if there were a contest, and he had to compete in measuring the shadows with the prisoners who had never moved out of the den, while his sight was still weak, and before his eyes had become steady (and the time which would be needed to acquire this new habit of sight might be very considerable), would he not be ridiculous? Men would say of him that up he went and down he came without his eyes; and that it was better not even to think of ascending; and if any one tried to loose another and lead him up to the light, let them only catch the offender, and they would put him to death.

No question, he said.

This entire allegory, I said, you may now append, dear Glaucon, 35 to the previous argument; the prison house is the world of sight, the light of the fire is the sun, and you will not misapprehend me if you interpret the journey upwards to be the ascent of the soul into the intellectual world according to my poor belief, which, at your desire, I have expressed—whether rightly or wrongly God knows. But, whether true or false, my opinion is that in the world of knowledge the idea of good appears last of all, and is seen only with an effort; and, when seen, is also inferred to be the universal author of all things beautiful and right, parent of light and of the lord of light in this visible world, and the immediate source of reason and truth in the intellectual; and that this is the power upon which he who would act rationally either in public or private life must have his eye fixed.

I agree, he said, as far as I am able to understand you.

Moreover, I said, you must not wonder that those who attain to this beatific vision are unwilling to descend to human affairs; for their souls are ever hastening into the upper world where they desire to dwell; which desire of theirs is very natural, if our allegory may be trusted.

Yes, very natural.

And is there anything surprising in one who passes from divine contemplations to the evil state of man, misbehaving himself in a ridiculous manner; if, while his eyes are blinking and before he has become accustomed to the surrounding darkness, he is compelled to fight in courts of law, or in other places, about the images or the shadows of images of justice, and is endeavoring to meet the conceptions of those who have never yet seen absolute justice?

Anything but surprising, he replied.   40

Anyone who has common sense will remember that the bewilderments of the eyes are of two kinds, and arise from two causes, either from coming out of the light or from going into the light, which is true of the mind's eye, quite as much as of the bodily eye; and he who remembers this when he sees anyone whose vision is perplexed and weak, will not be too ready to laugh; he will first ask whether that soul of man has come out of the brighter life, and is unable to see because unaccustomed to the dark, or having turned from darkness to the day is dazzled by excess of light. And he will count the one happy in his condition and state of being, and he will pity the other; or, if he have a mind to laugh at the soul which comes from below into the light, there will be more reason in this than in the laugh which greets him who returns from above out of the light into the den.

That, he said, is a very just distinction.

But then, if I am right, certain professors of education must be wrong when they say that they can put a knowledge into the soul which was not there before, like sight into blind eyes.

They undoubtedly say this, he replied.

Whereas, our argument shows that the power and capacity of 45 learning exists in the soul already; and that just as the eye was unable to turn from darkness to light without the whole body, so too the instrument of knowledge can only by the movement of the whole soul be turned from the world of becoming into that of being, and learn by degrees to endure the sight of being, and of the brightest and best of being, or in other words, of the good.

Very true.

And must there not be some art which will effect conversion in the easiest and quickest manner; not implanting the faculty of sight, for that exists already, but has been turned in the wrong direction, and is looking away from the truth?

Yes, he said, such an art may be presumed.

And whereas the other so-called virtues of the soul seem to be akin to bodily qualities, for even when they are not originally innate they can be implanted later by habit and exercise, the virtue of wisdom more than anything else contains a divine element which always remains, and by this conversion is rendered useful and profitable; or, on the other hand, hurtful and useless. Did you never observe the narrow intelligence flashing from the keen eye of a clever rogue—how eager he is, how clearly his paltry soul sees the way to his end; he is the reverse of blind, but his keen eyesight is forced into the service of evil, and he is mischievous in proportion to his cleverness?

Very true, he said.   50

But what if there had been a circumcision of such natures in the days of their youth; and they had been severed from those sensual pleasures, such as eating and drinking, which, like leaden weights, were attached to them at their birth, and which drag them down and turn the vision of their souls upon the things that are below—if, I say, they had been released from these impediments and turned in the opposite direction, the very same faculty in them would have seen the truth as keenly as they see what their eyes are turned to now.

Very likely.

Yes, I said; and there is another thing which is likely, or rather a necessary inference from what has preceded, that neither the uneducated and uninformed of the truth, nor yet those who never make an end of their education, will be able ministers of State; not the former, because they have no single aim of duty which is the rule of all their actions, private as well as public; nor the latter, because they will not act at all except upon compulsion, fancying that they are already dwelling apart in the islands of the blessed.

Very true, he replied.

Then, I said, the business of us who are the founders of the   55
State will be to compel the best minds to attain that knowledge which we have already shown to be the greatest of all—they must continue to ascend until they arrive at the good; but when they have ascended and seen enough we must not allow them to do as they do now.

What do you mean?

I mean that they remain in the upper world: but this must not be allowed; they must be made to descend again among the prisoners in the den, and partake of their labors and honors, whether they are worth having or not.

But is not this unjust? he said; ought we to give them a worse life, when they might have a better?

You have again forgotten, my friend, I said, the intention of the legislator, who did not aim at making any one class in the State happy above the rest; the happiness was to be in the whole State, and he held the citizens together by persuasion and necessity, making them benefactors of the State, and therefore benefactors of one another; to this end he created them, not to please themselves, but to be his instruments in binding up the State.

True, he said, I had forgotten.   60

Observe, Glaucon, that there will be no injustice in compelling our philosophers to have a care and providence of others; we shall explain to them that in other States, men of their class are not obliged to share in the toils of politics: and this is reasonable, for they grow up at their own sweet will, and the government would rather not have them. Being self-taught, they cannot be expected to show any gratitude for a culture which they have never received. But we have brought you into the world to be rulers of the hive, kings of yourselves and of the other citizens, and have educated you far better and more perfectly than they have been educated, and you are better able to share in the double duty. Wherefore each of you, when his turn comes, must go down to the general underground abode, and get the habit of seeing in the dark. When you have acquired the habit, you will see ten thousand times better than the inhabitants of the den, and you will know what the several images are, and what they represent, because you have seen the beautiful and just and good in their truth. And thus our State, which is also yours, will be a reality, and not a dream only, and will be administered in a spirit unlike that of other States, in which men fight with one another about shadows only and are distracted in the struggle for power, which in their eyes is a great good. Whereas the truth is that the State in which the rulers are most reluctant to govern is always the best and most quietly governed, and the State in which they are most eager, the worst.

Quite true, he replied.

And will our pupils, when they hear this, refuse to take their turn at the toils of State, when they are allowed to spend the greater part of their time with one another in the heavenly light?

Impossible, he answered; for they are just men, and the commands which we impose upon them are just; there can be no doubt that every one of them will take office as a stern necessity, and not after the fashion of our present rulers of State.

Yes, my friend, I said; and there lies the point. You must con- 65 trive for your future rulers another and a better life than that of a ruler, and then you may have a well-ordered State; for only in the State which offers this, will they rule who are truly rich, not in silver and gold, but in virtue and wisdom, which are the true blessings of life. Whereas if they go to the administration of public affairs, poor and hungering after their own private advantage, thinking that hence they are to snatch the chief good, order there can never be; for they will be fighting about office, and the civil and domestic broils which thus arise will be the ruin of the rulers themselves and of the whole State.

Most true, he replied.

And the only life which looks down upon the life of political ambition is that of true philosophy. Do you know of any other?

Indeed, I do not, he said.

For Discussion and Writing

1. What does the cave stand for in Plato's allegory? Make a list of the other elements in the allegory—chains, light, darkness, and so on— and explain what they represent.

2. Plato compares a number of things in this essay—the material world to the world of ideas, the life of the mind to the work of governing, silver and gold to virtue and wisdom. How does he use his comparisons to make his argument?

3. **connections** Though George Orwell, in "Shooting an Elephant" (p. 272), is a different kind of leader than the rulers in Plato's allegory, he is in a position of authority. Do you think there are points of connection between the two essays in this area? Can you consider Orwell's reflection on his actions, and the tangle of motivations behind them, in light of Plato's discussion of the potentially conflicting motivations of rulers?

4. Plato argues that working in public affairs and working for one's own private advantage cannot mix. How might contemporary politics bear out this assertion or contradict it?

5. **looking further** In "The Allegory of the Cave," legislators are described as aiming not "at making any one class in the State happy above the rest; the happiness was to be in the whole State" (par. 59). Consider contemporary politics through this statement. In what ways do you find the aim here ascribed to legislators to be shared by contemporary elected officials? In what ways do you not?

RICHARD RODRIGUEZ

Aria: Memoir of a Bilingual Childhood

Born in 1944 in San Francisco to Mexican immigrants, and raised in Sacramento, California, Richard Rodriguez is a foremost and sometimes controversial Chicano voice. Best known for his memoir Hunger of Memory: The Education of Richard Rodriguez *(1982), Rodriguez was a literary scholar and teacher until leaving the profession and becoming a full-time essayist. He is now a columnist and editor for the Pacific News Service, a regular essayist for PBS's* NewsHour with Jim Lehrer, *and a contributor to numerous magazines and newspapers. His latest book,* Darling *(2013), is a collection of stories Rodriguez has termed a "spiritual biography."*

"Aria: Memoir of a Bilingual Childhood" is taken from Hunger of Memory. *That book cemented Rodriguez's controversial reputation because of its stands against bilingual education and affirmative action. Knowing these stands might be controversial, he takes them firmly: Of bilingual voters' ballots, Rodriguez writes, "It is not enough to say that these schemes are foolish and certainly doomed" (par. 61). As you read "Aria," note other moments in which Rodriguez takes on ideas with which he disagrees.*

1

I remember to start with that day in Sacramento—a California now nearly thirty years past—when I first entered a classroom, able to understand some fifty stray English words.

The third of four children, I had been preceded to a neighborhood Roman Catholic school by an older brother and sister. But neither of them had revealed very much about their classroom experiences. Each afternoon they returned, as they left in the morning, always together, speaking in Spanish as they climbed the five steps of the porch. And their mysterious books, wrapped in shopping-bag paper, remained on the table next to the door, closed firmly behind them.

An accident of geography sent me to a school where all my classmates were white, many the children of doctors and lawyers and business executives. All my classmates certainly must have been uneasy on that first day of school—as most children are uneasy—to find themselves apart from their families in the first institution of their lives. But I was astonished.

The nun said, in a friendly but oddly impersonal voice, "Boys and girls, this is Richard Rodriguez." (I heard her sound out: *Rich-heard Road-ree-guess*.) It was the first time I had heard anyone name me in English. "Richard," the nun repeated more slowly, writing my name down in her black leather book. Quickly I turned to see my mother's face dissolve in a watery blur behind the pebbled glass door.

Many years later there is something called bilingual educa-   5
tion—a scheme proposed in the late 1960s by Hispanic-American social activists, later endorsed by a congressional vote. It is a program that seeks to permit non-English-speaking children, many from lower-class homes, to use their family language as the language of school. (Such is the goal its supporters announce.) I hear them and am forced to say no: it is not possible for a child—any child—ever to use his family's language in school. Not to understand this is to misunderstand the public uses of schooling and to trivialize the nature of intimate life—a family's "language."

Memory teaches me what I know of these matters; the boy reminds the adult. I was a bilingual child, a certain kind—socially disadvantaged—the son of working-class parents, both Mexican immigrants.

In the early years of my boyhood, my parents coped very well in America. My father had steady work. My mother managed at home. They were nobody's victims. Optimism and ambition led them to a house (our home) many blocks from the Mexican south side of town. We lived among *gringos* and only a block from the biggest, whitest houses. It never occurred to my parents that they couldn't live wherever they chose. Nor was the Sacramento of the fifties bent on teaching them a contrary lesson. My mother and father were more annoyed than intimidated by those two or three neighbors who tried initially to make us unwelcome. ("Keep your brats away from my sidewalk!") But despite all they achieved, perhaps because they had so much to achieve, any deep feeling of ease, the confidence of "belonging" in public was withheld from them both. They regarded the people at work, the faces in crowds, as very distant from us. They were the others, *los gringos*. That term was interchangeable in their speech with another, even more telling, *los americanos*.

I grew up in a house where the only regular guests were my relations. For one day, enormous families of relatives would visit and there would be so many people that the noise and the bodies would spill out to the backyard and front porch. Then, for weeks, no one came by. (It was usually a salesman who rang the doorbell.) Our house stood apart. A gaudy yellow in a row of white bungalows. We were the people with the noisy dog. The people who raised pigeons and chickens. We were the foreigners on the block. A few neighbors smiled and waved. We waved back. But no one in the family knew the names of the old couple who lived next door; until I was seven years old, I did not know the names of the kids who lived across the street.

In public, my father and mother spoke a hesitant, accented, not always grammatical English. And they would have to strain— their bodies tense—to catch the sense of what was rapidly said by *los gringos*. At home they spoke Spanish. The language of their Mexican past sounded in counterpoint to the English of public society. The words would come quickly, with ease. Conveyed through those sounds was the pleasing, soothing, consoling reminder of being at home.

During those years when I was first conscious of hearing, my mother and father addressed me only in Spanish; in Spanish I learned to reply. By contrast, English *(inglés)*, rarely heard in the house, was the language I came to associate with *gringos*. I learned my first words of English overhearing my parents speak to strangers. At five years of age, I knew just enough English for my mother to trust me on errands to stores one block away. No more.

I was a listening child, careful to hear the very different sounds of Spanish and English. Wide-eyed with hearing, I'd listen to sounds more than words. First, there were English *(gringo)* sounds. So many words were still unknown that when the butcher or the lady at the drugstore said something to me, exotic polysyllabic sounds would bloom in the midst of their sentences. Often, the speech of people in public seemed to me very loud, booming with confidence. The man behind the counter would literally ask, "What can I do for you?" But by being so firm and so clear, the sound of his voice said that he was a *gringo*; he belonged in public society.

I would also hear then the high nasal notes of middle-class American speech. The air stirred with sound. Sometimes, even now, when I have been traveling abroad for several weeks, I will hear what I heard as a boy. In hotel lobbies or airports, in Turkey or Brazil, some Americans will pass, and suddenly I will hear it again—the high sound of American voices. For a few seconds I will hear it with pleasure, for it is now the sound of *my* society—a reminder of home. But inevitably—already on the flight headed for home—the sound fades with repetition. I will be unable to hear it anymore.

When I was a boy, things were different. The accent of *los gringos* was never pleasing nor was it hard to hear. Crowds at Safeway or at bus stops would be noisy with sound. And I would be forced to edge away from the chirping chatter above me.

I was unable to hear my own sounds, but I knew very well that I spoke English poorly. My words could not stretch far enough to form complete thoughts. And the words I did speak I didn't know well enough to make into distinct sounds. (Listeners would usually lower their heads, better to hear what I was trying to say.) But it was one thing for *me* to speak English with difficulty. It was more troubling for me to hear my parents speak in public: their high-whining vowels and guttural consonants; their sentences that got stuck with "eh" and "ah" sounds; the confused syntax; the hesitant rhythm of sounds so different from the way *gringos* spoke. I'd notice, moreover, that my parents' voices were softer than those of *gringos* we'd meet.

I am tempted now to say that none of this mattered. In adult- 15 hood I am embarrassed by childhood fears. And, in a way, it didn't matter very much that my parents could not speak English with ease. Their linguistic difficulties had no serious consequences. My mother and father made themselves understood at the county hospital clinic and at government offices. And yet, in another way, it mattered very much—it was unsettling to hear my parents struggle with English. Hearing them, I'd grow nervous, my clutching trust in their protection and power weakened.

There were many times like the night at a brightly lit gasoline station (a blaring white memory) when I stood uneasily, hearing my father. He was talking to a teenaged attendant. I do not recall what they were saying, but I cannot forget the sounds my father made as he spoke. At one point his words slid together to form one word—sounds as confused as the threads of blue and green oil in the puddle next to my shoes. His voice rushed through what he had left to say. And, toward the end, reached falsetto notes, appealing to his listener's understanding. I looked away to the lights of passing automobiles. I tried not to hear anymore. But I heard only too well the calm, easy tones in the attendant's reply. Shortly afterward, walking toward home with my father, I shivered when he put his hand on my shoulder. The very first chance that I got, I evaded his grasp and ran on ahead into the dark, skipping with feigned boyish exuberance.

But then there was Spanish. *Español*: my family's language. *Español*: the language that seemed to me a private language. I'd hear strangers on the radio and in the Mexican Catholic church across town speaking in Spanish, but I couldn't really believe that Spanish was a public language, like English. Spanish speakers, rather, seemed related to me, for I sensed that we shared— through our language—the experience of feeling apart from *los gringos*. It was thus a ghetto Spanish that I heard and I spoke. Like those whose lives are bound by a barrio, I was reminded by Spanish of my separateness from *los otros, los gringos* in power. But more intensely than for most barrio children—because I did not live in a barrio—Spanish seemed to me the language of home. (Most days it was only at home that I'd hear it.) It became the language of joyful return.

A family member would say something to me and I would feel myself specially recognized. My parents would say something to me and I would feel embraced by the sounds of their words. Those sounds said: *I am speaking with ease in Spanish. I am addressing you in words I never use with* los gringos. *I recognize you as someone special, close, like no one outside. You belong with us. In the family.*
(Ricardo.)

At the age of five, six, well past the time when most other chil- 20 dren no longer easily notice the difference between sounds uttered at home and words spoken in public, I had a different experience.

I lived in a world magically compounded of sounds. I remained a child longer than most; I lingered too long, poised at the edge of language — often frightened by the sounds of *los gringos*, delighted by the sounds of Spanish at home. I shared with my family a language that was startlingly different from that used in the great city around us.

For me there were none of the gradations between public and private society so normal to a maturing child. Outside the house was public society; inside the house was private. Just opening or closing the screen door behind me was an important experience. I'd rarely leave home all alone or without reluctance. Walking down the sidewalk, under the canopy of tall trees, I'd warily notice the — suddenly — silent neighborhood kids who stood warily watching me. Nervously, I'd arrive at the grocery store to hear there the sounds of the *gringo* — foreign to me — reminding me that in this world so big, I was a foreigner. But then I'd return. Walking back toward our house, climbing the steps from the sidewalk, when the front door was open in summer, I'd hear voices beyond the screen door talking in Spanish. For a second or two, I'd stay, linger there, listening. Smiling, I'd hear my mother call out, saying in Spanish (words): "Is that you, Richard?" All the while her sounds would assure me: *You are home now; come closer; inside. With us.*

"*Sí,*" I'd reply.

Once more inside the house I would resume (assume) my place in the family. The sounds would dim, grow harder to hear. Once more at home, I would grow less aware of that fact. It required, however, no more than the blurt of the doorbell to alert me to listen to sounds all over again. The house would turn instantly still while my mother went to the door. I'd hear her hard English sounds. I'd wait to hear her voice return to soft-sounding Spanish, which assured me, as surely as did the clicking tongue of the lock on the door, that the stranger was gone.

Plainly, it is not healthy to hear such sounds so often. It is not healthy to distinguish public words from private sounds so easily. I remained cloistered by sounds, timid and shy in public, too dependent on voices at home. And yet it needs to be emphasized: I was an extremely happy child at home. I remember many nights when my father would come back from work, and I'd hear him call out to my mother in Spanish, sounding relieved. In Spanish, he'd sound light and free notes he never could manage in English. Some nights I'd jump up just at hearing his voice. With *mis hermanos* I would come running into the room where he was with my mother. Our laughing (so deep was the pleasure!) became screaming. Like others who know the pain of public alienation, we transformed the knowledge of our public separateness and made it consoling—the reminder of intimacy. Excited, we joined our voices in a celebration of sounds. *We are speaking now the way we never speak out in public. We are alone—together,* voices sounded, surrounded to tell me. Some nights, no one seemed willing to loosen the hold sounds had on us. At dinner, we invented new words. (Ours sounded Spanish, but made sense only to us.) We pieced together new words by taking, say, an English verb and giving it Spanish endings. My mother's instructions at bedtime would be lacquered with mock-urgent tones. Or a word like *sí* would become, in several notes, able to convey added measures of feeling. Tongues explored the edges of words, especially the fat vowels. And we happily sounded that military drum roll, the twirling roar of the Spanish *r*. Family language: my family's sounds. The voices of my parents and sisters and brother. Their voices insisting: *You belong here. We are family members. Related. Special to one another. Listen!* Voices singing and sighing, rising, straining, then surging, teeming with pleasure that burst syllables into fragments of laughter. At times it seemed there was steady quiet only when, from another room, the rustling whispers of my parents faded and I moved closer to sleep.

2

Supporters of bilingual education today imply that students like me miss a great deal by not being taught in their family's language. What they seem not to recognize is that, as a socially disadvantaged child, I considered Spanish to be a private language. What I needed to learn in school was that I had the right—and the obligation—to speak the public language of *los gringos*. The odd truth is that my first-grade classmates could have become bilingual, in the conventional sense of that word, more easily than I. Had they been taught (as upper-middle-class children are often taught early) a second language like Spanish or French, they could have regarded it simply as that: another public language. In my case such bilingualism could not have been so quickly achieved. What I did not believe was that I could speak a single public language.

Without question, it would have pleased me to hear my teachers address me in Spanish when I entered the classroom. I would have felt much less afraid. I would have trusted them and responded with ease. But I would have delayed—for how long postponed?—having to learn the language of public society. I would have evaded—and for how long could I have afforded to delay?—learning the great lesson of school, that I had a public identity.

Fortunately, my teachers were unsentimental about their responsibility. What they understood was that I needed to speak a public language. So their voices would search me out, asking me questions. Each time I'd hear them, I'd look up in surprise to see a nun's face frowning at me. I'd mumble, not really meaning to answer. The nun would persist, "Richard, stand up. Don't look at the floor. Speak up. Speak to the entire class, not just to me!" But I couldn't believe that the English language was mine to use. (In part, I did not want to believe it.) I continued to mumble. I resisted the teacher's demands. (Did I somehow suspect that once I learned public language my pleasing family life would be changed?) Silent, waiting for the bell to sound, I remained dazed, diffident, afraid.

Because I wrongly imagined that English was intrinsically a public language and Spanish an intrinsically private one, I easily noted the difference between classroom language and the language of home. At school, words were directed to a general audience of listeners. ("Boys and girls.") Words were meaningfully ordered. And the point was not self-expression alone but to make oneself understood by many others. The teacher quizzed: "Boys and girls, why do we use that word in this sentence? Could we think of a better word to use there? Would the sentence change its meaning if the words were differently arranged? And wasn't there a better way of saying much the same thing?" (I couldn't say. I wouldn't try to say.)

Three months. Five. Half a year passed. Unsmiling, ever watchful, my teachers noted my silence. They began to connect my behavior with the difficult progress my older sister and brother were making. Until one Saturday morning three nuns arrived at the house to talk to our parents. Stiffly, they sat on the blue living room sofa. From the doorway of another room, spying the visitors, I noted the incongruity—the clash of two worlds, the faces and voices of school intruding upon the familiar setting of home. I overheard one voice gently wondering, "Do your children speak only Spanish at home, Mrs. Rodriguez?" While another voice added, "That Richard especially seems so timid and shy."

That Rich-heard!   30

With great tact the visitors continued, "Is it possible for you and your husband to encourage your children to practice their English when they are home?" Of course, my parents complied. What would they not do for their children's well-being? And how could they have questioned the Church's authority which those women represented? In an instant, they agreed to give up the language (the sounds) that had revealed and accentuated our family's closeness. The moment after the visitors left, the change was observed. *"Ahora,* speak to us *en inglés,"* my father and mother united to tell us.

At first, it seemed a kind of game. After dinner each night, the family gathered to practice "our" English. (It was still then *inglés,* a language foreign to us, so we felt drawn as strangers to it.) Laughing, we would try to define words we could not pronounce. We played with strange English sounds, often over-anglicizing our pronunciations. And we filled the smiling gaps of our sentences with familiar Spanish sounds. But that was cheating, somebody shouted. Everyone laughed. In school, meanwhile, like my brother and sister, I was required to attend a daily tutoring session. I needed a full year of special attention. I also needed my teachers to keep my attention from straying in class by calling out, *Rich-heard*—their English voices slowly prying loose my ties to my other name, its three notes, *Ri-car-do.* Most of all I needed to hear my mother and father speak to me in a moment of seriousness in broken—suddenly heartbreaking—English. The scene was inevitable: one Saturday morning I entered the kitchen where my parents were talking in Spanish. I did not realize that they were talking in Spanish however until, at the moment they saw me, I heard their voices change to speak English. Those *gringo* sounds they uttered startled me. Pushed me away. In that moment of trivial misunderstanding and profound insight, I felt my throat twisted by unsounded grief. I turned quickly and left the room. But I had no place to escape to with Spanish. (The spell was broken.) My brother and sisters were speaking English in another part of the house.

Again and again in the days following, increasingly angry, I was obliged to hear my mother and father: "Speak to us *en inglés.*" *(Speak.)* Only then did I determine to learn classroom English. Weeks after, it happened: one day in school I raised my hand to volunteer an answer. I spoke out in a loud voice. And I did not think it remarkable when the entire class understood. That day, I moved very far from the disadvantaged child I had been only days earlier. The belief, the calming assurance that I belonged in public, had at last taken hold.

Shortly after, I stopped hearing the high and loud sounds of *los gringos.* A more and more confident speaker of English, I didn't trouble to listen to *how* strangers sounded, speaking to me. And there simply were too many English-speaking people in my day for me to hear American accents anymore. Conversations quickened. Listening to persons who sounded eccentrically pitched voices, I usually noted their sounds for an initial few seconds before I concentrated on *what* they were saying. Conversations became content-full. Transparent. Hearing someone's *tone* of voice — angry or questioning or sarcastic or happy or sad — I didn't distinguish it from the words it expressed. Sound and word were thus tightly wedded. At the end of a day, I was often bemused, always relieved, to realize how "silent," though crowded with words, my day in public had been. (This public silence measured and quickened the change in my life.)

At last, seven years old, I came to believe what had been techni- 35 cally true since my birth: I was an American citizen.

But the special feeling of closeness at home was diminished by then. Gone was the desperate, urgent, intense feeling of being at home; rare was the experience of feeling myself individualized by family intimates. We remained a loving family, but one greatly changed. No longer so close; no longer bound tight by the pleasing and troubling knowledge of our public separateness. Neither my older brother nor sister rushed home after school anymore. Nor did I. When I arrived home there would often be neighborhood kids in the house. Or the house would be empty of sounds.

Following the dramatic Americanization of their children, even my parents grew more publicly confident. Especially my mother. She learned the names of all the people on our block. And she decided we needed to have a telephone installed in the house. My father continued to use the word *gringo*. But it was no longer charged with the old bitterness or distrust. (Stripped of any emotional content, the word simply became a name for those Americans not of Hispanic descent.) Hearing him, sometimes, I wasn't sure if he was pronouncing the Spanish word *gringo* or saying gringo in English.

Matching the silence I started hearing in public was a new quiet at home. The family's quiet was partly due to the fact that, as we children learned more and more English, we shared fewer and fewer words with our parents. Sentences needed to be spoken slowly when a child addressed his mother or father. (Often the parent wouldn't understand.) The child would need to repeat himself. (Still the parent misunderstood.) The young voice, frustrated, would end up saying, "Never mind"—the subject was closed. Dinners would be noisy with the clinking of knives and forks against dishes. My mother would smile softly between her remarks; my father at the other end of the table would chew and chew at his food, while he stared over the heads of his children.

My *mother!* My *father!* After English became my primary language, I no longer knew what words to use in addressing my parents. The old Spanish words (those tender accents of sound) I had used earlier—*mamá* and *papá*—I couldn't use anymore. They would have been too painful reminders of how much had changed in my life. On the other hand, the words I heard neighborhood kids call *their* parents seemed equally unsatisfactory. *Mother* and *Father; Ma, Papa, Pa, Dad, Pop* (how I hated the all-American sound of that last word especially)—all these terms I felt were unsuitable, not really terms of address for *my* parents. As a result, I never used them at home. Whenever I'd speak to my parents, I would try to get their attention with eye contact alone. In public conversations, I'd refer to "my parents" or "my mother and father."

My mother and father, for their part, responded differently, as 40 their children spoke to them less. She grew restless, seemed troubled and anxious at the scarcity of words exchanged in the house. It was she who would question me about my day when I came home from school. She smiled at small talk. She pried at the edges of my sentences to get me to say something more.

(What?) She'd join conversations she overheard, but her intrusions often stopped her children's talking. By contrast, my father seemed reconciled to the new quiet. Though his English improved somewhat, he retired into silence. At dinner he spoke very little. One night his children and even his wife helplessly giggled at his garbled English pronunciation of the Catholic Grace before Meals. Thereafter he made his wife recite the prayer at the start of each meal, even on formal occasions, when there were guests in the house. Hers became the public voice of the family. On official business, it was she, not my father, one would usually hear on the phone or in stores, talking to strangers. His children grew so accustomed to his silence that, years later, they would speak routinely of his shyness. (My mother would often try to explain: Both his parents died when he was eight. He was raised by an uncle who treated him like little more than a menial servant. He was never encouraged to speak. He grew up alone. A man of few words.) But my father was not shy, I realized, when I'd watch him speaking Spanish with relatives. Using Spanish, he was quickly effusive. Especially when talking with other men, his voice would spark, flicker, flare alive with sounds. In Spanish, he expressed ideas and feelings he rarely revealed in English. With firm Spanish sounds, he conveyed confidence and authority English would never allow him.

The silence at home, however, was finally more than a literal silence. Fewer words passed between parent and child, but more profound was the silence that resulted from my inattention to sounds. At about the time I no longer bothered to listen with care to the sounds of English in public, I grew careless about listening to the sounds family members made when they spoke. Most of the time I heard someone speaking at home and didn't distinguish his sounds from the words people uttered in public. I didn't even pay much attention to my parents' accented and ungrammatical speech. At least not at home. Only when I was with them in public would I grow alert to their accents. Though, even then, their sounds caused me less and less concern. For I was increasingly confident of my own public identity.

I would have been happier about my public success had I not sometimes recalled what it had been like earlier, when my family had conveyed its intimacy through a set of conveniently private sounds. Sometimes in public, hearing a stranger, I'd hark

back to my past. A Mexican farmworker approached me downtown to ask directions to somewhere. *"¿Hijito . . . ?"* he said. And
his voice summoned deep longing. Another time, standing beside
my mother in the visiting room of a Carmelite convent, before the
dense screen which rendered the nuns shadowy figures, I heard
several Spanish-speaking nuns—their busy, singsong overlapping
voices—assure us that yes, yes, we were remembered, all our
family was remembered in their prayers. (Their voices echoed
faraway family sounds.) Another day, a dark-faced old woman—
her hand light on my shoulder—steadied herself against me as
she boarded a bus. She murmured something I couldn't quite
comprehend. Her Spanish voice came near, like the face of a
never-before-seen relative in the instant before I was kissed. Her
voice, like so many of the Spanish voices I'd hear in public,
recalled the golden age of my youth. Hearing Spanish then, I continued to be a careful, if sad, listener to sounds. Hearing a Spanish-
speaking family walking behind me, I turned to look. I smiled for
an instant, before my glance found the Hispanic-looking faces of
strangers in the crowd going by.

Today I hear bilingual educators say that children lose a degree
of "individuality" by becoming assimilated into public society.
(Bilingual schooling was popularized in the seventies, that decade
when middle-class ethnics began to resist the process of assimilation—the American melting pot.) But the bilingualists simplis-
tically scorn the value and necessity of assimilation. They do not
seem to realize that there are *two* ways a person is individualized.
So they do not realize that while one suffers a diminished sense
of *private* individuality by becoming assimilated into public society, such assimilation makes possible the achievement of *public*
individuality.

The bilingualists insist that a student should be reminded of
his difference from others in mass society, his heritage. But they
equate mere separateness with individuality. The fact is that only
in private—with intimates—is separateness from the crowd a
prerequisite for individuality. (An intimate draws me apart, tells
me that I am unique, unlike all others.) In public, by contrast, full
individuality is achieved, paradoxically, by those who are able to
consider themselves members of the crowd. Thus it happened for
me: only when I was able to think of myself as an American, no

longer an alien in *gringo* society, could I seek the rights and opportunities necessary for full public individuality. The social and political advantages I enjoy as a man result from the day that I came to believe that my name, indeed, is *Rich-heard Road-ree-guess*. It is true that my public society today is often impersonal. (My public society is usually mass society.) Yet despite the anonymity of the crowd and despite the fact that the individuality I achieve in public is often tenuous—because it depends on my being one in a crowd—I celebrate the day I acquired my new name. Those middle-class ethnics who scorn assimilation seem to me filled with decadent self-pity, obsessed by the burden of public life. Dangerously, they romanticize public separateness and they trivialize the dilemma of the socially disadvantaged.

My awkward childhood does not prove the necessity of bilin-   45
gual education. My story discloses instead an essential myth of childhood—inevitable pain. If I rehearse here the changes in my private life after my Americanization, it is finally to emphasize the public gain. The loss implies the gain: the house I returned to each afternoon was quiet. Intimate sounds no longer rushed to the door to greet me. There were other noises inside. The telephone rang. Neighborhood kids ran past the door of the bedroom where I was reading my schoolbooks—covered with shopping-bag paper. Once I learned public language, it would never again be easy for me to hear intimate family voices. More and more of my day was spent hearing words. But that may only be a way of saying that the day I raised my hand in class and spoke loudly to an entire roomful of faces, my childhood started to end.

3

I grew up victim to a disabling confusion. As I grew fluent in English, I no longer could speak Spanish with confidence. I continued to understand spoken Spanish. And in high school, I learned how to read and write Spanish. But for many years I could not pronounce it. A powerful guilt blocked my spoken words; an essential glue was missing whenever I'd try to connect words to form sentences. I would be unable to break a barrier of sound, to speak freely. I would speak, or try to speak, Spanish, and I would manage to utter halting, hiccuping sounds that betrayed my unease.

When relatives and Spanish-speaking friends of my parents came to the house, my brother and sisters seemed reticent to use Spanish, but at least they managed to say a few necessary words before being excused. I never managed so gracefully. I was cursed with guilt. Each time I'd hear myself addressed in Spanish, I would be unable to respond with any success. I'd know the words I wanted to say, but I couldn't manage to say them. I would try to speak, but everything I said seemed to me horribly anglicized. My mouth would not form the words right. My jaw would tremble. After a phrase or two, I'd cough up a warm, silvery sound. And stop.

It surprised my listeners to hear me. They'd lower their heads, better to grasp what I was trying to say. They would repeat their questions in gentle, affectionate voices. But by then I would answer in English. No, no, they would say, we want you to speak to us in Spanish. *(". . . en español.")* But I couldn't do it. *Pocho* then they called me. Sometimes playfully, teasingly, using the tender diminutive—*mi pochito*. Sometimes not so playfully, mockingly, *Pocho*. (A Spanish dictionary defines that word as an adjective meaning "colorless" or "bland." But I heard it as a noun, naming the Mexican-American who, in becoming an American, forgets his native society.) *"¡Pocho!"* the lady in the Mexican food store muttered, shaking her head. I looked up to the counter where red and green peppers were strung like Christmas tree lights and saw the frowning face of the stranger. My mother laughed somewhere behind me. (She said that her children didn't want to practice "our Spanish" after they started going to school.) My mother's smiling voice made me suspect that the lady who faced me was not really angry at me. But, searching her face, I couldn't find the hint of a smile.

Embarrassed, my parents would regularly need to explain their children's inability to speak flowing Spanish during those years. My mother met the wrath of her brother, her only brother, when he came up from Mexico one summer with his family. He saw his nieces and nephews for the very first time. After listening to me, he looked away and said what a disgrace it was that I couldn't speak Spanish, *"su proprio idioma."* He made that remark to my mother; I noticed, however, that he stared at my father.

I clearly remember one other visitor from those years. A long-time friend of my father from San Francisco would come to stay with us for several days in late August. He took great interest in   50 me after he realized that I couldn't answer his questions in Spanish. He would grab me as I started to leave the kitchen. He would ask me something. Usually he wouldn't bother to wait for my mumbled response. Knowingly, he'd murmur: "¿Ay Pocho, Pocho, adónde vas?" And he would press his thumbs into the upper part of my arms, making me squirm with currents of pain. Dumbly, I'd stand there, waiting for his wife to notice us, for her to call him off with a benign smile. I'd giggle, hoping to deflate the tension between us, pretending that I hadn't seen the glittering scorn in his glance.

I remember that man now, but seek no revenge in this telling. I recount such incidents only because they suggest the fierce power Spanish had for many people I met at home; the way Spanish was associated with closeness. Most of those people who called me a pocho could have spoken English to me. But they would not. They seemed to think that Spanish was the only language we could use, that Spanish alone permitted our close association. (Such persons are vulnerable always to the ghetto merchant and the politician who have learned the value of speaking their clients' family language to gain immediate trust.) For my part, I felt that I had somehow committed a sin of betrayal by learning English. But betrayal against whom? Not against visitors to the house exactly. No, I felt that I had betrayed my immediate family. I knew that my parents had encouraged me to learn English. I knew that I had turned to English only with angry reluctance. But once I spoke English with ease, I came to feel guilty. (This guilt defied logic.) I felt that I had shattered the intimate bond that had once held the family close. This original sin against my family told whenever anyone addressed me in Spanish and I responded, confounded.

But even during those years of guilt, I was coming to sense certain consoling truths about language and intimacy. I remember playing with a friend in the backyard one day, when my grandmother appeared at the window. Her face was stern with suspicion when she saw the boy (the gringo) I was with. In Spanish she called out to me, sounding the whistle of her ancient breath. My companion looked up and watched her intently as she lowered the window and moved, still visible, behind the light curtain, watching us both. He wanted to know what she had said. I started to tell him, to say—to translate her Spanish words into English. The problem was, however, that though I knew how to translate exactly *what* she had told me, I realized that any translation would distort the deepest meaning of her message: it had been directed only to me. This message of intimacy could never be translated because it was not *in* the words she had used but passed *through* them. So any translation would have seemed wrong; her words would have been stripped of an essential meaning. Finally, I decided not to tell my friend anything. I told him that I didn't hear all she had said.

This insight unfolded in time. Making more and more friends outside my house, I began to distinguish intimate voices speaking through *English*. I'd listen at times to a close friend's confidential tone or secretive whisper. Even more remarkable were those instances when, for no special reason apparently, I'd become conscious of the fact that my companion was speaking only to me. I'd marvel just hearing his voice. It was a stunning event: to be able to break through his words, to be able to hear this voice of the other, to realize that it was directed only to me. After such moments of intimacy outside the house, I began to trust hearing intimacy conveyed through my family's English. Voices at home at last punctured sad confusion. I'd hear myself addressed as an intimate at home once again. Such moments were never as raucous with sound as past times had been when we had had "private" Spanish to use. (Our English-sounding house was never to be as noisy as our Spanish-speaking house had been.) Intimate moments were usually soft moments of sound. My mother was in the dining room while I did my homework nearby. And she looked over at me. Smiled. Said something—her words said nothing very important. But her voice sounded to tell me *(We are together)* I was her son.

(Richard!)

Intimacy thus continued at home; intimacy was not stilled by 55 English. It is true that I would never forget the great change of my life, the diminished occasions of intimacy. But there would also be times when I sensed the deepest truth about language and intimacy: *Intimacy is not created by a particular language; it is created by intimates.* The great change in my life was not linguistic but social. If, after becoming a successful student, I no longer heard intimate voices as often as I had earlier, it was not because I spoke English rather than Spanish. It was because I used public language for most of the day. I moved easily at last, a citizen in a crowded city of words.

4

This boy became a man. In private now, alone, I brood over language and intimacy—the great themes of my past. In public I expect most of the faces I meet to be the faces of strangers. (How do you do?) If meetings are quick and impersonal, they have been efficiently managed. I rush past the sounds of voices attending only to the words addressed to me. Voices seem planed to an even surface of sound, soundless. A business associate speaks in a deep baritone, but I pass through the timbre to attend to his words. The crazy man who sells me a newspaper every night mumbles something crazy, but I have time only to pretend that I have heard him say hello. Accented versions of English make little impression on me. In the rush-hour crowd a Japanese tourist asks me a question, and I inch past his accent to concentrate on what he is saying. The Eastern European immigrant in a neighborhood delicatessen speaks to me through a marinade of sounds, but I respond to his words. I note for only a second the Texas accent of the telephone operator or the Mississippi accent of the man who lives in the apartment below me.

My city seems silent until some ghetto black teenagers board the bus I am on. Because I do not take their presence for granted, I listen to the sounds of their voices. Of all the accented versions of English I hear in a day, I hear theirs most intently. They are *the* sounds of the outsider. They annoy me for being loud—so self-sufficient and unconcerned by my presence. Yet for the same reason they seem to me glamorous. (A romantic gesture against public acceptance.) Listening to their shouted laughter, I realize my own quiet. Their voices enclose my isolation. I feel envious, envious of their brazen intimacy.

I warn myself away from such envy, however. I remember the black political activists who have argued in favor of using black English in schools. (Their argument varies only slightly from that made by foreign-language bilingualists.) I have heard "radical" linguists make the point that black English is a complex and intricate version of English. And I do not doubt it. But neither do I think that black English should be a language of public instruction. What makes black English inappropriate in classrooms is not something *in* the language. It is rather what lower-class speakers make of it. Just as Spanish would have been a dangerous language for me to have used at the start of my education, so black English would be a dangerous language to use in the schooling of teenagers for whom it reenforces feelings of public separateness. This seems to me an obvious point. But one that needs to be made. In recent years there have been attempts to make the language of the alien public language. "Bilingual education, two ways to understand . . . ," television and radio commercials glibly announce. Proponents of bilingual education are careful to say that they want students to acquire good schooling. Their argument goes something like this: children permitted to use their family language in school will not be so alienated and will be better able to match the progress of English-speaking children in the crucial first months of instruction. (Increasingly confident of their abilities, such children will be more inclined to apply themselves to their studies in the future.) But then the bilingualists claim another, very different goal. They say that children who use their family language in school will retain a sense of their individuality — their ethnic heritage and cultural ties. Supporters of bilingual education thus want it both ways. They propose bilingual schooling as a way of helping students acquire the skills of the classroom crucial for public success. But they likewise insist that bilingual instruction will give students a sense of their identity apart from the public.

Behind this screen there gleams an astonishing promise: one can become a public person while still remaining a private person. At the very same time one can be both! There need be no tension between the self in the crowd and the self apart from the crowd! Who would not want to believe such an idea? Who can be surprised that the scheme has won the support of many middle-class Americans? If the barrio or ghetto child can retain his separateness even while being publicly educated, then it is almost possible to believe that there is no private cost to be paid for public success. Such is the consolation offered by any of the current bilingual schemes. Consider, for example, the bilingual voters' ballot. In some American cities one can cast a ballot printed in several languages. Such a document implies that a person can exercise that most public of rights—the right to vote—while still keeping apart, unassimilated from public life.

It is not enough to say that these schemes are foolish and certainly doomed. Middle-class supporters of public bilingualism toy with the confusion of those Americans who cannot speak standard English as well as they can. Bilingual enthusiasts, moreover, sin against intimacy. An Hispanic-American writer tells me, "I will never give up my family language; I would as soon give up my soul." Thus he holds to his chest a skein of words, as though it were the source of his family ties. He credits to language what he should credit to family members. A convenient mistake. For as long as he holds on to words, he can ignore how much else has changed in his life.

It has happened before. In earlier decades, persons newly successful and ambitious for social mobility similarly seized upon certain "family words." Working-class men attempting political power took to calling one another "brother." By so doing they escaped oppressive public isolation and were able to unite with many others like themselves. But they paid a price for this union. It was a public union they forged. The word they coined to address one another could never be the sound *(brother)* exchanged by two in intimate greeting. In the union hall the word "brother" became a vague metaphor; with repetition a weak echo of the intimate sound. Context forced the change. Context could not be overruled. Context will always guard the realm of the intimate from public misuse.

Today nonwhite Americans call "brother" to strangers. And white feminists refer to their mass union of "sisters." And white middle-class teenagers continue to prove the importance of context as they try to ignore it. They seize upon the idioms of the black ghetto. But their attempt to appropriate such expressions invariably changes the words. As it becomes a public expression, the ghetto idiom loses its sound — its message of public separateness and strident intimacy. It becomes with public repetition a series of words, increasingly lifeless.

The mystery remains: intimate utterance. The communication of intimacy passes through the word to enliven its sound. But it cannot be held by the word. Cannot be clutched or ever quoted. It is too fluid. It depends not on word but on person.

My grandmother!   65

She stood among my other relations mocking me when I no longer spoke Spanish. *"Pocho,"* she said. But then it made no difference. (She'd laugh.) Our relationship continued. Language was never its source. She was a woman in her eighties during the first decade of my life. A mysterious woman to me, my only living grandparent. A woman of Mexico. The woman in long black dresses that reached down to her shoes. My one relative who spoke no word of English. She had no interest in *gringo* society. She remained completely aloof from the public. Protected by her daughters. Protected even by me when we went to Safeway together and I acted as her translator. Eccentric woman. Soft. Hard.

When my family visited my aunt's house in San Francisco, my grandmother searched for me among my many cousins. She'd chase them away. Pinching her granddaughters, she'd warn them all away from me. Then she'd take me to her room, where she had prepared for my coming. There would be a chair next to the bed. A dusty jellied candy nearby. And a copy of *Life en Español* for me to examine. "There," she'd say. I'd sit there content. A boy of eight. *Pocho*. Her favorite. I'd sift through the pictures of earthquake-destroyed Latin American cities and blond-wigged Mexican movie stars. And all the while I'd listen to the sound of my grandmother's voice. She'd pace round the room, searching through closets and drawers, telling me stories of her life. Her past. They were stories so familiar to me that I couldn't remember the first time I'd heard them. I'd look up sometimes to listen. Other times she'd look over at me. But she never seemed to expect a response. Sometimes I'd smile or nod. (I understood exactly what she was saying.) But it never seemed to matter to her one way or another. It was enough I was there. The words she spoke were almost irrelevant to that fact—the sounds she made. Content.

The mystery remained: intimate utterance.

I learn little about language and intimacy listening to those social activists who propose using one's family language in public life. Listening to songs on the radio, or hearing a great voice at the opera, or overhearing the woman downstairs singing to herself at an open window, I learn much more. Singers celebrate the human voice. Their lyrics are words. But animated by voice those words are subsumed into sounds. I listen with excitement as the words yield their enormous power to sound—though the words are never totally obliterated. In most songs the drama or tension results from the fact that the singer moves between word (sense) and note (song). At one moment the song simply "says"

something. At another moment the voice stretches out the words—
the heart cannot contain!—and the voice moves toward pure
sound. Words take flight.

Singing out words, the singer suggests an experience of sound   70
most intensely mine at intimate moments. Literally, most songs
are about love. (Lost love; celebrations of loving; pleas.) By simply
being occasions when sound escapes word, however, songs put
me in mind of the most intimate moments of my life.

Finally, among all types of song, it is the song created by lyric
poets that I find most compelling. There is no other public occasion of sound so important for me. Written poems exist on a page,
at first glance, as a mere collection of words. And yet, despite this,
without musical accompaniment, the poet leads me to hear the
sounds of the words that I read. As song, the poem passes between
sound and sense, never belonging for long to one realm or the
other. As public artifact, the poem can never duplicate intimate
sound. But by imitating such sound, the poem helps me recall the
intimate times of my life. I read in my room—alone—and grow
conscious of being alone, sounding my voice, in search of another.
The poem serves then as a memory device. It forces remembrance.
And refreshes. It reminds me of the possibility of escaping public
words, the possibility that awaits me in meeting the intimate.

The poems I read are not nonsense poems. But I read them
for reasons which, I imagine, are similar to those that make
children play with meaningless rhyme. I have watched them
before: I have noticed the way children create private languages
to keep away the adult; I have heard their chanting riddles that go
nowhere in logic but harken back to some kingdom of sound;
I have watched them listen to intricate nonsense rhymes, and I
have noted their wonder. I was never such a child. Until I was six
years old, I remained in a magical realm of sound. I didn't need
to remember that realm because it was present to me. But then
the screen door shut behind me as I left home for school. At last
I began my movement toward words. On the other side of initial sadness would come the realization that intimacy cannot be
held. With time would come the knowledge that intimacy must
finally pass.

I would dishonor those I have loved and those I love now to
claim anything else. I would dishonor our closeness by holding

on to a particular language and calling it my family language. Intimacy is not trapped within words. It passes through words. It passes. The truth is that intimates leave the room. Doors close. Faces move away from the window. Time passes. Voices recede into the dark. Death finally quiets the voice. And there is no way to deny it. No way to stand in the crowd, uttering one's family language.

The last time I saw my grandmother I was nine years old. I can tell you some of the things she said to me as I stood by her bed. I cannot, however, quote the message of intimacy she conveyed with her voice. She laughed, holding my hand. Her voice illumined disjointed memories as it passed them again. She remembered her husband, his green eyes, the magic name of Narciso. His early death. She remembered the farm in Mexico. The eucalyptus nearby. (Its scent, she remembered, like incense.) She remembered the family cow, the bell round its neck heard miles away. A dog. She remembered working as a seamstress. How she'd leave her daughters and son for long hours to go into Guadalajara to work. And how my mother would come running toward her in the sun—her bright yellow dress—to see her return. *"Mmmaaammmmáááá,"* the old lady mimicked her daughter (my mother) to her son. She laughed. There was the snap of a cough. An aunt came into the room and told me it was time I should leave. "You can see her tomorrow," she promised. And so I kissed my grandmother's cracked face. And the last thing I saw was her thin, oddly youthful thigh, as my aunt rearranged the sheet on the bed.

At the funeral parlor a few days after, I knelt with my relatives 75 during the rosary. Among their voices but silent, I traced, then lost, the sounds of individual aunts in the surge of the common prayer. And I heard at that moment what I have since heard often again—the sounds the women in my family make when they are praying in sadness. When I went up to look at my grandmother, I saw her through the haze of a veil draped over the open lid of the casket. Her face appeared calm—but distant and unyielding to love. It was not the face I remembered seeing most often. It was the face she made in public when the clerk at Safeway asked her some question and I would have to respond. It was her public face the mortician had designed with his dubious art.

For Discussion and Writing

1. What are the two educational philosophies Rodriguez describes?

2. Much of Rodriguez's essay is spent comparing the Spanish his parents spoke at home to the English they spoke outside it, "the language of their Mexican past" to "the English of public society" (par. 9). What is the point of including this material? How do these comparisons support his argument?

3. **connections** Rodriguez creates many moments where his point is illustrated in narrative—for example, the moment in school when he first hears his name in English (par. 4), and how the threat to his familial and cultural identity is represented in his seeing his mother's face "dissolve in a watery blur behind the pebbled glass door" (par. 4). Find similar moments in Langston Hughes's "Salvation" (p. 185). How do those moments add to Hughes's larger concern?

4. Do you agree with Rodriguez or with those who support bilingual education? Why?

5. **looking further** Research the politics of bilingualism in recent American history. What laws have been passed or proposed? What policies enacted or ended? What are the larger political arguments that have supported these developments?

MIKE ROSE

"I Just Wanna Be Average"

Born in 1944 to Italian immigrants and raised in South Central Los Angeles, Mike Rose is a professor of education at UCLA and an advocate for the democratization of the university and for creative teaching. His Lives on the Boundary: The Struggles and Achievements of America's Underprepared *(1989) investigated remedial education, and* Possible Lives: The Promise of Public Education in America *(1995) was the product of four years of research into teaching in America.*

"I Just Wanna Be Average," taken from Lives on the Boundary, *examines learning, knowledge, and expectations and is drawn from Rose's own experiences in school. Of knowledge, Rose writes, "It enabled me to do things in the world" (par. 37)—an idea at once simple and profound. Consider, as you read, the kinds of things that your education has allowed you to do. What else do you need to learn to "do things in the world"?*

It took two buses to get to Our Lady of Mercy. The first started deep in South Los Angeles and caught me at midpoint. The second drifted through neighborhoods with trees, parks, big lawns, and lots of flowers. The rides were long but were livened up by a group of South L.A. veterans whose parents also thought that Hope had set up shop in the west end of the county. There was Christy Biggars, who, at sixteen, was dealing and was, according to rumor, a pimp as well. There were Bill Cobb and Johnny Gonzales, grease-pencil artists extraordinaire, who left Nembutal-enhanced swirls of "Cobb" and "Johnny" on the corrugated walls of the bus. And then there was Tyrrell Wilson. Tyrrell was the coolest kid I knew. He ran the dozens like a metric halfback, laid down a rap that outrhymed and outpointed Cobb, whose rap was good but not great—the curse of a moderately soulful kid trapped in white skin. But it was Cobb who would sneak a radio onto the bus, and thus underwrote his patter with Little Richard, Fats

313

Domino, Chuck Berry, the Coasters, and Ernie K. Doe's mother-in-law, an awful woman who was "sent from down below." And so it was that Christy and Cobb and Johnny G. and Tyrrell and I and assorted others picked up along the way passed our days in the back of the bus, a funny mix brought together by geography and parental desire.

Entrance to school brings with it forms and releases and assessments. Mercy relied on a series of tests, mostly the Stanford-Binet, for placement, and somehow the results of my tests got confused with those of another student named Rose. The other Rose apparently didn't do very well, for I was placed in the vocational track, a euphemism for the bottom level. Neither I nor my parents realized what this meant. We had no sense that Business Math, Typing, and English–Level D were dead ends. The current spate of reports on the schools criticizes parents for not involving themselves in the education of their children. But how would someone like Tommy Rose, with his two years of Italian schooling, know what to ask? And what sort of pressure could an exhausted waitress apply? The error went undetected, and I remained in the vocational track for two years. What a place.

My homeroom was supervised by Brother Dill, a troubled and unstable man who also taught freshman English. When his class drifted away from him, which was often, his voice would rise in paranoid accusations, and occasionally he would lose control and shake or smack us. I hadn't been there two months when one of his brisk, face-turning slaps had my glasses sliding down the aisle. Physical education was also pretty harsh. Our teacher was a stubby ex-lineman who had played old-time pro ball in the Midwest. He routinely had us grabbing our ankles to receive his stinging paddle across our butts. He did that, he said, to make men of us. "Rose," he bellowed on our first encounter; me standing geeky in line in my baggy shorts. " 'Rose'? What the hell kind of name is that?"

"Italian, sir," I squeaked.

"Italian! Ho. Rose, do you know the sound a bag of shit makes   5
when it hits the wall?"

"No, sir."

"Wop!"

Sophomore English was taught by Mr. Mitropetros. He was a large, bejeweled man who managed the parking lot at the Shrine

Auditorium. He would crow and preen and list for us the stars he'd brushed against. We'd ask questions and glance knowingly and snicker, and all that fueled the poor guy to brag some more. Parking cars was his night job. He had little training in English, so his lesson plan for his day work had us reading the district's required text, *Julius Caesar*, aloud for the semester. We'd finished the play way before the twenty weeks was up, so he'd have us switch parts again and again and start again: Dave Snyder, the fastest guy at Mercy, muscling through Caesar to the breathless squeals of Calpurnia, as interpreted by Steve Fusco, a surfer who owned the school's most envied paneled wagon. Week ten and Dave and Steve would take on new roles, as would we all, and render a water-logged Cassius and a Brutus that are beyond my powers of description.

Spanish I—taken in the second year—fell into the hands of a new recruit. Mr. Montez was a tiny man, slight, five foot six at the most, soft-spoken and delicate. Spanish was a particularly rowdy class, and Mr. Montez was as prepared for it as a dolly maker at a hammer throw. He would tap his pencil to a room in which Steve Fusco was propelling spitballs from his heavy lips, in which Mike Dweetz was taunting Billy Hawk, a half-Indian, half-Spanish, reed-thin, quietly explosive boy. The vocational track at Our Lady of Mercy mixed kids traveling in from South L.A. with South Bay surfers and a few Slavs and Chicanos from the harbors of San Pedro. This was a dangerous miscellany: surfers and hodads and South-Central blacks all ablaze to the metronomic tapping of Hector Montez's pencil.

One day Billy lost it. Out of the corner of my eye I saw him 10 strike out with his right arm and catch Dweetz across the neck. Quick as a spasm, Dweetz was out of his seat, scattering desks, cracking Billy on the side of the head, right behind the eye. Snyder and Fusco and others broke it up, but the room felt hot and close and naked. Mr. Montez's tenuous authority was finally ripped to shreds, and I think everyone felt a little strange about that. The charade was over, and when it came down to it, I don't think any of the kids really wanted it to end this way. They had pushed and pushed and bullied their way into a freedom that both scared and embarrassed them.

Students will float to the mark you set. I and the others in the vocational classes were bobbing in pretty shallow water. Vocational education has aimed at increasing the economic opportunities of students who do not do well in our schools. Some serious programs succeed in doing that, and through exceptional teachers—like Mr. Gross in *Horace's Compromise*—students learn to develop hypotheses and troubleshoot, reason through a problem, and communicate effectively—the true job skills. The vocational track, however, is most often a place for those who are just not making it, a dumping ground for the disaffected. There were a few teachers who worked hard at education; young Brother Slattery, for example, combined a stern voice with weekly quizzes to try to pass along to us a skeletal outline of world history. But mostly the teachers had no idea of how to engage the imaginations of us kids who were scuttling along at the bottom of the pond.

And the teachers would have needed some inventiveness, for none of us was groomed for the classroom. It wasn't just that I didn't know things—didn't know how to simplify algebraic fractions, couldn't identify different kinds of clauses, bungled Spanish translations—but that I had developed various faulty and inadequate ways of doing algebra and making sense of Spanish. Worse yet, the years of defensive tuning out in elementary school had given me a way to escape quickly while seeming at least half alert. During my time in Voc. Ed., I developed further into a mediocre student and a somnambulant problem solver, and that affected the subjects I did have the wherewithal to handle: I detested Shakespeare; I got bored with history. My attention flitted here and there. I fooled around in class and read my books indifferently—the intellectual equivalent of playing with your food. I did what I had to do to get by, and I did it with half a mind.

But I did learn things about people and eventually came into my own socially. I liked the guys in Voc. Ed. Growing up where I did, I understood and admired physical prowess, and there was an abundance of muscle here. There was Dave Snyder, a sprinter and halfback of true quality. Dave's ability and his quick wit gave him a natural appeal, and he was welcome in any clique, though he always kept a little independent. He enjoyed acting the fool and could care less about studies, but he possessed a certain maturity and never caused the faculty much trouble. It was a testament to his independence that he included me among his friends—I eventually went out for track, but I was no jock.

Owing to the Latin alphabet and a dearth of *R*s and *S*s, Snyder sat behind Rose, and we started exchanging one-liners and became friends.

There was Ted Richard, a much-touted Little League pitcher. He was chunky and had a baby face and came to Our Lady of Mercy as a seasoned street fighter. Ted was quick to laugh and he had a loud, jolly laugh, but when he got angry he'd smile a little smile, the kind that simply raises the corner of the mouth a quarter of an inch. For those who knew, it was an eerie signal. Those who didn't found themselves in big trouble, for Ted was very quick. He loved to carry on what we would come to call philosophical discussions: What is courage? Does God exist? He also loved words, enjoyed picking up big ones like *salubrious* and *equivocal* and using them in our conversations—laughing at himself as the word hit a chuckhole rolling off his tongue. Ted didn't do all that well in school—baseball and parties and testing the courage he'd speculated about took up his time. His textbooks were *Argosy* and *Field and Stream*, whatever newspapers he'd find on the bus stop—from the *Daily Worker* to pornography—conversations with uncles or hobos or businessmen he'd meet in a coffee shop, *The Old Man and the Sea*. With hindsight, I can see that Ted was developing into one of those rough-hewn intellectuals whose sources are a mix of the learned and the apocryphal, whose discussions are both assured and sad.

And then there was Ken Harvey. Ken was good-looking in a 15 puffy way and had a full and oily ducktail and was a car enthusiast . . . a hodad. One day in religion class, he said the sentence that turned out to be one of the most memorable of the hundreds of thousands I heard in those Voc. Ed. years. We were talking about the parable of the talents, about achievement, working hard, doing the best you can do, blah-blah-blah, when the teacher called on the restive Ken Harvey for an opinion. Ken thought about it, but just for a second, and said (with studied, minimal affect), "I just wanna be average." That woke me up. Average? Who wants to be average? Then the athletes chimed in with the clichés that make you want to laryngectomize them, and the exchange became a platitudinous melee. At the time, I thought Ken's assertion was stupid, and I wrote him off. But his sentence has stayed with me all these years, and I think I am finally coming to understand it.

Ken Harvey was gasping for air. School can be a tremendously disorienting place. No matter how bad the school, you're going to encounter notions that don't fit with the assumptions and beliefs that you grew up with—maybe you'll hear these dissonant notions from teachers, maybe from the other students, and maybe you'll read them. You'll also be thrown in with all kinds of kids from all kinds of backgrounds, and that can be unsettling— this is especially true in places of rich ethnic and linguistic mix, like the L.A. basin. You'll see a handful of students far excel you in courses that sound exotic and that are only in the curriculum of the elite: French, physics, trigonometry. And all this is happening while you're trying to shape an identity, your body is changing, and your emotions are running wild. If you're a working-class kid in the vocational track, the options you'll have to deal with this will be constrained in certain ways: you're defined by your school as "slow"; you're placed in a curriculum that isn't designed to liberate you but to occupy you, or, if you're lucky, train you, though the training is for work the society does not esteem; other students are picking up the cues from your school and your curriculum and interacting with you in particular ways. If you're a kid like Ted Richard, you turn your back on all this and let your mind roam where it may. But youngsters like Ted are rare. What Ken and so many others do is protect themselves from such suffocating madness by taking on with a vengeance the identity implied in the vocational track. Reject the confusion and frustration by openly defining yourself as the Common Joe. Champion the average. Rely on your own good sense. Fuck this bullshit. Bullshit, of course, is everything you—and the others—fear is beyond you: books, essays, tests, academic scrambling, complexity, scientific reasoning, philosophical inquiry.

The tragedy is that you have to twist the knife in your own gray matter to make this defense work. You'll have to shut down, have to reject intellectual stimuli or diffuse them with sarcasm, have to cultivate stupidity, have to convert boredom from a malady into a way of confronting the world. Keep your vocabulary simple, act stoned when you're not or act more stoned than you are, flaunt ignorance, materialize your dreams. It is a powerful and effective defense—it neutralizes the insult and the frustration of being a vocational kid and, when perfected, it drives teachers up the wall, a delightful secondary effect. But like all strong magic, it exacts a price.

My own deliverance from the Voc. Ed. world began with sophomore biology. Every student, college prep to vocational, had to take biology, and unlike the other courses, the same person taught all sections. When teaching the vocational group, Brother Clint probably slowed down a bit or omitted a little of the fundamental biochemistry, but he used the same book and more or less the same syllabus across the board. If one class got tough, he could get tougher. He was young and powerful and very handsome, and looks and physical strength were high currency. No one gave him any trouble.

I was pretty bad at the dissecting table, but the lectures and the textbook were interesting: plastic overlays that, with each turned page, peeled away skin, then veins and muscle, then organs, down to the very bones that Brother Clint, pointer in hand, would tap out on our hanging skeleton. Dave Snyder was in big trouble, for the study of life—versus the living of it—was sticking in his craw. We worked out a code for our multiple-choice exams. He'd poke me in the back: once for the answer under *A*, twice for *B*, and so on; and when he'd hit the right one, I'd look up to the ceiling as though I were lost in thought. Poke: cytoplasm. Poke, poke: methane. Poke, poke, poke: William Harvey. Poke, poke, poke, poke: islets of Langerhans. This didn't work out perfectly, but Dave passed the course, and I mastered the dreamy look of a guy on a record jacket. And something else happened. Brother Clint puzzled over this Voc. Ed. kid who was racking up 98s and 99s on his tests. He checked the school's records and discovered the error. He recommended that I begin my junior year in the College Prep program. According to all I've read since, such a shift, as one report put it, is virtually impossible. Kids at that level rarely cross tracks. The telling thing is how chancy both my placement into and exit from Voc. Ed. was; neither I nor my parents had anything to do with it. I lived in one world during spring semester, and when I came back to school in the fall, I was living in another.

Switching to College Prep was a mixed blessing. I was an erratic student. I was undisciplined. And I hadn't caught onto the rules of the game: why work hard in a class that didn't grab my fancy? I was also hopelessly behind in math. Chemistry was hard;

toying with my chemistry set years before hadn't prepared me for the chemist's equations. Fortunately, the priest who taught both chemistry and second-year algebra was also the school's athletic director. Membership on the track team covered me; I knew I wouldn't get lower than a C. U.S. history was taught pretty well, and I did okay. But civics was taken over by a football coach who had trouble reading the textbook aloud—and reading aloud was the centerpiece of his pedagogy. College Prep at Mercy was certainly an improvement over the vocational program—at least it carried some status—but the social science curriculum was weak, and the mathematics and physical sciences were simply beyond me. I had a miserable quantitative background and ended up copying some assignments and finessing the rest as best I could. Let me try to explain how it feels to see again and again material you should once have learned but didn't.

You are given a problem. It requires you to simplify algebraic fractions or to multiply expressions containing square roots. You know this is pretty basic material because you've seen it for years. Once a teacher took some time with you, and you learned how to carry out these operations. Simple versions, anyway. But that was a year or two or more in the past, and these are more complex versions, and now you're not sure. And this, you keep telling yourself, is ninth- or even eighth-grade stuff.

Next it's a word problem. This is also old hat. The basic elements are as familiar as story characters: trains speeding so many miles per hour or shadows of buildings angling so many degrees. Maybe you know enough, have sat through enough explanations, to be able to begin setting up the problem: "If one train is going this fast . . ." or "This shadow is really one line of a triangle. . . ." Then: "Let's see . . ." "How did Jones do this?" "Hmmmm." "No." "No, that won't work." Your attention wavers. You wonder about other things: a football game, a dance, that cute new checker at the market. You try to focus on the problem again. You scribble on paper for a while, but the tension wins out and your attention flits elsewhere. You crumple the paper and begin daydreaming to ease the frustration.

The particulars will vary, but in essence this is what a number of students go through, especially those in so-called remedial classes. They open their textbooks and see once again the familiar and impenetrable formulas and diagrams and terms that have stumped them for years. There is no excitement here. *No* excitement. Regardless of what the teacher says, this is not a new challenge. There is, rather, embarrassment and frustration and, not surprisingly, some anger in being reminded once again of long-standing inadequacies. No wonder so many students finally attribute their difficulties to something inborn, organic: "That part of my brain just doesn't work." Given the troubling histories many of these students have, it's miraculous that any of them can lift the shroud of hopelessness sufficiently to make deliverance from these classes possible.

Through this entire period, my father's health was deteriorating with cruel momentum. His arteriosclerosis progressed to the point where a simple nick on his shin wouldn't heal. Eventually it ulcerated and widened. Lou Minton would come by daily to change the dressing. We tried renting an oscillating bed—which we placed in the front room—to force blood through the constricted arteries in my father's legs. The bed hummed through the night, moving in place to ward off the inevitable. The ulcer continued to spread, and the doctors finally had to amputate. My grandfather had lost his leg in a stockyard accident. Now my father too was crippled. His convalescence was slow but steady, and the doctors placed him in the Santa Monica Rehabilitation Center, a sun-bleached building that opened out onto the warm spray of the Pacific. The place gave him some strength and some color and some training in walking with an artificial leg. He did pretty well for a year or so until he slipped and broke his hip. He was confined to a wheelchair after that, and the confinement contributed to the diminishing of his body and spirit.

I am holding a picture of him. He is sitting in his wheelchair 25 and smiling at the camera. The smile appears forced, unsteady, seems to quaver, though it is frozen in silver nitrate. He is in his mid-sixties and looks eighty. Late in my junior year, he had a stroke and never came out of the resulting coma. After that, I would see him only in dreams, and to this day that is how I join him. Sometimes the dreams are sad and grisly and primal: my father lying in a bed soaked with his suppuration, holding me, rocking me. But sometimes the dreams bring him back to me healthy: him talking to me on an empty street, or buying some pictures to decorate our old house, or transformed somehow into someone strong and adept with tools and the physical.

Jack MacFarland couldn't have come into my life at a better time. My father was dead, and I had logged up too many years of scholastic indifference. Mr. MacFarland had a master's degree from Columbia and decided, at twenty-six, to find a little school and teach his heart out. He never took any credentialing courses, couldn't bear to, he said, so he had to find employment in a private system. He ended up at Our Lady of Mercy teaching five sections of senior English. He was a beatnik who was born too late. His teeth were stained, he tucked his sorry tie in between the third and fourth buttons of his shirt, and his pants were chronically wrinkled. At first, we couldn't believe this guy, thought he slept in his car. But within no time, he had us so startled with work that we didn't much worry about where he slept or if he slept at all. We wrote three or four essays a month. We read a book every two to three weeks, starting with the *Iliad* and ending up with Hemingway. He gave us a quiz on the reading every other day. He brought a prep school curriculum to Mercy High.

MacFarland's lectures were crafted, and as he delivered them he would pace the room jiggling a piece of chalk in his cupped hand, using it to scribble on the board the names of all the writers and philosophers and plays and novels he was weaving into his discussion. He asked questions often, raised everything from Zeno's paradox to the repeated last line of Frost's "Stopping by Woods on a Snowy Evening." He slowly and carefully built up our knowledge of Western intellectual history—with facts, with connections, with speculations. We learned about Greek philosophy, about Dante, the Elizabethan worldview, the Age of Reason, existentialism. He analyzed poems with us, had us reading sections from John Ciardi's *How Does a Poem Mean?*, making a potentially difficult book accessible with his own explanations. We gave oral reports on poems Ciardi didn't cover. We imitated the styles of Conrad, Hemingway, and *Time* magazine. We wrote and talked, wrote and talked. The man immersed us in language.

Even MacFarland's barbs were literary. If Jim Fitzsimmons, hung over and irritable, tried to smart-ass him, he'd rejoin with a flourish that would spark the indomitable Skip Madison—who'd lost his front teeth in a hapless tackle—to flick his tongue through the gap and opine, "good chop," drawing out the single "o" in stinging indictment. Jack MacFarland, this tobacco-stained intellectual, brandished linguistic weapons of a kind I hadn't encountered before. Here was this *egghead*, for God's sake, keeping some pretty difficult people in line. And from what I heard, Mike Dweetz and Steve Fusco and all the notorious Voc. Ed. crowd settled down as well when MacFarland took the podium. Though a lot of guys groused in the schoolyard, it just seemed that giving trouble to this particular teacher was a silly thing to do. Tomfoolery, not to mention assault, had no place in the world he was trying to create for us, and instinctively everyone knew that. If nothing else, we all recognized MacFarland's considerable intelligence and respected the hours he put into his work. It came to this: the troublemaker would look foolish rather than daring. Even Jim Fitzsimmons was reading *On the Road* and turning his incipient alcoholism to literary ends.

There were some lives that were already beyond Jack MacFarland's ministrations, but mine was not. I started reading again as I hadn't since elementary school. I would go into our gloomy little bedroom or sit at the dinner table while, on the television, Danny McShane was paralyzing Mr. Moto with the atomic drop, and work slowly back through *Heart of Darkness*, trying to catch the words in Conrad's sentences. I certainly was not MacFarland's best student; most of the other guys in College Prep, even my fellow slackers, had better backgrounds than I did. But I worked very hard, for MacFarland had hooked me. He tapped my old interest in reading and creating stories. He gave me a way to feel special by using my mind. And he provided a role model that wasn't shaped on physical prowess alone, and something inside me that I wasn't quite aware of responded to that. Jack MacFarland established a literacy club, to borrow a phrase of Frank Smith's, and invited me — invited all of us — to join.

There's been a good deal of research and speculation suggest- 30 ing that the acknowledgment of school performance with extrinsic rewards — smiling faces, stars, numbers, grades — diminishes the intrinsic satisfaction children experience by engaging in reading or writing or problem solving. While it's certainly true that we've created an educational system that encourages our best and brightest to become cynical grade collectors and, in general, have developed an obsession with evaluation and assessment, I must tell you that venal though it may have been, I loved getting good grades from MacFarland. I now know how subjective grades can be, but then they came tucked in the back of essays like bits of scientific data, some sort of spectroscopic readout that said, objectively and publicly, that I had made something of value. I suppose I'd been mediocre for too long and enjoyed a public redefinition. And I suppose the workings of my mind, such as they were, had been private for too long. My linguistic play moved into the world; . . . these papers with their circled, red B-pluses and A-minuses linked my mind to something outside it. I carried them around like a club emblem.

One day in the December of my senior year, Mr. MacFarland asked me where I was going to go to college. I hadn't thought much about it. Many of the students I teach today spent their last year in high school with a physics text in one hand and the Stanford catalog in the other, but I wasn't even aware of what "entrance requirements" were. My folks would say that they wanted me to go to college and be a doctor, but I don't know how seriously I ever took that; it seemed a sweet thing to say, a bit of supportive family chatter, like telling a gangly daughter she's graceful. The reality of higher education wasn't in my scheme of things: no one in the family had gone to college; only two of my uncles had completed high school. I figured I'd get a night job and go to the local junior college because I knew that Snyder and Company were going there to play ball. But I hadn't even prepared for that. When I finally said, "I don't know," MacFarland looked down at me— I was seated in his office—and said, "Listen, you can write."

My grades stank. I had A's in biology and a handful of B's in a few English and social science classes. All the rest were C's—or worse. MacFarland said I would do well in his class and laid down the law about doing well in the others. Still, the record for my first three years wouldn't have been acceptable to any four-year school. To nobody's surprise, I was turned down flat by USC and UCLA. But Jack MacFarland was on the case. He had received his bachelor's degree from Loyola University, so he made calls to old professors and talked to somebody in admissions and wrote me a strong letter. Loyola finally accepted me as a probationary student. I would be on trial for the first year, and if I did okay, I would be granted regular status. MacFarland also intervened to get me a loan, for I could never have afforded a private college without it. Four more years of religion classes and four more years of boys at one school, girls at another. But at least I was going to college. Amazing.

In my last semester of high school, I elected a special English course fashioned by Mr. MacFarland, and it was through this elective that there arose at Mercy a fledgling literati. Art Mitz, the editor of the school newspaper and a very smart guy, was the kingpin. He was joined by me and by Mark Dever, a quiet boy who wrote beautifully and who would die before he was forty. MacFarland occasionally invited us to his apartment, and those visits became the high point of our apprenticeship: we'd clamp on our training wheels and drive to his salon.

He lived in a cramped and cluttered place near the airport, tucked away in the kind of building that architectural critic Reyner Banham calls a *dingbat*. Books were all over: stacked, piled, tossed, and crated, underlined and dog eared, well worn and new. Cigarette ashes crusted with coffee in saucers or spilling over the sides of motel ashtrays. The little bedroom had, along two of its walls, bricks and boards loaded with notes, magazines, and over-sized books. The kitchen joined the living room, and there was a stack of German newspapers under the sink. I had never seen anything like it: a great flophouse of language furnished by City Lights and Café le Metro. I read every title. I flipped through paperbacks and scanned jackets and memorized names: Gogol, *Finnegans Wake*, Djuna Barnes, Jackson Pollock, *A Coney Island of the Mind*, F. O. Matthiessen's *American Renaissance*, all sorts of Freud, *Troubled Sleep*, Man Ray, *The Education of Henry Adams*, Richard Wright, *Film as Art*, William Butler Yeats, Marguerite Duras, *Redburn*, *A Season in Hell*, *Kapital*. On the cover of Alain-Fournier's *The Wanderer* was an Edward Gorey drawing of a young man on a road winding into dark trees. By the hotplate sat a strange Kafka novel called *Amerika*, in which an adolescent hero crosses the Atlantic to find the Nature Theater of Oklahoma. Art and Mark would be talking about a movie or the school newspaper, and I would be consuming my English teacher's library. It was heady stuff. I felt like a Pop Warner athlete on steroids.

Art, Mark, and I would buy stogies and triangulate from 35 MacFarland's apartment to the Cinema, which now shows X-rated films but was then L.A.'s premier art theater, and then to the musty Cherokee Bookstore in Hollywood to hobnob with beatnik homosexuals—smoking, drinking bourbon and coffee, and try-ing out awkward phrases we'd gleaned from our mentor's book-shelves. I was happy and precocious and a little scared as well, for

Hollywood Boulevard was thick with a kind of decadence that was foreign to the South Side. After the Cherokee, we would head back to the security of MacFarland's apartment, slaphappy with hipness.

Let me be the first to admit that there was a good deal of adolescent passion in this embrace of the avant-garde: self-absorption, sexually charged pedantry, an elevation of the odd and abandoned. Still it was a time during which I absorbed an awful lot of information: long lists of titles, images from expressionist paintings, new wave shibboleths, snippets of philosophy, and names that read like Steve Fusco's misspellings—Goethe, Nietzsche, Kierkegaard. Now this is hardly the stuff of deep understanding. But it was an introduction, a phrase book, a Baedeker to a vocabulary of ideas, and it felt good at the time to know all these words. With hindsight I realize how layered and important that knowledge was.

It enabled me to do things in the world. I could browse bohemian bookstores in far-off, mysterious Hollywood; I could go to the Cinema and see events through the lenses of European directors; and, most of all, I could share an evening, talk that talk, with Jack MacFarland, the man I most admired at the time. Knowledge was becoming a bonding agent. Within a year or two, the persona of the disaffected hipster would prove too cynical, too alienated to last. But for a time it was new and exciting: it provided a critical perspective on society, and it allowed me to act as though I were living beyond the limiting boundaries of South Vermont.

For Discussion and Writing

1. List the different teachers Rose writes about in this essay, adding a sentence to each name describing his significance for Rose.
2. This essay is from Rose's powerful book *Lives on the Boundary*. What boundaries does Rose write about here? What acts of classification do these boundaries serve?
3. **connections** Rose is put on the vocational track accidentally and remains there for two years because his parents are unequipped to help him. Compare his responses to the particular learning environment in which he found himself with those of Sherman Alexie in "The Joy of Reading and Writing: Superman and Me" (p. 22). How does it

feel to each? What larger significance does each find in the experience? What connections can you find between the larger meanings each writer reflects upon?

4. "Students will float to the mark you set," Rose writes (par. 11). Write about a time in your life when this was true of you, and reflect more generally on your life as a student. Have you found that your educational experiences thus far have pushed you to exceed what you originally thought was possible? What kinds of motivation are built into our educational system? Has traditional motivation (such as getting good grades) worked for you? What kind of an educational system might motivate *all* students?

5. **looking further**   Research the recent emphasis on standardized testing in public education through initiatives such as No Child Left Behind. What are the arguments for and against the increased use of testing? Do you find one set of arguments more compelling? If so, for what reasons? If not, are there further studies you think need to be done on the issue? Describe them.

OLIVER SACKS

My Periodic Table

Oliver Sacks (1933–2015) was a British neurologist and writer of more than fifteen books, many best sellers, most based on case studies of patients. He also wrote many pieces for the New Yorker, *the* New York Review of Books, *and the* London Review of Books. *His book* Awakenings *(1973) inspired a play by Harold Pinter, a documentary, and a feature film of the same name. Another book,* The Man Who Mistook His Wife for a Hat *(1985), a collection of case histories, was a best seller and the inspiration for a chamber opera, a theatrical adaptation by Peter Brooks, and an album title (Travis's* The Man Who*). Sacks also wrote about himself, in two memoirs and in two books that combined memoir and study of the brain,* The Mind's Eye *(2010) and* Hallucinations *(2012).*

Inspired early in his popular writing career by a review of his first book by his friend, the poet W. H. Auden, who said he should "be metaphorical, be mythical, be whatever you need," Sacks wrote about the science of mind and later, about himself, using the techniques of literature. It is this use that makes his work so inspirational of the art of others. As you read, pay attention not only to the story Sacks tells but to the ways in which he tells it.

I look forward eagerly, almost greedily, to the weekly arrival of journals like *Nature* and *Science,* and turn at once to articles on the physical sciences—not, as perhaps I should, to articles on biology and medicine. It was the physical sciences that provided my first enchantment as a boy.

In a recent issue of *Nature,* there was a thrilling article by the Nobel Prize–winning physicist Frank Wilczek on a new way of calculating the slightly different masses of neutrons and protons. The new calculation confirms that neutrons are very slightly heavier than protons—the ratio of their masses being 939.56563 to 938.27231—a trivial difference, one might think, but if it were

otherwise the universe as we know it could never have developed.
The ability to calculate this, Dr. Wilczek wrote, "encourages us to
predict a future in which nuclear physics reaches the level of precision and versatility that atomic physics has already achieved" —
a revolution that, alas, I will never see.

Francis Crick was convinced that "the hard problem" —
understanding how the brain gives rise to consciousness — would
be solved by 2030. "You will see it," he often said to my neurosci-
entist friend Ralph, "and you may, too, Oliver, if you live to my
age." Crick lived to his late 80s, working and thinking about consciousness till the last. Ralph died prematurely, at age 52, and
now I am terminally ill, at the age of 82. I have to say that I am not
too exercised by "the hard problem" of consciousness — indeed, I
do not see it as a problem at all; but I am sad that I will not see the
new nuclear physics that Dr. Wilczek envisages, nor a thousand
other breakthroughs in the physical and biological sciences.

A few weeks ago, in the country, far from the lights of the city, I
saw the entire sky "powdered with stars" (in Milton's words); such
a sky, I imagined, could be seen only on high, dry plateaus like
that of Atacama in Chile (where some of the world's most powerful telescopes are). It was this celestial splendor that suddenly
made me realize how little time, how little life, I had left. My
sense of the heavens' beauty, of eternity, was inseparably mixed
for me with a sense of transience — and death.

I told my friends Kate and Allen, "I would like to see such a sky   5
again when I am dying."

"We'll wheel you outside," they said.

I have been comforted, since I wrote in February about having
metastatic cancer, by the hundreds of letters I have received, the
expressions of love and appreciation, and the sense that (despite
everything) I may have lived a good and useful life. I remain very
glad and grateful for all this — yet none of it hits me as did that
night sky full of stars.

I have tended since early boyhood to deal with loss — losing
people dear to me — by turning to the nonhuman. When I was
sent away to a boarding school as a child of 6, at the outset of the
Second World War, numbers became my friends; when I returned
to London at 10, the elements and the periodic table became my
companions. Times of stress throughout my life have led me to

turn, or return, to the physical sciences, a world where there is no life, but also no death.

And now, at this juncture, when death is no longer an abstract concept, but a presence—an all-too-close, not-to-be-denied presence—I am again surrounding myself, as I did when I was a boy, with metals and minerals, little emblems of eternity. At one end of my writing table, I have element 81 in a charming box, sent to me by element-friends in England: it says, "Happy Thallium Birthday," a souvenir of my 81st birthday last July; then, a realm devoted to lead, element 82, for my just celebrated 82nd birthday earlier this month. Here, too, is a little lead casket, containing element 90, thorium, crystalline thorium, as beautiful as diamonds, and, of course, radioactive—hence the lead casket.

At the start of the year, in the weeks after I learned that I had cancer, I *felt* pretty well, despite my liver being half-occupied by metastases. When the cancer in my liver was treated in February by the injection of tiny beads into the hepatic arteries—a procedure called embolization—I felt awful for a couple of weeks but then super well, charged with physical and mental energy. (The metastases had almost all been wiped out by the embolization.) I had been given not a remission, but an intermission, a time to deepen friendships, to see patients, to write, and to travel back to my homeland, England. People could scarcely believe at this time that I had a terminal condition, and I could easily forget it myself.

This sense of health and energy started to decline as May moved into June, but I was able to celebrate my 82nd birthday in style. (Auden used to say that one should *always* celebrate one's birthday, no matter how one felt.) But now, I have some nausea and loss of appetite; chills in the day, sweats at night; and, above all, a pervasive tiredness, with sudden exhaustion if I overdo things. I continue to swim daily, but more slowly now, as I am beginning to feel a little short of breath. I could deny it before, but I *know* I am ill now. A CT scan on July 7 confirmed that the metastases had not only regrown in my liver but had now spread beyond it as well.

I started a new sort of treatment—immunotherapy—last week. It is not without its hazards, but I hope it will give me a few more good months. But before beginning this, I wanted to have a little fun: a trip to North Carolina to see the wonderful lemur research center at Duke University. Lemurs are close to the ancestral stock from which all primates arose, and I am happy to think that one of my own ancestors, 50 million years ago, was a little tree-dwelling creature not so dissimilar to the lemurs of today. I love their leaping vitality, their inquisitive nature.

Next to the circle of lead on my table is the land of bismuth: naturally occurring bismuth from Australia; little limousine-shaped ingots of bismuth from a mine in Bolivia; bismuth slowly cooled from a melt to form beautiful iridescent crystals terraced like a Hopi village; and, in a nod to Euclid and the beauty of geometry, a cylinder and a sphere made of bismuth.

Bismuth is element 83. I do not think I will see my 83rd birthday, but I feel there is something hopeful, something encouraging, about having "83" around. Moreover, I have a soft spot for bismuth, a modest gray metal, often unregarded, ignored, even by metal lovers. My feeling as a doctor for the mistreated or marginalized extends into the inorganic world and finds a parallel in my feeling for bismuth.

I almost certainly will not see my polonium (84th) birthday, nor would I want any polonium around, with its intense, murderous radioactivity. But then, at the other end of my table—my periodic table—I have a beautifully machined piece of beryllium (element 4) to remind me of my childhood, and of how long ago my soon-to-end life began. 15

For Discussion and Writing

1. Why do you think Sacks titles his essay the way he does?

2. Sacks grounds his essay in the physical. Read back through the essay and note the significant pieces of matter he mentions, and describe how he uses each to drive the story or reveal a feeling or a truth.

3. **connections** This essay and Brian Doyle's "Joyas Voladores" (p. 132) are in many ways very different—the immediate subject, the structure, and the style of each could not in some ways be more dissimilar. Yet they share certain concerns. What are those concerns? How does each essay raise them and explore them? How are the way each frames these concerns, the issues and feelings each brings up, similar? In what ways are they different?

4. How do you imagine you would feel if you were in Sacks's position—that is, if you were near the end of your life, and knew it? Reflect on this any way you like, whether straightforwardly with a short reflection on how you imagine you would feel, what you would

think, and how you would spend your final days, or creatively, with an imagined account like that Sacks writes. Then evaluate this account. Is it how you wish you could act ideally, or how you realistically think you would act? Is there no difference?

5. **looking further** Do some research on the different ways people think about and react to death—in different cultures, according to different belief systems, depending on manner of death, and so forth. What are the commonalities and differences? What are some of the different ways people can think and feel about death? How do their different worldviews allow them to deal with those thoughts and feelings? If you are yourself in a similar situation, compare your own actions and reactions to his.

Me Talk Pretty One Day

*Born in 1956 in Johnston City, New York, David Sedaris grew up in
Raleigh, North Carolina. He is a playwright (in collaboration with his
sister Amy) and an essayist whose work has been featured regularly on
National Public Radio and in the essay collections* Naked *(1997),*
Dress Your Family in Corduroy and Denim *(2004),* When You Are
Engulfed in Flames *(2008), and* Let's Explore Diabetes with Owls
(2013), as well as the short story collection Squirrel Seeks Chipmunk:
A Modest Bestiary *(2010). Sedaris's work tends toward the satiric, but
even the most wickedly pointed of his pieces are marked by an ironic
stance that includes the author among those humans whose folly must
be satirized. This insistence on turning his satiric eye on himself is evident in "Me Talk Pretty One Day," taken from the collection of the same
name (2000), in which he recounts his efforts to learn French, to the
chagrin of his teacher and to his own evident amusement.*

At the age of forty-one, I am returning to school and have to think
of myself as what my French textbook calls "a true debutant."
After paying my tuition, I was issued a student ID, which allows
me a discounted entry fee at movie theaters, puppet shows, and
Festyland, a far-flung amusement park that advertises with bill-
boards picturing a cartoon stegosaurus sitting in a canoe and eating what appears to be a ham sandwich.

I've moved to Paris with hopes of learning the language. My
school is an easy ten-minute walk from my apartment, and on the
first day of class I arrived early, watching as the returning students
greeted one another in the school lobby. Vacations were recounted,
and questions were raised concerning mutual friends with names
like Kang and Vlatnya. Regardless of their nationalities, everyone
spoke in what sounded to me like excellent French. Some accents
were better than others, but the students exhibited an ease and
confidence I found intimidating. As an added discomfort, they

were all young, attractive, and well dressed, causing me to feel not unlike Pa Kettle trapped backstage after a fashion show.

The first day of class was nerve-racking because I knew I'd be expected to perform. That's the way they do it here—it's everybody into the language pool, sink or swim. The teacher marched in, deeply tanned from a recent vacation, and proceeded to rattle off a series of administrative announcements. I've spent quite a few summers in Normandy, and I took a monthlong French class before leaving New York. I'm not completely in the dark, yet I understood only half of what this woman was saying.

"If you have not *meimslsxp* or *lgpdmurct* by this time, then you should not be in this room. Has everyone *apzkiubjxow*? Everyone? Good, we shall begin." She spread out her lesson plan and sighed, saying, "All right, then, who knows the alphabet?"

It was startling because (a) I hadn't been asked that question in 5 a while and (b) I realized, while laughing, that I myself did *not* know the alphabet. They're the same letters, but in France they're pronounced differently. I know the shape of the alphabet but had no idea what it actually sounded like.

"Ahh." The teacher went to the board and sketched the letter *a*. "Do we have anyone in the room whose first name commences with an *ahh*?"

Two Polish Annas raised their hands, and the teacher instructed them to present themselves by stating their names, nationalities, occupations, and a brief list of things they liked and disliked in this world. The first Anna hailed from an industrial town outside of Warsaw and had front teeth the size of tombstones. She worked as a seamstress, enjoyed quiet times with friends, and hated the mosquito.

"Oh, really," the teacher said. "How very interesting. I thought that everyone loved the mosquito, but here, in front of all the world, you claim to detest him. How is it that we've been blessed with someone as unique and original as you? Tell us, please."

The seamstress did not understand what was being said but knew that this was an occasion for shame. Her rabbity mouth huffed for breath, and she stared down at her lap as though the appropriate comeback were stitched somewhere alongside the zipper of her slacks.

The second Anna learned from the first and claimed to love 10 sunshine and detest lies. It sounded like a translation of one of those Playmate of the Month data sheets, the answers always

written in the same loopy handwriting. "Turn-ons: Mom's famous
five-alarm chili! Turnoffs: insecurity and guys who come on too
strong!!!!"

The two Polish Annas surely had clear notions of what they
loved and hated, but like the rest of us, they were limited in terms
of vocabulary, and this made them appear less than sophisticated.
The teacher forged on, and we learned that Carlos, the Argentine
bandonion player, loved wine, music, and, in his words, "making
sex with the womens of the world." Next came a beautiful young
Yugoslav who identified herself as an optimist, saying that she
loved everything that life had to offer.

The teacher licked her lips, revealing a hint of the saucebox we
would later come to know. She crouched low for her attack,
placed her hands on the young woman's desk, and leaned close,
saying, "Oh yeah? And do you love your little war?"

While the optimist struggled to defend herself, I scrambled to
think of an answer to what had obviously become a trick question. How often is one asked what he loves in this world? More to
the point, how often is one asked and then publicly ridiculed for
his answer? I recalled my mother, flushed with wine, pounding
the tabletop late one night, saying, "Love? I love a good steak
cooked rare. I love my cat, and I love . . ." My sisters and I leaned
forward, waiting to hear our names. "Tums," our mother said. "I
love Tums."

The teacher killed some time accusing the Yugoslavian girl of
masterminding a program of genocide, and I jotted frantic notes
in the margins of my pad. While I can honestly say that I love leaf-
ing through medical textbooks devoted to severe dermatological
conditions, the hobby is beyond the reach of my French vocabulary, and acting it out would only have invited controversy.

When called upon, I delivered an effortless list of things that I   15
detest: blood sausage, intestinal pâtés, brain pudding. I'd learned
these words the hard way. Having given it some thought, I then
declared my love for IBM typewriters, the French word for *bruise*,
and my electric floor waxer. It was a short list, but still I managed
to mispronounce *IBM* and assign the wrong gender to both the
floor waxer and the typewriter. The teacher's reaction led me to
believe that these mistakes were capital crimes in the country of
France.

"Were you always this *palicmkrexis*?" she asked. "Even a *fiu-
scrzsa ticiwelmun* knows that a typewriter is feminine."

I absorbed as much of her abuse as I could understand, thinking—but not saying—that I find it ridiculous to assign a gender
to an inanimate object incapable of disrobing and making an
occasional fool of itself. Why refer to crack pipe or Good Sir
Dishrag when these things could never live up to all that their sex
implied?

The teacher proceeded to belittle everyone from German Eva,
who hated laziness, to Japanese Yukari, who loved paintbrushes
and soap. Italian, Thai, Dutch, Korean, and Chinese—we all left
class foolishly believing that the worst was over. She'd shaken us
up a little, but surely that was just an act designed to weed out the
deadweight. We didn't know it then, but the coming months
would teach us what it was like to spend time in the presence of a
wild animal, something completely unpredictable. Her tempera-
ment was not based on a series of good and bad days but, rather,
good and bad moments. We soon learned to dodge chalk and protect our heads and stomachs whenever she approached us with a
question. She hadn't yet punched anyone, but it seemed wise to
protect ourselves against the inevitable.

Though we were forbidden to speak anything but French, the
teacher would occasionally use us to practice any of her five fluent languages.

"I hate you," she said to me one afternoon. Her English was 20
flawless. "I really, really hate you." Call me sensitive, but I couldn't
help but take it personally.

After being singled out as a lazy *kfdtinvfm*, I took to spending
four hours a night on my homework, putting in even more time
whenever we were assigned an essay. I suppose I could have gotten by with less, but I was determined to create some sort of identity for myself: David the hard worker, David the cut-up. We'd
have one of those "complete this sentence" exercises, and I'd fool
with the thing for hours, invariably settling on something like "A
quick run around the lake? I'd love to! Just give me a moment
while I strap on my wooden leg." The teacher, through word and
action, conveyed the message that if this was my idea of an identity, she wanted nothing to do with it.

My fear and discomfort crept beyond the borders of the classroom and accompanied me out onto the wide boulevards. Stopping for a coffee, asking directions, depositing money in my bank
account: these things were out of the question, as they involved

having to speak. Before beginning school, there'd been no shutting me up, but now I was convinced that everything I said was wrong. When the phone rang, I ignored it. If someone asked me a question, I pretended to be deaf. I knew my fear was getting the best of me when I started wondering why they don't sell cuts of meat in vending machines.

My only comfort was the knowledge that I was not alone. Huddled in the hallways and making the most of our pathetic French, my fellow students and I engaged in the sort of conversation commonly overheard in refugee camps.

"Sometime me cry alone at night."

"That be common for I, also, but be more strong, you. Much work and someday you talk pretty. People start love you soon. Maybe tomorrow, okay." 25

Unlike the French class I had taken in New York, here there was no sense of competition. When the teacher poked a shy Korean in the eyelid with a freshly sharpened pencil, we took no comfort in the fact that, unlike Hyeyoon Cho, we all knew the irregular past tense of the verb *to defeat*. In all fairness, the teacher hadn't meant to stab the girl, but neither did she spend much time apologizing, saying only, "Well, you should have been *vkkdyo* more *kdeynfulh*."

Over time it became impossible to believe that any of us would ever improve. Fall arrived and it rained every day, meaning we would now be scolded for the water dripping from our coats and umbrellas. It was mid-October when the teacher singled me out, saying, "Every day spent with you is like having a cesarean section." And it struck me that, for the first time since arriving in France, I could understand every word that someone was saying.

Understanding doesn't mean that you can suddenly speak the language. Far from it. It's a small step, nothing more, yet its rewards are intoxicating and deceptive. The teacher continued her diatribe and I settled back, bathing in the subtle beauty of each new curse and insult.

"You exhaust me with your foolishness and reward my efforts with nothing but pain, do you understand me?"

The world opened up, and it was with great joy that I 30 responded, "I know the thing that you speak exact now. Talk me more, you, plus, please, plus."

For Discussion and Writing

1. The kind of language-learning approach described in this essay is called "immersion." Explain the metaphor. Is it appropriate? What are its implications?

2. Describe the way in which Sedaris presents the dialogue of the students as they attempt to speak French. What effect does this achieve?

3. **connections**   In telling his story, Sedaris does not present himself as entirely heroic—he is not afraid to appear foolish. George Orwell, in "Shooting an Elephant" (p. 272), also chooses not to portray himself as flawless. Compare the effects of these choices and the motivations of the writers for making them.

4. Write about a time when you encountered a teacher or other authority figure with whom you had a problem. Did the friction make you want to give up or to work harder, either to please this person or show him or her what you could do?

5. **looking further**   One way of doing research is not to turn to written sources such as books or articles but to do interviews. Your assignment, should you choose to accept it (or be assigned it), is to interview a fellow student (in class or not) about his or her experience of classrooms. Come up with a list of questions (e.g., best and worst classroom experiences, teachers liked and not liked, how he or she learns best), identify an interview subject, and ask these questions and any others that come up during the interview. After the interview, write up a summary of what your subject said, what you got out of it about your subject's experience of classrooms, and any larger thoughts about education.

BRENT STAPLES

Just Walk on By: Black Men and Public Space

Brent Staples, born in 1951 in Chester, Pennsylvania, has a doctorate in psychology and has taught, but he has built a career as a reporter and columnist. He is on the editorial board of the New York Times, *where he writes on education, culture, and politics. He has also contributed to* Ms., Harper's, *and other magazines. Staples's memoir,* Parallel Time: Growing Up in Black and White *(1994), tells the story of his youth and that of his younger brother, whose violent life followed a very different path.*

"Just Walk on By" originally appeared in Ms. *As you read, think about why this piece might be appropriate for a publication intended primarily for women.*

My first victim was a woman—white, well dressed, probably in her early twenties. I came upon her late one evening on a deserted street in Hyde Park, a relatively affluent neighborhood in an otherwise mean, impoverished section of Chicago. As I swung onto the avenue behind her, there seemed to be a discreet, uninflammatory distance between us. Not so. She cast back a worried glance. To her, the youngish black man—a broad six feet two inches with a beard and billowing hair, both hands shoved into the pockets of a bulky military jacket—seemed menacingly close. After a few more quick glimpses, she picked up her pace and was soon running in earnest. Within seconds she disappeared into a cross street.

That was more than a decade ago, I was twenty-two years old, a graduate student newly arrived at the University of Chicago. It was in the echo of that terrified woman's footfalls that I first began to know the unwieldy inheritance I'd come into—the ability to alter public space in ugly ways. It was clear that she thought herself the quarry of a mugger, a rapist, or worse. Suffering a bout of insomnia, however, I was stalking sleep, not defenseless wayfarers. As a softy who is scarcely able to take a knife to a raw chicken—let alone hold one to a person's throat—I was surprised, embarrassed, and dismayed all at once. Her flight made me feel like an accomplice in tyranny. It also made it clear that I was indistinguishable from the muggers who occasionally seeped into the area from the surrounding ghetto. That first encounter, and those that followed, signified that a vast, unnerving gulf lay between nighttime pedestrians—particularly women—and me. And I soon gathered that being perceived as dangerous is a hazard in itself. I only needed to turn a corner into a dicey situation, or crowd some frightened, armed person in a foyer somewhere, or make an errant move after being pulled over by a policeman. Where fear and weapons meet—and they often do in urban America—there is always the possibility of death.

In that first year, my first away from my hometown, I was to become thoroughly familiar with the language of fear. At dark, shadowy intersections, I could cross in front of a car stopped at a traffic light and elicit the *thunk, thunk, thunk, thunk* of the driver—black, white, male, or female—hammering down the door locks. On less traveled streets after dark, I grew accustomed to but never comfortable with people crossing to the other side of the street rather than pass me. Then there were the standard unpleasantries with policemen, doormen, bouncers, cabdrivers, and others whose business it is to screen out troublesome individuals *before* there is any nastiness.

I moved to New York nearly two years ago and I have remained an avid night walker. In central Manhattan, the near-constant crowd cover minimizes tense one-on-one street encounters. Elsewhere—in SoHo, for example, where sidewalks are narrow and tightly spaced buildings shut out the sky—things can get very taut indeed.

After dark, on the warrenlike streets of Brooklyn where I live, 5 I often see women who fear the worst from me. They seem to have set their faces on neutral, and with their purse straps strung across their chests bandolier-style, they forge ahead as though bracing themselves against being tackled. I understand, of course, that the danger they perceive is not a hallucination. Women are particularly vulnerable to street violence, and young black males are drastically overrepresented among the perpetrators of that

violence. Yet these truths are no solace against the kind of alienation that comes of being ever the suspect, a fearsome entity with
whom pedestrians avoid making eye contact.

It is not altogether clear to me how I reached the ripe old age of
twenty-two without being conscious of the lethality nighttime
pedestrians attributed to me. Perhaps it was because in Chester,
Pennsylvania, the small, angry industrial town where I came of
age in the 1960s, I was scarcely noticeable against a backdrop of
gang warfare, street knifings, and murders. I grew up one of the
good boys, had perhaps a half-dozen fistfights. In retrospect, my
shyness of combat has clear sources.

As a boy, I saw countless tough guys locked away; I have since
buried several, too. They were babies, really—a teenage cousin, a
brother of twenty-two, a childhood friend in his mid-twenties—
all gone down in episodes of bravado played out in the streets. I
came to doubt the virtues of intimidation early on. I chose, perhaps unconsciously, to remain a shadow—timid, but a survivor.

The fearsomeness mistakenly attributed to me in public places
often has a perilous flavor. The most frightening of these confu-
sions occurred in the late 1970s and early 1980s, when I worked
as a journalist in Chicago. One day, rushing into the office of a
magazine I was writing for with a deadline story in hand, I was
mistaken for a burglar. The office manager called security and,
with an ad hoc posse, pursued me through the labyrinthine halls,
nearly to my editor's door. I had no way of proving who I was. I
could only move briskly toward the company of someone who
knew me.

Another time I was on assignment for a local paper and killing
time before an interview. I entered a jewelry store on the city's
affluent Near North Side. The proprietor excused herself and
returned with an enormous red Doberman pinscher straining at
the end of a leash. She stood, the dog extended toward me, silent
to my questions, her eyes bulging nearly out of her head. I took a
cursory look around, nodded, and bade her good night.

Relatively speaking, however, I never fared as badly as another 10
black male journalist. He went to nearby Waukegan, Illinois, a
couple of summers ago to work on a story about a murderer who
was born there. Mistaking the reporter for the killer, police
officers hauled him from his car at gunpoint and but for his
press credentials would probably have tried to book him. Such

episodes are not uncommon. Black men trade tales like this all the time.

Over the years, I learned to smother the rage I felt at so often being taken for a criminal. Not to do so would surely have led to madness. I now take precautions to make myself less threatening. I move about with care, particularly late in the evening. I give a wide berth to nervous people on subway platforms during the wee hours, particularly when I have exchanged business clothes for jeans. If I happen to be entering a building behind some people who appear skittish, I may walk by, letting them clear the lobby before I return, so as not to seem to be following them. I have been calm and extremely congenial on those rare occasions when I've been pulled over by the police.

And on late-evening constitutionals I employ what has proved to be an excellent tension-reducing measure: I whistle melodies from Beethoven and Vivaldi and the more popular classical composers. Even steely New Yorkers hunching toward nighttime destinations seem to relax, and occasionally they even join in the tune. Virtually everybody seems to sense that a mugger wouldn't be warbling bright, sunny selections from Vivaldi's *Four Seasons*. It is my equivalent of the cowbell that hikers wear when they know they are in bear country.

For Discussion and Writing

1. How does Staples describe himself? How is he sometimes seen by others?

2. Staples begins his essay by discussing the effect of his presence on another person. However, others' reactions to his presence affect him in return, and he spends much of the essay explaining the emotional and practical effects he experiences as a consequence of his interactions. How is the complication and paradox of these situations expressed by the last sentence about Staples's whistling classical music being the "equivalent of the cowbell that hikers wear when they know they are in bear country" (par. 12)?

3. **connections**   Compare Staples's reaction to race-inflected encounters to James Baldwin's reaction to the encounter in the restaurant in "Notes of a Native Son" (p. 44). What might the differences tell us about the individuals and their respective times?

4. The person with whom you find yourself identifying in a story sometimes depends on your own identity. With whom did you identify at

the start of Staples's essay, and how did it affect your reading of the full piece?

5. **looking further**   Imagine a response to "Just Walk on By" that takes issue with the tactics Staples employs in order to avoid frightening people with his mere presence. What arguments might someone make against his choice to accommodate the irrational fears of others? On what basis might objections to this practice be raised?

JOHN JEREMIAH SULLIVAN

Feet in Smoke

John Jeremiah Sullivan was born in Louisville, Kentucky, in 1974, and raised across the Ohio River in Albany, Indiana. An essayist and long-form journalist, Sullivan is a contributing writer to the New York Times Magazine, *a contributing editor at* Harper's, *and southern editor of the* Paris Review. *He has written two books,* Blood Horses: Notes of a Sportswriter's Son *(2004) and* Pulphead: Essays *(2011).*

"Feet in Smoke" tells an unusual family story that is memorable in itself. However, Sullivan makes his account of the event even more memorable, and meaningful, by including both the telling details that led critic James Wood to call him "a fierce noticer" and the thoughtful reflection that readers value in his work. As you read, note the details that Sullivan notices and the ways he incorporates them.

On the morning of April 21, 1995, my elder brother, Worth (short for Elsworth), put his mouth to a microphone in a garage in Lexington, Kentucky, and in the strict sense of having been "shocked to death," was electrocuted. He and his band, the Moviegoers, had stopped for a day to rehearse on their way from Chicago to a concert in Tennessee, where I was in school. Just a couple of days earlier, he had called to ask if there were any songs I wanted to hear at the show. I asked for something new, a song he'd written and played for me the last time I'd seen him, on Christmas Day. Our holidays always end the same way, with the two of us up late drinking and trying out our "tunes" on each other. There's something biologically satisfying about harmonizing with a sibling. We've gotten to where we communicate through music, using guitars the way fathers and sons use baseball, as a kind of emotional code. Worth is seven years older than I am, an age difference that can make brothers strangers. I'm fairly sure the first time he ever felt we had anything to talk about was the day he caught me in his basement bedroom at our old house in Indiana, trying to teach myself how to play "Radio Free Europe" on a black Telecaster he'd forbidden me to touch.

The song I had asked for, "Is It All Over," was not a typical Moviegoers song. It was simpler and more earnest than the infectious pop-rock they made their specialty. The changes were still unfamiliar to the rest of the band, and Worth had been about to lead them through the first verse, had just leaned forward to sing the opening lines—"Is it all over? I'm scanning the paper / For someone to replace her"—when a surge of electricity arced through his body, magnetizing the mike to his chest like a tiny but obstinate missile, searing the first string and fret into his palm, and stopping his heart. He fell backward and crashed, already dying.

Possibly you know most of this already. I got many of my details from a common source, an episode of *Rescue 911* (the reality show hosted by William Shatner) that aired about six months after the accident. My brother played himself in the dramatization, which was amusing for him, since he has no memory whatsoever of the real event. For the rest of us, his family and friends, the segment is hard to watch.

The story Shatner tells, which ends at the moment we learned that my brother would live, is different from the story I know. But his version offers a useful reminder of the danger, where medical emergencies are involved, of talking too much about "miracles." Not to knock the word—the staff at Humana Hospital in Lexington called my brother's case "miraculous," and they've seen any number of horrifying accidents and inexplicable recoveries— but it tends to obscure the human skill and coolheadedness that go into saving somebody's life. I think of Liam, my brother's best friend and bandmate, who managed not to fall apart while he cradled Worth in his arms until help arrived, and who'd warned him when the band first started practicing to put on his Chuck Taylors, the rubber soles of which were the only thing that kept him from being zapped into a more permanent fate than the one he did endure. I think of Captain Clarence Jones, the fireman and paramedic who brought Worth back to life, strangely with two hundred joules of pure electric shock (and who later responded to my grandmother's effusive thanks by giving all the credit to the Lord). Without people like these and doubtless others whom I never met and Shatner didn't mention, there would have been no miracle.

It was afternoon when I heard about the accident from my father, who called and told me flatly that my brother had been "hurt." I asked if Worth would live, and there was a nauseating pause before his "I don't know." I got in the car and drove from Tennessee to Lexington, making the five-hour trip in about three and a half hours. In the hospital parking lot I was met by two of my uncles on my mother's side, fraternal twins, both of them Lexington businessmen. They escorted me up to the ICU and, in the elevator, filled me in on Worth's condition, explaining that he'd flatlined five times in the ambulance on the way to the hospital, his heart locked in something that Captain Jones, in his interview for *Rescue 911,* diagnosed as "asystole," which Jones described as "just another death-producing rhythm." As I took him to mean, my brother's pulse had been almost one continuous beat, like a drumroll, but feeble, not actually sending the blood anywhere. By the time I showed up, his heart was at least beating on its own power, but a machine was doing all his breathing for him. The worst news had to do with his brain, which we were told displayed 1 percent activity, vegetable status.

In the waiting room, a heavyset nurse who looked to be in her sixties came up and introduced herself as Nancy. She took me by the hand and led me through two silent, automatic glass doors into Intensive Care. My brother was a nightmare of tubes and wires, dark machines silently measuring every internal event, a pump filling and emptying his useless lungs. The stench of dried spit was everywhere in the room. His eyes were closed, his every muscle slack. It seemed that only the machines were still alive, possessed of some perverse will that wouldn't let them give up on this body.

I stood frozen, staring at him. The nurse spoke to me from the corner of the room in an unexpected tone of admonishment, which stung me at the time and even in retrospect seems hard to account for. "It ain't like big brother's gonna wake up tomorrow and be all better," she said. I looked at her stupidly. Had I not seemed shocked enough?

"Yes, I realize that," I said, and asked to be alone. When the door closed behind me, I went up to the side of the bed. Worth and I have different fathers, making us half brothers, technically, though he was already living with my dad when I was born, which means that I've never known life without him. Nonetheless we look nothing alike. He has thick dark hair and olive skin and was probably the only member of our family in the hospital that night with green as opposed to blue eyes. I leaned over into his face. The normal flush of his cheeks had gone white, and his lips were parted to admit the breathing tube. There was no sign of anything, of life or struggle or crisis, only the gruesomely robotic sounds of the oxygen machine pumping air into his chest and drawing it out again. I heard my uncles, their voices composed with strain, telling me about the 1 percent brain activity. I leaned closer, putting my mouth next to my brother's right ear. "Worth," I said, "it's John."

Without warning, all six feet and four inches of his body came to life, writhing against the restraints and what looked like a thousand invasions of his orifices and skin. His head reared back, and his eyes swung open on me. The pupils were almost nonexistent. They stayed open only for the briefest instant, focusing loosely on mine before falling shut. But what an instant! As a volunteer fireman in college, I had once helped to pull a dead man out of an overturned truck, and I remember the look of his open eyes as I handed him to the next person in line—I'd been expecting pathos, some shadow of whatever had been the last thought to cross his mind, but his eyes were just marbles, mere things. My brother's eyes had been nothing like that. They were, if anything, the terrified eyes of a man who was trying to climb out of a well: the second he moves, he slips back to the bottom. Worth's head fell back onto the pillow motionless, his body exhausted from that brief effort at reentering the world. I put down his hand, which I'd taken without knowing it, and stepped back into the hallway.

Worth spent that night, and the second day and night, in a coma. 10 There were no outward signs of change, but the machines began to pick up indications of increased brain function. The neurosurgeon, an Irishman, explained to us (in what must have been, for him, child's language) that the brain is itself an electrical machine, and that the volts that had flowed from my brother's vintage Gibson amplifier and traumatized his body were in some sense still racing around in his skull. There was a decent chance, the doctor said, that he would emerge from the coma, but no one could say what would be left; no one could say who would emerge. The period of waiting comes back to me as a collage of awful food, nurses' cautious encouragement, and the disquieting presence of my brother supine in his bed, an oracle who could answer all our questions but refused to speak. We rotated in and out of his room like tourists circulating through a museum.

"On the third day" (I would never have said it myself, but Shatner does it for me on the show), Worth woke up. The nurses led us into his room, their faces almost proud, and we found him sitting up—gingerly resting on his elbows, with heavy-lidded eyes, as if at any moment he might decide he liked the coma better and slip back into it. His face lit up like a simpleton's whenever one of us entered the room, and he greeted each of us by our names in a barely audible rasp. He seemed to know us, but hadn't the slightest idea what we were all doing there, or where "there" might be—though he did come up with theories on the last point over the next two weeks, chief among them a wedding reception, a high school poker game, and at one point some kind of holding cell.

I've tried many times over the years to describe for people the person who woke up from that electrified near-death, the one who remained with us for about a month before he went back to being the person we'd known and know now. It would save one a lot of trouble to be able to say "it was like he was on acid," but that wouldn't be quite true. Instead, he seemed to be living one of those imaginary acid trips we used to pretend to be on in junior high, before we tried the real thing and found out it was slightly less magical—"Hey, man, your nose is like a star or something, man." He had gone there. My father and I kept notes, neither of us aware that the other was doing it, trying to get down all of Worth's little disclosures before they faded. I have my own list here in front of me. There's no best place to begin. I'll just transcribe a few things:

> Squeezed my hand late on the night of the 23rd. Whispered, "That's the human experience."
>
> While eating lunch on the 24th, suddenly became convinced that I was impersonating his brother. Demanded to see my ID. Asked me, "Why

would you want to impersonate John?" When I protested, "But, Worth, don't I look like John?" he replied, "You look exactly like him. No wonder you can get away with it."

On the day of the 25th, stood up from his lunch, despite my attempts to restrain him, spilling the contents of his tray everywhere. Glanced at my hands, tight around his shoulders, and said, "I am not . . . repulsed . . . by man-to-man love. But I'm not into it."

Evening of the 25th. Gazing at own toes at end of bed, remarked, "That'd make a nice picture: Feet in Smoke."

Day of the 26th. Referred to heart monitor as "a solid, congealed bag of nutrients."

Night of the 26th. Tried to punch me with all his strength while I worked with Dad and Uncle John to restrain him in his bed, swinging and missing me by less than an inch. The IV tubes were tearing loose from his arms. His eyes were terrified, helpless. I think he took us for fascist goons.

Evening of the 27th. Unexpectedly jumped up from his chair, a perplexed expression on his face, and ran to the wall. Rubbed palms along a small area of the wall, like a blind man. Turned. Asked, "Where's the piñata?" Shuffled into hallway. Noticed a large nurse walking away from us down the hall. Muttered, "If she's got our piñata, I'm gonna be pissed."

The experience went from tragedy to tragicomedy to outright farce on a sliding continuum, so it's hard to pinpoint just when one let onto another. He was the most delightful drunk you'd ever met—I had to follow him around the hospital like a sidekick to make sure he didn't fall, because he couldn't stop moving, couldn't concentrate on anything for longer than a second. He became a holy fool. He looked down into his palm, where the fret and string had burned a deep, red cross into his skin, and said, "Hey, it'd be stigmata if there weren't all those ants crawling in it." He introduced my mother and father to each other as if they'd never met, saying, "Mom, meet Dad; Dad, meet Dixie Jean." Asked by the neurosurgeon if he knew how to spell his own name, he said, "Well, doctor, if you were Spenser, you might spell it w-o-r-t-h-E."

Another of the nurses, when I asked her if he'd ever be normal again, said, "Maybe, but wouldn't it be wonderful just to have him like this?" She was right; she humbled me. I can't imagine anything more hopeful or hilarious than having a seat at the spectacle of my brother's brain while it reconstructed reality. Like a lot of people, I'd always assumed, in a sort of cut-rate Hobbesian way, that the center of the brain, if you could ever find it, would inevitably be a pretty dark place, that whatever is good or beautiful about being human is a result of our struggles against everything innate, against physical nature. My brother changed my mind about all that. Here was a consciousness reduced to its matter, to a ball of crackling synapses—words that he knew how to use but couldn't connect to the right things; strange new objects for which he had to invent names; unfamiliar people who approached and receded like energy fields—and it was a good place to be, you might even say a poetic place. He had touched death, or death had touched him, but he seemed to find life no less interesting for having done so.

There is this one other remark: *a dicey thing*   15
    Late afternoon of April 25. The window slats casting bars of shadow all over his room in the ICU. I had asked my mom and dad if they'd mind giving me a moment alone with him, since I still wasn't sure he knew quite who I was. I did know he wasn't aware of being inside a hospital; his most recent idea was that we were all back at my grandparents' house having a party, and at one point he slipped loose and went to the nurses' station to find out whether his tux was ready. Now we were sitting there in his room. Neither of us was speaking. Worth was jabbing a fork into his Jell-O, and I was just watching, waiting to see what would come out. Earlier that morning, he'd been scared by the presence of so many "strangers," and I didn't want to upset him any more. Things went on in silence like this for maybe five minutes.
    Very quietly, he began to weep, his shoulders heaving with the force of emotion. I didn't touch him. A minute went by. I asked, "Worth, why are you crying?"
    "I was thinking of the vision I had when I knew I was dead."
    Certain that I'd heard him right, I asked him again anyway. He repeated it in the same flat tone: "I was thinking of the vision I had when I knew I was dead."
    How could he know he'd been dead, when he didn't even know 20
we were in a hospital, or that anything unusual had happened to him? Had a sudden clarity overtaken him?
    "What was it? What was your vision?"
    He looked up. The tears were gone. He seemed calm and serious. "I was on the banks of the River Styx," he said. "The boat came to

row me across, but . . . instead of Charon, it was Huck and Jim.
Only, when Huck pulled back his hood, he was an old man . . . like,
ninety years old or something."

My brother put his face in his hands and cried a little more.
Then he seemed to forget all about it. According to my notes, the
next words out of his mouth were, "Check this out—I've got the
Andrews Sisters in my milkshake."

We've never spoken of it since. It's hard to talk to my brother
about anything related to his accident. He has a monthlong tape
erasure in his memory that starts the second he put his lips to
that microphone. He doesn't remember the shock, the ambulance,
having died, coming back to life. Even when it was time for him
to leave the hospital, he had managed only to piece together that
he was late for a concert somewhere, and my last memory of him
from that period is his leisurely wave when I told him I had to go
back to school. "See you at the show," he called across the parking lot. When our family gets together, the subject of his accident
naturally bobs up, but he just looks at us with a kind of suspicion.
It's a story about someone else, a story he thinks we might be
fudging just a bit.

When I can't sleep I still sometimes will try to decipher that   25
vision. My brother was never much of a churchgoer (he pro-
claimed himself a deist at age fifteen) but had been an excellent
student of Latin in high school. His teacher, a sweet and brilliant
old bun-wearing woman named Rank, drilled her classes in classical mythology. Maybe when it came time for my brother to have
his near-death experience, to reach down into his psyche and pull
up whatever set of myths would help him make sense of the fear,
he reached for the ones he'd found most compelling as a young
man. For most people, that involves the whole tunnel-of-light
business; for my brother, the underworld.

The question of where he got Huck and Jim defeats me. My
father was a great Mark Twain fanatic—he got fired from the
only teaching job he ever held for keeping the first graders in at
recess, to make them listen to records of an actor reading the
master's works—and he came up with the only clue: the accident
had occurred on the eighty-fifth anniversary of Twain's death, in
1910.

I'm just glad they decided to leave my brother on this side of
the river.

For Discussion and Writing

1. Why did the event at the center of this essay appear on television?

2. "Feet in Smoke" has strong narrative pull—that is, it is the kind of writing that you do not want to put down until you are finished. How does Sullivan achieve this in his writing, from sentence to sentence and in the larger structure of the essay? Is it all about finding out what happens to his brother, or are there other things that provide narrative momentum?

3. **connections** Compare this essay and Brian Doyle's "Joyas Voladores" (p. 132). Both essays reflect on the fragility of life, but do so in very different ways. How does each author bring up the subject? How does each frame it? What do they have to say about it?

4. Write about Sullivan's use of humor in "Feet in Smoke." While one would not call this a funny essay, it includes some very funny moments. When do they occur? Why do you think Sullivan includes them?

5. **looking further** "Feet in Smoke" is an excellent example of the personal essay. It tells a compelling story of an event important to the writer and also points to larger areas of experience, truths, ideas, and mysteries that might be relevant to any reader's life. What larger topics does Sullivan's essay point to? Pick one and run with it a little bit. What do we know about the workings of the heart, or the brain? What does it mean to call something a miracle or a successful medical intervention against long odds?

A Modest Proposal

Born in 1667 in Ireland and raised there by English parents, Jonathan Swift was dean of St. Patrick's Cathedral in Dublin and a prolific poet, satirist, and pamphleteer. While he is best known today for his satiric novel Gulliver's Travels *(1726) and for "A Modest Proposal," his political pamphlets and essays on behalf of Irish causes had great impact and are themselves masterpieces of political irony. Swift's work is thought by some to reveal a misanthropic, skeptical, and hopeless heart, but there always exists in his writing the possibility of alternatives, the hope for improvement. In "A Modest Proposal," Swift writes, "Therefore I repeat, let no man talk to me of these and the like expedients, till he has at least some glimpse of hope that there will be ever some hearty and sincere attempt to put them in practice" (par. 30). As you read this essay and try to tease out Swift's messages, keep this idea in mind.*

In 1729, when "A Modest Proposal" was published, years of drought were exacerbated by a crop failure that caused thousands of Irish to starve to death, and this suffering was essentially ignored by English landowners. "A Modest Proposal" is Swift's response to this tragedy.

It is a melancholy object to those who walk through this great town or travel in the country, when they see the streets, the roads, and cabin doors, crowded with beggars of the female sex, followed by three, four, or six children, all in rags and importuning every passenger for an alms. These mothers instead of being able to work for their honest livelihood, are forced to employ all their time in strolling to beg sustenance for their helpless infants: who as they grow up either turn thieves for want of work, or leave their dear native country to fight for the pretender in Spain, or sell themselves to the Barbadoes.

I think it is agreed by all parties that this prodigious number of children in the arms, or on the backs, or at the heels of their mothers, and frequently of their fathers, is in the present deplorable state of the kingdom a very great additional grievance; and, therefore, whoever could find out a fair, cheap, and easy method of making these children sound, useful members of the commonwealth, would deserve so well of the public as to have his statue set up for a preserver of the nation.

But my intention is very far from being confined to provide only for the children of professed beggars; it is of a much greater extent, and shall take in the whole number of infants at a certain age who are born of parents in effect as little able to support them as those who demand our charity in the streets.

As to my own part, having turned my thoughts for many years upon this important subject, and maturely weighed the several schemes of our projectors, I have always found them grossly mistaken in their computation. It is true, a child just dropped from its dam may be supported by her milk for a solar year, with little other nourishment; at most not above the value of 2s., which the mother may certainly get, or the value in scraps, by her lawful occupation of begging; and it is exactly at one year old that I propose to provide for them in such a manner as instead of being a charge upon their parents or the parish, or wanting food and raiment for the rest of their lives, they shall on the contrary contribute to the feeding, and partly to the clothing, of many thousands.

There is likewise another great advantage in my scheme, that   5
it will prevent those voluntary abortions, and that horrid practice of women murdering their bastard children, alas! too frequent among us! sacrificing the poor innocent babes I doubt more to avoid the expense than the shame, which would move tears and pity in the most savage and inhuman breast.

The number of souls in this kingdom being usually reckoned one million and a half, of these I calculate there may be about 200,000 couples whose wives are breeders; from which number I subtract 30,000 couples who are able to maintain their own children (although I apprehend there cannot be so many, under the present distress of the kingdom); but this being granted, there will remain 170,000 breeders. I again subtract 50,000 for those women who miscarry, or whose children die by accident or disease within the year. There only remain 120,000 children of poor parents annually born. The question therefore is, how this number shall be reared and provided for? which, as I have already said, under the present situation of affairs, is utterly impossible by all the methods hitherto proposed. For we can neither employ them in handicraft of agriculture; we neither build houses (I mean in the country) nor cultivate land; they can very seldom pick up a livelihood by stealing, till they arrive at six years old, except where they are of towardly parts, although I confess they learn the rudiments much earlier; during which time they can, however, be properly looked upon only as probationers; as I have been informed by a principal gentleman in the county of Cavan, who protested to me that he never knew above one or two instances under the age of six, even in a part of the kingdom so renowned for the quickest proficiency in that art.

I am assured by our merchants, that a boy or a girl before twelve years old is no salable commodity; and even when they come to this age they will not yield above 3£. or 3£. 2s. 6d. at most on the exchange; which cannot turn to account either to the parents or kingdom, the charge of nutriment and rags having been at least four times that value.

I shall now therefore humbly propose my own thoughts, which I hope will not be liable to the least objection.

I have been assured by a very knowing American of my acquaintance in London, that a young healthy child well nursed is at a year old a most delicious, nourishing, and wholesome food, whether stewed, roasted, baked, or broiled; and I make no doubt that it will equally serve in a fricassee or a ragout.

I do therefore humbly offer it to public consideration that of 10 the 120,000 children already computed, 20,000 may be reserved for breed, whereof only one-fourth part to be males; which is more than we allow to sheep, black cattle, or swine; and my reason is, that these children are seldom the fruits of marriage, a circumstance not much regarded by our savages; therefore one male will be sufficient to serve four females. That the remaining 100,000 may, at a year old, be offered in sale to the persons of quality and fortune through the kingdom; always advising the mother to let them suck plentifully in the last month, so as to render them plump and fat for a good table. A child will make two dishes at an entertainment for friends; and when the family dines alone, the fore and hind quarter will make a reasonable dish, and seasoned with a little pepper or salt will be very good boiled on the fourth day, especially in winter.

I have reckoned upon a medium that a child just born will weigh 12 pounds, and in a solar year, if tolerably nursed, will increase to 28 pounds.

I grant this food will be somewhat dear, and therefore very proper for landlords, who, as they have already devoured most of the parents, seem to have the best title to the children.

Infants' flesh will be in season throughout the year, but more plentiful in March, and a little before and after: for we are told by a grave author, an eminent French physician, that fish being a prolific diet, there are more children born in Roman Catholic countries about nine months after Lent than at any other season; therefore, reckoning a year after Lent, the markets will be more glutted than usual, because the number of popish infants is at least three to one in this kingdom: and therefore it will have one other collateral advantage, by lessening the number of papists among us.

I have already computed the charge of nursing a beggar's child (in which list I reckon all cottagers, laborers, and four-fifths of the farmers) to be about 2s. per annum, rags included; and I believe no gentleman would repine to give 10s. for the carcass of a good fat child, which, as I have said, will make four dishes of excellent nutritive meat, when he has only some particular friend or his own family to dine with him. Thus the squire will learn to be a good landlord, and grow popular among the tenants; the mother will have 8s. net profit, and be fit for work till she produces another child.

Those who are more thrifty (as I must confess the times 15 require) may flay the carcass; the skin of which artificially dressed will make admirable gloves for ladies, and summer boots for fine gentlemen.

As to our city of Dublin, shambles may be appointed for this purpose in the most convenient parts of it, and butchers we may be assured will not be wanting: although I rather recommend buying the children alive, and dressing them hot from the knife as we do roasting pigs.

A very worthy person, a true lover of his country, and whose virtues I highly esteem, was lately pleased in discoursing on this matter to offer a refinement upon my scheme. He said that many gentlemen of this kingdom, having of late destroyed their deer, he conceived that the want of venison might be well supplied by the bodies of young lads and maidens, not exceeding fourteen years of age nor under twelve; so great a number of both sexes in every country being now ready to starve for want of work and service; and these to be disposed of by their parents, if alive, or otherwise by their nearest relations. But with due deference to so excellent a friend and so deserving a patriot, I cannot be altogether in his sentiments; for as to the males, my American acquaintance assured me from frequent experience that their flesh was generally tough and lean, like that of our schoolboys by continual exercise, and their taste disagreeable; and to fatten them would not answer the charge. Then as to the females, it would, I think, with humble submission be a loss to the public, because they soon would become breeders themselves: and besides, it is not improbable that some scrupulous people might be apt to censure such a practice (although indeed very unjustly), as a little bordering upon cruelty; which, I confess, has always been with me the strongest objection against any project, how well soever intended.

But in order to justify my friend, he confessed that this expedient was put into his head by the famous Psalmanazar, a native of the island Formosa, who came from thence to London about twenty years ago: and in conversation told my friend, that in his country when any young person happened to be put to death, the executioner sold the carcass to persons of quality as a prime dainty; and that in his time the body of a plump girl of fifteen, who was crucified for an attempt to poison the emperor, was sold to his imperial majesty's prime minister of state, and other great mandarins of the court, in joints from the gibbet, at 400 crowns. Neither indeed can I deny, that if the same use were made of several plump young girls in this town, who without one single groat to their fortunes cannot stir abroad without a chair, and appear at the playhouse and assemblies in foreign fineries which they never will pay for, the kingdom would not be the worse.

Some persons of a desponding spirit are in great concern about the vast number of poor people, who are aged, diseased, or maimed, and I have been desired to employ my thoughts what course may be taken to ease the nation of so grievous an encumbrance. But I am not in the least pain upon that matter, because it is very well known that they are every day dying and rotting by cold and famine, and filth and vermin, as fast as can be reasonably expected. And as to the young laborers, they are now in as hopeful condition: They cannot get work, and consequently pine away for want of nourishment, to a degree that if at any time they are accidentally hired to common labor, they have not strength to perform it; and thus the country and themselves are happily delivered from the evils to come.

I have too long digressed, and therefore shall return to my sub- 20 ject. I think the advantages by the proposal which I have made are obvious and many, as well as of the highest importance.

For first, as I have already observed, it would greatly lessen the number of papists, with whom we are yearly overrun, being the principal breeders of the nation as well as our most dangerous enemies; and who stay at home on purpose to deliver the kingdom to the Pretender, hoping to take their advantage by the absence of so many good Protestants, who have chosen rather to leave their country than stay at home and pay tithes against their conscience to an Episcopal curate.

Secondly, The poor tenants will have something valuable of their own, which by law may be made liable to distress and help to pay their landlord's rent, their corn and cattle being already seized, and money a thing unknown.

Thirdly, Whereas the maintenance of 100,000 children from two years old and upward, cannot be computed at less that 10s. a-piece per annum, the nation's stock will be thereby increased £50,000 per annum, beside the profit of a new dish introduced to the tables of all gentlemen of fortune in the kingdom who have any refinement in taste. And the money will circulate among ourselves, the goods being entirely of our own growth and manufacture.

Fourthly, The constant breeders beside the gain of 8s. sterling per annum by the sale of their children, will be rid of the charge of maintaining them after the first year.

Fifthly, This food would likewise bring great custom to taverns, 25 where the vintners will certainly be so prudent as to procure the best receipts for dressing it to perfection, and consequently have their houses frequented by all the fine gentlemen, who justly value themselves upon their knowledge in good eating; and a skilful cook who understands how to oblige his guests, will contrive to make it as expensive as they please.

Sixthly, This would be a great inducement to marriage, which all wise nations have either encouraged by rewards or enforced by laws and penalties. It would increase the care and tenderness of mothers toward their children, when they were sure of a settlement for life to the poor babes, provided in some sort by the public, to their annual profit instead of expense. We should see an honest emulation among the married women, which of them would bring the fattest child to the market. Men would become as fond of their wives during the time of their pregnancy as they are now of their mares in foal, their cows in calf, their sows when they are ready to farrow; nor offer to beat or kick them (as is too frequent a practice) for fear of a miscarriage.

Many other advantages might be enumerated. For instance, the addition of some thousand carcasses in our exportation of barreled beef, the propagation of swine's flesh, and improvement in the art of making good bacon, so much wanted among us by the great destruction of pigs, too frequent at our table; which are no way comparable in taste or magnificence to a well-grown, fat, yearling child, which roasted whole will make a considerable figure at a lord mayor's feast or any other public entertainment. But this and many others I omit, being studious of brevity.

Supposing that 1,000 families in this city would be constant customers for infants' flesh, besides others who might have it at merry-meetings, particularly at weddings and christenings, I compute that Dublin would take off annually about 20,000 carcasses; and the rest of the kingdom (where probably they will be sold somewhat cheaper) the remaining 80,000.

I can think of no one objection that will possibly be raised against this proposal unless it should be urged that the number of people will be thereby much lessened in the kingdom. This I freely own, and it was indeed one principal design in offering it to the world. I desire the reader will observe, that I calculate my remedy for this one individual kingdom of Ireland and for no other that ever was, is, or I think ever can be upon earth. Therefore let no man talk to me of other expedients: of taxing our absentees at 5s. a pound: of using neither clothes nor household furniture except what is of our own growth and manufacture: of utterly rejecting the materials and instruments that promote foreign luxury: of curing the expensiveness of pride, vanity, idleness, and gaming in our women: of introducing a vein of parsimony, prudence, and temperance: of learning to love our country, in the want of which we differ even from Laplanders and the inhabitants

of Topinamboo: of quitting our animosities and factions, nor acting any longer like the Jews, who were murdering one another at
the very moment their city was taken: of being a little cautious
not to sell our country and conscience for nothing: of teaching
landlords to have at least one degree of mercy toward their tenants: lastly, of putting a spirit of honesty, industry, and skill into
our shopkeepers; who, if a resolution could now be taken to buy
only our native goods, would immediately unite to cheat and exact
upon us in the price the measure, and the goodness, nor could
ever yet be brought to make one fair proposal of just dealing,
though often and earnestly invited to it.

Therefore I repeat, let no man talk to me of these and the like   30
expedients, till he has at least some glimpse of hope that there
will be ever some hearty and sincere attempt to put them in
practice.

But as to myself, having been wearied out for many years
with offering vain, idle, visionary thoughts, and at length utterly
despairing of success, I fortunately fell upon this proposal; which,
as it is wholly new, so it has something solid and real, of no
expense and little trouble, full in our own power, and whereby we
can incur no danger in disobliging England. For this kind of commodity will not bear exportation, the flesh being of too tender a
consistence to admit a long continuance in salt, although perhaps
I could name a country which would be glad to eat up our whole
nation without it.

After all, I am not so violently bent upon my own opinion as
to reject any offer proposed by wise men, which shall be found
equally innocent, cheap, easy, and effectual. But before something of that kind shall be advanced in contradiction to my
scheme, and offering a better, I desire the author or authors will
be pleased maturely to consider two points. First, as things now
stand, how they will be able to find food and raiment for 100,000
useless mouths and backs. And secondly, there being a round million of creatures in human figure throughout this kingdom,
whose subsistence put into a common stock would leave them in
debt 2,000,000£. sterling, adding those who are beggars by profession to the bulk of farmers, cottagers, and laborers, with the
wives and children who are beggars in effect; I desire those politicians who dislike my overture, and may perhaps be so bold as to
attempt an answer, that they will first ask the parents of these

mortals, whether they would not at this day think it a great happiness to have been sold for food at a year old in the manner I prescribe, and thereby have avoided such a perpetual scene of misfortunes as they have since gone through by the oppression of landlords, the impossibility of paying rent without money or trade, the want of common sustenance, with neither house nor clothes to cover them from the inclemencies of the weather, and the most inevitable prospect of entailing the like or greater miseries upon their breed for ever.

I profess, in the sincerity of my heart, that I have not the least personal interest in endeavoring to promote this necessary work, having no other motive than the public good of my country, by advancing our trade, providing for infants, relieving the poor, and giving some pleasure to the rich. I have no children by which I can propose to get a single penny; the youngest being nine years old, and my wife past childbearing.

For Discussion and Writing

1. List the ways in which the proposal is presented that make it appear rational.
2. If there exists a "typical" method for making an argument, Swift's method here is not it. What is the real point Swift is arguing, and how does it relate to the apparent point the speaker makes?
3. **connections** Swift's use of a persona—here, the "projector" who makes this proposal—involves the use of irony to make a political point, while Thomas Jefferson's Declaration of Independence (p. 193) is straightforward. Why might these texts' differing strategies be appropriate for their political goals?
4. Write a short response to "A Modest Proposal" focusing on the experience of reading it. How do your responses—to the beginning, to the moment when the proposal is laid out, to the handling of objections—change?
5. **looking further** Read up on conditions in Ireland at the time this essay was written. What different factors contributed to Ireland's dire state? Think about the contemporary world, and perhaps do a little more research on places where poverty and hunger are rampant. Do you see parallels? Are there ways in which Swift's non-ironic suggestions for improving Ireland's situation might be applicable?

AMY TAN

Mother Tongue

Amy Tan, born in 1952, was raised in northern California. Formerly a business writer, Tan is now a novelist. She is best known for her first book, The Joy Luck Club *(1989), but has also written* The Kitchen God's Wife *(1991),* The Bonesetter's Daughter *(2001),* Saving Fish from Drowning *(2005), and* The Valley of Amazement *(2013). Her fiction is rooted in her experiences as the child of Chinese immigrants growing up and living in American culture.*

In "Mother Tongue," Tan describes the variety of Englishes she uses. In doing so, she addresses the connections between languages and cultures, but in her writing she also demonstrates what she says about herself in the essay: "I am a writer. And by that definition, I am someone who has always loved language" (par. 2). As you read, note the ways in which this love for language manifests itself.

I am not a scholar of English or literature. I cannot give you much more than personal opinions on the English language and its variations in this country or others.

I am a writer. And by that definition, I am someone who has always loved language. I am fascinated by language in daily life. I spend a great deal of my time thinking about the power of language—the way it can evoke an emotion, a visual image, a complex idea, or a simple truth. Language is the tool of my trade. And I use them all—all the Englishes I grew up with.

Recently, I was made keenly aware of the different Englishes I do use. I was giving a talk to a large group of people, the same talk I had already given to half a dozen other groups. The nature of the talk was about my writing, my life, and my book, *The Joy Luck Club*. The talk was going along well enough, until I remembered one major difference that made the whole talk sound wrong. My mother was in the room. And it was perhaps the first time she had heard me give a lengthy speech, using the kind of English I have never used with her. I was saying things like "The intersection of

362

memory upon imagination" and "There is an aspect of my fiction that relates to thus-and-thus"—a speech filled with carefully wrought grammatical phrases, burdened, it suddenly seemed to me, with nominalized forms, past perfect tenses, conditional phrases, all the forms of standard English that I had learned in school and through books, the forms of English I did not use at home with my mother.

Just last week, I was walking down the street with my mother, and I again found myself conscious of the English I was using, the English I do use with her. We were talking about the price of new and used furniture and I heard myself saying this: "Not waste money that way." My husband was with us as well, and he didn't notice any switch in my English. And then I realized why. It's because over the twenty years we've been together I've often used that same kind of English with him, and sometimes he even uses it with me. It has become our language of intimacy, a different sort of English that relates to family talk, the language I grew up with.

So you'll have some idea of what this family talk I heard sounds like, I'll quote what my mother said during a recent conversation which I videotaped and then transcribed. During this conversation, my mother was talking about a political gangster in Shanghai who had the same last name as her family's, Du, and how the gangster in his early years wanted to be adopted by her family, which was rich by comparison. Later, the gangster became more powerful, far richer than my mother's family, and one day showed up at my mother's wedding to pay his respects. Here's what she said in part:

"Du Yusong having business like fruit stand. Like off the street kind. He is Du like Du Zong—but not Tsung-ming Island people. The local people call putong, the river east side, he belong to that side local people. That man want to ask Du Zong father take him in like become own family. Du Zong father wasn't look down on him, but didn't take seriously, until that man big like become a mafia. Now important person, very hard to inviting him. Chinese way, came only to show respect, don't stay for dinner. Respect for making big celebration, he shows up. Mean gives lots of respect. Chinese custom. Chinese social life that way. If too important won't have to stay too long. He come to my wedding. I didn't see, I heard it. I gone to boy's side, they have YMCA dinner. Chinese age I was nineteen."

You should know that my mother's expressive command of English belies how much she actually understands. She reads the *Forbes* report, listens to *Wall Street Week*, converses daily with her stockbroker, reads all of Shirley MacLaine's books with ease — all kinds of things I can't begin to understand. Yet some of my friends tell me they understand 50 percent of what my mother says. Some say they understand 80 to 90 percent. Some say they understand none of it, as if she were speaking pure Chinese. But to me, my mother's English is perfectly clear, perfectly natural. It's my mother tongue. Her language, as I hear it, is vivid, direct, full of observation and imagery. That was the language that helped shape the way I saw things, expressed things, made sense of the world.

Lately, I've been giving more thought to the kind of English my mother speaks. Like others, I have described it to people as "broken" or "fractured" English. But I wince when I say that. It has always bothered me that I can think of no other way to describe it other than "broken," as if it were damaged and needed to be fixed, as if it lacked a certain wholeness and soundness. I've heard other terms used, "limited English," for example. But they seem just as bad, as if everything is limited, including people's perceptions of the limited English speaker.

I know this for a fact, because when I was growing up, my mother's "limited" English limited *my* perception of her. I was ashamed of her English. I believed that her English reflected the quality of what she had to say. That is, because she expressed them imperfectly her thoughts were imperfect. And I had plenty of empirical evidence to support me: the fact that people in department stores, at banks, and at restaurants did not take her seriously, did not give her good service, pretended not to understand her, or even acted as if they did not hear her.

My mother has long realized the limitations of her English 10 as well. When I was fifteen, she used to have me call people on the phone to pretend I was she. In this guise, I was forced to ask for information or even to complain and yell at people who had been rude to her. One time it was a call to her stockbroker in New York. She had cashed out her small portfolio and it just so happened we were going to go to New York the next week, our very first trip outside California. I had to get on the phone and say in an adolescent voice that was not very convincing, "This is Mrs. Tan."

And my mother was standing in the back whispering loudly, "Why he don't send me check, already two weeks late. So mad he lie to me, losing me money."

And then I said in perfect English, "Yes, I'm getting rather concerned. You had agreed to send the check two weeks ago, but it hasn't arrived."

Then she began to talk more loudly. "What he want, I come to New York tell him front of his boss, you cheating me?" And I was trying to calm her down, make her be quiet, while telling the stockbroker, "I can't tolerate any more excuses. If I don't receive the check immediately, I am going to have to speak to your manager when I'm in New York next week." And sure enough, the following week there we were in front of this astonished stockbroker, and I was sitting there red-faced and quiet, and my mother, the real Mrs. Tan, was shouting at his boss in her impeccable broken English.

We used a similar routine just five days ago, for a situation that was far less humorous. My mother had gone to the hospital for an appointment, to find out about a benign brain tumor a CAT scan had revealed a month ago. She said she had spoken very good English, her best English, no mistakes. Still, she said, the hospital did not apologize when they said they had lost the CAT scan and she had come for nothing. She said they did not seem to have any sympathy when she told them she was anxious to know the exact diagnosis, since her husband and son had both died of brain tumors. She said they would not give her any more information until the next time and she would have to make another appointment for that. So she said she would not leave until the doctor called her daughter. She wouldn't budge. And when the doctor finally called her daughter, me, who spoke in perfect English—lo and behold—we had assurances the CAT scan would be found, promises that a conference call on Monday would be held, and apologies for any suffering my mother had gone through for a most regrettable mistake.

I think my mother's English almost had an effect on limiting 15 my possibilities in life as well. Sociologists and linguists probably will tell you that a person's developing language skills are more influenced by peers. But I do think that the language spoken in the family, especially in immigrant families which are more insular, plays a large role in shaping the language of the child. And I believe that it affected my results on achievement tests, IQ tests, and the SAT. While my English skills were never judged as poor, compared to math, English could not be considered my strong suit. In grade school I did moderately well, getting perhaps B's, sometimes B-pluses, in English and scoring perhaps in the sixtieth or seventieth percentile on achievement tests. But those scores were not good enough to override the opinion that my true abilities lay in math and science, because in those areas I achieved A's and scored in the ninetieth percentile or higher.

This was understandable. Math is precise; there is only one correct answer. Whereas, for me at least, the answers on English tests were always a judgment call, a matter of opinion and personal experience. Those tests were constructed around items like fill-in-the-blank sentence completion, such as "Even though Tom was ____, Mary thought he was ____." And the correct answer always seemed to be the most bland combinations of thoughts, for example, "Even though Tom was shy, Mary thought he was charming," with the grammatical structure "even though" limiting the correct answer to some sort of semantic opposites, so you wouldn't get answers like, "Even though Tom was foolish, Mary thought he was ridiculous." Well, according to my mother, there were very few limitations as to what Tom could have been and what Mary might have thought of him. So I never did well on tests like that.

The same was true with word analogies, pairs of words in which you were supposed to find some sort of logical, semantic relationship—for example, "Sunset is to nightfall as ____ is to ____." And here you would be presented with a list of four possible pairs, one of which showed the same kind of relationship: red is to stoplight, bus is to arrival, chills is to fever, yawn is to boring. Well, I could never think that way. I knew what the tests were asking, but I could not block out of my mind the images already created by the first pair, "sunset is to nightfall"—and I would see a burst of colors against a darkening sky, the moon rising, the lowering of a curtain of stars. And all the other pairs of words—red, bus, stoplight, boring—just threw up a mass of confusing images, making it impossible for me to sort out something as logical as saying: "A sunset precedes nightfall" is the same as "a chill precedes a fever."

The only way I would have gotten that answer right would have been to imagine an associative situation, for example, my being disobedient and staying out past sunset, catching a chill at night, which turns into feverish pneumonia as punishment, which indeed did happen to me.

I have been thinking about all this lately, about my mother's English, about achievement tests. Because lately I've been asked, as a writer, why there are not more Asian Americans represented in American literature. Why are there few Asian Americans enrolled in creative writing programs? Why do so many Chinese students go into engineering? Well, these are broad sociological questions I can't begin to answer. But I have noticed in surveys—in fact, just last week—that Asian students, as a whole, always do significantly better on math achievement tests than in English. And this makes me think that there are other Asian-American students whose English spoken in the home might also be described as "broken" or "limited." And perhaps they also have teachers who are steering them away from writing and into math and science, which is what happened to me.

Fortunately, I happen to be rebellious in nature and enjoy the challenge of disproving assumptions made about me. I became an English major my first year in college, after being enrolled as pre-med. I started writing nonfiction as a freelancer the week after I was told by my former boss that writing was my worst skill and I should hone my talents toward account management.

But it wasn't until 1985 that I finally began to write fiction. And at first I wrote using what I thought to be wittily crafted sentences, sentences that would finally prove I had mastery over the English language. Here's an example from the first draft of a story that later made its way into *The Joy Luck Club*, but without this line: "That was my mental quandary in its nascent state." A terrible line, which I can barely pronounce.

Fortunately, for reasons I won't get into today, I later decided I should envision a reader for the stories I would write. And the reader I decided upon was my mother, because these were stories about mothers. So with this reader in mind—and in fact she did read my early drafts—I began to write stories using all the Englishes I grew up with: the English I spoke to my mother, which for lack of a better term might be described as "simple"; the

English she used with me, which for lack of a better term might be described as "broken"; my translation of her Chinese, which could certainly be described as "watered down"; and what I imagined to be her translation of her Chinese if she could speak in perfect English, her internal language, and for that I sought to preserve the essence, but neither an English nor a Chinese structure. I wanted to capture what language ability tests can never reveal: her intent, her passion, her imagery, the rhythms of her speech, and the nature of her thoughts.

Apart from what any critic had to say about my writing, I knew I had succeeded where it counted when my mother finished reading my book and gave me her verdict: "So easy to read."

For Discussion and Writing

1. List the different Englishes Tan describes, defining each.
2. Of her mother's English, Tan writes, "That was the language that helped shape the way I saw things, expressed things, made sense of the world" (par. 7). How was the effect of her mother's English positive, and how was it negative?
3. **connections**   Richard Rodriguez, in "Aria: Memory of a Bilingual Childhood" (p. 289), expresses a complicated set of feelings about his linguistic inheritances and what they mean to him and to the world around him. Compare his feelings to Tan's as expressed in "Mother Tongue." How does each deal with the way the world thinks of their language(s)?
4. Do you use different Englishes yourself? Even if English is your sole language, consider how your use of it changes depending on circumstances and audience. Write an essay in which you describe the different ways you speak and the meaning of these differences.
5. **looking further**   When literary writing—particularly fiction—attempts literal representation of accented or region-, race-, ethnicity-, or class-inflected English speech in dialogue, it is often said to be "doing dialect." At times in U.S. history, this practice has been seen not as an attempt at realism but rather as the product of prejudice, or at least as a means of unintentionally confirming stereotypes about people who don't speak Standard English. Read up on this practice and check out some examples. What do you think about it? Is it possible to make any kind of blanket judgment? Are there some cases where you think this technique is acceptable, and others you think are offensive?

HENRY DAVID THOREAU

Civil Disobedience

Henry David Thoreau was born in 1817 and raised in Concord, Massachusetts, living there for most of his life. Along with Ralph Waldo Emerson, Thoreau was one of the most important thinkers of his time in America and is still widely read today. Walden (1854), the work for which he is best known, is drawn from the journal he kept during his two-year-long stay in a cabin on Walden Pond. In Walden, Thoreau explores his interests in naturalism, individualism, and self-sufficiency.

Thoreau is also remembered for his essay "Civil Disobedience" (1849), an early, influential statement of this tactic of protest later practiced by Mahatma Gandhi and, under the leadership of Martin Luther King Jr., by many in the civil rights movement. As you work your way through this essay, keep an eye out not just for the arguments Thoreau makes in support of his larger point but the well-crafted ways in which he makes them.

I heartily accept the motto—"That government is best which governs least,"[1] and I should like to see it acted up to more rapidly and systematically. Carried out, it finally amounts to this, which also I believe—"That government is best which governs not at all"; and when men are prepared for it, that will be the kind of government which they will have. Government is at best but an expedient; but most governments are usually, and all governments are sometimes, inexpedient. The objections which have been brought against a standing army, and they are many and weighty, and deserve to prevail, may also at last be brought against a standing government. The standing army is only an arm of the standing government. The government itself, which is only the mode which

---

1. **governs least:** Possibly a reference to "The best government is that which governs least," the motto of the *United States Magazine and Democratic Review* (1837–1859), or "the less government we have, the better," from Ralph Waldo Emerson's "Politics" (1844). [Ed.]

the people have chosen to execute their will, is equally liable to be abused and perverted before the people can act through it. Witness the present Mexican war,[2] the work of comparatively a few individuals using the standing government as their tool; for in the outset the people would not have consented to this measure.

This American government — what is it but a tradition, a recent one, endeavoring to transmit itself unimpaired to posterity but each instant losing some of its integrity? It has not the vitality and force of a single living man; for a single man can bend it to his will. It is a sort of wooden gun to the people themselves. But it is not the less necessary for this; for the people must have some complicated machinery or other, and hear its din, to satisfy that idea of government which they have. Governments show thus how successfully men can be imposed on, even impose on themselves, for their own advantage. It is excellent, we must all allow. Yet this government never of itself furthered any enterprise but by the alacrity with which it got out of its way. *It* does not keep the country free. *It* does not settle the West. *It* does not educate. The character inherent in the American people has done all that has been accomplished; and it would have done somewhat more if the government had not sometimes got in its way. For government is an expedient by which men would fain succeed in letting one another alone; and, as has been said, when it is most expedient the governed are most let alone by it. Trade and commerce, if they were not made of India-rubber, would never manage to bounce over the obstacles which legislators are continually putting in their way; and, if one were to judge these men wholly by the effects of their actions and not partly by their intentions, they would deserve to be classed and punished with those mischievous persons who put obstructions on the railroads.

But to speak practically and as a citizen, unlike those who call themselves no-government men,[3] I ask for, not at once no government, but *at once* a better government. Let every man make known what kind of government would command his respect, and that will be one step toward obtaining it.

---

2. **the present Mexican war:** Abolitionists considered the U.S.–Mexican War (1846–1848) an effort to extend slavery into former Mexican territory. [Ed.]
3. **no-government men:** Anarchists. [Ed.]

After all, the practical reason why, when the power is once in the hands of the people, a majority are permitted, and for a long period continue, to rule is not because they are most likely to be in the right, nor because this seems fairest to the minority but because they are physically the strongest. But a government in which the majority rule in all cases cannot be based on justice, even as far as men understand it. Can there not be a government in which majorities do not virtually decide right and wrong but conscience?—in which majorities decide only those questions to which the rule of expediency is applicable? Must the citizen ever for a moment, or in the least degree, resign his conscience to the legislator? Why has every man a conscience then? I think that we should be men first and subjects afterward. It is not desirable to cultivate a respect for the law, so much as for the right. The only obligation which I have a right to assume is to do at any time what I think right. It is truly enough said that a corporation has no conscience; but a corporation of conscientious men is a corporation *with* a conscience. Law never made men a whit more just; and, by means of their respect for it, even the well-disposed are daily made the agents of injustice. A common and natural result of an undue respect for law is that you may see a file of soldiers, colonel, captain, corporal, privates, powder-monkeys,[4] and all, marching in admirable order over hill and dale to the wars, against their wills, ay, against their common sense and consciences, which makes it very steep marching indeed and produces a palpitation of the heart. They have no doubt that it is a damnable business in which they are concerned; they are all peaceably inclined. Now, what are they? Men at all? or small movable forts and magazines at the service of some unscrupulous man in power? Visit the Navy-Yard, and behold a marine, such a man as an American government can make, or such as it can make a man with its black arts—a mere shadow and reminiscence of humanity, a man laid out alive and standing, and already, as one may say, buried under arms with funeral accompaniments, though it may be—

Not a drum was heard, not a funeral note,
As his corse to the rampart we hurried;

4. **powder monkeys:** The boys who carried gunpowder for soldiers. [Ed.]

Not a soldier discharged his farewell shot
O'er the grave where our hero we buried.[5]

The mass of men serve the state thus, not as men mainly, but as   5
machines, with their bodies. They are the standing army, and the
militia, jailers, constables, posse comitatus,[6] &c. In most cases
there is no free exercise whatever of the judgment or of the moral
sense; but they put themselves on a level with wood and earth and
stones; and wooden men can perhaps be manufactured that will
serve the purpose as well. Such command no more respect than
men of straw or a lump of dirt. They have the same sort of worth
only as horses and dogs. Yet such as these even are commonly
esteemed good citizens. Others—as most legislators, politicians,
lawyers, ministers, and office-holders—serve the state chiefly
with their heads; and, as they rarely make any moral distinctions,
they are as likely to serve the Devil, without *intending* it, as God. A
very few, as heroes, patriots, martyrs, reformers in the great
sense, and *men*, serve the state with their consciences also and so
necessarily resist it for the most part; and they are commonly
treated as enemies by it. A wise man will only be useful as a man
and will not submit to be "clay" and "stop a hole to keep the wind
away,"[7] but leave that office to his dust at least:

> I am too high-born to be propertied,
> To be a secondary at control,
> Or useful serving-man and instrument
> To any sovereign state throughout the world.[8]

He who gives himself entirely to his fellow-men appears to
them useless and selfish; but he who gives himself partially to
them is pronounced a benefactor and philanthropist.

How does it become a man to behave toward this American
government today? I answer, that he cannot without disgrace
be associated with it. I cannot for an instant recognize that

---

5. From "The Burial of Sir John Moore at Corunna" by Charles Wolfe (1791–1823).
[Ed.]
6. **posse comitatus:** Literally, "the power of the county"; a sheriff's posse. [Ed.]
7. From *Hamlet*, V.i.226–227. [Ed.]
8. From *King John*, V.ii.79–82. [Ed.]

political organization as *my* government which is the *slave's* government also.

All men recognize the right of revolution; that is, the right to refuse allegiance to, and to resist the government when its tyranny or its inefficiency are great and unendurable. But almost all say that such is not the case now. But such was the case, they think, in the Revolution of '75. If one were to tell me that this was a bad government because it taxed certain foreign commodities brought to its ports, it is most probable that I should not make an ado about it, for I can do without them. All machines have their friction; and possibly this does enough good to counterbalance the evil. At any rate, it is a great evil to make a stir about it. But when the friction comes to have its machine, and oppression and robbery are organized, I say let us not have such a machine any longer. In other words, when a sixth of the population of a nation which has undertaken to be the refuge of liberty are slaves, and a whole country is unjustly overrun and conquered by a foreign army and subjected to military law, I think that it is not too soon for honest men to rebel and revolutionize. What makes this duty the more urgent is the fact that the country so overrun is not our own, but ours is the invading army.

Paley,[9] a common authority with many on moral questions, in his chapter on the "Duty of Submission to Civil Government," resolves all civil obligation into expediency; and he proceeds to say, "that so long as the interest of the whole society requires it, that is, so long as the established government cannot be resisted or charged without public inconveniency, it is the will of God that the established government be obeyed, and no longer. . . . This principle being admitted, the justice of every particular case of resistance is reduced to a computation of the quantity of the danger and grievance on the one side, and of the probability and expense of redressing it on the other." Of this, he says, every man shall judge for himself. But Paley appears never to have contemplated those cases to which the rule of expediency does not apply, in which a people, as well as an individual, must do justice, cost what it may. If I have unjustly wrested a plank from a drowning man, I must restore it to him though I drown myself. This,

9. **Paley:** William Paley (1743–1805), an English theologian and philosopher. [Ed.]

according to Paley, would be inconvenient. But he that would save his life, in such a case, shall lose it. This people must cease to hold slaves and to make war on Mexico, though it cost them their existence as a people.

In their practice, nations agree with Paley; but does anyone 10 think that Massachusetts does exactly what is right at the present crisis?

A drab of state, a cloth-o'-silver slut,
To have her train borne up, and her soul trail in the dirt.[10]

Practically speaking, the opponents to a reform in Massachusetts are not a hundred thousand politicians at the South but a hundred thousand merchants and farmers here, who are more interested in commerce and agriculture than they are in humanity, and are not prepared to do justice to the slave and to Mexico, cost what it may. I quarrel not with far-off foes but with those who, near at home, co-operate with, and do the bidding of, those far away, and without whom the latter would be harmless. We are accustomed to say that the mass of men are unprepared; but improvement is slow because the few are not materially wiser or better than the many. It is not so important that many should be as good as you as that there be some absolute goodness somewhere; for that will leaven the whole lump. There are thousands who are in opinion opposed to slavery and to the war who yet in effect do nothing to put an end to them; who, esteeming themselves children of Washington and Franklin, sit down with their hands in their pockets and say that they know not what to do, and do nothing; who even postpone the question of freedom to the question of free trade, and quietly read the prices-current along with the latest advices from Mexico after dinner and, it may be, fall asleep over them both. What is the price-current of an honest man and patriot today? They hesitate and they regret and sometimes they petition; but they do nothing in earnest and with effect. They will wait, well-disposed, for others to remedy the evil, that they may no longer have it to regret. At most, they give only a cheap vote, and a feeble countenance and God-speed, to the right, as it goes by them. There are nine hundred and ninety-nine

10. From Cyril Tourneur's *The Revenger's Tragedy* (1607). [Ed.]

patrons of virtue to one virtuous man. But it is easier to deal with the real possessor of a thing than with the temporary guardian of it.

All voting is a sort of gaming, like checkers or backgammon, with a slight moral tinge to it, a playing with right and wrong, with moral questions; and betting naturally accompanies it. The character of the voters is not staked. I cast my vote, perchance, as I think right; but I am not vitally concerned that that right should prevail. I am willing to leave it to the majority. Its obligation, therefore, never exceeds that of expediency. Even voting *for the right* is *doing* nothing for it. It is only expressing to men feebly your desire that it should prevail. A wise man will not leave the right to the mercy of chance, nor wish it to prevail through the power of the majority. There is but little virtue in the action of masses of men. When the majority shall at length vote for the abolition of slavery, it will be because they are indifferent to slavery, or because there is but little slavery left to be abolished by their vote. *They* will then be the only slaves. Only *his* vote can hasten the abolition of slavery who asserts his own freedom by his vote.

I hear of a convention to be held at Baltimore, or elsewhere, for the selection of a candidate for the Presidency, made up chiefly of editors, and men who are politicians by profession; but I think, what is it to any independent, intelligent, and respectable man what decision they may come to? Shall we not have the advantage of his wisdom and honesty nevertheless? Can we not count upon some independent votes? Are there not many individuals in the country who do not attend conventions? But no: I find that the responsible man, so called, has immediately drifted from his position, and despairs of his country when his country has more reason to despair of him. He forthwith adopts one of the candidates thus selected as the only *available* one, thus proving that he is himself *available* for any purposes of the demagogue. His vote is of no more worth than that of any unprincipled foreigner or hireling native who may have been bought. O for a man who is a *man* and, as my neighbor says has a bone in his back which you cannot pass your hand through! Our statistics are at fault: the population has been returned too large. How many *men* are there to a square thousand miles in this country? Hardly one. Does not America offer any inducement for men to settle here? The

American has dwindled into an Odd Fellow[11]—one who may be known by the development of his organ of gregariousness and a manifest lack of intellect and cheerful self-reliance; whose first and chief concern, on coming into the world, is to see that the Almshouses are in good repair; and, before yet he has lawfully donned the virile garb, to collect a fund for the support of the widows and orphans that may be; who, in short, ventures to live only by the aid of the Mutual Insurance Company, which has promised to bury him decently.

It is not a man's duty, as a matter of course, to devote himself to the eradication of any, even the most enormous wrong; he may still properly have other concerns to engage him; but it is his duty, at least, to wash his hands of it and, if he gives it no thought longer, not to give it practically his support. If I devote myself to other pursuits and contemplations, I must first see, at least, that I do not pursue them sitting upon another man's shoulders. I must get off him first, that he may pursue his contemplations too. See what gross inconsistency is tolerated. I have heard some of my townsmen say, "I should like to have them order me out to help put down an insurrection of the slaves, or to march to Mexico—see if I would go"; and yet these very men have each directly by their allegiance and so indirectly, at least, by their money, furnished a substitute. The soldier is applauded who refuses to serve in an unjust war by those who do not refuse to sustain the unjust government which makes the war; is applauded by those whose own act and authority he disregards and sets at naught; as if the State were penitent to that degree that it hired one to scourge it while it sinned, but not to that degree that it left off sinning for a moment. Thus, under the name of Order and Civil Government, we are all made at last to pay homage to and support our own meanness. After the first blush of sin comes its indifference; and from immoral it becomes, as it were, *un*moral, and not quite unnecessary to that life which we have made.

The broadest and most prevalent error requires the most disinterested virtue to sustain it. The slight reproach to which the virtue of patriotism is commonly liable, the noble are most likely to incur. Those who, while they disapprove of the character and

---

11. **Odd Fellow:** A member of the Independent Order of Odd Fellows, a fraternal organization originating in England in the mid-1700s. [Ed.]

measures of a government, yield to it their allegiance and support, are undoubtedly its most conscientious supporters, and so
frequently the most serious obstacles to reform. Some are petitioning the State to dissolve the Union, to disregard the requisitions of the President. Why do they not dissolve it themselves — the
union between themselves and the State — and refuse to pay their
quota into its treasury? Do not they stand in the same relation to
the State that the State does to the Union? And have not the same
reasons prevented the State from resisting the Union which have
prevented them from resisting the State?

How can a man be satisfied to entertain an opinion merely, 15
and enjoy *it*? Is there any enjoyment in it if his opinion is that he
is aggrieved? If you are cheated out of a single dollar by your
neighbor, you do not rest satisfied with knowing that you are
cheated, or with saying that you are cheated, or even with petitioning him to pay you your due; but you take effectual steps at
once to obtain the full amount and see that you are never cheated
again. Action from principle, the perception and the performance
of right, changes things and relations; it is essentially revolutionary and does not consist wholly with anything which was. It not
only divides states and churches, it divides families; ay, it divides
the *individual*, separating the diabolical in him from the divine.

Unjust laws exist: shall we be content to obey them, or shall we
endeavor to amend them and obey them until we have succeeded,
or shall we transgress them at once? Men generally, under such a
government as this, think that they ought to wait until they have
persuaded the majority to alter them. They think that if they
should resist the remedy would be worse than the evil. *It* makes
it worse. Why is it not more apt to anticipate and provide for
reform? Why does it not cherish its wise minority? Why does it
cry and resist before it is hurt? Why does it not encourage its citizens to be on the alert to point out its faults and *do* better than
it would have them? Why does it always crucify Christ and excom-
municate Copernicus and Luther[12] and pronounce Washington
and Franklin rebels?

---

12. **Copernicus and Luther:** Nicolaus Copernicus (1473–1543) was the Polish
founder of modern astronomy; Martin Luther (1483–1546) was a German monk
who was integral to the Protestant Reformation. [Ed.]

One would think that a deliberate and practical denial of its authority was the only offense never contemplated by government; else why has it not assigned its definite, its suitable and proportionate penalty? If a man who has no property refuses but once to earn nine shillings for the State, he is put in prison for a period unlimited by any law that I know, and determined only by the discretion of those who placed him there; but if he should steal ninety times nine shillings from the State, he is soon permitted to go at large again.

If the injustice is part of the necessary friction of the machine of government, let it go, let it go: perchance it will wear smooth— certainly the machine will wear out. If the injustice has a spring or a pulley or a rope or a crank exclusively for itself, then perhaps you may consider whether the remedy will not be worse than the evil; but if it is of such a nature that it requires you to be the agent of injustice to another, then I say break the law. Let your life be a counter friction to stop the machine. What I have to do is to see, at any rate, that I do not lend myself to the wrong which I condemn.

As for adopting the ways which the State has provided for remedying the evil, I know not of such ways. They take too much time, and a man's life will be gone. I have other affairs to attend to. I came into this world, not chiefly to make this a good place to live in, but to live in it, be it good or bad. A man has not everything to do, but something; and because he cannot do *everything*, it is not necessary that he should do *something* wrong. It is not my business to be petitioning the Governor or the Legislature any more than it is theirs to petition me; and if they should not hear my petition what should I do then? But in this case the State has provided no way: its very Constitution is the evil. This may seem to be harsh and stubborn and unconciliatory; but it is to treat with the utmost kindness and consideration the only spirit that can appreciate or deserves it. So is all change for the better, like birth and death, which convulse the body.

I do not hesitate to say that those who call themselves Aboli- 20 tionists should at once effectually withdraw their support, both in person and property, from the government of Massachusetts, and not wait till they constitute a majority of one before they suffer the right to prevail through them. I think that it is enough if they have God on their side, without waiting for that other one.

Moreover, any man more right than his neighbors constitutes a majority of one already.

I meet this American government or its representative, the State government, directly and face to face once a year—no more—in the person of its tax-gatherer; this is the only mode in which a man situated as I am necessarily meets it; and it then says distinctly, Recognize me; and the simplest, the most effectual and, in the present posture of affairs, the indispensablest mode of treating with it on this head, of expressing your little satisfaction with and love for it, is to deny it then. My civil neighbor, the tax-gatherer, is the very man I have to deal with—for it is, after all, with men and not with parchment that I quarrel—and he has voluntarily chosen to be an agent of the government. How shall he ever know well what he is and does as an officer of the government, or as a man, until he is obliged to consider whether he shall treat me, his neighbor, for whom he has respect, as a neighbor and well-disposed man, or as a maniac and disturber of the peace, and see if he can get over this obstruction to his neighborliness without a ruder and more impetuous thought or speech corresponding with his action. I know this well, that if one thousand, if one hundred, if ten men whom I could name—if ten *honest* men only—ay, if *one* HONEST man in this State of Massachusetts, *ceasing to hold slaves*, were actually to withdraw from this copartnership and be locked up in the county jail therefor, it would be the abolition of slavery in America. For it matters not how small the beginning may seem to be: what is once well done is done forever. But we love better to talk about it: that we say is our mission. Reform keeps many scores of newspapers in its service but not one man. If my esteemed neighbor,[13] the State's ambassador, who will devote his days to the settlement of the question of human rights in the Council Chamber, instead of being threatened with the prisons of Carolina, were to sit down the prisoner of Massachusetts, that State which is so anxious to foist the sin of slavery upon her sister—though at present she can discover only an act of inhospitality to be the ground of a

---

13. **esteemed neighbor:** Thoreau is referring to Samuel Hoar, a Massachusetts congressman who was sent to South Carolina to protest the seizure and enslavement of black sailors. He was threatened and forced out of the state without securing the justice he sought. [Ed.]

quarrel with her—the Legislature would not wholly waive the subject the following winter.

Under a government which imprisons any unjustly, the true place for a just man is also a prison. The proper place today, the only place which Massachusetts has provided for her freer and less desponding spirits is in her prisons, to be put out and locked out of the State by her own act, as they have already put themselves out by their principles. It is there that the fugitive slave and the Mexican prisoner on parole and the Indian come to plead the wrongs of his race should find them; on that separate but more free and honorable ground where the State places those who are not *with* her but *against* her—the only house in a slave State in which a free man can abide with honor. If any think that their influence would be lost there, and their voices no longer afflict the ear of the State, that they would not be as an enemy within its walls, they do not know by how much truth is stronger than error, nor how much more eloquently and effectively he can combat injustice who has experienced a little in his own person. Cast your whole vote, not a strip of paper merely, but your whole influence. A minority is powerless while it conforms to the majority; it is not even a minority then; but it is irresistible when it clogs by its whole weight. If the alternative is to keep all just men in prison or give up war and slavery, the State will not hesitate which to choose. If a thousand men were not to pay their tax-bills this year, that would not be a violent bloody measure, as it would be to pay them, and enable the State to commit violence and shed innocent blood. This is, in fact, the definition of a peaceable revolution, if any such is possible. If the tax-gatherer or any other public officer asks me, as one has done, "But what shall I do?" my answer is, "If you really wish to do anything, resign your office." When the subject has refused allegiance and the officer has resigned his office, then the revolution is accomplished. But even suppose blood should flow. Is there not a sort of blood shed when the conscience is wounded? Through this wound a man's real manhood and immortality flow out, and he bleeds to an everlasting death. I see this blood flowing now.

I have contemplated the imprisonment of the offender rather than the seizure of his goods—though both will serve the same purpose—because they who assert the purest right, and consequently are most dangerous to a corrupt State, commonly have not spent much time in accumulating property. To such the State renders comparatively small service, and a slight tax is wont to appear exorbitant, particularly if they are obliged to earn it by special labor with their hands. If there were one who lived wholly without the use of money, the State itself would hesitate to demand it of him. But the rich man—not to make any invidious comparison—is always sold to the institution which makes him rich. Absolutely speaking, the more money, the less virtue; for money comes between a man and his objects and obtains them for him; and it was certainly no great virtue to obtain it. It puts to rest many questions which he would otherwise be taxed to answer; while the only new question which it puts is the hard but superfluous one, how to spend it. Thus his moral ground is taken from under his feet. The opportunities of living are diminished in proportion as what are called the "means" are increased. The best thing a man can do for his culture when he is rich is to endeavor to carry out those schemes which he entertained when he was poor. Christ answered the Herodians according to their condition. "Show me the tribute-money," said he—and one took a penny out of his pocket—if you use money which has the image of Caesar on it, and which he has made current and valuable, that is, if *you are men of the State* and gladly enjoy the advantages of Caesar's government, then pay him back some of his own when he demands it; "Render therefore to Caesar that which is Caesar's, and to God those things which are God's"[14]—leaving them no wiser than before as to which was which; for they did not wish to know.

When I converse with the freest of my neighbors, I perceive that whatever they may say about the magnitude and seriousness of the question, and their regard for the public tranquillity, the long and the short of the matter is that they cannot spare the protection of the existing government, and they dread the consequences to their property and families of disobedience to it. For my own part, I should not like to think that I ever rely on the protection of the State. But if I deny the authority of the State when it presents its tax-bill, it will soon take and waste all my property and so harass me and my children without end. This is hard. This makes it impossible for a man to live honestly, and at the same

14. "Render therefore . . . which are God's": Matthew 22:19–22. [Ed.]

time comfortably, in outward respects. It will not be worth the while to accumulate property; that would be sure to go again. You must hire or squat somewhere and raise but a small crop and eat that soon. You must live within yourself and depend upon yourself always tucked up and ready for a start, and not have many affairs. A man may grow rich in Turkey even, if he will be in all respects a good subject of the Turkish government. Confucius said: "If a state is governed by the principles of reason, poverty and misery are subjects of shame; if a state is not governed by the principles of reason, riches and honors are the subjects of shame." No; until I want the protection of Massachusetts to be extended to me in some distant Southern port, where my liberty is endangered, or until I am bent solely on building up an estate at home by peaceful enterprise, I can afford to refuse allegiance to Massachusetts and her right to my property and life. It costs me less in every sense to incur the penalty of disobedience to the State than it would to obey. I should feel as if I were worth less in that case.

Some years ago the State met me in behalf of the Church and 25 commanded me to pay a certain sum toward the support of a clergyman whose preaching my father attended, but never I myself. "Pay," it said, "or be locked up in the jail." I declined to pay. But, unfortunately, another man saw fit to pay it. I did not see why the schoolmaster should be taxed to support the priest, and not the priest the schoolmaster; for I was not the State's schoolmaster, but I supported myself by voluntary subscription. I did not see why the lyceum[15] should not present its tax-bill and have the State to back its demand, as well as the Church. However, at the request of the selectmen, I condescended to make some such statement as this in writing: — "Know all men by these presents, that I, Henry Thoreau, do not wish to be regarded as a member of any incorporated society which I have not joined." This I gave to the town clerk; and he has it. The State, having thus learned that I did not wish to be regarded as a member of that church, has never made a like demand on me since; though it said that it must adhere to its original presumption that time. If I had known how to name them, I should then have signed off in detail from all the societies which I never signed on to; but I did not know where to find a complete list.

15. **lyceum:** A hall where public lectures are held. [Ed.]

I have paid no poll-tax for six years. I was put into a jail once on this account, for one night; and, as I stood considering the walls of solid stone, two or three feet thick, the door of wood and iron, a foot thick, and the iron grating which strained the light, I could not help being struck with the foolishness of that institution which treated me as if I were mere flesh and blood and bones, to be locked up. I wondered that it should have concluded at length that this was the best use it could put me to and had never thought to avail itself of my services in some way. I saw that if there was a wall of stone between me and my townsmen, there was a still more difficult one to climb or break through before they could get to be as free as I was. I did not for a moment feel confined, and the walls seemed a great waste of stone and mortar. I felt as if I alone of all my townsmen had paid my tax. They plainly did not know how to treat me but behaved like persons who are underbred. In every threat and in every compliment there was a blunder; for they thought that my chief desire was to stand on the other side of that stone wall. I could not but smile to see how industriously they locked the door on my meditations, which followed them out again without let or hindrance, and *they* were really all that was dangerous. As they could not reach me, they had resolved to punish my body; just as boys, if they cannot come at some person against whom they have a spite, will abuse his dog. I saw that the State was half-witted, that it was timid as a lone woman with her silver spoons, and that it did not know its friends from its foes, and I lost all my remaining respect for it and pitied it.

Thus the State never intentionally confronts a man's sense, intellectual or moral, but only his body, his senses. It is not armed with superior wit or honesty but with superior physical strength. I was not born to be forced. I will breathe after my own fashion. Let us see who is the strongest. What force has a multitude? They only can force me who obey a higher law than I. They force me to become like themselves. I do not hear of *men* being *forced* to live this way or that by masses of men. What sort of life were that to live? When I meet a government which says to me, "Your money or your life," why should I be in haste to give it my money? It may be in a great strait and not know what to do: I cannot help that. It must help itself; do as I do. It is not worth the while to snivel about it. I am not responsible for the successful working of the machinery of society. I am not the son of the engineer. I perceive that, when an acorn and a chestnut fall side by side, the one does not remain inert to make way for the other, but both obey their own laws and spring and grow and flourish as best they can till one, perchance, overshadows and destroys the other. If a plant cannot live according to its nature, it dies; and so a man.

The night in prison was novel and interesting enough. The prisoners in their shirt-sleeves were enjoying a chat and the evening air in the doorway when I entered. But the jailer said, "Come, boys, it is time to lock up"; and so they dispersed, and I heard the sound of their steps returning into the hollow apartments. My room-mate was introduced to me by the jailer as "a first-rate fellow and a clever man." When the door was locked, he showed me where to hang my hat and how he managed matters there. The rooms were whitewashed once a month; and this one, at least, was the whitest, most simply furnished, and probably the neatest apartment in the town. He naturally wanted to know where I came from and what brought me there; and when I had told him, I asked him in my turn how he came there, presuming him to be an honest man, of course; and, as the world goes, I believe he was. "Why," said he, "they accuse me of burning a barn; but I never did it." As near as I could discover, he had probably gone to bed in a barn when drunk and smoked his pipe there; and so a barn burnt. He had the reputation of being a clever man, had been there some three months waiting for his trial to come on, and would have to wait as much longer; but he was quite domesticated and contented, since he got his board for nothing and thought that he was well treated.

He occupied one window, and I the other; and I saw that if one stayed there long, his principal business would be to look out the window. I had soon read all the tracts that were left there and examined where former prisoners had broken out and where a grate had been sawed off and heard the history of the various occupants of that room; for I found that even here there was a history and a gossip which never circulated beyond the walls of the jail. Probably this is the only house in the town where verses are composed, which afterward printed in a circular form but not published. I was shown quite a long list of verses which were composed by some young men who had been detected in an attempt to escape, who avenged themselves by signing them.

I pumped my fellow-prisoner as dry as I could, for fear I should 30
never see him again; but at length he showed me which was my
bed and left me to blow out the lamp.

It was like travelling into a far country, such as I had never
expected to behold, to lie there for one night. It seemed to me that
I never had heard the town-clock strike before, nor the evening
sounds of the village; for we slept with the windows open, which
were inside the grating. It was to see my native village in the light
of the Middle Ages, and our Concord was turned into a Rhine
stream, and visions of knights and castles passed before me. They
were the voices of old burghers that I heard in the streets. I was
an involuntary spectator and auditor of whatever was done and
said in the kitchen of the adjacent village-inn—a wholly new and
rare experience to me. It was a closer view of my native town. I
was fairly inside of it. I never had seen its institutions before. This
is one of its peculiar institutions; for it is a shire town.[16] I began to
comprehend what its inhabitants were about.

In the morning our breakfasts were put through the hole in the
door, in small oblong-square tin pans, made to fit, and holding
a pint of chocolate, with brown bread and an iron spoon. When
they called for the vessels again, I was green enough to return
what bread I had left; but my comrade seized it and said that I
should lay that up for lunch or dinner. Soon after he was let out to
work at haying in a neighboring field, whither he went every day,
and would not be back till noon; so he bade me good-day, saying
that he doubted if he should see me again.

When I came out of prison—for someone interfered and paid
that tax—I did not perceive that great changes had taken place
on the common, such as he observed who went in a youth and
emerged a tottering and gray-headed man; and yet a change
had to my eyes come over the scene—the town and State and
country—greater than any that mere time could effect. I saw yet
more distinctly the State in which I lived. I saw to what extent the
people among whom I lived could be trusted as good neighbors
and friends; that their friendship was for summer weather only;
that they did not greatly propose to do right; that they were a distinct race from me by their prejudices and superstitions, as the
Chinamen and Malays are; that, in their sacrifices to humanity,

16. **shire town:** A town with a court, county offices, and jails. [Ed.]

they ran no risks, not even to their property; that, after all, they were not so noble but they treated the thief as he had treated them and hoped, by a certain outward observance and a few prayers, and by walking in a particular straight though useless path from time to time, to save their souls. This may be to judge my neighbors harshly; for I believe that many of them are not aware that they have such an institution as the jail in their village.

It was formerly the custom in our village, when a poor debtor came out of jail, for his acquaintances to salute him, looking through their fingers, which were crossed to represent the grating of a jail window, "How do ye do?" My neighbors did not thus salute me but first looked at me and then at one another as if I had returned from a long journey. I was put into jail as I was going to the shoemaker's to get a shoe which was mended. When I was let out the next morning I proceeded to finish my errand, and having put on my mended shoe, joined a huckleberry party who were impatient to put themselves under my conduct; and in half an hour—for the horse was soon tackled—was in the midst of a huckleberry field on one of our highest hills two miles off, and then the State was nowhere to be seen.

This is the whole history of "My Prisons."   35

I have never declined paying the highway tax, because I am as desirous of being a good neighbor as I am of being a bad subject; and as for supporting schools I am doing my part to educate my fellow countrymen now. It is for no particular item in the tax-bill that I refuse to pay it. I simply wish to refuse allegiance to the State, to withdraw and stand aloof from it effectually. I do not care to trace the course of my dollar, if I could, till it buys a man or a musket to shoot one with—the dollar is innocent—but I am concerned to trace the effects of my allegiance. In fact, I quietly declare war with the State, after my fashion, though I will still make what use and get what advantage of her I can, as is usual in such cases.

If others pay the tax which is demanded of me from a sympathy with the State, they do but what they have already done in their own case, or rather they abet injustice to a greater extent than the State requires. If they pay the tax from a mistaken interest in the individual taxed, to save his property, or prevent his going to jail, it is because they have not considered wisely how far they let their private feelings interfere with the public good.

This, then, is my position at present. But one cannot be too much on his guard in such a case, lest his action be biased by obstinacy or an undue regard for the opinions of men. Let him see that he does only what belongs to himself and to the hour.

I think sometimes, Why, this people mean well; they are only ignorant; they would do better if they knew how: why give your neighbors this pain to treat you as they are not inclined to? But I think again, this is no reason why I should do as they do or permit others to suffer much greater pain of a different kind. Again, I sometimes say to myself, When many millions of men, without heat, without ill will, without personal feeling of any kind, demand of you a few shillings only, without the possibility, such is their constitution, of retracting or altering their present demand, and without the possibility, on your side, of appeal to any other millions, why expose yourself to this overwhelming brute force? You do not resist cold and hunger, the winds and the waves, thus obstinately; you quietly submit to a thousand similar necessities. You do not put your head into the fire. But just in proportion as I regard this as not wholly a brute force but partly a human force, and consider that I have relations to those millions as to so many millions of men, and not of mere brute or inanimate things, I see that appeal is possible, first and instantaneously, from them to the Maker of them, and secondly, from them to themselves. But if I put my head deliberately into the fire, there is no appeal to fire or to the Maker of fire, and I have only myself to blame. If I could convince myself that I have any right to be satisfied with men as they are, and to treat them accordingly, and not according, in some respects, to my requisitions and expectations of what they and I ought to be, then, like a good Mussulman[17] and fatalist, I should endeavor to be satisfied with things as they are and say it is the will of God. And, above all, there is this difference between resisting this and a purely brute or natural force, that I can resist this with some effect; but I cannot expect, like Orpheus,[18] to change the nature of the rocks and trees and beasts.

I do not wish to quarrel with any man or nation. I do not wish to 40 split hairs, to make fine distinctions, or set myself up as better than

17. **Mussulman:** A Muslim. [Ed.]
18. **Orpheus:** In Greek mythology, Orpheus's music was so affecting that his songs could charm rocks, trees, and animals. [Ed.]

my neighbors. I seek rather, I may say, even an excuse for conform-
ing to the laws of the land. I am but too ready to conform to them.
Indeed, I have reason to suspect myself on this head; and each year,
as the tax-gatherer comes round, I find myself disposed to review
the acts and position of the general and State governments, and
the spirit of the people, to discover a pretext for conformity.

> We must affect our country as our parents;
> And if at any time we alienate
> Our love or industry from doing it honor,
> We must respect effects and teach the soul
> Matter of conscience and religion,
> And not desire of rule or benefit.[19]

I believe that the State will soon be able to take all my work of
this sort out of my hands, and then I shall be no better a patriot
than my fellow-countrymen. Seen from a lower point of view, the
Constitution, with all its faults, is very good; the law and the
courts are very respectable; even this State and this American
government are, in many respects, very admirable and rare
things, to be thankful for, such as a great many have described
them; but seen from a point of view a little higher, they are what I
have described them; seen from a higher still, and the highest,
who shall say what they are, or that they are worth looking at or
thinking of at all?

However, the government does not concern me much, and I
shall bestow the fewest possible thoughts on it. It is not many
moments that I live under a government, even in this world. If a
man is thought-free, fancy-free, imagination-free, that which *is
not* never for a long time appearing *to be* to him, unwise rulers or
reformers cannot fatally interrupt him.

I know that most men think differently from myself; but those
whose lives are by profession devoted to the study of these or
kindred subjects content me as little as any. Statesmen and legislators, standing so completely within the institution, never
distinctly and nakedly behold it. They speak of moving society
but have no resting-place without it. They may be men of a certain
experience and discrimination and have no doubt invented

---

19. From George Peele's *Battle of Alcazar* (acted 1588–1589; printed 1594). [Ed.]

ingenious and even useful systems, for which we sincerely thank them; but all their wit and usefulness lie within certain not very wide limits. They are wont to forget that the world is not governed by policy and expediency. Webster[20] never goes behind government and so cannot speak with authority about it. His words are wisdom to those legislators who contemplate no essential reform in the existing government; but for thinkers, and those who legislate for all time, he never once glances at the subject. I know of those whose serene and wise speculations on this theme would soon reveal the limits of his mind's range and hospitality. Yet, compared with the cheap professions of most reformers, and the still cheaper wisdom and eloquence of politicians in general, his are almost the only sensible and valuable words, and we thank Heaven for him. Comparatively, he is always strong, original, and, above all, practical. Still his quality is not wisdom but prudence. The lawyer's truth is not Truth but consistency, or a consistent expediency. Truth is always in harmony with herself and is not concerned chiefly to reveal the justice that may consist with wrong-doing. He well deserves to be called, as he has been called, the Defender of the Constitution. There are really no blows to be given by him but defensive ones. He is not a leader but a follower. His leaders are the men of '87.[21] "I have never made an effort," he says, "and never propose to make an effort; I have never countenanced an effort, and never mean to countenance an effort, to disturb the arrangement as originally made, by which the various States came into the Union." Still thinking of the sanction which the Constitution gives to slavery, he says, "Because it was a part of the original compact—let it stand." Notwithstanding his special acuteness and ability, he is unable to take a fact out of its merely political relations and behold it as it lies absolutely to be disposed of by the intellect—what, for instance, it behooves a man to do here in America today with regard to slavery but ventures, or is driven, to make some such desperate answer as the following, while professing to speak absolutely, and as a private man—from which what new and singular code of social duties might be inferred? "The manner," says he, "in which the governments of those States where slavery exists are to regulate it, is for their own

20. **Webster:** Daniel Webster, the secretary of state from 1841 to 1843. [Ed.]
21. **men of '87:** The men who wrote the Constitution in 1787. [Ed.]

consideration, under their responsibility to their constituents, to the general laws of propriety, humanity, and justice, and to God. Associations formed elsewhere, springing from a feeling of humanity, or any other cause, have nothing whatever to do with it. They have never received any encouragement from me, and they never will."

They who know of no purer sources of truth, who have traced up its stream no higher, stand, and wisely stand, by the Bible and the Constitution, and drink at it there with reverence and humility; but they who behold where it comes trickling into this lake or that pool gird up their loins once more and continue their pilgrimage toward its fountain-head.

No man with a genius for legislation has appeared in America. They are rare in the history of the world. There are orators, politicians, and eloquent men by the thousand; but the speaker has not yet opened his mouth to speak who is capable of settling the much-vexed questions of the day. We love eloquence for its own sake and not for any truth which it may utter or any heroism it may inspire. Our legislators have not yet learned the comparative value of free-trade and of freedom, of union, and of rectitude, to a nation. They have no genius or talent for comparatively humble questions of taxation and finance, commerce and manufacturers and agriculture. If we were left solely to the wordy wit of legislators in Congress for our guidance, uncorrected by the seasonable experience and the effectual complaints of the people, America would not long retain her rank among the nations. For eighteen hundred years, though perchance I have no right to say it, the New Testament has been written; yet where is the legislator who has wisdom and practical talent enough to avail himself of the light which it sheds on the science of legislation?

The authority of government, even such as I am willing to 45 submit to—for I will cheerfully obey those who know and can do better than I, and in many things even those who neither know nor can do so well—is still an impure one: to be strictly just, it must have the sanction and consent of the governed. It can have no pure right over my person and property but what I concede to it. The progress from an absolute to a limited monarchy, from a limited monarchy to a democracy, is a progress toward a true respect for the individual. Even the Chinese philosopher[22] was wise enough to

22. the Chinese philosopher: Most likely Confucius. [Ed.]

regard the individual as the basis of the empire. Is a democracy such as we know it the last improvement possible in government? Is it not possible to take a step further towards recognizing and organizing the rights of man? There will never be a really free and enlightened State until the State comes to recognize the individual as a higher and independent power, from which all its own power and authority are derived, and treats him accordingly. I please myself with imagining a State at last which can afford to be just to all men and to treat the individual with respect as a neighbor; which even would not think it inconsistent with its own repose if a few were to live aloof from it, not meddling with it, nor embraced by it, who fulfilled all the duties of neighbors and fellow-men. A State which bore this kind of fruit and suffered it to drop off as fast as it ripened would prepare the way for a still more perfect and glorious State, which also I have imagined but not yet anywhere seen.

For Discussion and Writing

1. What two specific situations is Thoreau most unhappy about?
2. For a document that has proven so important in world history, "Civil Disobedience" seems quite personal. What about the way that Thoreau presents himself and the way he addresses his readers makes it feel this way?
3. **connections**   Thoreau argues that an undue respect for law's ability to ensure justice leads men to fight in wars "against their common sense and consciences" (par. 4). Why does James Boswell, in "On War" (p. 66), say that soldiers go to war? Would Thoreau agree or disagree with Boswell's thoughts on the matter? How?
4. Thoreau's writing has been remembered not only because its ideas remain appealing but because he states them memorably. Write about what you think it is that makes his writing stylistically memorable. Look at the way he sometimes uses mottoes or aphorisms, and think about how they work in terms of word choice and structure. Look also at the way he strings his thoughts together, how he builds his argument, how he strikes emotional chords.
5. **looking further**   While "Civil Disobedience" was important to Mahatma Gandhi and Martin Luther King Jr., it was also inspirational for many in the Vietnam-era antiwar movement. Do a little research into contemporary protest movements at home and abroad. Was this essay important to members of these movements too? If not explicitly read by them, do you see evidence that the principles championed by Thoreau had some influence? How? If not, were other statements of protest influential to them, or other principles?

JAMES THURBER

The Subjunctive Mood

James Thurber (1894–1961) was a cartoonist and writer. Best known for the cartoons and stories he wrote for the New Yorker *over a career that spanned four decades, Thurber had thirty-five books published under his name. Thurber's talent was wide ranging—he wrote journalism, humor, serious fiction, drama, and biography, and drew cartoons that have been a lasting influence on the art form. His story "The Secret Life of Walter Mitty" is among his best-known works; the titular character has become iconic, and the story was made into a motion picture in 1947 and again in 2013.*

While Thurber was multitalented, much of his best work is marked by humor. His sense of humor became a large part of the New Yorker's *identity, and it was in turn shaped by that magazine's sophisticated, urbane style. As you read "The Subjunctive Mood," which was published in 1929, think about its sense of humor and how you think the essay might be received if published today.*

The importance of correct grammar in the home can not be overestimated. Two young people should make sure that each is rhetorically sound before they get married, because grammatical precision, particularly in mood, is just as important as anything else. Rhetoric and sex, in fact, are so closely related that when one becomes confused they both become confused. Take the subjunctive. Fowler[1], in his book on modern English usage, says the subjunctive is dying, but adds that there are still a few truly living uses, which he groups under "Alives, Revivals, Survivals, and Arrivals." Let us examine the all too common domestic situation where the husband arrives just after another gentleman has departed—or just after he thinks another gentleman has departed

1. Henry Fowler (1858–1933) wrote *A Dictionary of English Usage*, an iconic British style guide that was first published in 1926. [Ed.]

(Suppositional Departures lead to just as much bitterness, and even more subjunctives, than Actual Departures).

The wife, in either case, is almost sure to go into the subjunctive—very likely before any accusation is made. Among the most common subjunctives which she will be inclined to use are those of indignation and hauteur, such as "Be that as it may," "Far be it from me," etc.

For the moment, she is safe enough in the subjunctive, because her husband has probably gone into it, too, using "Would God I were," "If there be justice," and so on. Wives select the subjunctive usually because it is the best mood in which to spar for time, husbands because it lends itself most easily to ranting and posturing. As long as they both stay in it they are safe. Misunderstandings are almost certain to arise, however, when the husband goes into the indicative, as he is pretty sure to do. He usually does this preparatory to dismissing his suspicions, a step toward which every husband is impelled by his natural egotism. First he will begin with a plain past-tense indicative *if*-clause—just to show that he knows who the man is—prior to dismissing him.

"If George Spangrell was here," the husband will begin, lighting a cigarette, "I . . ."

"Well, what would you do if he *were?*" demands the wife.   5

The confusion, which begins at this point, is pretty intricate. The husband has gone into the indicative, but his wife has stayed in the subjunctive and, furthermore, she thinks that he is still there, too. Thus she thinks he intended to say: "If George Spangrell was here [that is, now] I would tell him what I think of him, the low scoundrel." There is no excuse for a wife prematurely imputing such a suspicion or such a rhetorical monstrosity to her husband. What he probably intended to say was merely something like this: "If George Spangrell was here, I wouldn't like it, but of course I know he wasn't, dear." However, misunderstandings now begin to pile up. The husband is instantly made suspicious by her "What would you do if he *were?*" He considers her "were" tantamount to "is." (This quick-tempered construction, of course, makes the "would" in his wife's sentence ridiculous, for, had she meant "is" instead of "were," she would have substituted "will" for "would.") The situation is much too involved now, however, for the husband to make an effort to parse anything. He instantly abandons all grammatical analysis, and begins to look about, peering into the wardrobe, swishing under beds with a cane or mop-handle.

His wife now has the advantage of him, not only in mood, but in posture. A woman must naturally view with disdain and contempt any man who is down on all fours unless he has taken that position for the purpose of playing horse with some children—an extenuation which we need not discuss here. To meet her on even terms, the husband should walk, not crawl, from wardrobe to chaise-longue, using the mandatory subjunctive in a firm voice, as follows: "If anyone be in (or under) there, let him come out!" ["Come out" is better here than "emerge" because stronger, but a husband should not fall into the colloquial "Come on out of that!" He may, however, if he so wishes, address the gentleman, whether he be present or not, as "Spangrell" but never "Mr. Spangrell" (Hypocritical Dignification) and certainly never as "George"—the use of the given name being in extreme bad taste where no endearment is intended.]

The wife of course will resent all these goings-on, and the quarrel that results will probably last late into the night.

There are several ways to prevent a situation like this. In the first place, when a husband says "was" a wife should instantly respond with "wasn't." Most husbands will take a "wasn't" at its face value, because it preserves their egotism and self-respect. On the other hand, "if . . . were" is always dangerous. Husbands have come to know that a wife's "if . . . were" usually means that what she is presenting as purely hypothetical is, in reality, a matter of fact. Thus, if a wife begins, one evening after an excellent dinner, "Dear, what would you do if I were the sort of woman who had, etc.," her husband knows full well that it is going to turn out that she is the sort of woman who has. Husbands are suspicious of all subjunctives. Wives should avoid them. Once a woman has "if . . . were'd" a Mr. Spangrell, her husband is, nine times out of ten, going to swish under the chaise-longue. Even if he finds no-one, the situation becomes extremely awkward, and there is of course always the plaguey hundredth chance that he may discover a strange cane or pair of gloves.

The best of all ways out is for the husband to go instantly into 10 the future indicative and say, with great dignity, "I shall go down to the drugstore." Ordinarily his wife would reply, "Oh, no you won't," but with all the doubt and suspicion in the air, she will be

inclined to humor him and let him have his way. She is certain to,
if Spangrell is in the clothes hamper.

For Discussion and Writing

1. What is the subjunctive mood?
2. How would you classify the mode in which this essay is written? Is it argumentative? Narrative? Both? Explain your answer by referring to the features that distinguish these different modes.
3. **connections** How does Thurber use humor in this essay—that is, how does he write so as to be funny, and to what end? Compare Thurber's use of humor to Nancy Mairs's in "On Being a Cripple" (p. 226). How does she write to be funny? What is her purpose for doing so? How do the two essays compare on both counts?
4. Write a brief humorous essay. Then write a reflection on the process of writing to be funny. What was the experience like? Was it easy? Hard? In what ways? Was there anything surprising about it?
5. **looking further** While this essay is funny, the narrative it constructs is about marital infidelity, something that is often not felt to be amusing in real life. Do some research on this phenomenon in contemporary life. What kind of information can you collect? What information do you think is more important? What kind of information is less important? Do you think it is an appropriate subject for humor, based on the information you've gathered? Why, or why not?

MIYA TOKUMITSU

In the Name of Love

Miya Tokumitsu is a contributing editor at the quarterly magazine
Jacobin *and the author of* Do What You Love: And Other Lies about
Success and Happiness *(2015). She has a Ph.D. in art history from the*
University of Pennsylvania and writes cultural criticism as well as
scholarship.
  Though the subject of this essay and of Tokumitsu's book is far from
her scholarly specialization—Northern European Renaissance and
Baroque art—it is interesting to think about how the author's back-
ground informs her take on the world(s) of work. As you read, take into
account where the author is coming from, in both senses.

"Do what you love. Love what you do."
  The commands are framed and perched in a living room that
can only be described as "well-curated." A picture of this room
appeared first on a popular design blog, but has been pinned,
tumbl'd, and liked thousands of times by now.
  Lovingly lit and photographed, this room is styled to inspire
Sehnsucht, roughly translatable from German as a pleasurable
yearning for some utopian thing or place. Despite the fact that it
introduces exhortations to labor into a space of leisure, the "do
what you love" living room—where artful tchotchkes abound
and work is not drudgery but love—is precisely the place all those
pinners and likers long to be. The diptych arrangement suggests a
secular version of a medieval house altar.
  There's little doubt that "do what you love" (DWYL) is now the
unofficial work mantra for our time. The problem is that it leads
not to salvation, but to the devaluation of actual work, including
the very work it pretends to elevate—and more importantly, the
dehumanization of the vast majority of laborers.
  Superficially, DWYL is an uplifting piece of advice, urging us to   5
ponder what it is we most enjoy doing and then turn that activity

396

into a wage-generating enterprise. But why should our pleasure be for profit? Who is the audience for this dictum? Who is not?

By keeping us focused on ourselves and our individual happiness, DWYL distracts us from the working conditions of others while validating our own choices and relieving us from obligations to all who labor, whether or not they love it. It is the secret handshake of the privileged and a worldview that disguises its elitism as noble self-betterment. According to this way of thinking, labor is not something one does for compensation, but an act of self-love. If profit doesn't happen to follow, it is because the worker's passion and determination were insufficient. Its real achievement is making workers believe their labor serves the self and not the marketplace.

Aphorisms have numerous origins and reincarnations, but the generic and hackneyed nature of DWYL confounds precise attribution. Oxford Reference links the phrase and variants of it to Martina Navratilova and François Rabelais, among others. The Internet frequently attributes it to Confucius, locating it in a misty, Orientalized past. Oprah Winfrey and other peddlers of positivity have included it in their repertoires for decades, but the most important recent evangelist of the DWYL creed is deceased Apple CEO Steve Jobs.

His graduation speech to the Stanford University class of 2005 provides as good an origin myth as any, especially since Jobs had already been beatified as the patron saint of aestheticized work well before his early death. In the speech, Jobs recounts the creation of Apple, and inserts this reflection:

> You've got to find what you love. And that is as true for your work as it is for your lovers. Your work is going to fill a large part of your life, and the only way to be truly satisfied is to do what you believe is great work. And the only way to do great work is to love what you do.

In these four sentences, the words "you" and "your" appear eight times. This focus on the individual is hardly surprising coming from Jobs, who cultivated a very specific image of himself as a worker: inspired, casual, passionate—all states agreeable with ideal romantic love. Jobs telegraphed the conflation of his besotted worker-self with his company so effectively that his black turtleneck and blue jeans became metonyms for all of Apple and the labor that maintains it.

But by portraying Apple as a labor of his individual love, Jobs 10 elided the labor of untold thousands in Apple's factories, conveniently hidden from sight on the other side of the planet—the very labor that allowed Jobs to actualize his love.

The violence of this erasure needs to be exposed. While "do what you love" sounds harmless and precious, it is ultimately self-focused to the point of narcissism. Jobs's formulation of "do what you love" is the depressing antithesis to Henry David Thoreau's utopian vision of labor for all. In "Life without Principle," Thoreau wrote,

> . . . it would be good economy for a town to pay its laborers so well that they would not feel that they were working for low ends, as for a livelihood merely, but for scientific, even moral ends. Do not hire a man who does your work for money, but him who does it for the love of it.

Admittedly, Thoreau had little feel for the proletariat (it's hard to imagine someone washing diapers for "scientific, even moral ends," no matter how well-paid). But he nonetheless maintains that society has a stake in making work well-compensated and meaningful. By contrast, the twenty-first-century Jobsian view demands that we all turn inward. It absolves us of any obligation to or acknowledgment of the wider world, underscoring its fundamental betrayal of all workers, whether they consciously embrace it or not.

One consequence of this isolation is the division that DWYL creates among workers, largely along class lines. Work becomes divided into two opposing classes: that which is lovable (creative, intellectual, socially prestigious) and that which is not (repetitive, unintellectual, undistinguished). Those in the lovable work camp are vastly more privileged in terms of wealth, social status, education, society's racial biases, and political clout, while comprising a small minority of the workforce.

For those forced into unlovable work, it's a different story. Under the DWYL credo, labor that is done out of motives or needs other than love (which is, in fact, most labor) is not only demeaned but erased. As in Jobs's Stanford speech, unlovable but socially necessary work is banished from the spectrum of consciousness altogether.

Think of the great variety of work that allowed Jobs to spend even 15 one day as CEO: his food harvested from fields, then transported

strong words

across great distances. His company's goods assembled, packaged, shipped. Apple advertisements scripted, cast, filmed. Lawsuits processed. Office wastebaskets emptied and ink cartridges filled. Job creation goes both ways. Yet with the vast majority of workers effectively invisible to elites busy in their lovable occupations, how can it be surprising that the heavy strains faced by today's workers (abysmal wages, massive child care costs, et cetera) barely register as political issues even among the liberal faction of the ruling class?

In ignoring most work and reclassifying the rest as love, DWYL may be the most elegant anti-worker ideology around. Why should workers assemble and assert their class interests if there's no such thing as work?

"Do what you love" disguises the fact that being able to choose a career primarily for personal reward is an unmerited privilege, a sign of that person's socioeconomic class. Even if a self-employed graphic designer had parents who could pay for art school and cosign a lease for a slick Brooklyn apartment, she can self-righteously bestow DWYL as career advice to those covetous of her success.

If we believe that working as a Silicon Valley entrepreneur or a museum publicist or a think-tank acolyte is essential to being true to ourselves—in fact, to loving ourselves—what do we believe about the inner lives and hopes of those who clean hotel rooms and stock shelves at big-box stores? The answer is: nothing.

Yet arduous, low-wage work is what ever more Americans do and will be doing. According to the US Bureau of Labor Statistics, the two fastest-growing occupations projected until 2020 are "Personal Care Aide" and "Home Care Aide," with average salaries of $19,640 per year and $20,560 per year in 2010, respectively. Elevating certain types of professions to something worthy of love necessarily denigrates the labor of those who do unglamorous work that keeps society functioning, especially the crucial work of caregivers.

If DWYL denigrates or makes dangerously invisible vast 20 swaths of labor that allow many of us to live in comfort and to do what we love, it has also caused great damage to the professions it portends to celebrate, especially those jobs existing within institutional structures. Nowhere has the DWYL mantra been more

devastating to its adherents than in academia. The average
Ph.D. student of the mid-2000s forwent the easy money of finance
and law (now slightly less easy) to live on a meager stipend in
order to pursue their passion for Norse mythology or the history
of Afro-Cuban music.

The reward for answering this higher calling is an academic
employment marketplace in which around 41 percent of American
faculty are adjunct professors—contract instructors who usually
receive low pay, no benefits, no office, no job security, and no long-
term stake in the schools where they work.

There are many factors that keep Ph.D.s providing such
high-skilled labor for such extremely low wages, including path
dependency and the sunk costs of earning a Ph.D., but one of the
strongest is how pervasively the DWYL doctrine is embedded in
academia. Few other professions fuse the personal identity of
their workers so intimately with the work output. This intense
identification partly explains why so many proudly left-leaning
faculty remain oddly silent about the working conditions of their
peers. Because academic research should be done out of pure
love, the actual conditions of and compensation for this labor
become afterthoughts, if they are considered at all.

In "Academic Labor, the Aesthetics of Management, and the
Promise of Autonomous Work," Sarah Brouillette writes of academic faculty,

> . . . our faith that our work offers non-material rewards, and is more inte-
> gral to our identity than a "regular" job would be, makes us ideal employ-
> ees when the goal of management is to extract our labor's maximum
> value at minimum cost.

Many academics like to think they have avoided a corporate
work environment and its attendant values, but Marc Bousquet
notes in his essay "We Work" that academia may actually provide
a model for corporate management:

> How to emulate the academic workplace and get people to work at a high
> level of intellectual and emotional intensity for fifty or sixty hours a week
> for bartenders' wages or less? Is there any way we can get our employees
> to swoon over their desks, murmuring "I love what I do" in response to
> greater workloads and smaller paychecks? How can we get our workers

to be like faculty and deny that they work at all? How can we adjust our corporate culture to resemble campus culture, so that our workforce will fall in love with their work too?

No one is arguing that enjoyable work should be less so. But 25 emotionally satisfying work is still work, and acknowledging it as such doesn't undermine it in any way. Refusing to acknowledge it, on the other hand, opens the door to the most vicious exploitation and harms all workers.

Ironically, DWYL reinforces exploitation even within the so-called lovable professions where off-the-clock, underpaid, or unpaid labor is the new norm: reporters required to do the work of their laid-off photographers, publicists expected to Pin and Tweet on weekends, the 46 percent of the workforce expected to check their work email on sick days. Nothing makes exploitation go down easier than convincing workers that they are doing what they love.

Instead of crafting a nation of self-fulfilled, happy workers, our DWYL era has seen the rise of the adjunct professor and the unpaid intern—people persuaded to work for cheap or free, or even for a net loss of wealth. This has certainly been the case for all those interns working for college credit or those who actually purchase ultra-desirable fashion-house internships at auction. (Valentino and Balenciaga are among a handful of houses that auctioned off month-long internships. For charity, of course.) The latter is worker exploitation taken to its most extreme, and as an ongoing Pro Publica investigation reveals, the unpaid intern is an ever larger presence in the American workforce.

It should be no surprise that unpaid interns abound in fields that are highly socially desirable, including fashion, media, and the arts. These industries have long been accustomed to masses of employees willing to work for social currency instead of actual wages, all in the name of love. Excluded from these opportunities, of course, is the overwhelming majority of the population: those who need to work for wages. This exclusion not only calcifies economic and professional immobility, but insulates these industries from the full diversity of voices society has to offer.

And it's no coincidence that the industries that rely heavily on interns—fashion, media, and the arts—just happen to be the

402 MIYA TOKUMITSU

feminized ones, as Madeleine Schwartz wrote in *Dissent*. Yet another damaging consequence of DWYL is how ruthlessly it works to extract female labor for little or no compensation. Women comprise the majority of the low-wage or unpaid workforce; as care workers, adjunct faculty, and unpaid interns, they outnumber men. What unites all of this work, whether performed by G.E.D.s or Ph.D.s, is the belief that wages shouldn't be the primary motivation for doing it. Women are supposed to do work because they are natural nurturers and are eager to please; after all they've been doing uncompensated child care, elder care, and housework since time immemorial. And talking money is unladylike anyway.

The DWYL dream is, true to its American mythology, superfi- 30
cially democratic. Ph.D.s can do what they love, making careers that indulge their love of the Victorian novel and writing thoughtful essays in the *New York Review of Books*. High school grads can also do it, building prepared food empires out of their Aunt Pearl's jam recipe. The hallowed path of the entrepreneur always offers this way out of disadvantaged beginnings, excusing the rest of us for allowing those beginnings to be as miserable as they are. In America, everyone has the opportunity to do what he or she loves and get rich.

Do what you love and you'll never work a day in your life! Before succumbing to the intoxicating warmth of that promise, it's critical to ask, "Who, exactly, benefits from making work feel like nonwork?" "Why *should* workers feel as if they aren't working when they are?" Historian Mario Liverani reminds us that "ideology has the function of presenting exploitation in a favorable light to the exploited, as advantageous to the disadvantaged."

In masking the very exploitative mechanisms of labor that it fuels, DWYL is, in fact, the most perfect ideological tool of capitalism. It shunts aside the labor of others and disguises our own labor to ourselves. It hides the fact that if we acknowledged all of our work as work, we could set appropriate limits for it, demanding fair compensation and humane schedules that allow for family and leisure time.

And if we did that, more of us could get around to doing what it is we *really* love.

For Discussion and Writing

1. What does the author use the acronym "DWYL" to stand for? What does she think of it?

2. Make a list of the different kinds of evidence Tokumitsu uses in her argument.

3. **connections** Read "In the Name of Love" alongside Barbara Ehrenreich's "Serving in Florida" (p. 136). In what ways are the two about different subjects? In what ways do they overlap? Are there points of agreement and/or disagreement?

4. Write about work in your own life. What kind of work do you want to do when you finish school? What kind of work do you do now? What do you value most in work? How much it pays? How much you enjoy it? How much it helps other people?

5. **looking further** Do some research into national labor trends. What industries employ the most people? What kinds of jobs do most people have? What industries were the biggest employers fifty years ago? Why do you think things have changed as they have, and what effects do you think these changes have had on workers?

E. B. WHITE

Once More to the Lake

Born in Mount Vernon, New York, in 1899, E. B. White was an editor, essayist, and writer of children's books. He is identified in some circles as the writer of sketches, poems, editorials, and essays for the young New Yorker *magazine and in others as the author of the children's books* Stuart Little *(1945) and* Charlotte's Web *(1952). He is also known for his revision of William Strunk Jr.'s* The Elements of Style *(1959).*

White's involvement with The Elements of Style *highlights what is for many the most important element of his writing—his style. As you read "Once More to the Lake," look for telling details in his descriptions and take note of the kinds of words he chooses.*

One summer, along about 1904, my father rented a camp on a lake in Maine and took us all there for the month of August. We all got ringworm from some kittens and had to rub Pond's Extract on our arms and legs night and morning, and my father rolled over in a canoe with all his clothes on; but outside of that the vacation was a success and from then on none of us ever thought there was any place in the world like that lake in Maine. We returned summer after summer—always on August 1 for one month. I have since become a salt-water man, but sometimes in summer there are days when the restlessness of the tides and the fearful cold of the sea water and the incessant wind that blows across the afternoon and into the evening make me wish for the placidity of a lake in the woods. A few weeks ago this feeling got so strong I bought myself a couple of bass hooks and a spinner and returned to the lake where we used to go, for a week's fishing and to revisit old haunts.

I took along my son, who had never had any fresh water up his nose and who had seen lily pads only from train windows. On the journey over to the lake I began to wonder what it would be like.

I wondered how time would have marred this unique, this holy spot—the coves and streams, the hills that the sun set behind, the camps and the paths behind the camps. I was sure that the tarred road would have found it out, and I wondered in what other ways it would be desolated. It is strange how much you can remember about places like that once you allow your mind to return into the grooves that lead back. You remember one thing, and that suddenly reminds you of another thing. I guess I remembered clearest of all the early mornings, when the lake was cool and motionless, remembered how the bedroom smelled of the lumber it was made of and of the wet woods whose scent entered through the screen. The partitions in the camp were thin and did not extend clear to the top of the rooms, and as I was always the first up I would dress softly so as not to wake the others, and sneak out into the sweet outdoors and start out in the canoe, keeping close along the shore in the long shadows of the pines. I remembered being very careful never to rub my paddle against the gunwale for fear of disturbing the stillness of the cathedral.

The lake had never been what you would call a wild lake. There were cottages sprinkled around the shores, and it was in farming country although the shores of the lake were quite heavily wooded. Some of the cottages were owned by nearby farmers, and you would live at the shore and eat your meals at the farmhouse. That's what our family did. But although it wasn't wild, it was a fairly large and undisturbed lake and there were places in it that, to a child at least, seemed infinitely remote and primeval.

I was right about the tar: it led to within half a mile of the shore. But when I got back there, with my boy, and we settled into a camp near a farmhouse and into the kind of summertime I had known, I could tell that it was going to be pretty much the same as it had been before—I knew it, lying in bed the first morning, smelling the bedroom and hearing the boy sneak quietly out and go off along the shore in a boat. I began to sustain the illusion that he was I, and therefore, by simple transposition, that I was my father. This sensation persisted, kept cropping up all the time we were there. It was not an entirely new feeling, but in this setting it grew much stronger. I seemed to be living a dual existence. I would be in the middle of some simple act, I would be picking up a bait box or laying down a table fork, or I would be saying something, and suddenly it would be not I but my father who was saying the words or making the gesture. It gave me a creepy sensation.

We went fishing the next morning. I felt the same damp moss 5 covering the worms in the bait can, and saw the dragonfly alight on the tip of my rod as it hovered a few inches from the surface of the water. It was the arrival of this fly that convinced me beyond any doubt that everything was as it always had been, that the years were a mirage and that there had been no years. The small waves were the same, chucking the rowboat under the chin as we fished at anchor, and the boat was the same boat, the same color green and the ribs broken in the same places, and under the floorboards the same fresh-water leavings and débris—the dead helgramite, the wisps of moss, the rusty discarded fishhook, the dried blood from yesterday's catch. We stared silently at the tips of our rods, at the dragonflies that came and went. I lowered the tip of mine into the water, tentatively, pensively dislodging the fly, which darted two feet away, poised, darted two feet back, and came to rest again a little farther up the rod. There had been no years between the ducking of this dragonfly and the other one—the one that was part of memory. I looked at the boy, who was silently watching his fly, and it was my hands that held his rod, my eyes watching. I felt dizzy and didn't know which rod I was at the end of.

We caught two bass, hauling them in briskly as though they were mackerel, pulling them over the side of the boat in a businesslike manner without any landing net, and stunning them with a blow on the back of the head. When we got back for a swim before lunch, the lake was exactly where we had left it, the same number of inches from the dock, and there was only the merest suggestion of a breeze. This seemed an utterly enchanted sea, this lake you could leave to its own devices for a few hours and come back to, and find that it had not stirred, this constant and trustworthy body of water. In the shallows, the dark, water-soaked sticks and twigs, smooth and old, were undulating in clusters on the bottom against the clean ribbed sand, and the track of the mussel was plain. A school of minnows swam by, each minnow with its small individual shadow, doubling the attendance, so clear and sharp in the sunlight. Some of the other campers were in swimming, along the shore, one of them with a cake of soap, and the water felt thin and clear and unsubstantial. Over the years there had been this person with the cake of soap, this cultist, and here he was. There had been no years.

Up to the farmhouse to dinner through the teeming, dusty field, the road under our sneakers was only a two-track road. The middle track was missing, the one with the marks of the hooves and the splotches of dried, flaky manure. There had always been three tracks to choose from in choosing which track to walk in; now the choice was narrowed down to two. For a moment I missed terribly the middle alternative. But the way led past the tennis court, and something about the way it lay there in the sun reassured me; the tape had loosened along the backline, the alleys were green with plantains and other weeds, and the net (installed in June and removed in September) sagged in the dry noon, and the whole place steamed with midday heat and hunger and emptiness. There was a choice of pie for dessert, and one was blueberry and one was apple, and the waitresses were the same country girls, there having been no passage of time, only the illusion of it as in a dropped curtain—the waitresses were still fifteen; their hair had been washed, that was the only difference—they had been to the movies and seen the pretty girls with the clean hair.

Summertime, oh, summertime, pattern of life indelible, the fade-proof lake, the woods unshatterable, the pasture with the sweetfern and the juniper forever and ever, summer without end; this was the background, and the life along the shore was the design, the cottages with their innocent and tranquil design, their tiny docks with the flagpole and the American flag floating against the white clouds in the blue sky, the little paths over the roots of the trees leading from camp to camp and the paths leading back to the outhouses and the can of lime for sprinkling, and at the souvenir counters at the store the miniature birchbark canoes and the postcards that showed things looking a little better than they looked. This was the American family at play, escaping the city heat, wondering whether the newcomers in the camp at the head of the cove were "common" or "nice," wondering whether it was true that the people who drove up for Sunday dinner at the farmhouse were turned away because there wasn't enough chicken.

It seemed to me, as I kept remembering all this, that those times and those summers had been infinitely precious and worth saving. There had been jollity and peace and goodness. The arriving (at the beginning of August) had been so big a business in itself, at the railway station the farm wagon drawn up, the first smell of the pine-laden air, the first glimpse of the smiling farmer, and the great importance of the trunks and your father's enormous authority in such matters, and the feel of the wagon under you for the long ten-mile haul, and at the top of the last long hill catching the first view of the lake after eleven months of not seeing this cherished body of water. The shouts and cries of the other campers when they saw you, and the trunks to be unpacked, to give up their rich burden. (Arriving was less exciting nowadays, when you sneaked up in your car and parked it under a tree near the camp and took out the bags and in five minutes it was all over, no fuss, no loud wonderful fuss about trunks.)

Peace and goodness and jollity. The only thing that was wrong 10 now, really, was the sound of the place, an unfamiliar nervous sound of the outboard motors. This was the note that jarred, the one thing that would sometimes break the illusion and set the years moving. In those other summertimes all motors were inboard; and when they were at a little distance, the noise they made was a sedative, an ingredient of summer sleep. They were one-cylinder and two-cylinder engines, and some were make-and-break and some were jump-spark, but they all made a sleepy sound across the lake. The one-lungers throbbed and fluttered, and the twin-cylinder ones purred and purred, and that was a quiet sound, too. But now the campers all had outboards. In the daytime, in the hot mornings, these motors made a petulant, irritable sound; at night, in the still evening when the afterglow lit the water, they whined about one's ears like mosquitoes. My boy loved our rented outboard, and his great desire was to achieve single-handed mastery over it, and authority, and he soon learned the trick of choking it a little (but not too much), and the adjustment of the needle valve. Watching him I would remember the things you could do with the old one-cylinder engine with the heavy flywheel, how you could have it eating out of your hand if you got really close to it spiritually. Motorboats in those days didn't have clutches, and you would make a landing by shutting off the motor at the proper time and coasting in with a dead rudder. But there was a way of reversing them, if you learned the trick, by cutting the switch and putting it on again exactly on the final dying revolution of the flywheel, so that it would kick back against compression and begin reversing. Approaching a dock in a strong following breeze, it was difficult to slow up sufficiently by the ordinary coasting method, and if a boy felt he had complete mastery over his motor, he was tempted to keep it running beyond its time and then reverse it a few feet from the dock. It took a cool nerve, because if you threw the switch a twentieth of a second too soon you would catch the flywheel when it still had speed enough to go up past center, and the boat would leap ahead, charging bull-fashion at the dock.

We had a good week at the camp. The bass were biting well and the sun shone endlessly, day after day. We would be tired at night and lie down in the accumulated heat of the little bedrooms after the long hot day and the breeze would stir almost imperceptibly outside and the smell of the swamp drift in through the rusty screens. Sleep would come easily and in the morning the red squirrel would be on the roof, tapping out his gay routine. I kept remembering everything, lying in bed in the mornings—the small steamboat that had a long rounded stern like the lip of a Ubangi, and how quietly she ran on the moonlight sails, when the older boys played their mandolins and the girls sang and we ate doughnuts dipped in sugar, and how sweet the music was on the water in the shining night, and what it had felt like to think about girls then. After breakfast we would go up to the store and the things were in the same place—the minnows in a bottle, the plugs and spinners disarranged and pawed over by the youngsters from the boys' camp, the Fig Newtons and the Beeman's gum. Outside, the road was tarred and cars stood in front of the store. Inside, all was just as it had always been, except there was more Coca-Cola and not so much Moxie and root beer and birch beer and sarsaparilla. We would walk out with the bottle of pop apiece and sometimes the pop would backfire up our noses and hurt. We explored the streams, quietly, where the turtles slid off the sunny logs and dug their way into the soft bottom; and we lay on the town wharf and fed worms to the tame bass. Everywhere we went I had trouble making out which was I, the one walking at my side, the one walking in my pants.

One afternoon while we were there at that lake a thunderstorm came up. It was like the revival of an old melodrama that I had seen long ago with childish awe. The second-act climax of the drama of the electrical disturbance over a lake in America had not changed in any important respect. This was the big scene, still the big scene. The whole thing was so familiar, the first feeling of oppression and heat and a general air around camp of not wanting to go very far away. In midafternoon (it was all the same) a curious darkening of the sky, and a lull in everything that had made life tick; and then the way the boats suddenly swung the other way at their moorings with the coming of a breeze out of the new quarter, and the premonitory rumble. Then the kettle drum, then the snare, then the bass drum and cymbals, then crackling light against the dark, and the gods grinning and licking their chops in the hills. Afterward the calm, the rain steadily rustling in the calm lake, the return of light and hope and spirits, and the campers running out in joy and relief to go swimming in the rain, their bright cries perpetuating the deathless joke about how they were getting simply drenched, and the children screaming with delight at the new sensation of bathing in the rain, and the joke about getting drenched linking the generations in a strong indestructible chain. And the comedian who waded in carrying an umbrella.

When the others went swimming, my son said he was going in, too. He pulled his dripping trunks from the line where they had hung all through the shower and wrung them out. Languidly, and with no thought of going in, I watched him, his hard little body, skinny and bare, saw him wince slightly as he pulled up around his vitals the small, soggy, icy garment. As he buckled the swollen belt, suddenly my groin felt the chill of death.

For Discussion and Writing

1. Why does White describe the lake as "fade-proof" and the woods as "unshatterable" (par. 8)?

2. White uses description to give a fairly simple story great richness. Note and explain the effectiveness of five descriptive moments in the essay.

3. **connections** As long as there has been writing, the natural world has served writers as a subject in its own right and as vehicle for expressing other things. Read "Once More to the Lake" next to Brian Doyle's "Joyas Voladores" (p. 132) with this idea in mind. How does each writer use the natural world? How does each essay use nature as topic? How does each use it as vehicle?

4. Describe a childhood trip you remember well. Try to borrow descriptive devices from White.

5. **looking further** White reads the changes on and around the lake in terms of his own mortality. How else might they be read? Literary critics with ecological concerns sometimes read works of art for what they reveal about our attitudes toward the natural world and our place in it. Try to read "Once More to the Lake" in this way. What can you say about the way "nature" is thought of and treated by people within the essay as well as by its author?

COLSON WHITEHEAD

The Loser Edit

*Colson Whitehead is an American writer of fiction and nonfiction.
He is the author of six novels, including* The Intuitionist *(1999),*
John Henry Days *(2001),* Zone One *(2011), and his most recent,*
The Underground Railroad *(2016), which follows much of his earlier fiction in its focus on African American history and in its inven-
tive reimagining of the past. He has also written two books of
nonfiction, including a poker memoir,* The Noble Hustle *(2014).
Whitehead began his writing life as a reviewer at the New York alternative weekly the* Village Voice *and continues to write shorter essays
for publications such as the* New York Times Magazine *and the*
New Yorker.*

*One of Whitehead's enduring interests in his fiction is the way in
which individuals and groups construct narratives through which they
understand their lives and their history. As you read "The Loser Edit,"
think about how Whitehead pursues this interest here.*

If you have ever watched a reality TV show and said, "He's going
home tonight," you know what the "loser edit" is. I imagine it
started as a matter of practicality. If you have 20 contestants, they
can't all receive equal airtime. When an obscure character gets
the heave-ho, the producers have to cobble together a coherent
story line. Intersperse the snippets across the hour, and we can
identify sins and recognizable human frailty that need to be punished. Anyone tuning in for the first time catches up quickly. The
loser edit is not just the narrative arc of a contestant about to be
chopped, or voted off the island, whatever the catchphrase. It is
the plausible argument of failure.

The concept first bubbled up out of the pop-cultural ether
when competitive reality shows hit upon their formula, in the
form of *Survivor* and *The Amazing Race.* TV enthusiasts—part
fan, part Roland Barthes with a TiVo—congregated on online

message boards like Television Without Pity, creating a new slang
with which to dis and deconstruct their favorites.

Fifteen years later, the critical language used to carve up the
phonies, saints and sad-sack wannabes of reality shows has
migrated, and the loser edit has become a limber metaphor for
exploring our own real-world failures. Fate doles out ideas for
subplots—fire her, dump him, all species of mortification—and
we eagerly run with them, cutting loser narratives for friends and
enemies, the people we have demoted to the status of mere character. Everybody's setbacks or degradations have been foreshad-
owed if we look hard enough at the old tape. We arrange the
sequences, borrowing from cultural narratives of disgrace, sifting
through the available footage with a bit of hindsight—and in
turn, we endure our own loser edits when we stumble.

With so many media bloggers staggering under daily content
quotas, rooting through the digital-content vaults, we can now
assemble the montage of public shame more quickly than ever. A
few weeks ago, NBC told Brian Williams to pack his knives and
go. Cue the supercut of Williams spinning different accounts of
dangerous helicopter rides in Iraq, the gradual embellishments
creeping in over the years. Cue Williams in a Hurricane Katrina
documentary telling us how he heard that a man committed suicide in the Superdome, juxtaposed with an interview years later
in which he says he "watched" that suicide actually happen. *How
could we have missed it?*

It was inevitable that Bill Cosby would receive a thorough loser   5
edit after his army of accusers began stepping forward. There
were too many sleuths nosing around for clues, downloading
ancient standup routines, tapping search words into digital scans
of out-of-print books: "cocktail hour," "consent," "things America's
favorite dad said that are creepy in retrospect." Is he really joking
about dosing women with Spanish fly on a 1969 comedy album?
On a talk show in 1991? *It was right in front of us all along.* Embed
the clip, tweet it out. This Cosby edit is on VHS, recorded over the
videotape of your childhood illusions, and it cannot be undone. If
that can be erased, what else?

How stupid of them to leave all that incriminating evidence
out there.

The footage of *your* loser edit is out there as well, waiting.
Taken from the surveillance camera of the gas station where you

bought a lottery ticket like a chump. From the A.T.M. that recorded you taking out money for the romantic evening that went bust. From inside the black domes on the ceiling of the train station, the lenses that captured your slow walk up the platform stairs after the doomed excursion. From all the cameras on all the street corners, entryways and strangers' cellphones, building the digital dossier of your days. Maybe we can't clearly make out your face in every shot, but everyone knows it's you. We know you like to slump. Our entire lives as B-roll, shot and stored away to be recut and reviewed at a moment's notice when the plot changes: the divorce, the layoff, the lawsuit. Any time the producers decide to raise the stakes.

Occasionally, on a *Top Chef* or a *Project Runway*, a contestant suffers a monstrous loser edit, one that lasts a whole season. The unlucky contestant isn't sent home at the end of the night, but is instead doomed to perform personality deficits episode after episode. The supporting player trapped first by an aspect of himself or herself, and then by editors who won't let him or her escape the casting. We need a goat.

Perhaps you have a personal acquaintance with this phenomenon, slogging through months and months of your own terrible editing. The audience takes in the spectacle, pressing pause for a quick trip to the kitchen so they won't miss a second of your humiliation: this is destination television. Your co-workers rewind your loser's reel, speculating over why you didn't get that promotion, where it all started to go wrong. *If you ask me, it goes back to the Peterson account.* Your ex's buddies pass the potato chips and barely pay attention, texting pals, making jokes on Twitter—they knew before the first commercial break that you were being voted off the island. Your friends and family, who of course love you very much, are tuning in, even though they know all of your story lines by heart. They've seen this episode before. *There he goes again.*

When life gets the drop on us, we have to submit to the framing. We leave too many traces of our failures, too much material for a ruthless editor to work with. As if we didn't already have one in our heads—cutting and splicing a lifetime of bad decisions and bonehead moves into an existential montage of boobery: 10

"Why did I say that?"

"What's wrong with me?"

"Why do I keep falling for that?"

Memory is the most malicious cutter of all, preserving, recasting, panning in slow motion across the awful bits so that we retain every detail.

Can we escape our editing? In their wisdom, the philosopher-consumers of Television Without Pity also identified the loser edit's opposite number and antiparticle: the winner edit. If there's a loser edit, there has to be a winner edit. Makes sense. Over the course of a season, the inevitable winner thrives. He or she will suffer some setbacks for drama and suspense, sure, but the groundwork for victory is established challenge by challenge, week by week. It has been written, by fate or the producers, pick your deity. It cannot be reversed.

You know the golden boys and girls who sail through life without care, recipients of an enviable winner edit that lasts season after season. Untouchable. Everyone else has to do it by himself or herself, assembling our edits through a thousand compulsive Facebook tweaks, endless calibrations of Twitter personas, Instagram posts filtered of all disturbance. *Should I wear glasses in my profile pic? How do I express solidarity with the freedom fighters?* The exaggerations and elisions on your dating profile, and the ridiculous yet oddly calming amount of time you spent choosing the proper font for your résumé. *I hear employers associate Calibri with diligence and follow-through.* Marshal the flattering anecdotes, string them together into a leitmotif of confidence and sophistication. Cut when this scene establishes the perfect pitch of self-deprecation, cut before everyone can see your humility for the false modesty it is.

Do you think it's working? Did you get away with it today?

We give ourselves loser edits and winner edits all the time, to clasp meaning onto experience. Sometimes you render both kinds of edits in the same day, maybe even the same afternoon, deleting certain scenes from your memory, fooling with the contrast, as reality presses on you and directs your perceptions. Pull it off, and maybe you'll make it to bedtime. Why do you think they call it *Survivor?*

Splice and snip. The contradictory evidence falls to the cutting-room floor, and we assert order, shape a narrative, any narrative, out of the chaos. Whether you tend to give yourself a loser edit to feed that goblin part of your psyche or you fancy the winner's edit

16 COLSON WHITEHEAD

for the camouflage and safety it provides, it's better than having no arc at all. If we're going down, let us at least be a protagonist, have a story line, not be just one of those miserable players in the background. A cameo's stand-in. The loser edit, with all its savage cuts, is confirmation that you exist. The winner edit, even in its artifice, is a gesture toward optimism, the expectation of rewards waiting for that better self. Whenever he or she shows up, Take the footage you need. Burn the rest.

20

olson Whitehead, "The Loser Edit," originally published under the title "Life without Pity" from *The New York Times*, March 8, 2015 © 2015 The New York Times. All rights reserved. Used by permission and protected by the Copyright Laws of the United States. The printing, copying, redistribution, or retransmission of this Content without express written permission is prohibited.

For Discussion and Writing

1. What is a loser edit? What phenomenon outside of reality TV does Whitehead use it as a metaphor for?

2. Whitehead's work is admired in part for the strength of its style. One aspect of this style is the creation of memorable phrases. Make a list of phrases from the essay that you find memorable. What different kinds of phrases can you find? What makes them memorable? What do you think Whitehead uses them to do?

3. **connections** Whitehead makes interesting use of the second person in this essay, at times implicating his readers in a way that merely assuming they're out there (the way most essayists do) could not. Read "The Loser Edit" alongside Jamaica Kincaid's "The Ugly Tourist" (p. 206). How does each address readers? What kind of audience does each assume? To what end does each address its audience in the way it does?

4. Think of a moment when you asked yourself the kinds of questions Whitehead says we ask ourselves after the fact ("Why did I say that?"). Are there events you look back on that give you that feeling? Do you learn from moments like this? Do you try to forget them and move on?

5. **looking further** Reality TV is a relatively new phenomenon, historically, and yet it has taken over popular culture. Read up on the history of the genre and on its current manifestations, and using this research and Whitehead's essay, reflect on what the phenomenon might tell us about American culture. What kinds of stories do we find ourselves telling about ourselves and each other? What does that say about the way our society is organized, what it values, how it treats individuals?

VIRGINIA WOOLF

Professions for Women

Born Adeline Virginia Stephen in London in 1882, Virginia Woolf is one of the most important writers not just of her time but of all literary history. A modernist, Woolf, along with contemporaries such as James Joyce, T. S. Eliot, Ezra Pound, and Gertrude Stein, revolutionized literature by inventing new forms that explored the rich inner lives of their subjects. She is known especially for the novels Mrs. Dalloway *(1925) and* To the Lighthouse *(1927) but also for the nonfiction and feminist* A Room of One's Own *(1929).*

One section of A Room of One's Own *is devoted to the imagining of a sister of William Shakespeare, equally talented but, because of the possibilities available to women of her time and place, unable to create masterpieces as he had. Woolf imagines this counterfactual in order to argue for expanded possibilities for women. As you read "Professions for Women," think of it (as Woolf did) as a sequel to* A Room of One's Own, *and consider the ways it further reflects on its concerns but also raises some new ones of its own.*

When your secretary invited me to come here, she told me that your Society is concerned with the employment of women and she suggested that I might tell you something about my own professional experiences. It is true I am a woman; it is true I am employed; but what professional experiences have I had? It is difficult to say. My profession is literature; and in that profession there are fewer experiences for women than in any other, with the exception of the stage—fewer, I mean, that are peculiar to women. For the road was cut many years ago—by Fanny Burney, by Aphra Behn, by Harriet Martineau, by Jane Austen, by George Eliot—many famous women, and many more unknown and forgotten, have been before me, making the path smooth, and regulating my steps. Thus, when I came to write, there were very few material obstacles in my way. Writing was a reputable and harmless occupation. The family peace was not broken by the scratching of a pen. No demand was made upon the family purse. For ten and sixpence one can buy paper enough to write all the plays of Shakespeare—if one has a mind that way. Pianos and models, Paris, Vienna and Berlin, masters and mistresses, are not needed by a writer. The cheapness of writing paper is, of course, the reason why women have succeeded as writers before they have succeeded in the other professions.

But to tell you my story—it is a simple one. You have only got to figure to yourselves a girl in a bedroom with a pen in her hand. She had only to move that pen from left to right—from ten o'clock to one. Then it occurred to her to do what is simple and cheap enough after all—to slip a few of those pages into an envelope, fix a penny stamp in the corner, and drop the envelope into the red box at the corner. It was thus that I became a journalist; and my effort was rewarded on the first day of the following month—a very glorious day it was for me—by a letter from an editor containing a cheque for one pound ten shillings and sixpence. But to show you how little I deserve to be called a professional woman, how little I know of the struggles and difficulties of such lives, I have to admit that instead of spending that sum upon bread and butter, rent, shoes and stockings, or butcher's bills, I went out and bought a cat—a beautiful cat, a Persian cat, which very soon involved me in bitter disputes with my neighbours.

What could be easier than to write articles and to buy Persian cats with the profits? But wait a moment. Articles have to be about something. Mine, I seem to remember, was about a novel by a famous man. And while I was writing this review, I discovered that if I were going to review books I should need to do battle with a certain phantom. And the phantom was a woman, and when I came to know her better I called her after the heroine of a famous poem, The Angel in the House. It was she who used to come between me and my paper when I was writing reviews. It was she who bothered me and wasted my time and so tormented me that at last I killed her. You who come of a younger and happier generation may not have heard of her—you may not know what I mean by the Angel in the House. I will describe her as shortly as I can. She was intensely sympathetic. She was immensely charming. She was utterly unselfish. She excelled in the difficult arts of family life. She sacrificed herself daily. If there was chicken, she took the leg; if there was a draught she sat in it—in short she was so constituted that she never had a mind or a wish of her own, but preferred to sympathize always with the minds and wishes of others. Above all—I need not say it—she was pure. Her purity was supposed to be her chief beauty—her blushes, her great grace. In those days—the last of Queen Victoria—every house had its Angel. And when I came to write I encountered her with the very first words. The shadow of her wings fell on my page; I heard the rustling of her skirts in the room. Directly, that is to say, I took my pen in my hand to review that novel by a famous man, she slipped behind me and whispered: "My dear, you are a young woman. You are writing about a book that has been written by a man. Be sympathetic; be tender; flatter; deceive; use all the arts and wiles of our sex. Never let anybody guess that you have a mind of your own. Above all, be pure." And she made as if to guide my pen. I now record the one act for which I take some credit to myself, though the credit rightly belongs to some excellent ancestors of mine who left me a certain sum of money—shall we say five hundred pounds a year?—so that it was not necessary for me to depend solely on charm for my living. I turned upon her and caught her by the throat. I did my best to kill her. My excuse, if I were to be had up in a court of law, would be that I acted in self-defence. Had I not killed her she would have killed me. She would have plucked the heart out of my writing. For, as I found, directly I put pen to paper, you cannot review even a novel without having a mind of your own, without expressing what you think to be the truth about human relations, morality, sex. And all these questions, according to the Angel of the House, cannot be dealt with freely and openly by women; they must charm, they must conciliate, they must—to put it bluntly—tell lies if they are to succeed. Thus, whenever I felt the shadow of her wing or the radiance of her halo upon my page, I took up the inkpot and flung it at her. She died hard. Her fictitious nature was of great assistance to her. It is far harder to kill a phantom than a reality. She was always creeping back when I thought I had despatched her. Though I flatter myself that I killed her in the end, the struggle was severe; it took much time that had better have been spent upon learning Greek grammar; or in roaming the world in search of adventures. But it was a real experience; it was an experience that was bound to befall all women writers at that time. Killing the Angel in the House was part of the occupation of a woman writer.

But to continue my story. The Angel was dead; what then remained? You may say that what remained was a simple and common object—a young woman in a bedroom with an inkpot. In other words, now that she had rid herself of falsehood, that young woman had only to be herself. Ah, but what is "herself"? I mean, what is a woman? I assure you, I do not know. I do not believe that you know. I do not believe that anybody can know until she has expressed herself in all the arts and professions open to human skill. That indeed is one of the reasons why I have come here out of respect for you, who are in process of showing us by your experiments what a woman is, who are in process of providing us, by your failures and successes, with that extremely important piece of information.

But to continue the story of my professional experiences. I   5
made one pound ten and six by my first review; and I bought a Persian cat with the proceeds. Then I grew ambitious. A Persian cat is all very well, I said; but a Persian cat is not enough. I must have a motor car. And it was thus that I became a novelist—for it is a very strange thing that people will give you a motor car if you will tell them a story. It is a still stranger thing that there is nothing so delightful in the world as telling stories. It is far pleasanter than writing reviews of famous novels. And yet, if I am to obey your secretary and tell you my professional experiences as a novelist, I must tell you about a very strange experience that befell me as a novelist. And to understand it you must try first to imagine a novelist's state of mind. I hope I am not giving away professional secrets if I say that a novelist's chief desire is to be as unconscious as possible. He has to induce in himself a state of perpetual lethargy. He wants life to proceed with the utmost quiet and regularity. He wants to see the same faces, to read the same books, to do the same things day after day, month after month, while he is writing, so that nothing may break the illusion in which he is living—so that nothing may disturb or disquiet the mysterious nosings about, feelings round, darts, dashes and sudden discoveries of that very shy and illusive spirit, the imagination. I suspect that this state is the same both for men and women. Be that as it may, I want you to imagine me writing a novel in a

state of trance. I want you to figure to yourselves a girl sitting with a pen in her hand, which for minutes, and indeed for hours, she never dips into the inkpot. The image that comes to my mind when I think of this girl is the image of a fisherman lying sunk in dreams on the verge of a deep lake with a rod held out over the water. She was letting her imagination sweep unchecked round every rock and cranny of the world that lies submerged in the depths of our unconscious being. Now came the experience, the experience that I believe to be far commoner with women writers than with men. The line raced through the girl's fingers. Her imagination had rushed away. It had sought the pools, the depths, the dark places where the largest fish slumber. And then there was a smash. There was an explosion. There was foam and confusion. The imagination had dashed itself against something hard. The girl was roused from her dream. She was indeed in a state of the most acute and difficult distress. To speak without figure she had thought of something, something about the body, about the passions which it was unfitting for her as a woman to say. Men, her reason told her, would be shocked. The consciousness of—what men will say of a woman who speaks the truth about her passions had roused her from her artist's state of unconsciousness. She could write no more. The trance was over. Her imagination could work no longer. This I believe to be a very common experience with women writers—they are impeded by the extreme conventionality of the other sex. For though men sensibly allow themselves great freedom in these respects, I doubt that they realize or can control the extreme severity with which they condemn such freedom in women.

These then were two very genuine experiences of my own. These were two of the adventures of my professional life. The first—killing the Angel in the House—I think I solved. She died. But the second, telling the truth about my own experiences as a body, I do not think I solved. I doubt that any woman has solved it yet. The obstacles against her are still immensely powerful—and yet they are very difficult to define. Outwardly, what is simpler than to write books? Outwardly, what obstacles are there for a woman rather than for a man? Inwardly, I think, the case is very different; she has still many ghosts to fight, many prejudices to overcome. Indeed it will be a long time still, I think, before a woman can sit down to write a book without finding a phantom

to be slain, a rock to be dashed against. And if this is so in literature, the freest of all professions for women, how is it in the new
professions which you are now for the first time entering?

Those are the questions that I should like, had I time, to ask
you. And indeed, if I have laid stress upon these professional
experiences of mine, it is because I believe that they are, though
in different forms, yours also. Even when the path is nominally
open—when there is nothing to prevent a woman from being a
doctor, a lawyer, a civil servant—there are many phantoms and
obstacles, as I believe, looming in her way. To discuss and define
them is I think of great value and importance; for thus only can
the labour be shared, the difficulties be solved. But besides this, it
is necessary also to discuss the ends and the aims for which we
are fighting, for which we are doing battle with these formidable
obstacles. Those aims cannot be taken for granted; they must be
perpetually questioned and examined. The whole position, as I
see it—here in this hall surrounded by women practising for the
first time in history I know not how many different professions—is one of extraordinary interest and importance. You have
won rooms of your own in the house hitherto exclusively owned
by men. You are able, though not without great labour and effort,
to pay the rent. You are earning your five hundred pounds a year.
But this freedom is only a beginning—the room is your own, but
it is still bare. It has to be furnished; it has to be decorated; it has
to be shared. How are you going to furnish it, how are you going
to decorate it? With whom are you going to share it, and upon
what terms? These, I think are questions of the utmost importance and interest. For the first time in history you are able to ask
them; for the first time you are able to decide for yourselves what
the answers should be. Willingly would I stay and discuss those
questions and answers—but not to-night. My time is up; and I
must cease.

For Discussion and Writing

1. What is the Angel in the House?
2. Think about narrative form in this essay. Woolf claims early in it that
   her story "is a simple one" (par. 2). Is it? If not, how does she complicate it? Why does she claim early on that it is?

3. **connections**   Woolf asks, "[W]hat is a woman?" (par. 4) not in isolation but as part of her story of becoming a writer. Read this essay alongside Joan Didion's "On Keeping a Notebook" (p. 116). How is Didion's essay in part implicitly about the explicit subject of Woolf's essay? Where do you think Didion's exploration of the story of her writing life touches on the same concerns as Woolf's? Is there an Angel in Didion's house?

4. On one of her motivations for becoming a novelist, Woolf writes, "[I]t is a very strange thing that people will give you a motor car if you will tell them a story" (par. 5). While it is a luxury to do work that you love, if you could choose a profession purely out of interest, while being realistic (e.g., no professional basketball players) and selecting something that would pay (give you a motor car), what would it be? Why? Do you think you will end up doing it? Why, or why not?

5. **looking further**   Find one or two examples of people who have successfully built careers in the field you would like to work in. They can be famous enough to have online biographies you can consult or they can be people you interview. How did they get there? What did they have to do in terms of schooling, training, and other work to prepare themselves and gain entry into their field? What obstacles did they encounter, and how did they overcome them?

DAVE ZIRIN

Pre-Game

Dave Zirin is an American sportswriter. He writes about the politics of professional and college sports for the magazine the Nation. *He also hosts one podcast called* Edge of Sports *and cohosts another. Zirin is the author of eight books on the history and politics of sports, including books on John Carlos, Muhammad Ali, and the economics of team ownership.*

"Pre-Game" is drawn from Zirin's 2013 book Game Over: How Politics Has Turned the Sports World Upside Down. *As you read, keep that subtitle in mind, in particular the historical narrative it implies—that things are changing in sports—and watch for how that narrative appears in the essay.*

In March 2012, the Miami Heat chose to put down their basketballs and put on their hoodies. As a team, they stood shoulder to shoulder and did what we are told athletes no longer do: made a conscious political stand for justice. The entire Heat roster—from stars LeBron James, Dwyane Wade, and Chris Bosh to South Dakota's Mike Miller to the nearly forty-year-old reserve Juwan Howard—stood as one for seventeen-year-old Trayvon Martin, who had been recently killed by armed self-appointed "neighborhood watch leader" George Zimmerman. While Martin's killer had a nine-millimeter, the teenager had nothing but a pack of Skittles and a can of Arizona iced tea in his pocket. Trayvon was wearing a hoodie when he died, which some pundits in their infinite wisdom believed made him "suspicious" and worthy of being pursued.

Of all the teams in the league, the Heat were the most shocking yet also most appropriate to step up and be heard. It was shocking because the Heat are often painted as being a collection of prima donnas, as allegedly superficial as the town they call home. It was also appropriate because this was Trayvon's favorite team, and he was killed after leaving his house during halftime of the NBA All-Star Game, where he was watching James and Wade perform.

Given the outrage over Trayvon Martin's death, particularly in southern Florida, the Heat's powerful gesture hardly came out of the blue. What may be surprising for many fans is that "the King" himself, LeBron James, drove the effort. The March 2012 team photo was reportedly James's idea and was first posted to his personal Twitter account with the hashtag #WeWantJustice.

James later said, "It was very emotional, an emotional day for all of us. Taking that picture, we're happy that we're able to shed light on the situation that we feel is unjust." His teammate Wade commented to the Associated Press, "This situation hit home for me because last Christmas, all my oldest son wanted as a gift was hoodies. So when I heard about this a week ago, I thought of my sons. I'm speaking up because I feel it's necessary that we get past the stereotype of young, black men."

Since he was a teenager, "King James" has been pegged as potentially the greatest basketball player alive. He's a Fortune 500 company with legs and, thus far, has a very carefully crafted apolitical image. He is also someone who was raised by a single mother in Akron, Ohio, at times so poor that they were living in a car. He has everything, as well as memories of having had nothing. Perhaps this is why he once said that his dream is to be "a global icon like Muhammad Ali." We've rarely seen evidence of his efforts to achieve this dream, but the hoodie photo could be a result of the Ali in him straining to be heard.

At the Heat's home game the following Friday night, James and several of his teammates took the floor with messages such as "RIP Trayvon Martin" and "We want justice" scrawled on their sneakers. Their actions inspired others across the NBA. Players spanning the gamut—from stars, like Steve Nash and Carmelo Anthony, to less famous jocks, such as Will Bynum and Brandon Knight—spoke out to raise awareness. Anthony, the high-profile star of the New York Knicks, changed his own Twitter picture to show him in a hoodie with "I am Trayvon Martin" superimposed over his body.

Detroit Pistons center Greg Monroe explained to the *Detroit Free Press* why so many players wanted to say something. "These kids come from the same neighborhoods we walked—or worse. And we see the same news everybody sees. When we turn on CNN, we don't have a special CNN channel. When we get pulled over, there's no special millionaire cops. We're just paid to play basketball."

To put it a different way, athletes aren't cartoon characters or robots. They are a part of this world. We are often told that today's athletes have no stake, as their forebears did, in fighting for change. At one time, athletes, particularly athletes of color and women athletes, had a self-interest in broader struggles against discrimination, but no longer. The argument goes that we are now somehow a "postracial, postpolitical" society. But while there are more people than ever telling us that the world has changed, injustice, discrimination, and inequality of opportunity still rule the land.

In the real world, any change at all has been incremental and hard-won. In the sports world, there's been a different kind of change and it couldn't be more dramatic. Over the last thirty years, the athletic-industrial complex has transformed itself into a trillion-dollar, global entity. One way it's done this is by making its product and its players as explicitly apolitical as possible. From Peyton Manning to Derek Jeter to Danica Patrick, the dominant message projected by athletes has been that it's far more important to be a brand than an individual, and that a modern jock should never sacrifice commercial concerns for political principle. This credo echoes Jesse Owens, the great Olympic star, who once said, "The only time the black fist has significance is when there's money inside."

ESPN, twenty-four-hour talk radio, and a seemingly bottom-less appetite for distraction have exploded the size of our sports world—and its profits—into the stratosphere. In conjunction with this expansion, politics has also been actively discouraged by management and slammed by sports columnists. Legendary sportscaster Howard Cosell toward the end of his life dubbed it rule number one of "the jockocracy": sports and politics just don't mix.

Yet over the last several years, the specter of politics has been haunting sports. Cosell's Golden Rule has been repeatedly and flagrantly breached. More athletes are speaking out across the political spectrum as a series of revolutions, occupations, and protests

10

has defined the global landscape. The real world is gaining on the sports world and the sports world is starting to look over its shoulder. . . . As I hope to show, whether we see ourselves as sports fans or not, we all have a stake in understanding why the sports page is insufficient for understanding sports.

THE WALL BETWEEN SPORTS AND POLITICS IS BREACHED

On Cinco de Mayo in 2010, the NBA's Phoenix Suns went where no American sports team had gone before. In their playoff game against the San Antonio Spurs, the squad took to the court wearing jerseys that read simply "Los Suns." They were coming out as one against Arizona's Senate Bill 1070, which critics said would codify racial profiling by criminalizing anyone suspected of being an undocumented immigrant. This was the first time in U.S. sports history that an entire team—from owner to general manager to players—had expressed any kind of unified political stance. This audacious move by the Suns was perhaps the most publicized moment of a low-frequency sea change in the world of sports.

There were the members of the Green Bay Packers who stood—and continue to stand—behind the workers of Wisconsin under attack by the state's Governor Scott Walker.

There were the soccer players and clubs in the Middle East who played a leading role in the Arab Spring and, with unprecedented impact, are helping shape their revolutions.

There were the two NFL players—Pro Bowler Brendon 15 Ayanbadejo and New Orleans Saints Super Bowl hero Scott Fujita—who spoke out in favor of LGBT marriage equality in the fall of 2009. (They have been joined by basketball star Steve Nash, New England Patriot Rob Gronkowski, New York Giant Michael Strahan, New York Ranger Sean Avery, Charles Barkley, Michael Irvin, and other players willing to speak out on what was recently a taboo locker room subject.)

Other political explosions have recently detonated inside the world of sports. Labor lockouts in the NFL and NBA have brought a taste of the broader economic crisis that provoked the Occupy movement into this supposedly privileged space. The explosive child-molestation charges at Penn State University and broader issues of corruption in the NCAA have raised political questions that speak to the very role we expect our universities to play. College athletes in the "revenue-producing" sports of football and basketball have signed petitions to form organizations and unshackle themselves from an ugly, utterly corrupt system.

Discussions about Tim Tebow, Jeremy Lin, Caster Semenya, and many others have created a buzz and a dialogue beyond the confines of sports radio. When Boston Bruins goalie Tim Thomas turned down the team's invitation to go to the White House after they won the 2011 Stanley Cup, he wasn't content with quiet protest and instead posted a Tea Party–influenced monologue on his Facebook page. When Joel Ward, a black player for the Washington Capitals, scored a playoff-clinching goal on Thomas in 2012, the racist bile on Twitter was so intense that players and the media felt compelled to respond.

The more recent political eruptions are in many respects a hangover from the 2008 elections, when an unprecedented number of athletes went public in support of Barack Obama's candidacy and the efforts to elect an African American president. Some of the most commercially successful—and therefore some of the most commercially vulnerable—jocks became involved in the campaign. LeBron James wore Obama T-shirts to games and all-star players like Baron Davis and Chauncey Billups vocally supported his candidacy. Boston Celtics star Kevin Garnett wore sneakers with "Vote for Change" scrawled on their sides. Then Denver Nuggets star Carmelo Anthony pledged that he would score forty-four points in a game in honor of the future forty-fourth president (he only scored twenty-eight, which was, one can assume, not a tribute to Woodrow Wilson). When Billups was asked if he was concerned that his public support of Obama would hurt his endorsement chances, he said, "Like I give a shit."

As it turns out, a whole new generation of "Jocks for Justice" is rejecting the yoke of apathy and speaking out about the world. NBA players like Nash, Etan Thomas, and Joakim Noah, as well as NFL players Scott Fujita and Adalius Thomas, raised objections against the U.S. war in Iraq. Even Ultimate Fighting champion Jeff "the Snowman" Monson took to distributing antiwar pamphlets on his way to the "Octagon" and was arrested protesting at the 2008 Republican National Convention. As Martina Navratilova said to *Sports Illustrated* in 2008, "It's like athletes

have woken up to what actors and musicians have known forever:
I have this amazing platform—why not use it?"

These small acts of solidarity may seem negligible—but they   20
matter. Whether we like it or not, athletes are role models; it's
worth asking, then, what are they in fact modeling?

While not every athlete acts like his life's ambition off the playing field is to be featured on *MTV Cribs*, the media loves to highlight the salacious and scandalous. It's not just the worst
examples, like football player Ben Roethlisberger, who was investigated twice for rape, or Adam "Pac Man" Jones getting in trouble
with the law at "gentleman's clubs." As a rule, the pro athletes
who engage in the most mindless conspicuous consumption are
the ones who tend to be highlighted.

If, instead of modeling crass materialism, more athletes chose
to display a broader sense of community awareness—no matter
the issue or politics—we'd all be better off. Even when I personally disagree with the politics of an athlete (see Tim Tebow), the
mere fact that he is saying anything has the potential to initiate
a dialogue more full and involving than anything we get from
Capitol Hill.

Having athletes risk their prime perch in society for the greater
good also becomes a kind of weather vane, a crackling signal that
we have entered a new era. In 1968, political struggle was part of
the oxygen of the sports world. The people and the games we
watched were shaped by the struggles in the streets.

In a time that has seen revolts from the Middle East to the Midwest, we can look at the facts on the ground and note that the citadel of American sports has also been breached. The apolitical
1990s were dubbed the "vacation from history." Well, vacation is
over and history has returned with a vengeance—severe enough
to cross the moat and enter the locker room.

Why are more athletes speaking out? Some point to social   25
media as a critical delivery system for a generation of athletes
who don't trust "old school" reporters. Hundred-and-forty-
character bursts and Facebook posts offer the ability to speak
without a filter directly to fans.

Another theory is that players are now actually encouraged, for
commercial reasons, to "define their own brand." I spoke at a
seminar for NBA rookies where the dominant theme was how
players could distinguish themselves and create a memorable

persona for their audience. Just repeating clichés by rote, like "We give 150 percent and play one game at a time," is now seen as a liability. But the most compelling reason is simply, as Greg Monroe said, that the world is changing and athletes are a part of that world.

But speaking out still has a cost. We saw this in May 2011, after al-Qaeda leader and "9/11 mastermind" Osama bin Laden was killed by U.S. Navy SEALs. In the aftermath of his assassination, the sports world embraced the public eruption of patriotism. From the spontaneous cheers of forty thousand fans in Philadelphia to amped "Military Appreciation Night" celebrations at stadiums around the country, the sports world exulted in the euphoria of bin Laden's dramatic demise.

Yet some athletes dared to buck the trend—and, in the process, learned a tough lesson about the limits of free speech in the jockocracy. Chris Douglas-Roberts, former Memphis basketball all-American and Milwaukee Buck, responded to bin Laden's death with a litany of reasons why he wasn't joining the party, tweeting, among other things, "It took 919,967 deaths to kill that one guy. It took 10 years & 2 Wars to kill that guy. It cost us (USA) roughly $1,188,263,000,000 to kill that guy. But we winning though. Haaaa. (Sarcasm)."

Profanity, threats, and the general belief that he was "stupid" and a "moron" who should shut his "dumb [expletive] mouth" because he is "not intelligent" came rolling in. Douglas-Roberts tried to hit back, tweeting: "What I'm sayin has nothing to do with 9/11 or that guy (Bin Laden). I still feel bad for the 9/11 families but I feel EQUALLY bad for the war families. . . . People are telling me to get out of America now b/c I'm against MORE INNOCENT people dying everyday? B/c I'm against a 10 year WAR? Whatever happened to our freedom of speech? What I've learned tonight, athletes shouldn't have perspectives. But I don't care. We feel certain ways about things TOO."

Rashard Mendenhall, the Pro Bowl running back for the 30 Pittsburgh Steelers, raised eyebrows even higher with his comments, writing, "[For] those of you who said you want to see Bin Laden burn in hell and piss on his ashes, I ask how would God feel about your heart? . . . What kind of person celebrates death?" Mendenhall then took it further and voiced his doubts about the official story of the 9/11 attacks, causing *Sports Illustrated*'s senior football writer Don Banks to write a piece titled "Mendenhall Just the Latest NFL Player to Spout Utter Nonsense."

The outrage intensified to the point where Steelers president Art Rooney II, a big money bundler for President Obama and the U.S. ambassador to Ireland, had to actually issue a formal statement about a tweet, writing, "I have not spoken with Rashard so it is hard to explain or even comprehend what he meant with his recent Twitter comments. The entire Steelers' organization is very proud of the job our military personnel have done and we can only hope this leads to our troops coming home soon."

Whether or not you supported some or all the wars of the last decade, it should be clear that the guardians of jock culture are trying to teach athletes a lesson: you have signed away your right to have an opinion beyond your choice of sneaker or sports drink. This is something that runs very deeply in the marrow of our sports world: the idea that athletes, particularly athletes of color, should just "shut up and play."

Douglas-Roberts and Mendenhall also unintentionally exposed the most bizarre contradiction of this no-politics rule. Players are strongly encouraged by management, family, and the media to follow the rules and "never talk politics" — but whether we choose to acknowledge it or not, a politically charged atmosphere pervades all of professional sports. I don't just say that because I live in a town where people root for a team called the Redskins. I say so because at every sporting event we are encouraged to collectively celebrate the displays of nationalism, patriotism, and military might that festoon every corner. In addition, the politics of big business and big sponsorship deals saturate sports arenas. At one point, baseball owners wanted to put ads for *Spider-Man 2* on every second base, and only backed away when fans erupted in outrage. Even college football players, so-called amateurs, are trussed in ads to a degree that would shame NASCAR. If only the owners of pro sports teams could create a red, white, and blue beer, they might collectively keel over in joy.

But throughout history, we've also seen athletes take this setup and stand it on its head. This has happened when they have used their exalted, hypercommercialized platform to say something about the world and then dare those in power to shut them up. There is a reason we associate people like Jackie Robinson with the civil rights movement; Muhammad Ali with the 1960s; Billie

Jean King with the women's movement; or 1968 Olympian Tom Waddell, the founder of the Gay Games, with LGBT rights. This history indicates that sports is never just a spectacle—that it has a potential to tap into sentiments for social change.

Our sports culture shapes societal attitudes, relationships, and 35 power arrangements. It is where cultural meanings—our very notions of who we are and how we see each other, not only as Americans but also as individuals—play out. It frames the ways in which we understand and discuss issues of gender, race, and class. And, as ever, it is crucial for understanding how these norms and power structures have been negotiated, struggled with, and resisted.

For Discussion and Writing

1. What does Zirin mean when he claims that athletes "are a part of this world" (par. 8)? In what way could people think athletes are not a part of this world? What does it mean for Zirin that they are?

2. Rather than presenting both sides disinterestedly, Zirin takes a strong position in "Pre-Game." How does he take that position? List five or six ways in which he presses his point. Does he argue from evidence and proof or through use of rhetoric, or some combination of the two?

3. **connections** The surge in political awareness and political speech among the athletes Zirin describes in "Pre-Game" is significant, but what does Zirin have to say about its effect? Think about this question in the light of Malcolm Gladwell's "Small Change" (p. 169). Social media play a role in many of the moments of protest Zirin discusses; would they have had the same impact without the Internet? How might Zirin respond to Gladwell?

4. College and professional sports in the United States are billion-dollar industries. In 2013, networks paid a total of $20.4 billion for the broadcast rights to National Football League games. How do you feel about the place of sports in society that this fact reflects? Are you a fan, do you question national priorities, or do you not care? Do you think there are positive or negative ramifications for the place sports hold in our economy and culture?

5. **looking further** Zirin alludes to the controversy over the name of the Washington, DC, National Football League team. Research this issue, summarizing the arguments on both sides and listing the positions taken for and against. Based on your research, where do you stand? Why?

Documentation Guide

Engaging with the work of others is an important part of academic writing. When writing formal essays about the works in *50 Essays*, or when you refer in your writing to other outside sources, you need to acknowledge these sources. When you summarize, paraphrase, or quote outside sources in your writing, it is crucial that you properly acknowledge them. It is important for two reasons. First, it demonstrates that you are joining the intellectual discussion, writing not just about your own ideas and about your own experience but in conversation with the ideas and experiences of others. Second, it is your ethical responsibility to acknowledge when the words and ideas that appear in your work do not originate with you; if you don't, you will be guilty of plagiarism, a serious academic offense carrying serious consequences and also an act of dishonesty.

Documentation is the word for the activity of acknowledging sources. There are different systems or styles of documentation; the style most often used in English and the humanities is that recommended by the Modern Language Association (MLA). Below are some examples of the most common kinds of documentation in MLA style; consult the *MLA Handbook*, eighth edition, at style/mla .org for additional information and models.

MLA PARENTHETICAL CITATIONS

MLA style is fairly simple. When you need to cite a source, you do so in a parenthetical in-text citation. Rather than use footnotes or endnotes, you insert, before the period at the end of the sentence, a parenthetical reference that lets readers know the source and, usually, where in the source the particular material can be found. If the source is clear from the sentence itself, you need only include a page number in parentheses; if the source is not clear, including the author's name along with the page number will be enough to allow the reader to find the source in the list of works cited, which you will include at the end of your essay (guidelines for which follow this section). Below are some examples of the most common kinds of parenthetical citations. There are a number of exceptions to these general rules; you'll find these below too.

ONE AUTHOR

The Emigrants begins: "At the end of September 1970, shortly before I took up my position in Norwich, I drove out to Hingham with Clara in search of somewhere to live" (Sebald 3).

TWO AUTHORS

According to the Enlightenment, "thinking is the creation of unified, scientific order and the derivation of factual knowledge from principles" (Horkheimer and Adorno 83).

THREE OR MORE AUTHORS

As one letter to the editor of an intellectual journal put it: "Eighteen months later, the CIA is still stonewalling" (Blakey et al. 65).

UNKNOWN AUTHOR

Of the avian flu, a recent editorial states: "Nobody has the foggiest idea whether a pandemic will arrive in the near future or how severe one might be, but federal officials argue, persuasively, that we have to brace ourselves for the worst" ("Vaccine Capacity" A22).

SOURCE WITHOUT PAGE NUMBERS

As a recent article on the Web periodical *Inside Higher Education* explains, in many federal agencies, "it is standard practice for external groups to formally ask officials to begin a process to review a specific rule or set of rules" (Lederman).

INDIRECT SOURCE

In his autobiography, Ford wrote, "If I'm remembered, it will probably be for healing the land" (qtd. in Patterson 94).

MLA LIST OF WORKS CITED

The works cited list is the place where your reader can go to find out more information about the sources cited in your parenthetical citations. Follow these guidelines for the format for this list, which should be given its own page or pages: it should be organized alphabetically by author's last name or first major word in the title; it should be double-spaced; each entry should begin at the left margin; and the second (and all following) lines of an entry should be indented one tab (or five spaces, or one half inch).

Books

ONE AUTHOR

Cohen, Samuel. *After the End of History: American Fiction in the 1990s*. U of Iowa P, 2009.

TWO AUTHORS

Mohlenbrock, Robert H., and Paul M. Thomson, Jr. *Flowering Plants: Smartweeds to Hazelnuts*. 2nd ed., Southern Illinois UP, 2009.

THREE OR MORE AUTHORS

Cunningham, Stewart, et al. *Media Economics*. Palgrave Macmillan, 2015.

TWO OR MORE BOOKS BY THE SAME AUTHOR

García, Cristina. *Dreams of Significant Girls*. Simon and Schuster, 2011.

---. *The Lady Matador's Hotel*. Scribner, 2010.

BOOK WITH AN EDITOR OR TRANSLATOR

Ullmann, Regina. *The Country Road: Stories*. Translated by Kurt Beals, New Directions Publishing, 2015.

WORK IN AN ANTHOLOGY

Hughes, Langston. "Salvation." *50 Essays*, edited by Samuel Cohen, 5th ed., Bedford/St. Martin's, 2017, pp. 185–87.

MULTIVOLUME WORK

Stark, Freya. *Letters*. Edited by Lucy Moorehead, Compton Press, 1974–82. 8 vols.

EDITION OTHER THAN THE FIRST

Eagleton, Terry. *Literary Theory: An Introduction*. 3rd ed., U of Minnesota P, 2008.

Periodicals

ARTICLE IN A JOURNAL

Matchie, Thomas. "Law versus Love in *The Round House*." *Midwest Quarterly*, vol. 56, no. 4, Summer 2015, pp. 353–64.

ARTICLE IN A MONTHLY MAGAZINE

Bryan, Christy. "Ivory Worship." *National Geographic*, Oct. 2012, pp. 28–61.

ARTICLE IN A WEEKLY MAGAZINE

Grossman, Lev. "A Star Is Born." *Time*, 2 Nov. 2015, pp. 30–39.

ARTICLE IN A NEWSPAPER

Bray, Hiawatha. "As Toys Get Smarter, Privacy Issues Emerge." *The Boston Globe*, 10 Dec. 2015, p. C1.

EDITORIAL OR LETTER TO THE EDITOR

"The Road toward Peace." *The New York Times*, 15 Feb. 1945, p. 18. Editorial.

Electronic Sources

ENTIRE WEB SITE

Transparency International. *Transparency International: The Global Coalition against Corruption*. 2015, www.transparency.org/.

SHORT WORK FROM A WEB SITE

"Social and Historical Context: Vitality." *Arapesh Grammar and Digital
Language Archive Project*, Institute for Advanced Technology in the
Humanities, www.arapesh.org/socio_historical_context_vitality.php.
Accessed 22 Mar. 2016.

WORK FROM A SUBSCRIPTION SERVICE

Fahey, John A. "Recalling the Cuban Missile Crisis." *The Washington Post*, 28
Oct. 2012, p. A16. Letter. *LexisNexis Library Express*, www.lexisnexis
.com/hottopics/lnpubliclibraryexpress/.

ONLINE BOOK

Piketty, Thomas. *Capital in the Twenty-First Century*. Translated by Arthur
Goldhammer, Harvard UP, 2014. *Google Books*, books.google.com
/books?isbn=0674369556.

ARTICLE IN AN ONLINE PERIODICAL

Leonard, Andrew. "The Surveillance State High School." *Salon*, 27 Nov.
2012, www.salon.com/2012/11/27/the_surveillance_state_high
_school/.

E-MAIL

Thornbrugh, Caitlin. "Coates Lecture." Received by Rita Anderson, 20 Oct.
2015. E-mail.

Other Sources

ADVERTISEMENT

AT&T. *National Geographic*, Dec. 2015, p. 14. Advertisement.

INTERVIEW

Putin, Vladimir. Interview by Charlie Rose. *Charlie Rose: The Week*, PBS, 19
June 2015.

GOVERNMENT DOCUMENT

United States, Department of Agriculture, Food and Nutrition Service, Child
Nutrition Programs. *Eligibility Manual for School Meals: Determining
and Verifying Eligibility. National School Lunch Program*, July 2015,
www.fns.usda.gov/sites/default/files/cn/SP40_CACFP18_SFSP20
-2015a1.pdf.

FILM, VIDEO, OR DVD

Scott, Ridley, director. *The Martian*. Performances by Matt Damon, Jessica
Chastain, Kristen Wiig, and Kate Mara, Twentieth Century Fox, 2015.

TELEVISION OR RADIO PROGRAM

"Free Speech on College Campuses." *Washington Journal*, narrated by Peter
Slen, C-SPAN, 27 Nov. 2015.

Glossary of Writing Terms

Allusion A reference to an artistic work, person, place, or event about which readers are assumed to already know. The relevance of the reference is also not usually explained: Readers are assumed to understand the connection between the writer's subject and the thing referred to. As a result of these assumptions, allusion is an economical way of making a point, as it crams a lot of information into a few words. When Judith Ortiz Cofer, in "The Myth of the Latin Woman: I Just Met a Girl Named Maria" (p. 103), refers to popular songs (as she does in her title, to a song from the musical *West Side Story*), she is making allusions—assuming that we will be familiar with her references and that we will understand the connections she is trying to make between popular songs and stereotypes.

Analogy An extended comparison. An analogy explains features of one thing by reference to features shared with something more commonly known and understood. In "A Modest Proposal" (p. 353), Jonathan Swift makes an analogy between the treatment of the poor in Ireland and a hypothetical, imagined treatment that would be unthinkable and impossible, but, if considered in a certain way, is not far from what is actually happening to them. Swift presents the analogy indirectly—it may not be until you are far into the essay until you realize what he's doing—but the power of the connection is the greater for it.

Argument Writing that attempts to prove a point through reasoning. Argument presses its case by using logic and by supporting its logic with examples and **evidence**. When Thomas Jefferson, in "The Declaration of Independence" (p. 193), makes his case for why the American colonies should be given their independence, he introduces his list like this: "The history of the present King of Great Britain is a history of repeated injuries and usurpations, all having in direct object the establishment of an absolute Tyranny over these States. To prove this, let Facts be submitted to a candid world" (par. 6). Making a **claim** and then making the transition to supporting examples, Jefferson's writing is argument.

Audience   As actors have audiences who can see and hear them, writers have readers. Having a sense of audience is important in writing because we write differently depending on who we think will be reading our work. If the audience is specific, we write in such a way that will appeal to a small group; if it is general, we write in such a way that as many people as possible will listen to, and be able to hear, what we have to say. It is especially easy to see considerations of audience in speeches, as in public documents such as Thomas Jefferson's Declaration of Independence (p. 193), but it can also be seen in works in which writers are trying to explain their experiences to readers who might not have had such experiences themselves, as in Brent Staples's "Just Walk on By: Black Men and Public Space" (p. 339).

Cause and effect   Analysis of events or situations in which reasons are sought and effects are considered. Writers tracing the chain of events leading to a present situation or arguing the consequences of a future decision are doing cause and effect writing. In "Why Don't We Complain?" (p. 72), William F. Buckley Jr. makes his focus on cause and effect explicit: he is asking what the cause of a particular phenomenon is—"why" it exists. Over the course of his essay, he describes the phenomenon, offers examples of it, and attempts to venture some possible explanations of the cause of it, as many cause and effect essays do. In this case, the cause of a behavior—failure or reluctance to complain— is explained by a larger cultural development: an increased sense of helplessness. He then goes on to explain *that* phenomenon as the product of even larger historical developments: technologization and centralization of political and economic power. To take exception to Buckley's argument, one thus has to refute at least two layers of cause and effect explanations.

Claim   What an argument tries to prove; often called a **thesis**. In "The Paranoid Style of American Policing" (p. 99), Ta-Nehisi Coates makes an argument that police violence against the community delegitimizes the police force in the eyes of the people. His claim is straightforward: when citizens cannot trust the police, the system is broken. Supporting that claim requires evidence and the well-reasoned addressing of opposing viewpoint, but the claim itself remains simple and clear.

Classification and division   The sorting out of elements into classes or groups, or the separation of something into its parts. Classification and division are used when a writer wants to break something down into its elements or group a number of things in order to analyze them. When Mike Rose talks about different kinds of teachers and students in " 'I Just Wanna Be Average' " (p. 313), he is classifying; when Amy Tan in "Mother

Tongue" (p. 362) breaks down her language use into the various Englishes she uses, she is dividing.

Cliché An old, tired expression that writers should avoid like the plague. "Like the plague" is an example of cliché. When drafting and especially when revising, writers scan their work for words and phrases that have that less-than-fresh feeling and strike them out. "Like the plague," for example, can be replaced with a new, concrete image, which "like the plague" must have been at one time (closer to the time of the plague itself, perhaps). The uniqueness of a writer's voice comes in part from the words chosen. Using well-worn, often-chosen phrases can be thought of, then, as a lost opportunity.

Comparison and contrast Examination of similarities and differences. One usually but not always appears with the other. Bharati Mukherjee's "Two Ways to Belong in America" (p. 267) shows in its first sentence that differences often arise between similar things, and so that comparison and contrast often go together: "This is a tale of two sisters from Calcutta, Mira and Bharati, who have lived in the United States for some 35 years, but who find themselves on different sides in the current debate over the status of immigrants" (par. 1).

Conclusion The ending of an **essay**, which should bring the writer's point home in a few sentences or even a **paragraph** or two. Good conclusions do more than repeat a **thesis**, and they can even sometimes point the way to extensions of the thesis, but they should not introduce entirely new thoughts. Conclusions can also be funny, as when Swift, at the end of "A Modest Proposal" (p. 353), insists he has no personal interest at stake in his **ironic** proposal that the people of Ireland eat their infants as, in his words, "I have no children by which I can propose to get a single penny; the youngest being nine years old, and my wife past childbearing" (par. 33).

Definition Explanation of the nature of a word, thing, or idea. **Essays** that define may use many other kinds of writing, such as **description**, **exposition**, and **narration**. Definition essays often are really redefinition essays: they attempt to make us understand something we thought we already understood. When Nancy Mairs writes, in "On Being a Cripple" (p. 226), "As a cripple, I swagger" (par. 2), she is embracing a label that others have tried not to use and she is redefining what it means.

Description Depiction through sensory evidence. Description is not just visual: it can use details of touch, smell, taste, and hearing. These concrete details can support a specific **argument**, give the reader a sense of immediacy, or establish a mood. Description, while tied to the concrete, can also use **metaphor**, as when Richard Rodriguez writes in "Aria: Memoir of a Bilingual Childhood" (p. 289), "At one point his words slid together to form one word—sounds as confused as the threads of blue and green oil in the puddle next to my shoes" (par. 16).

Diction   Word choice. Diction can be characterized in terms of level of formality (formal or informal), concreteness (specific or abstract), and other choices that reflect a level appropriate to the writer's subject and **audience**. Diction is a central vehicle by which a writer makes her meaning clear, and it is a major element of a writer's style as well, and so of her tone. The Declaration of Independence (p. 193) is an excellent example of careful word choice. In this important document, Thomas Jefferson had to make every word count, and in his choice of words, some repeated, such as *equal, usurpations, tyrant,* and *independent,* Jefferson made his meaning very clear indeed.

Draft   An unfinished **essay**. A draft may have a **conclusion**, but it has not been completely revised, edited, and proofread. When still in the draft stage, writers can rethink not just the structure of their essay but their ideas as well.

Essay   A short nonfiction piece of writing. A writer should present one main idea in an essay. There are different kinds of essays—scholarly and personal, formal and informal—and many that mix these different kinds of writing.

Evidence   The facts that support an **argument**. Evidence takes different forms depending on the kind of writing in which it appears, but it generally is concrete, agreed-on information that can be pointed to as example or proof. In "Serving in Florida" (p. 136), Barbara Ehrenreich supports the narrative of her experiences living as a low-income worker with both a detailed survey of the living conditions of her coworkers and statistical support gleaned from research. Ehrenreich's argument is strengthened by inclusion of these different kinds of evidence.

Exemplification   Providing specific instances in support of general ideas. In "On Compassion" (p. 40), Barbara Lazear Ascher tells a number of anecdotes that serve as examples of encounters between the less fortunate and those who offer help.

Exposition   Writing that explains. Rather than showing, as in **narrative**, exposition tells. A majority of **essays** contain some exposition because they need to convey information, give background, or tell how events occurred or processes work. Lars Eighner uses exposition in "On Dumpster Diving" (p. 146) to explain who scavenges from Dumpsters, how they do it, how things in Dumpsters get there, and many other things related to Dumpster diving.

Fallacy A logical error. Fallacies weaken an argument. They include the making of false choices, the false assigning of cause (as in saying that because something happened after something else, the first event caused the second), the making of false generalizations, and many others.

Five-paragraph essay You should be familiar with this format from high school. It is taught because it provides an easy template for composition: an introductory **paragraph**, which contains your **thesis statement**; three body paragraphs laying out three **arguments**, pieces of **evidence**, or other kinds of support for your **thesis**; and a final concluding paragraph restating the thesis and summarizing the material in the body. While it can be a useful tool for beginning writers, it is confining and tends to encourage uninspiring, unimaginative writing. You will notice that none of the authors in this book use that format, and you shouldn't either. It is the **cliché** of writing essays, and, like actual clichés, should be avoided — like the plague.

Introduction The beginning of an **essay**; it should generally state a writer's main point. An introduction can include a **thesis statement** and can even begin to develop the **thesis**, but it can also simply pose a question, the answer to which will be the essay's thesis, or it can begin with a **story**, out of which the thesis will come. William F. Buckley Jr.'s "Why Don't We Complain?" (p. 72) is a good example of this kind of introduction.

Irony Verbal irony is writing that says one thing while it means something else, often the opposite of what it says (sarcasm is one form of verbal irony). The difference between literal meaning and implicit meaning is often used to suggest the difference between what a situation or person seems or pretends to be and what it or he really is. This use of irony is the reason irony often appears in satirical writing (writing that mocks a situation or idea). Jonathan Swift's "A Modest Proposal" (p. 353) is entirely ironic; the difficulty lies in figuring out what meaning Swift intends, since the literal meaning is certainly not his message. When something occurs that is counter to what is expected (what people often refer to when they say something is ironic), it is sometimes called situational irony. An example of this latter form of irony can be seen in the conclusion of Langston Hughes's "Salvation" (p. 185).

Metaphor Metaphor can be understood as a figure of speech (a nonliteral use of language) that says one thing *is* another or, in the form of simile, as a figure of speech that says one thing is *like* another. In both cases, the writer is trying to explain one thing by means of comparing it to another, more familiar thing. One example of the metaphor that makes a comparison by saying one thing is another comes from E. B. White's "Once More to the Lake" (p. 404): "It took a cool nerve, because if you threw the switch a twentieth of a second too soon you would catch the flywheel when it still had speed enough to go up past center, and the boat would leap ahead, charging bull-fashion at the dock" (par. 10). Note that this metaphor does not say explicitly that the boat is a bull; rather it says that the boat would *leap* and *charge bull-fashion*.

Narration   Telling a **story**, or giving an account of an event. Narration is a part of many different kinds of writing. Writers often tell an anecdote, or short narrative often told to make a point, as support for an **argument**. Some **essays** are almost entirely narration, but usually the events of the story lead to some kind of **conclusion**. George Orwell's "Shooting an Elephant" (p. 272) is largely narration and leads him to a very specific conclusion, as can be seen when he writes, of the story he tells, "It was a tiny incident in itself, but it gave me a better glimpse than I had had before of the real nature of imperialism—the real motives for which despotic governments act" (par. 3).

Paragraph   A series of sentences, set off by an initial indentation or a blank line, that develop a main idea. Paragraphs often have **topic sentences** that state that main idea, followed by sentences that offer support.

Paraphrase   A rephrasing of a section of a work into one's own words. A paraphrase is different from a **summary** in that it includes the details of a work and so is of similar length to the original; a paraphrase is similar to a summary in that both attempt to give some sense of another work without using its words.

Plagiarism   Using another person's words or ideas in one's own work without acknowledgment.

Point of view   The angle from which a writer sees his or her subject. No matter how objective or impartial a writer claims to be, he or she is always writing from a point of view influenced by age, race, gender, and economic and social status, to name just a few factors. In the personal essay "How It Feels to Be Colored Me" (p. 188), Zora Neale Hurston acknowledges writing from her own point of view.

Prewriting   Writing that happens before drafting. Prewriting is an early stage in the writing process during which writers brainstorm, come up with topics and theses, and begin to work on ways to develop them.

Process analysis   Explaining how to do something, how others do it, or how certain things occur. Often process analysis supports another aim—

to make a point or to tell one's own **story**, for example. When Malcolm X tells the story of his self-education in "Learning to Read" (p. 240), for example, he explains the process he went through to teach himself to read and also describes how he learned about the history of Africa and African Americans.

Quotation The inclusion of the words of another in one's own work, indicated by surrounding quotation marks. Used to convey a sense of the person who wrote or spoke those words, or to reproduce a phrase or sentence or more that perfectly captures some meaning the writer wishes also to convey, or to borrow some authority from an expert or eyewitness. Gloria Anzaldúa's "How to Tame a Wild Tongue" (p. 27) demonstrates a number of uses of quotation.

Revision The stage in the process of writing after a first **draft** is written when writers reexamine their work and try to improve it. This improvement consists of more than editing and proofreading—it also includes reevaluating the structure, the supporting **evidence**, the **thesis**, and even the topic. All good writers revise their work.

Rhetoric The effective use of language; also, the study of effective language use. The term can also be used negatively, as when it is said that a particular argument is really just using rhetoric, that is, using words persuasively (perhaps by making emotional appeals) without actually making a solid **argument**.

Story A **narrative**. The term is used in a number of different senses—to indicate a narrative within a nonfiction piece, to label a news article in a newspaper or magazine, or to name the genre of short fiction. Many, perhaps most, effective essays tell some kind of story.

Style The way a writer writes. Any of the choices writers make while writing—about **diction**, sentence length, structure, rhythm, and figures of speech—that make their work sound like them. The **tone** of a particular work can be due in part to a writer's style. James Baldwin is known for his distinctive style, one aspect of which is the mixing of formal, sometimes biblical, language and an everyday, conversational style, as in this sentence from "Notes of a Native Son" (p. 44): "I had declined to believe in that apocalypse which had been central to my father's vision; very well, life seemed to be saying, here is something that will certainly pass for an apocalypse until the real thing comes along" (par. 2).

Summary A condensation, in one's own words, of a work. Summaries consist of the main points of the work; supporting points, examples, and other kinds of support are left out.

Synthesis The use of outside sources to gather information and opinions, in order to develop ideas, amass evidence, and support arguments. Synthesis enables writers to do more than simply express their opinion—it enables them to enter the conversation about their topic already being held in the wider world. It also allows them to complicate their ideas, to see more than one side, and to marshal information and logical arguments in the service of their position.

Thesis The main idea in a piece of writing, which the work is trying to argue or explore. Also sometimes known as the **claim**, a term which also has a more specific meaning related to argumentation. The thesis can be explicit, as in essays that make an argument (as in Alan Burdick's "The Truth about Invasive Species," p. 79), or implicit or even secondary, as in some narrative essays (as in Cristina Henríquez's "Lunch," p. 182).

Thesis statement A sentence or group of sentences, usually appearing early in a piece of writing, that announce the thesis. The thesis statement often states plainly what the work as a whole is to be about, but it can take many forms, as in the following from Stephanie Ericsson's "The Ways We Lie" (p. 159), in which she makes an assertion and follows with a question: "We lie. We all do. We exaggerate, we minimize, we avoid confrontation, we spare people's feelings, we conveniently forget, we keep secrets, we justify lying to the big-guy institutions. Like most people, I indulge in small falsehoods and still think of myself as an honest person. Sure I lie, but it doesn't hurt anything. Or does it?" (par. 3).

Tone Attitude toward subject, readers, and even the writer and work itself; also sometimes mood or atmosphere more generally. Achieved through **style** as well as content. In his indictment of King George III in the Declaration of Independence (p. 193), Thomas Jefferson writes, "He has abdicated Government here, by declaring us out of his Protection and waging War against us. He has plundered our seas, ravaged our Coasts, burnt our towns, and destroyed the lives of our people" (pars. 20–21). His tone in this passage comes from his choice of words, the shape of his sentences, and his imagery.

Topic sentence The sentence in which the writer states a **paragraph**'s main idea. The topic sentence often appears at or near the beginning of the paragraph. When Gloria Anzaldúa in "How to Tame a Wild Tongue" (p. 27) begins a paragraph, "Chicanos, after 250 years of Spanish/Anglo colonization, have developed significant differences in the Spanish we speak" (par. 18), we should suspect the rest of the paragraph will develop that idea, perhaps with examples of these differences (and we would be right).

Transitions   The connective tissue among sentences, ideas, and **paragraphs**. Transitions help readers follow writers through their ideas and see the connections among the parts of an **argument** or the relation between scenes in a **narrative**. Through the use of transitional words *(therefore, nonetheless, then)*, phrases *(on the other hand, as a result, in the same way)*, effects (such as repetition or parallel sentence structures), and even whole paragraphs, good writers include signposts to show readers the direction the argument or story is going. Nancy Mairs in "On Being a Cripple" (p. 226) begins many of her paragraphs with transitions that help readers follow the line of her thought. Some examples: "Lest I begin to sound like Pollyanna, however, let me say that I don't like having MS" (par. 9); "Along with this fear that people are secretly accepting shoddy goods comes a relentless pressure to please" (par. 18); "This gentleness is part of the reason that I'm not sorry to be a cripple" (par. 32).

Acknowledgments *(continued from p. ii)*

Lars Eighner, "On Dumpster Diving," an excerpt from *Travels with Lizbeth*, © 1993 by Lars Eighner. Reprinted by permission of St. Martin's Press, LLC. All rights reserved.

Stephanie Ericsson, "The Ways We Lie," Copyright © 1992 by Stephanie Ericsson. Originally published by *The Utne Reader*. Reprinted by permission of Dunham Literary, Inc. as agent for the author.

Malcolm Gladwell, "Small Change: Why the Revolution Will Not Be Tweeted," *New Yorker Magazine*, October 4, 2010. Copyright © 2010 by Malcolm Gladwell. Reprinted by permission.

Cristina Henríquez, "Lunch: Dinner in Panama," *The New Yorker*, Family Dinner, September 3, 2007. Reprinted by permission of the author.

Langston Hughes, "Salvation" from *THE BIG SEA* by Langston Hughes. Copyright © 1940 by Langston Hughes. Copyright renewed 1968 by Arna Bontemps and George Houston Bass. Reprinted by permission of Hill and Wang, a division of Farrar, Straus and Giroux, LLC.

Camden Joy, "Surviving Sinatra" from *Lost Joy* by Camden Joy, published by Verse Chorus Press, © 2002, 2015. Reprinted by permission.

Jamaica Kincaid, "The Ugly Tourist," excerpt from *A Small Place* by Jamaica Kincaid. Copyright © 1988 by Jamaica Kincaid. Reprinted by permission of Farrar, Straus and Giroux, LLC.

Stephen King, "Reading to Write." Reprinted with the permission of Scribner, a division of Simon & Schuster, Inc., from *On Writing: A Memoir of the Craft* by Stephen King. Copyright © 2000 by Stephen King. All rights reserved.

Verlyn Klinkenborg, "Our Vanishing Night: Most City Skies Have Become Virtually Empty of Stars." *National Geographic Magazine*. National Geographic Society. Nov. 2008.

Audre Lorde, "The Fourth of July," from *Zami: A New Spelling of My Name*— published by Crossing Press. Copyright © 1982, 2006 by Audre Lorde. Used herewith by permission of the Charlotte Sheedy Literary Agency.

Nancy Mairs, "On Being a Cripple," from *Plaintext* by Nancy Mairs. Copyright © 1986 by The Arizona Board of Regents. Reprinted by permission of the University of Arizona Press.

Malcolm X, "Learning to Read" from *THE AUTOBIOGRAPHY OF MALCOLM X*, as told to Alex Haley, copyright © 1964 by Alex Haley and Malcolm X. Copyright © 1965 by Alex Haley and Betty Shabazz. Used by permission of Ballantine Books, an imprint of Random House, a division of Penguin Random House LLC. All rights reserved. Any third party use of this material, outside of this publication, is prohibited. Interested parties must apply directly to Penguin Random House LLC for permission.

John McPhee, "The Search for Marvin Gardens" from *PIECES OF THE FRAME* by John McPhee. Copyright © 1975, renewed 2003 by John McPhee. Reprinted by permission of Farrar, Straus and Giroux, LLC.

Lydia Millet, "Victor's Hall" originally published under the title "Stuffed with an Agenda." From *The New York Times*, April 5, 2015 © 2015 The New York Times. All rights reserved. Used by permission and protected by the Copyright Laws of the United States. The printing, copying, redistribution, or retransmission of this Content without express written permission is prohibited.

Bharati Mukherjee, "Two Ways to Belong to America," by Bharati Mukherjee. Copyright © 1996 by Bharati Mukherjee. Originally published in *The New York Times*. Reprinted by permission of the author.

George Orwell, "Shooting an Elephant," from *Shooting an Elephant and Other Essays* by George Orwell. Copyright © 1946 by Sonia Brownell Orwell; copyright © renewed 1974 by Sonia Orwell. Reprinted by permission of Houghton Mifflin Harcourt Publishing Company. All rights reserved.

Richard Rodriguez, "Aria: Memoir of a Bilingual Childhood." From *Hunger of Memory: The Education of Richard Rodriguez* by Richard Rodriguez. Reprinted by permission of David R. Godine, Publisher, Inc. Copyright © 1982 by Richard Rodriguez.

Mike Rose, "'I Just Wanna Be Average.'" Reprinted with the permission of Free Press, a Division of Simon & Schuster, Inc., from *Lives on the Boundary: The Struggles and Achievements of America's Underprepared* by Mike Rose. Copyright © 1989 by Mike Rose. All rights reserved.

Oliver Sacks, "My Periodic Table," by Oliver Sacks, originally published in *The New York Times*, currently collected in *GRATITUDE*. Copyright © 2015 by Oliver Sacks, used by permission of The Wylie Agency LLC.

David Sedaris, "Me Talk Pretty One Day." First published in *Esquire* and reprinted by permission of Don Congdon Associates, Inc. Copyright © 1999 by David Sedaris.

Brent Staples, "Just Walk on By: Black Men and Public Space." Copyright © 1986 by Brent Staples. Reprinted by permission of the author.

John Jeremiah Sullivan, "Feet in Smoke" from *Pulphead: Essays* by John Jeremiah Sullivan. Copyright © 2011 by John Jeremiah Sullivan. Reprinted by permission of Farrar, Straus and Giroux, LLC.

Amy Tan, "Mother Tongue," Copyright © 1989 by Amy Tan. First appeared in *The Threepenny Review*. Reprinted by permission of the author and Sandra Dijkstra Literary Agency.

James Thurber, "The Subjunctive Mood." Originally titled "Our Own Modern English Usage," *The New Yorker Magazine* (August 17, 1929). © Condé Nast. Used by permission of Condé Nast.

Miya Tokumitsu, "In the Name of Love" by Miya Tokumitsu, *Jacobin Magazine*, https://www.jacobinmag.com/2014/01/in-the-name-of-love/. Reprinted by permission.

E. B. White, "Once More to the Lake," from *One Man's Meat*, by E. B. White. Copyright © 1941 by E. B. White. Reprinted by permission of Tilbury House, Publishers and ICM Partners.

Colson Whitehead, "The Loser Edit," originally published under the title "Life without Pity" from *The New York Times*, March 8, 2015 © 2015 The New York Times. All rights reserved. Used by permission and protected by the Copyright Laws of the United States. The printing, copying, redistribution, or retransmission of this Content without express written permission is prohibited.

Dave Zirin, excerpt from *Game Over: How Politics Has Turned the Sports World Upside Down*. Copyright © 2013 by Dave Zirin. Reprinted by permission of The New Press, www.thenewpress.com.

Index of Authors and Titles

451